Historical Dictionary of Sacred Music

Joseph P. Swain

The Scarecrow Press, Inc.
Lanham, Maryland • Toronto • Oxford
2006

SCARECROW PRESS, INC.

Published in the United States of America
by Scarecrow Press, Inc.
A wholly owned subsidiary of
The Rowman & Littlefield Publishing Group, Inc.
4501 Forbes Boulevard, Suite 200, Lanham, Maryland 20706
www.scarecrowpress.com

PO Box 317
Oxford
OX2 9RU, UK

British Library Cataloguing in Publication Information Available

Library of Congress Cataloging-in-Publication Data

Swain, Joseph Peter.
  Historical dictionary of sacred music / Joseph P. Swain.
    p. cm.
  Appendices contain texts of the Roman Catholic and Anglican rites, and of
Shema and Kaddish.
  Includes bibliographical references.
  ISBN-13: 978-0-8108-5530-4 (hardcover : alk. paper)
  ISBN-10: 0-8108-5530-5 (hardcover : alk. paper)
  1. Church music–Dictionaries. 2. Synagogue music–Dictionaries. I. Title.
ML102.C5S83   2007
781.7003–dc22   2006019324

Contents

Editor's Foreword

One thing nearly all religions have in common is a role for music. That is a basic theme, but the variations on it are countless. In some religions, denominations thereof, or sects, music can assume a primary position in the liturgy, while in others it is scarcely present. In some contexts, sacred music is very tightly defined, allowing very little development or change, while in others it is constantly evolving, keeping up with musical trends in the secular world, and sometimes moving so close to secular music as to be scarcely recognizable as "sacred." This music may be mere imitation of precedent, slavishly copying what went before, or it can become incredibly creative and innovative. It may be composed by clerics, church musicians, or rank outsiders, including some of the greatest figures of the age, like Bach, Beethoven, and Mozart. Whatever its role, music is an important aspect of religion, and one that certainly deserves more attention.

That is partly the purpose of this *Historical Dictionary of Sacred Music*, which focuses both on the common theme and many of the variations. Most of the dictionary entries are inevitably devoted to music in the Christian churches of the West, since that is where it has developed and flourished most. But there are also many entries on other traditions—Buddhist, Hindu, and Islamic, and also forms of shamanism. Although there are fewer references to specific composers or works elsewhere, this dictionary does provide a view of the types of music, the instruments, and the role of music in many different settings. What they all have in common is dealt with more specifically in the introduction. And the chronology follows some of the main trends. As always, the bibliography is an important part of the book, and this time it is particularly useful in helping readers obtain further information on those aspects in which they are most keenly interested or know less about.

This first volume on music in our series on literature and the arts was written by Joseph P. Swain, who is familiar with the topic from different angles. Most important, he has taught music history and theory for more than 25 years at Phillips Academy and Colgate University. Dr. Swain has also written many articles and books on music, including sacred music. But he is also a practitioner, as organist and director of music at St. Malachy's Church in Sheburne, New York, as well as music director of the Tapestry All-Centuries Singers in Clinton, New York. So he knows what is of most interest to students and musicians, and in this book he has compiled an impressive amount of information that can be of use to specialists but also to a curious and informed general public.

Jon Woronoff
Series Editor

Preface

This *Historical Dictionary of Sacred Music* provides in one volume basic information about the most important traditions, persons, places, technical terms, and documents of sacred music. It also provides an extensive bibliography if the reader requires more information about any of the entries. It is intended for musicians at all levels—students of sacred music, interested lay persons, and composers of sacred music who need technical advice about traditions, texts, and usages. The dictionary assumes a basic musical vocabulary (e.g., "key," "strophic form," "Baroque") and some familiarity with religious concepts and liturgical practices (e.g., "Virgin Mary," "Allah," "Bible").

The dictionary covers the most important aspects of the sacred music of Buddhism, Christianity, Confucianism, Hinduism, Islam, Judaism, and certain other smaller groups. The cross references frequently indicate an analogous entry in other religious traditions, even when there is no direct historical relation, in order to highlight commonalities that otherwise might be missed. Owing to the nature of sacred music and its histories (discussed in the Introduction), as well as the most likely public for the dictionary, the great majority of entries concern Christianity and Judaism.

About one third of the entries are biographical: mostly composers but also key religious figures (e.g., Martin Luther), writers (e.g., Boethius), and publishers who influenced significantly the course of sacred music. Composers who are very famous but not especially for their sacred music (e.g., Ludwig van Beethoven) will have surprisingly brief entries tailored specifically to the part of their oeuvre that is sacred, or none at all. Also omitted are composers whose names live in the history of sacred music because of a single outstanding work (e.g., *Miserere* of Gregorio Allegri), but there is instead an entry for the work itself. Not included are performers and scholars of sacred music. In a single volume dealing with such a vast subject area, it was thought best to keep the music itself front and center, and in any case the state of scholarship may be assessed in the Bibliography.

Another third of the entries concern themselves with the various genres, or types of sacred music (e.g., cantata, mass, songs of the *hajj*). Something over one tenth deal with technical terms (e.g., Alleluia, *hazan*, pipe organ, psalm tone, qī'rat). Other types of entries include important documents and sources (e.g., Genevan Psalter, *Oktoēchos* of Severus, Old Hall Manuscript), places, institutions (e.g., Chapel Royal), important events (e.g., Council of Trent), and significant compositions (e.g., Requiem of Gabriel Fauré) which include performance duration and requirements. There is also an appendix which gives texts and translations of the Christian and Jewish prayers most frequently set to music.

There is no attempt to characterize the various religions in the dictionary itself with entries such as "Buddhism" or "Anglicanism." A reader may get a foothold in one entry such as "Buddhist chant" and thereafter the cross-references should lead to the other relevant entries. In the interest of packing as much hard information into a single volume as possible, furthermore, I have not tried to describe the way any kind of sacred music sounds, or the sounds of sacred music themselves, nearly impossible anyway, except when precise and technical terms will serve (e.g., "six-voice imitative texture," "mode 1 melody"). Objective facts—definitions, names, dates, places, orders of worship, etc.—make up most of the information. Such treatment of the music may strike some as rather cold, but it allows a much greater coverage, and besides, no writing substitutes for hearing the music itself.

The compiler's problem with such a vast and diverse subject as sacred music is not the acquisition of information but rather deciding what to include and what to omit. Some entries may merit their places because of intrinsic worth, such as Monteverdi's *Vespers of the Blessed Virgin (1610)*, a magnificent but unique composition without significant influence, but more often precious space is allotted to persons or events that affected the course of sacred music history in some way. Thus, Giovanni da Palestrina has more lines than Orlandus Lassus. The latter is one of the great geniuses of the Western tradition whose sacred music represents every bit as great an artistic achievement as Palestrina's, but Palestrina became the icon of proper sacred music for later centuries while Lassus' reputation unjustly faded. And while John Wesley is less widely known among musicians than Beethoven, the Methodist founder exercises a much wider influence on Christian music today than did the great German composer's few contributions—great as they may be. The relevance for the present day, the end product of historical influence, is inevitably a weighty consideration. While many traditions and musical practices of sacred music today trace their origins back millennia, recent events within the Western traditions, particularly persons, receive slightly more emphasis.

Many people—scholars, teachers, ministers, and rabbis—have generously given me their expert advice in many areas, without which I could not have finished the book. In particular, I would like to recognize the contributions of Mr. Stephen Best, Dr. Noël Bisson, Prof. John Ross Carter, Rabbi Garson Herzfeld, Prof. Omid Safi, Mr. Mark Shiner, Rabbi Michael Tayvah, and Fr. Jerome Weber.

The Humanities Division of Colgate University generously provided funds for two student research assistants, Heather Wick, who compiled a list of potential biographies, and Annabel Truesdell, who researched and wrote some of the shorter ones (signaled in the dictionary by "at").

I must also recognize Jon Woronoff of Scarecrow Press, who supported my idea for such a historical dictionary from the outset and offered much valuable advice along the way.

My deepest appreciation to all who supported this project.

Chronology

c. 1000 B. C.   Rule of King David, traditional author and compiler of the Book of Psalms.

c. 420 B. C.   Synagogues established; divine service ordained by the Sanhedrin.

A. D. 70   Destruction of the Temple in Jerusalem by the Romans; instrumental music in Jewish worship is prohibited as a sign of mourning.

c. 400   *Oktoēchos* of Severus collection of Byzantine hymn texts. St. Romanos develops *kontakion* hymn form for Byzantine liturgy.

c. 500   System of accents for chanting the Hebrew Scriptures brought into use by the Masoretes. First wave of *bhajan*, popular Hindu songs, in India.

590–604   Pontificate of St. Gregory the Great.

c. 622   The Prophet Muhammed institutes the call to prayer, the *'adhān*.

c. 700   Role of the Jewish *hazzan* changes from caretaker to chanter of the Scriptures and leader of song.

711   Muslims invade the Iberian peninsula.

c. 760   Yehudai Gaon of Sura standardizes the synagogal chant.

c. 850   Byzantine chant brought to Slavic peoples by Sts. Cyril and Methodius.

c. 875   First Jewish *siddur* compiled by Rav Amram.

c. 900   Earliest sources of Gregorian chant, recorded in staffless neumes at St. Gall and Laon. *Musica enchiriadis*, earliest source of polyphonic mass propers and ordinaries. Earliest sources of Byzantine chant with decipherable melodies.

c. 950   Abū'l-Faradj al-Isfahāni compiles *Kitāb al-Aghāni* ("Book of Songs"). Aaron Ben Asher founds the Tiberian system of Biblical accents.

c. 996   First Winchester Troper preserves music and text of *Quem quaeritis* liturgical drama.

c. 1000   Precise pitch notation of Gregorian chant using staves; Hartker Antiphoner. Earliest written sources of *sāmavedic* chant.

c. 1025   Guido d'Arezzo introduces staff lines to express pitch height in chants more precisely and a system of sight-singing.

c. 1050   Second Winchester Troper preserves first practical book of polyphony.

1085   Fall of Toledo; Mozarabic rite suppressed in Spain.

c. 1100   Earliest Missinai melodies. Earliest notated *piyyutim*. Jayadeva composes the *Gīta-Govinda* in India.

c. 1160   *Magnus Liber Organi* collection of organum begins to be compiled. Earliest notated Chinese *ya-yüeh*.

c. 1350   Guillaume de Machaut composes *La Messe de Nostre Dame*, first mass cycle by a single composer.

c. 1425–35   Earliest cantus firmus masses by Leonel Power and John Dunstable.

1409   Süleyman Celibi composes the *mawlīd* called the "Way to Salvation."

c. 1425   Rabbi Jacob Molin standardizes the Ashkenazic synagogue liturgy.

c. 1450   Guillaume Dufay's *Missa Se La Face Ay Pale* uses a secular tune as cantus firmus. Practices of chanting in Ashkenazic liturgy, standardized by Jacob Molin, are compiled.

1484 Puranda Dasa, composer of Hindu *kirtana*, born in India.

c. 1490 Earliest alphabetic pitch notation for Russian chant. Earliest extant polyphonic Requiem, composed by Johannes Ockeghem.

c. 1475–1500 Structural imitation becomes standard texture for polyphonic masses and motets, particularly notable in the works of Josquin Desprez.

1524 Earliest printed collections of Lutheran chorales.

1526 Martin Luther's *Deutsche Messe* (German Mass).

1540 Constance Songbook published.

1545–1563 Council of Trent enacts reforms in Roman Catholic liturgical music.

1547 Heinrich Glarean publishes his *Dodechachordon* updating the theoretical recognition of church modes to 12.

1550 John Merbecke publishes *Booke of Common Praier Noted* (London).

1562 Third Genevan Psalter published.

1567 *Missa Papae Marcelli* by Giovanni da Palestrina published.

1586 Lucas Osiander's *Fünfftzig geistliche Lieder und Psalmen* (Nuremburg), first printed collection of cantional chorales with melody in the soprano voice.

1587 Israel Najara brings out first printed collection of devotional poems (*zemirotim*) in Safed.

1594 The organ is used as part of a Sabbath ritual in Prague.

1614–1615 Publication in Rome of the so-called Medicean chantbooks containing revisions of traditional Latin chants.

1623 Salamone Rossi publishes *Ha-Shirim Asher Li'Shlomo*, settings of traditional Jewish liturgical texts to modern musical style, in Venice.

1629 Rabbi Leone da Modena founds a Jewish music academy in Venice.

1652–1656   Patriarch Nikon promotes polyphony in Russian chant.

1700   Erdmann Neumeister publishes *Geistliche Cantaten statt einer Kirchen-Music*, poetic texts for liturgy modeled after Italian operatic conventions.

1707   First hymnal of Isaac Watts, *Hymns and Spiritual Songs*, setting psalm paraphrases.

1707–1708   Johann Sebastian Bach's earliest authenticated cantatas performed at Mühlhausen.

1712   B. H. Brocke publishes *Der für die Sünden der Welt gemarterte und sterbende Jesus*, a popular paraphrase of the passion story set by Telemann and Handel among others.

1717–1718   George Frederic Handel's Chandos Anthems.

1723   **December 25:** First performance of J. S. Bach's Magnificat, St. Thomas Church, Leipzig, Saxony (Germany).

1724   **April 7:** First performance of J. S. Bach's St. John Passion.

1727   **April 11:** First performance of J. S. Bach's St. Matthew Passion. **October 27:** First performance of Handel's Coronation Anthems.

1734   **December 25–27:** First performance of J. S. Bach's Christmas Oratorio, Parts I–III.

1737   First Methodist hymnal compiled by John Wesley.

1739   Publication of Part III of J. S. Bach's *Clavier-Übung*.

1741   **14 September:**   Handel completes the orchestration to *Messiah*.

1749   Completion of J. S. Bach's Mass in B Minor.

c. 1750   R. Israel Bal Shem Tov founds Hassidism and teaches a significant spirituality for congregational singing.

1791   Requiem by Wolfgang Amadeus Mozart.

1801   *A Collection of Spiritual Songs and Hymns*, first hymnal for African-American use published in Philadelphia.

1803 First printed collection of spirituals published in Philadelphia.

1815 Israel Jacobson introduces the organ to synagogue liturgy in Berlin.

1822 Israel Lovy introduces four-voiced choral singing to synagogue liturgy in Paris.

1823 *Missa Solemnis* by Ludwig van Beethoven.

1826 Salomon Sulzer begins modernizing the Jewish cantorate in Vienna.

1829 **11 March:** Revival of J. S. Bach's St. Matthew Passion in Berlin, credited with igniting an explosion of interest in Bach's music.

c. 1830 Chrysanthus of Madytus reforms the Byzantine chant notation.

1837 Prosper Guéranger founds the abbey of St. Pierre at Solesmes, France, a center for the revival of Gregorian chant. **December 5:** Premiere of Requiem by Hector Berlioz in Paris.

1838 Solomon Sulzer publishes Vol. 1 of *Schir Zion*.

1846 **26 August:** Premiere of Felix Mendelssohn's *Elijah* in Birmingham.

1861 *Hymns Ancient and Modern* published in England.

1870 The Ceciliam movement publishes the so-called Ratisbon Edition of Latin chant.

1874 **22 May:** Premiere of Giuseppe Verdi's Requiem in Milan.

1882 The Congress of Arezzo introduces the Solesmes versions of traditional Latin chant.

1894 **17 May:** Premiere of Gabriel Fauré's Requiem.

1896 First edition of the modern chant book *Liber Usualis*.

1903 **22 November:** Pope St. Pius X promulgates *Tra le sollecitudini* (*Motu proprio*) regulating music of the Roman Catholic Church.

1921 Mass in G minor by Ralph Vaughn Williams.

1926 *Sancta Civitas*, cantata by Edward Elgar.

1932 Oratorio-opera *Moses und Aron* composed by Arnold Schoenberg.

1945 *Missa Cantuariensis* by Edmund Rubbra.

1947 *Messe Solennelle "Salve Regina"* by Jean Langlais.

1948 Mass for chorus, soloists, and 10 winds by Igor Stravinksy.

1949 Taizé interdenominational community founded.

1956 *20th-Century Folk Mass* composed by Geoffrey Beaumont.

1960 *Missa Super Modos Duodecimales*, a mass composed with serial technique, by Anton Heiler.

1963 **4 December:** Second Vatican Council in Rome promulgates the *Constitution on the Sacred Liturgy*.

1964 *Misa Criolla* by Ariel Ramirez.

1965 *Passio et mors Domini nostri Jesu Christi secundum Lucam* by Krzyztof Penderecki. *Chichester Psalms* by Leonard Bernstein.

1974 Magnificat by Penderecki.

1979 Publication of *Graduale Triplex*, comparing modern chant notation with earliest sources.

2000 *Lamentations and Praises* of John Tavener.

Introduction

Sacred music is a universal phenomenon of humanity. Where there is faith, there is music to express it. Every major religious tradition and most minor ones have music and have it in abundance and variety. There is music to accompany ritual and music purely for devotion, music for large congregations and music for trained soloists, music that sets holy words, and music without words at all. In some traditions, the relation between music and religious ritual is so intimate that it is inaccurate to speak of the music accompanying the ritual. Rather, to perform the ritual is to sing, and to sing the ritual is to perform it.

WHAT IS SACRED MUSIC?

That kind of intimacy begs the question whether the tones uttered during the ritual are properly considered music in the usual sense at all. In traditional Islam, the heightened speech or cantillation used to read the *Qur'ān* in religious rites is not so considered by imams, even though it might possibly be written down by ethnomusicologists with pitch notation; it is simply the proper way to proclaim the *Qur'ān*. Any devotional music outside the mosque is suspect as a temptation of the secular world (although in certain sects popular religious music associated with particular festivals and temple rites has developed). In this case, and that of Theravada Buddhism, too, and certain early Christian sects, the term "sacred music" is nearly empty.

In Hindu India, on the other hand, virtually all of the arts, until very recent times, owe their inspiration to religion, and even the Hindustani and Karnatic classical music performed in concert halls comprises texts drawn on sacred themes. "Sacred music" in this context is nearly redundant.

So a direct translation of "sacred music" into certain other cultures may well elicit a kind of puzzlement. In the West, the line demarcating sacred from secular music is clearer than anywhere else. Yet, even in a Western context, what counts as "sacred music" is not simply a matter of the music heard in a church or synagogue. The category appears to admit of degree—works can be more or less sacred.

The most sacred would be liturgical music, music explicitly required as part of a ritual, such as a sung mass, a psalm in a vespers service, or a required proper hymn. Next would come devotional music apart from liturgy, either personal or public: processional songs, Italian *laude*, songs from the *Sacred Harp* collection sung in homes, etc. These two categories dominate the middles ages and Renaissance in Europe and the early colonial period of North America and represent the sacred/secular distinction at its strongest, secular music being any sort neither liturgical nor devotional.

Thereafter, the categories branch out and the distinction blurs. A third kind of Western music often considered sacred, but not without qualification, is music composed on Bible stories or lives of saints but with little connection to liturgy or to private devotions and often belonging to no particular sect of Christianity. Such compositions flourished after the invention of opera just before 1600, when art music in general began to acquire strong narrative and dramatic properties and to take on a larger role in public entertainment, to reach into the growing middle and mercantile classes, to attain, in short, the status of an art to be contemplated for its own sake without having to accompany some cultural activity. Certain kinds of composition, particularly instrumental genres, could cross over from the strictly liturgical to much more worldly, even commercial uses. "Christmas" concertos, such as Arcangelo Corelli's famous op. 6, no. 8 (c. 1690, pub. 1714), accompanied a liturgy but doubled as household music. Franz Joseph Haydn's "Seven Last Words of Our Saviour from the Cross," originally composed as orchestral meditations for a Lenten service in Cadiz (1787), became famous through more accessible versions for string quartet (1787) and piano (not arranged by Haydn). Other works, such as Johann Kuhnau's "Biblical" Sonatas (1700) for keyboard, have no liturgical role whatever. The oratorio trod the same path, beginning within the church as an extra-liturgical devotion in 17th-century Rome and quickly making its way into the courts and eventually the theater. The most famous exemplar, Handel's *Messiah*, which he entitled *A Sacred Oratorio*, embodies the paradox of this kind of sacred music: the entire text is Biblical, minimally adapted, and yet tickets were sold for the first performance, which took place in a large public hall in Dublin in 1742.

The translocation from church to concert hall also produced a large repertory of works composed in liturgical forms but which live on chiefly as concert works: a fourth category of symphonic masses, cantatas, motets, and sacred songs that are the bread and butter of choral societies throughout the western world. Once again, many of these originated as, or were at least intended to be, liturgical works, but the logistical requirements for their execution—large orchestras and choruses—were climbing just as interest in liturgical music and in Christianity in general was declining rapidly at the onset of the 19th century. Some works, with Ludwig van Beethoven's massive *Missa Solemnis* (1823) perhaps setting the trend, landed in the concert hall chiefly because they demand extraordinary performance forces and overwhelm the liturgy by sheer length, but few churches can afford the regular performance of even a comparatively modest mass by Franz Schubert.

SACRED MUSIC AND HISTORY

This rich and wonderfully varied repertory grew up chiefly in Christian Europe because that tradition failed to do what religious traditions elsewhere practiced as a matter of principle—to resist history.

Music, generally speaking, lends itself least to preservation of all the fine arts, and composition with and performance from notation is still a peculiarly Western tradition that distinguishes it from the other musics of the world, sacred or secular. Many religious traditions have positively discouraged any writing of music, preferring to hand it on by rote from elder to novice in oral tradition. Thus, singers of Coptic chant spend 20 years or more learning their repertory, and the samāvedic chanters of the Hindu tradition attain such mastery that some can recite whole passages from memory in reverse or begin at any point within many volumes of scripture.[1] Strictly speaking, music known only through oral tradition has no history because we can know only its present form. There is no way of telling whether it was different in the past, and mere prose accounts of what happened, numerous in some traditions, operate at a great remove from the actual music and give little specific sense of it. History is difficult if not impossible without written records.

Yet it is a curious coincidence that a number of different religious traditions began developing a means of writing their music around the turn of the second millennium A. D: the earliest Gregorian chant books about 900; Byzantine chant books from the 10th century; *samāvedic* chant from the 11th century; Jewish *piyyutim* in the 11th century; Chinese *ya-yüeh* from the 12th century. The reason, at least in some of these cases, is that the repertory of sacred chant had grown too large to be committed to memory reliably, and so notation was invented to prevent the inevitable creeping change that always accompanies the more casual oral traditions such as folk music. Here, in black and white, is a second obstacle to a history of sacred music—the resistance to change itself. For if the music is ever constant, then there is no history, and this state of affairs is exactly what many religious traditions have tried to achieve, and in the main they have succeeded. The proper musical setting of a sacred text is considered immutable, a reflection of the divine perfection that never needs improvement. Inventing new formulae for such chants would be as abhorrent for a Copt as altering the text of the Gospels for most Christians.

Early on in Europe, this attitude seems to have relaxed compared to other traditional cultures. Lois Ibsen al Faruqi suggests that the central conception of God changed from one of transcendence and immutability to a more personal, humanist image and therefore allowed changes in modes of worshipping Him.[2] Somehow the West adopted a different standard for what transmitted the sense of the sacred: rather than being an immutable facet of the Word, the music could develop and change and continue to convey the Word with reverence and awe as long as it did not emulate the music of the secular world. It is impossible to say when this change of attitude came about, but it is certain that Christian communities were composing new hymns, that is, non-Biblical texts to be sung, by the fourth century. Whatever the explanation, the dissociation of the sacred semantic in music—the sense of what is holy in music—from the Biblical text itself is what allows sacred music in the West to have so rich a history.

THE KEY EVENTS IN THE WEST

The most important developments in the history of sacred music in the West are four. The first was this allowance of change in sacred chanting and new compositions that could be admitted to liturgy. This relaxed conception of sacred music made possible everything that followed.

The second key event was the invention of polyphony about A. D. 1000. Not only is the sounding of simultaneous and coordinated melodies the foundation of all Western art music both sacred and secular, but it created a means for compositional creativity while remaining faithful to a venerable musical tradition, a technique that would serve for centuries in many different guises. The technique is the cantus firmus: a traditional chant, often sung slowly and repeatedly, accompanied by melodic inventions of the composer. From this simple premise grew the great repertory of motets, cyclic cantus firmus masses, and all the subgenres we know as "classical polyphony" as composed by Guillaume Du Fay, Josquin Desprez, Giovanni da Palestrina, Orlandus Lassus, William Byrd, and their colleagues and disciples. The origins of this style in chant remained audible even when a composition did not quote a traditional melody, as often happened by the 16th century.

The third signal event was the Reformation as widespread disputes about the very nature of sacred music arose for the first time since Antiquity. Martin Luther's chief and lasting reform of the Roman Catholic mass promoted congregational singing from its customary peripheral role in extra-liturgical processions to a central place in Eucharistic liturgy. Jean Calvin's reform was much more reactionary. By permitting only psalm texts to be sung, he temporarily restored the ancient and immutable union of music with the Word of God that had been abandoned by Western Christianity at least 12 centuries before.

The fourth key event was the invention of opera in the last decade of the 16th century. Opera clarified once and for all differences in compositional techniques, materials, and above all sound that had increasingly separated music in the church from music at court. Two ways of composing—sometimes called the *stile antico* ("ancient style") and the *stile moderno* ("modern style")—had become essentially separate languages. Opera made this separation explicit by creating a new musical institution, musical theater. Composers trained in the old church style quickly succumbed to the temptation to set sacred texts in an operatic manner that could have no link with the traditional chant. In abandoning traditional chant and its polyphonic descendants, would sacred music finally lose its mark of distinction?

THE DISTINCTION OF SACRED MUSIC

Despite great variety in culture and creed throughout the world, a fundamental conception of the character of sacred music is held largely in common: it is chant. All the religious traditions seem to have some form of it, though there are distinctive traditions to be sure. Its sound is iconic of religious music.

In most types of chant, three musical qualities combine. First, it is pure vocal music: while some kinds of Eastern chanting uses clappers, bells, or other percussion to articulate liturgy, accompaniment by instruments in the Western sense of doubling melodies or adding harmonies is alien to most chant traditions. Second, it is monophonic: one note at a time, without harmonization. Third, it is non-metric, or in "free rhythm": regular beats and time measures are usually absent, as is the periodic accenting of such beats that is the essence of meter.

If the substrate of a sacred music tradition is its chant, the development, complication, flowering, and enrichment of that tradition—in short, its history—comes from modifying one or more of these three critical features of chant. The history of Western sacred music, with significant correspondences in other traditions, can be conceived as processes of adding instruments to a purely vocal sonority, adding new melodies to a single line to create polyphony, and replacing free rhythm with metric rhythm. Sometimes one kind of change may dominate and proceed independently for a period; at other times these processes affect one another essentially.

Like traditional Islam and certain Buddhist sects, early Christianity regarded music with some suspicion as a symbol of paganism and the sinful, secular world, and particularly instrumental music, which had long associations with Greek and Roman rites. Thus the earliest Christian liturgical music seems to have consisted entirely of psalms, sung after the Jewish manner, with antiphonal singing introduced fairly early on. Nevertheless, by the 10th century the organ had secured a place as the one instrument allowed to accompany chant, and the exclusive reliance on this one versatile instrument, as well as its very antiquity, are what make the pipe organ by far the single most powerful instrumental symbol of the sacred in the West even today.

About the same time that the organ moved into the church, the chant acquired a new, festival mode of presentation: polyphony, more than one melody sung simultaneously. At first the additional melody was as simple as could be, merely doubling the original chant melody note for note at a predetermined consonant interval such as the perfect fifth, a short step away from the normal occurrence of singing in octaves by men and boys. The true breakthrough came in southern France in the first half of the 12th century with the elaboration of the added melody by allowing several of its notes to be sung against a sustained single note of the original chant, a cantus firmus. For the first time, polyphony consisted of simultaneous melodies that were melodically and rhythmically independent to an ever-greater degree, one of the hallmarks of the Western musical tradition. But the syntax of polyphony depended heavily on the occurrence of certain harmonic consonances, mainly the perfect octave and perfect fifth, and as the coordination of the two, then three, and by the turn of the 13th century, four melodies to make these consonances at the right moment required a means of measuring the time with much greater precision than chant had ever wanted. The solution, developed in France from the 12th through the mid-14th centuries and ending with the invention of modern mensural notation, threatened to rob church music of its free flowing rhythm by constraining notes to be countable in terms of a standard time unit, or beat, and then by organizing those beats into metric groups defined by recurring accents. Meter, the sign of dance, had come to the church as a practical necessity of polyphony.

To be sure, introducing precise time measure into church music did not convert the mystical chant into dance music at a stroke, for the element of meter, while discrete in one sense, in other senses admits of degree. Meter can be strong and regular, as in dance, but also weak, irregular, and ephemeral as in the sacred polyphony of Palestrina and his colleagues of the high Renaissance. Even certain kinds of chant, such as hymns, have a vague periodicity deriving from the poetic meter of their texts. As it grew fierce by the 14th century, the very independence of melody that required the adoption of time measure in the first place ironically ensured a less periodic distribution of melodic accents, so that the resulting meter in the sacred polyphony is weak. Indeed, much of the genius of Catholic polyphony through the 15th and 16th centuries lay in its preservation of something like a mystical, chant-like rhythmic flow despite a coordinated texture of six simultaneous melodies or more.

Thus, Renaissance polyphony avoided the principal danger of all these modifications to chant: that the result would sound like secular court music. Having long abandoned the premise of other world religions, that liturgical music embodied a divine essence and therefore should never change, Christian authorities instead sought to maintain an essential distinction between music for the liturgy and that heard in the secular world of court and workplace. Despite the introduction of the organ, polyphony, and meter, a strategy of maintaining the traditional chant as the core of liturgical music while the innovations slowly accrued around it largely succeeded in maintaining this distinction. Nevertheless, the "corruption and depravity" of Catholic church music became a contentious matter with the onset of the Reformation in the early 16th century, with Martin Luther and Jean Calvin radically reforming many of its practices in order to keep secular influences at bay.

The psalmody promoted by Calvin and brought to life in the *Genevan Psalter* attempted a return to the purity of chant while simplifying its rhythmic subtleties so that musically untrained congregants could sing it. Spurning all the creative sacred poetry of the medieval Latin hymns, Calvin permitted only the Biblical psalms, metricized to facilitate learning and memorization, set to simple tunes. He preferred no harmonization at all; the tunes in the *Genevan Psalter* and its imitators have simple note-against-note arrangements. Instruments were forbidden. The result is an ascetic sacred song clearly set apart from the music of the world. Many of its spare characteristics, through necessity if not theological principle, crossed the Atlantic and flourished in the numerous sects descended from Calvin in the American colonies.

The Lutheran chorale and the Anglican hymn did not quarrel so much with Catholic musical aesthetics, adapting in fact many Catholic hymns, as make congregational singing possible through texts in the vernacular languages and a stronger metric profile in their melodies or adaptations. They, too, established a character of hymnody sufficiently distinct from contemporary secular music.

On the defensive, Catholic authorities responded to a number of the reformer's criticisms in the final years of the Council of Trent (1545–1563) while yet affirming the propriety of polyphony for liturgy. They also moved to restrict the use of instruments besides the organ that had been slowly creeping into liturgy, and thus gave the *a cappella* aesthetic for church music its moment of reference. They insisted that the sacred texts, often rendered unintelligible in motets by complex overlap of voices in polyphony, be set in clearer textures. They tried to outlaw "profane" melodies of erotic madrigals from being heard as *cantus firmi* in masses, and to prevent the adventurous Italian secular chromaticism from infecting the modal purity of Catholic polyphony. In affirming the polyphonic tradition, the Church rejected for four more centuries the Protestant ideal of congregational singing and kept sacred music in the hands of trained professional singers, at least officially. But by insisting on certain key elements of the musical language—voices only, melodies without chromaticism, and polyphonic texture—they also managed to keep their sacred music apart from the world, maintaining that critical sacred/secular distinction at the very moment European music experienced a fundamental reorientation.

The 16th century was the first in the history of Western music that showed a clear demarcation between the sound of art music for the churches and art music for the courts, salons, intellectual academies, and other secular locales. One can speak of a Renaissance secular musical language, or at least a dialect, distinct from the reigning language of sacred music in which every musician was trained. Naturally, as when any two language groups have close contact, there were mutual influences, and it was still common for secular compositions such as Heinrich Isaac's farewell to his home city "*Innsbruck, ich muß dich lassen*" to be adapted as *contrafacta* to sacred hymnody merely by changing the text. By stopping this process, the fathers of the Council of Trent widened the gap and preserved a style of music in a "pure" state, much as Renaissance humanists restored the Latin language to its "pure" classical state. With the development of ever more tempting secular styles in the 17th century, Catholic, Lutheran, and Anglican church musicians would be forced to choose between them and the iconic sacred polyphony frozen in the 16th century.

The greatest temptations came from the invention of opera at the turn of the 17th century in Florence and Rome, a new genre that rapidly spread over all of Europe and transformed the conception of music from a primarily lyrical art devoted to contemplation of God and man to a conception of music as a dramatic art, capable of conveying character and action. The inventors redeployed the elements of late-16th-century secular music to create the new textures of recitative and aria, which, when properly combined with modern functional harmony, founded the musical language of the Baroque, rhythmically driven and metrically much more dancelike than any polyphonist would have ever desired. Most churchmen could not resist. Operalike genres of sacred concerto, sacred symphony, oratorio, Neapolitan mass, and church cantata sprouted to accommodate sacred texts. In sound, their arias and recitatives are indistinguishable from their secular counterparts. Only the occasional polyphonic chorus recalled the sacred semantic. Even that distinction weakened, as choruses found their way into coronations, French opera, and other secular celebrations as well as oratorio. Thus, many of Johann Sebastian Bach's magnificent church cantatas are reworked secular pieces, made sacred by a Pietistic text and perhaps the inclusion of a Lutheran chorale.[3]

The greatly compromised sacred semantic, to say nothing of the scientific revolution or the Enlightenment, caused a serious decline in the fortunes of Lutheran and Anglican music beginning in the late 18th century. Leading composers were not attracted by a sacred music that merely aped opera and symphony and other secular genres while giving up their flexibility. As a youth, Wolfgang Amadeus Mozart had a permanent appointment at the Salzburg Cathedral, but he could not wait to escape to Vienna for a much less secure career writing opera. Neither did anyone want to compose in an academic musical language frozen in the past. Paradoxically, recovery of that past, restoration of musical traditions that connoted the transcendent, became the answer to the sorry contemporary situation in the 19th century. This was the time of the Cecillian movement beginning in Germany, the recovery and revival of Gregorian chant at Solesmes, and the Oxford movement in England.[4] This was when Palestrina was most idealized.

Such efforts flouted the main aesthetic impulse of the culture at large in the later 19th and 20th centuries: the demand for originality in high degree, for near absolute individuality in art. The terms of the conflict were clear: to be artists, modernizers composed and promoted sacred music, if at all, in their contemporary idiom, flouting the unwritten law observed since the middle ages that required liturgical music to be distinct from secular; traditionalists campaigned to restore the distinction by reviving musical languages whose sacred semantics were beyond doubt. The conflict affected non-Western and non-Christian traditions within reach. Cantor Solomon Sulzer of Austria provoked controversy when he arranged traditional Jewish chants in contemporary idiom and brought the organ into the synagogue. Already in the previous century Peter the Great had reinforced the new polyphony added to Russian *znamennïy* chant by importing Western notation, driving the dissident "Old Believers" into the mountains.

The principal thrust of the 19th century liturgical movement—the Cecilians and Oxford proponents in particular—wanted to restore a vibrant spirituality to liturgies grown tired and perfunctory, and some of these activists saw congregational singing as one means to this end. For Catholics, this would mean recognizing a practice that, it could well be argued, had been simmering beneath the surface for centuries, even bubbling up in isolated regions here and there without official blessing; for Protestants it meant merely the revival of a liturgical reform that had been part of their very foundation.

Such spirited congregational singing, ironically enough, had already flowered for two centuries in the cultural backwater of America. (Latin America had adopted the old Roman Catholic musical traditions early on, with cathedrals in Mexico City, Lima, and Rio di Janiero boasting music equal in quality to the greatest in Europe.) The seeds of a rough democratization of sacred music sown by Luther and especially Calvin found fertile ground in the American colonies, with their largely dissident Protestant distrust of central authorities and privileged classes, including highly trained musicians. Congregational psalmody was the order of the day in the 17th and 18th centuries, with singing schools springing up to teach whole congregations how to do it better and better. At the same time the black slaves, who had no teachers or authorities to follow, created their spirituals. These songs in turn fertilized the Gospel song tradition that arose from the populist religious movement known as the Second Awakening in the 19th century, a tradition very much alive today.

In the American environment where music that most people heard was homemade, it is perhaps not surprising that the European problem of maintaining a sacred semantic distinct from the secular was not a live issue. The simple stanzas of Isaac Watts were enough to make a song sacred, almost regardless of its musical material. This attitude has remained the hallmark of much American sacred music through the 20th century, particularly in Evangelical churches, which have adopted in their music one popular style after another. The praise choruses composed in the last half of the century have only their words to distinguish them from commercial music heard on radio and television. More recently, the mainline Protestant churches have begun to abandon their traditional hymnodies for songs of this type, following the American Catholics who seized upon the exception clauses in the Second Vatican Council's *Constitution on the Sacred Liturgy* (1963) to use folk revival music and its rhythmically simpler derivatives in the 1980s and 1990s for their masses.

CONTINUING CONTENTIONS

Despite the pervasive influence of this American populism in sacred music, felt now even in Europe, sentiments like those of the Cecilian and Oxford movements that yearn for a restoration of "solemnity" to liturgy—in other words a truly distinct and sacred semantic—are easy to find. Controversies about what sacred music should sound like are common in many congregations and show no sign of abating. They generally take on one of three forms.

One dispute, important in any evangelical religious tradition seeking to spread its message beyond a local culture, is about catholicity versus local custom. Should everyone use the same music as a sign of religious unity, or should indigenous musical traditions, which often attract converts, play a role in rituals? The pendulum swings back and forth throughout the history of sacred music in the West, with periods of intense local invention countered by a pruning from a central authority, often signaled by new liturgical books.

A second kind of dispute, typical of older traditions, concerns congregational singing versus professional ministry. Congregational singing seems to respond to a universal human desire to praise the divine in communal song; examples are found in every major religion. But such music routinely contains elements of popular music with its association with the secular world, which is why Maimonides opposed the singing of *piyyutim* (hymns) in synagogue services. And music for congregations must be very simple. Sacred music of the highest artistic standards generally demands a highly trained class of musicians, who resist abandoning their long years of training and simplifying their art for the sake of the commoner. They ask, "Should not the highest, most sublime form of praise be offered to the divine?"

The last kind of dispute, the interests of tradition versus those of artistic creativity, is an eruption of a tension inherent in the art of sacred music. Sacred music is music, after all, a fine art, and therefore requires artists, not mere craftsmen, who by nature want to create beauty, not merely replicate it, through music and who by training are equipped to do it. But sacred music must also be sacred. For some religions this has meant that the music received must be handed on without change, for to change it risks profanation. God is the same yesterday, today, and forever; so is the music that best praises Him. Obviously this leaves the musician in an artistic dilemma, one that some traditionalist religions solve by refusing to regard their chant as music at all. For Western Christianity, the artist's dilemma was accommodated for many centuries by allowing enough change to satisfy the creator while insisting that the essence of the music remain to set it apart from music of the world. In the last two centuries since the Enlightenment, this strategy has failed on many counts. Whether it may be recovered, and whether it should be, remains to be seen.

"What is the nature of sacred music?" is the question at the center of all these contentions, a question that admits a continuum of answers, as history has shown. At one extreme is the belief that the music, as music, imbues no sacred qualities at all; rather, everything is in the text being sung or the ritual being enacted. This kind of sacred music never remains static for long; why should it? At the opposite end we find the music bound so tightly to the holy word that it cannot be changed, no more than the Bible, the Qur'ān, or the Vedas could be revised. Between these extremes lie every variety of compromise, highly attuned to the historical moment, responding to the particular desires to praise the divine as well as the deeper, eternal ones. As cultures evolve through time, so do these particular desires and also the music that carries them upward.

NOTES

1. Wayne Howard, *Sāmavedic Chant* (New Haven: Yale University Press, 1977), ch.1.

2. "What Makes 'Religious Music' Religious?" in *Sacred Sound: Music in Religious Thought and Practice*, ed. Joyce Irwin (Chico, Calif.: Scholars Press), 1983, pp. 27–29.

3. Even as monumental a sacred work as Bach's *Mass in B Minor* contains a reworking of a secular cantata: the Osanna is a recomposition of "Preise dein Glücke," BW 215. See George Stauffer, *Bach: The Mass in B Minor* (New York: Schirmer, 1997), 49.

4. Strictly speaking, the Oxford writers, also known as Tractarians, aimed at theological, not liturgical renewal, but a revival of interest in liturgy was one of its most practical effects in the latter half of the 19th century.

The Dictionary

– A –

ABENDMUSIK (**Ger. "Evening music"**). A series of sacred music concerts given at the Marienkirche in Lübeck, Germany. They may have begun under the direction of Franz Tunder (1614–1667), **organist** from 1641–1667, as organ recitals, but their repertory expanded to include **sacred concertos** and **oratorios** under the direction of **Dietrich Buxtehude**. The series at Marienkirche ceased in 1810, but since then the term has come to mean "concerts in church."

A CAPPELLA (It. "in the manner of the chapel"). Choral music sung without **instrumental** accompaniment. The strict practice of the Sistine Chapel in **Rome** may have originated the term, but since the 19th century it has been used to describe any ensemble singing without instruments. Whether Roman Catholic **polyphony** was supported by the **pipe organ** or other instruments doubling the voices in other places during the Middle Ages and Renaissance is controversial. *See also* INSTRUMENTS, USE OF.

A COLLECTION OF PSALMS AND HYMNS (Charles Town, So. Carolina, 1737). The first of a series of Methodist hymnals, the first compiled by **John Wesley**, containing 70 **hymns**, 35 by **Isaac Watts** and several by **Charles Wesley**.

A COLLECTION OF SPIRITUAL SONGS AND HYMNS SELECTED FROM VARIOUS AUTHORS BY RICHARD ALLEN, AFRICAN MINISTER (Philadelphia, 1801). Influential first hymnal designed for the specific use of an African-American congregation, containing 54 **hymn** texts (no tunes) by Allen, **Isaac**

1

Watts, Charles and **John Wesley**, and other Methodist and Baptist authors.

ADAM OF ST. VICTOR (died Paris, 1146). A charter of Notre Dame cathedral lists "Subdeacon Adam" as a signatory. About 1133, "Adam Precentor" moved to the Abbey of St. Victor. He is believed to have contributed significantly to the creation of more than 100 **sequence** texts composed in Paris in the early 12th century.

'ADHĀN. Islamic call to prayer, one of the two forms of compulsory mosque music, instituted by the Prophet between 622 and 624. Originally a simple announcement, it can range from monotonic **chant** to ornate melody sung five times per day by **muezzins** from the minarets of mosques as a summons, then immediately again as *iqamā*, the beginning of prayer.

Transmitted by oral tradition, the melody varies widely by locality. Military bands of **drummers** accompanied *'adhān* from the 10th to 19th centuries in some places.

In modern times the *'adhān* of Egypt have become the most influential and are imitated abroad. Loudspeakers and radio broadcasts, often at great, distorted volumes, have diminished the role of the muezzin in some areas. *See also QĪRA.*

AGNUS DEI. *See* MASS; Appendix IA5 for text.

AHLE, JOHANN RUDOLF (24 December 1625, Mühlhausen, Thuringia, Germany–9 July 1673, Mühlhausen). Elected **organist** of St. Blasius in Mühlhausen in 1654. He composed **motets, sacred concertos**, and sacred part-songs. Some of the latter are still sung.

AKATHISTOS **HYMN.** Famous **Byzantine** *kontakion*, its anonymous text, containing two *prooimia* followed by 24 strophes in honor of the Virgin Mary, dates from as early as the sixth century, but the earliest known melodic setting, highly **melismatic**, dates from a 13th-century *psaltikon*. Its text remained unabbreviated even after the singing of complete *kontakia* was suppressed in the eighth century. Originally for the Feast of the Annunciation, the **hymn** is now sung on the vigil of the fifth Sunday in Lent.

AKOLOUTHIAI (**Gk. "orders of service"**). Manuscripts containing **Byzantine chant**. The earliest is dated 1336; about 20 of those discovered so far also date from the 14th century and 40 more from the 15th. More than 100 composers are cited, including **Joannes Glykys**, Nikephoros Ethikos (fl. c. 1300), **Joannes Koukouzeles**, **Xenos Korones**, Joannes Kladas (fl. c. 1400), and **Manuel Chrysaphes**.

The manuscripts contain some simple chants for liturgical texts but are mostly occupied with the elaborate **kalophonic chant** for the same texts. Because these relatively new melodies replaced older ones, each manuscript may reflect the preferences of its monastery or compiler.

ĀLĀP (**Sans. "conversation"**). A non-**metric** improvisational introduction preceding the establishment of *tāla* common in much Hindu devotional and art music. It presents the *rāga* to be used for the entire composition. It may last from a few minutes to an hour, although those associated with devotional genres are typically short. The earliest notated examples date from the 13th century. *See also DHRUPAD.*

ALBRIGHT, WILLIAM (20 October 1944, Gary, Indiana–17 September 1998, Ann Arbor, Mich.). Student of **Olivier Messiaen**, his *Organbook I* (1967) is a collection of practical works for liturgy, while *Organbook II* (1971) incorporates electronic sounds. He also composed three **masses**, a dozen **hymns**, **anthems**, and **motets.**

ALLEGRI, GREGORIO. *See MISERERE.*

ALLELUIA. Latin spelling of the Hebrew expression for "praise the Lord," which also refers to a **proper chant** of the Roman Catholic **mass**, sung immediately preceding the Gospel except during Lent.

In the **Gregorian** tradition, the Alleluia is a **responsorial** chant that includes a **proper psalm** verse. The **cantor**(s) begin by singing "Alleluia," which the choir repeats and then appends a **melismatic** extension of the last syllable, called the *jubilus*. The cantor follows with the psalm verse, the choir joining in for its conclusion. Then the Alleluia is sung again as before, except that the choir does not repeat the cantor's music, but sings the *jubilus* only.

In modern liturgy the **congregation**, taking the place of the choir, mimics the cantor exactly, who then follows with a **versicle**, to which the congregation responds with one more iteration of the Alleluia tune. Some modern settings ignore the ancient tradition of singing the word "Alleluia" three times to symbolize the Trinity. *See also HALLELUJAH.*

ALMA REDEMPTORIS MATER. See VOTIVE ANTIPHON.

ALTERNATIM. A specific kind of **antiphony,** by which traditional **chant** alternates with newly composed **polyphony**, almost always using the traditional response as a **cantus firmus**. In vocal music *alternatim* is usually practiced for the verses of a **psalm** or **canticle**. In an **organ mass**, *alternatim* is applied to the **ordinary** and **proper** prayers of the liturgy, with organ **versets** substituting for the chant at certain traditional points.

AMALAR (AMALARIUS) OF METZ (c. 775, northern France–c. 850, Metz?). He provided a direct account of ninth-century plainchant practice and performance, comparing Frankish and Roman sources and discussing antiphonal singing. His largest and best-known work is the *Liber officialis* (c. 823, rev. ed. 831). (at)

AMBROSE, ST. (c. 333, Trier, Germany–4 April, 397, Milan). The "Father of Christian **Hymnology**," he was elected Bishop of Milan in 374 and introduced the eastern practices of **antiphonal** and **congregational** singing into the liturgy as part of a **psalm** vigil service, which consequently spread widely. That he composed the text for the **Te Deum** was discredited in the 19th century, but scholars believe he did write as many as 14 traditionally attributed texts, and certainly *Aeterne rerum conditor, Deus creator omnium, Iam surgit hora tertia,* and *Intende qui regis Israel.*

AMBROSIAN CHANT. Chant sung in Roman Catholic liturgies in the diocese of Milan, Italy, traditionally attributed to **St. Ambrose** of

Milan but now discredited, whose prestige helped ensure its survival as a distinct repertory despite the growing dominance of **Gregorian chant** through the Middle Ages. The earliest sources date from the 11th and 12th centuries, significantly later than the earliest Gregorian sources. Versions of some Ambrosian chants also survive in the **Byzantine** rite.

ANDREW OF CRETE, ST. (Andrew Hierosolymites, Andrew of Jerusalem, c. 660, Damascus–c. 740, Mytilene, Crete). Byzantine **hymnographer** and homilist, he is the first identified who wrote in the Syriac **modal** system and the first known composer of **kanons**, including the Great Kanon, consisting of 250 strophes, still sung during Lent. (at)

ANDRIESSEN, HENDRIK (17 September 1892, Haarlem, Netherlands–12 April 1981, Heemstede). Famous **organist** who composed 16 **masses** including the *Missa in Honorem Ss Cordis* (1919), *Missa Diatonica* (1935), and *Missa Christus Rex* (1938) and many other sacred works, principally for chorus or organ. He experimented with **modal**, serial, and modernist tonal techniques. (at)

ANERIO, GIOVANNI FRANCESCO (c. 1567, Rome–buried 12 June 1630, Graz, Austria). Organist and priest who introduced the vernacular **oratorio** with his *Teatro Armonico Spirituale* (1619), written for the Oratory of St. Filippo Neri. It contains the earliest surviving obbligato **instrumental** parts in Rome. He also composed several **masses**, 83 **motets**, and *Selva armonica* (1617), a collection of Latin motets and *madrigali spirituali* in Italian for one to four voices representating the latest trends. *See also* MEDICEAN CHANT.

ANGLICAN CHANT. Method of **chanting psalms** and **canticles** in four-voiced harmony used by the Anglican Church (See figure 1.).

The first half of each verse is chanted without **meter** on the first harmony for as long as the number of syllables demands, until the pointing of the text indicates the next harmony. The last few syllables are then sung to measured beats, always in whole, half, or quarter-note values. The second half of the psalm verse follows similarly,

Figure 1. Anglican chant.

with one additional measure for finality. The tradition owes something to both the unmetered **Gregorian psalm tones** and the English practice of **faburden**, or improvised **polyphony**.

The earliest sources of Anglican chant are examples in **Thomas Morley**'s *A Plaine and Easie Introduction to Practicall Musike* (1597) and a small number of 17th-century sources. Robert Janes published a system of text pointing in *The Psalter or Psalms of David* (1837), and most of the chanting formulas in modern service books date from the 19th century.

ANIMUCCIA, GIOVANNI (c. 1500, Florence–c. 20 March 1571, Rome). *Magister cantorum* at Cappella Giulia of the Vatican from 1555 until his death, between the two tenures of **Giovanni da Palestrina**. His two publications of *Laude* spirituali (1563, 1570) for the *Congregazione dell'* **Oratorio** of St. Filippo Neri, where he was the first *maestro di cappella*, uses a simple **homorhythmic** style in preference to complex Flemish **counterpoint** to attract attendance. (at)

ANTHEM. A **polyphonic** setting of a Christian text, usually Biblical, in English, excluding **ordinaries** of the **mass** and traditional **canticles** such as **Magnificat**. The term dates from the 11th century, an English cognate of **antiphon**. English-language sacred music suddenly rose in status when the first *Booke of Common Praier* (1549) replaced liturgical Latin with English. By the 17th century, "anthem" commonly referred to sacred vocal music of the Anglican Church.

Early post-Reformation sources, the Wanley and Lumley Part-books (c. 1546–1548 and c. 1549), contain mostly anonymous anthems setting texts from the Bible, from the *Booke of Common Praire*, and **metrical psalms** in four-voiced textures typical of Flemish **counterpoint**. Clarity of diction was important. Anthems continued to parallel continental developments in the late 16th century, including explicit use of solo singers in **verse anthems**, which began to outnumber **full anthems** by the turn of the 17th century. After the Restoration, Matthew Locke (c. 1621–1677) and Humphrey Pelham (1647/8–1674) brought from their European travels **operatic** textures and the use of **organ** and various solo **instruments** to articulate with voices ever more ambitious musical structures, culminating in the **Coronation Anthems** of **George Frideric Handel**. Interest in anthem composition declined along with interest in Anglican liturgy generally from the latter half of the 18th century onward, although interest revived somewhat in the 20th century. Such as were composed, up to the present, reflect the musical idioms of their times.

In **Morning** and **Evening Prayer**, the anthem should occur after the third collect, according to the 1662 rubric.

ANTIPHON. Chant preceding and following a chanted **psalm** or **canticle** with text from the Bible or hagiography. The term and its association with **psalmody** has been traced to **St. Ambrose** in the late fourth century, and some documents indicate a performance practice of splitting the choir to sing in **antiphony**. The choir may sing the antiphon in alternation with verses of the psalm, or sets of verses, or may frame the psalm by singing the antiphon once before it begins and once after it ends. In any case, the **psalm tone** for chanting the psalm is chosen according to the **mode** of the antiphon for the particular occasion. Some scholars believe that the melodies of the older antiphons derive from the formulas of the psalm tones.

Antiphons will occur first of all whenever psalms are sung in Roman Catholic liturgy, principally in the **divine office**, but also in certain **propers** of the **mass**. Actions of the celebrant—his entrance (introit), prayer over the gifts (offertory), and prayers during communion—are thought to have been at one time accompanied by psalms and antiphons. In the **Gregorian** tradition (ninth century), only the antiphons, without psalm verses, remain at offertory and communion; with the Introit enough psalm verses are sung to cover the procession. *See also* BYZANTINE CHANT; PSALM TONE; *STICHERON*; VOTIVE ANTIPHON.

ANTIPHONAL. Liturgical book containing the **chants** for singing the **divine office**.

ANTIPHONY. Performance practice of dividing a choir into two, each semichoir singing a portion of a **chanted** composition in response to the other. The triumphal return of David from his defeat of Goliath and the Philistines may be the earliest written evidence of antiphony (1 Samuel 18:7). **Psalmody** is most commonly sung antiphonally, each semichoir taking a verse, but **antiphons** and **responsories** may also be sung this way.

Anglicans call singers who sit with the dean (first **cantor**) on the south side of the chancel *decani*; those with the cantor on the north side, *cantori*. See *also ALTERNATIM*; *CORI SPEZZATI*; GREGORIAN CHANT.

AQUINAS, ST. THOMAS (late 1224 or early 1225, Roccasecca, Italy–9 March 1274, Fossanova). Preeminent Roman Catholic theologian who wrote texts for *Lauda Sion Salvatore* (Corpus Christi **sequence**), and the **hymns** *Pange Lingua*, *Adoro Te Devote*, *Verbum Supernum Prodiens*, *Sacris Solemnis*. (at)

ARIA. Operatic composition developing from the late 16th century for solo singer with **instrumental** accompaniment characterized by a clear **meter** and significant musical structure such as strophic, ABA (*da capo*), sonata form, etc., which usually requires much repetition of short phrases of sung text. Arias for more than one singer are termed duets, trios, etc. A large group singing an aria is a chorus.

The aria conveys a character's emotional reaction to a dramatic situation. In sacred music, this function is largely confined to **oratorios** and **passions**. Otherwise, segments of a Neapolitan style **mass** or verses within a church **cantata** were commonly set as arias to make them musically substantial without explicit dramatic function. *See also* RECITATIVE.

ARS NOVA (**Lat. "the new art"**). System of **mensural** rhythmic notation developed in late 13th-century France that determines the duration of a note by its shape, essentially the concept used in the West ever since, except in tablature. *See also* MOTET; POLYPHONY.

ASHFORD, EMMA LOUISE (HINDLE) (27 March 1850, Newark, Del.–22 September 1930, Nashville, Tenn.). She wrote more than 250 **anthems**, 50 sacred songs, 24 sacred duets, more than 200 voluntaries, plus **cantatas**, **gospel songs**, and *Ashford's Organ Instructor*. (at)

ASMATIKON. Liturgical book of **Byzantine chant** compiled for the trained choir (*psaltai*) as contrasted with the soloist's *psaltikon*. **Responsorial** chants divided between soloist and choir will likewise be divided between the books; both are required for a complete performance. The surviving copies date from the 13th and early 14th century, mostly from south Italy. They contain chants for *koinōnika* (communion) in the **divine liturgy**, refrains for *prokeimena* and *troparia*, *hypakoai*, *kontakia*, and **ordinary** chants for the **divine office** including the *eisdikon*, *trisagion*, and *cheroubikon*.

AUGUSTINE (AUGUSTINUS AURELIUS), ST. (13 November 354–28 August 430). Great Doctor of the Christian Church, his theological writings and sermons touch on **Ambrosian chant** and his book *De Musica* (391) is an early theory of rhythm and **meter**.

AVE MARIA (**Lat. "Hail, Mary"**). The most popular prayer invoking the intercession of the Blessed Virgin Mary. Its full text may be **chanted** as a self-contained prayer and has been set **polyphonically** as a **motet** many times, although the chant has no traditional liturgical role. Truncated versions serve as **offertories** for the fourth Sunday of Advent and for certain Marian feasts, although there is a different melody for the Feast of the Immaculate Conception (December 8). Yet another chant melody sets a truncated version as an **antiphon** for second **vespers** of two feasts: the Annunciation (March 25) and the Holy Rosary (October 7).

AVE MARIA . . . VIRGO SERENA. Famous four-voiced **motet** of **Josquin Desprez** often cited as an early example *par excellence* of the technique of structural **imitation**, which he did so much to perfect. The strophic text is a pastiche of a **sequence** sung at the Feast of the Annunciation, a well-known 15th-century prayer, and a common invocation at the end. Josquin composes a different type of imitative texture for each strophe, including strict, free, and paired **imitation**, and an apparently **homophonic** passage that hides a **canon**. The piece may come from Milan in the 1470s, and it requires about five minutes to sing.

AVE REGINA COELORUM. See VOTIVE ANTIPHON.

AYIN. Islamic ritual dance associated with the Sufi order of Mevlevi, founded by Jalāl al-dīn Rūmī (1207–1273) and now centered in Konya, Turkey. The roughly 100 surviving *ayin* compositions date from the 16th century, although the earliest musical notation is 18th century. Qu'rānic recitations frame an address to the Prophet (*na't*), **instrumental preludes**, four Turkish songs (*selam*) on texts by Rumi, and an instrumental **postlude**. Traditional instruments include end-blown flutes, **drum**, and in some areas types of lute and fiddle. *See also* DHIKR; KIRTANA; MADĪH; QĪRA; SAMA.

– B –

BACH, JOHANN SEBASTIAN (21 March 1685 Eisenach, Thuringia, [modern Germany]–23 July 1750, Leipzig). In his own day, J. S. Bach was recognized within German-speaking principalities as an outstanding performing musician, particularly on keyboard **instruments,** and by connoisseurs as one of the great composers of the time. Today his work continues to influence sacred music more than that of any other single composer, and even in the secular repertories Bach's voice is so predominant in the Western tradition that the year of his death has been traditionally observed as the end of the Baroque period. He composed masterworks in every genre of the early 18th century except opera.

Bach concentrated on whatever kind of composition was demanded by the church or court post he held at a given time. His first two important appointments, as **organist** to the New Church at Arnstadt from 1703–1707 and then to St. Blasius's in Mühlhausen (both in Thuringia) from 1707–1708, produced early organ pieces (e.g., *Toccata and Fugue in D minor*, BWV 565) and a small number of church **cantatas** (e.g., *"Gott ist mein König,"* BWV 70). Next, he was appointed organist and chamber musician at the court of Saxe-Weimar from 1708–1717 where he composed the great bulk of his keyboard works, including didactic collections (e.g., *Orgelbüchlein*, c. 1713–1715, BWV 599–644). His promotion to concertmaster in March 1714 required the composition once per month of a church cantata for small instrumental and vocal ensemble in order to fit into the confined space of the chapel at the Weimar castle (e.g., *Himmelskönig, sei willkommen*, BWV 182). In 1717, he moved to Cöthen (Thuringia) to be *kapellmeister* to Prince Leopold where he directed an ensemble of professional court musicians. Here, Bach composed or collected much of his secular concertos, suites (including those for solo violin and cello), sonatas, and other ensemble works (e.g., Brandenburg Concertos). In 1723, Bach was elected **cantor** of St. Thomas Church by the town council of Leipzig. He remained in this post until his death.

As *Thomaskantor,* Bach had to supervise the music at four churches (St. Thomas, St. Nicholas, St. Paul's, and the New Church) and the musical education of students at the St. Thomas school. In the 1720s, according to Bach's obituary, he composed five liturgical cycles of about 60 church cantatas each for the **Lutheran** church year, only three of which survive, as well as at least two **passions** (**St. John**, 1724, BWV 245 and **St. Matthew**, 1727, BWV 244), as well as the **Magnificat** (1723, BWV 243) and a number of secular cantatas and keyboard works. Toward 1730, he became increasingly unhappy with the lack of support for his program from the town authorities. The prodigious compositional production of more than one cantata per week at the beginning of his Leipzig tenure fell off. Thereafter he often **parodied** older compositions to meet liturgical demands (e.g., **The Christmas Oratorio**, 1734, BWV 248) and devoted himself increasingly to secular compositions for the local Collegium Musicum and to compilations of a speculative nature such as the "Goldberg" Variations" (1742 pubd., BWV 988), the "Musical Offering" (1747 pubd.), and the "Art of Fugue" (1742–1750; pubd. 1751, BWV 1080). In these encyclopedic works, Bach explores the limits of his musical style, the technical possibilities of his inherited language. Even his last major composition, the **Mass in B minor** (BWV 232), is such an exploration, since there is no known commission for its Credo, Sanctus, or Agnus Dei. Thus Bach's last two decades adumbrate the modern composer who creates after his own inspiration rather than for a particular event or liturgy.

In 1950, Wolfgang Schmieder published his *Bach-Werke-Verzeichnis*, a catalog of Bach's works (rev. ed. 1990). His BWV numeration, running to more than 1,070 works, is the most common way of precisely identifying a Bach composition today. The catalog, however, is not chronological but categorical; BWV numbers cannot be trusted to indicate priority of composition even within a category.

Bach's music influenced the sacred repertory of the Christian West in at least five areas. Accounting by breadth of dispersal and frequency of hearing, his music exercises the widest sphere of influence through his four-voiced **chorale** harmonizations. Many of these originated as movements, usually concluding, from his church cantatas. First collected by Bach's son, Carl Phillip Emmanuel (1714–1788), in 1765 and 1769, they have since populated the **hymn** repertories of Lutheran, Anglican, Roman Catholic, and other Christian churches. The soprano melodies were, of course, already traditional in Bach's time; he added alto, tenor, and bass voices, resulting in arrangements of exceptionally inventive harmonic goals, animated inner part-writing, and dissonances that, while at times strident, never violate the syntax of his native musical language. Music students the world over study Bach chorales because they capture in miniature the synthesis of harmonic function and **counterpoint** that is the essence of the Western tradition.

Next most influential is the organ music, which stands at the summit of the entire organ repertory. There are five categories: improvisational genres (*stylus phantasticus*), **fugues, sonatas, chorale preludes**, and transcriptions.

The improvisational genres include works with titles such as **prelude, toccata**, and **fantasia**. Bach was an incomparable improviser on the keyboard, and these works are thought to be derived from such extemporaneous performances that might occur at the beginning of a liturgy or as part of an organ recital. Typical of these works are passages with discontinuous meter, disjointed phrasing, chromatic wandering, extended sequential modulations, and other devices suggesting invention on the spot. Because they are not rhythmically unified in the manner of most Baroque instrumental compositions, rather like instrumental **recitative**, they present a tentative and unclosed structure and often do not stand alone but introduce a following fugue.

Bach's name is almost synonymous with fugue, for he explored this technique more comprehensively, by far, than anyone else has ever done. The most explicit compendia are the two collections of *The Well-Tempered Clavier* (c. 1722, BWV 846–69 and 1742, BWV 870–93, not for organ but harpsichord or clavichord), in which Bach presents the player with 24 preludes and fugues from two to five voices, of every type, one for each of the major and minor keys, and *The Art of Fugue* (1742–1750, pubd. 1751, BWV 1080), which treats a single **subject** to the various traditional contrapuntal devices: simple **imitation**, double and triple counterpoint, inversion, and retrograde.

The six trio sonatas (late 1720s, BWV 525–30) are thought to be among his most difficult because they require intricate passagework to be played with constant independence of the two hands and feet. The transcriptions of concertos by Antonio Vivaldi, Giuseppe Torelli, and other masters come from Bach's early career as a means of learning the highly influential Italian manner. He often enlivened the simpler Italian textures by adding inner parts and fast bass rhythms.

The chorale preludes take a traditional chorale as their compositional premise, usually as a sustained **cantus firmus**. The four important collections of these are the **Orgelbüchlein**, Part III of the *Clavier-Übung* (1739 publ., BWV 669–89), a set known as *The Great Eighteen* (after 1740, BWV 651–68), and the *Schubler Chorales* (1748–1749 publ., BWV 645–50). Again, Bach explores every means of raising the humble chorale to undreamed of artistic heights: as a cantus firmus in soprano, alto, tenor, or bass, in **canon**, in a highly ornamented version, as the subject of a fugue and as canonic variations (on *Vom Himmel hoch*, 1747, BWV 769). Although the chorale may be drawn out slowly, Bach's unflagging accompanying voices never fail to maintain an intense Baroque rhythmic continuity throughout.

Bach often combined these genres and crossed categorical boundaries within a single work. Improvisatory toccatas may have tightly composed fugal sections. Late in life, he transcribed a number of vocal pieces for organ (e.g., two in the *Schubler Chorales*). Trio texture is common throughout the organ works, and of course the chorale prelude concept underlies all his "chorale" cantatas.

Third most influential would be Bach's church cantatas, passions, and masses. When Bach was *Thomaskantor*, these comprised his principal compositional responsibility. The cantatas, using Biblical texts with commentary, would be sung directly after the readings from Scripture in the Lutheran mass before the homily and so act as a musical exegesis of the day's lessons. Longer cantatas would be performed in two parts, one before and the other after the homily. Bach's *St. John Passion* and *St. Matthew Passion* occupy an analogous position in the Good Friday **vespers** liturgy but on a much larger scale, especially the *St. Matthew Passion*, of which the music alone lasts nearly three hours.

Because the liturgical reforms of Martin Luther authorized both Latin versions of the mass ordinaries as well as German chorale substitutes, Bach composed four masses consisting of only Kyrie and Gloria movements (1733–1739, BWV 232–36) that might be used more frequently than the cantatas whose texts destined them for a particular feast. The Mass in B minor began as such a pair; the Credo, Sanctus, and Agnus Dei were added only at the end of his life. Each of the four smaller masses has a Kyrie chorus of a single movement and a five-part Gloria in the form of three arias sandwiched between opening and closing choruses. The music in 19 of the 24 movements has been traced to previously composed cantatas.

Today, only isolated movements of Bach cantatas, masses, and passions find their way into liturgies. Instead, they form an essential component of the concert choral repertory.

The last but by no means inconsiderable influence on modern sacred music would be Bach's music for instrumental ensemble: works for solo violin, cello, and flute; the sonatas for solo instrument and **continuo**; trio sonatas; and the many concertos. Although Bach would not have used any of this music in liturgy without some accompanying sacred text, today it is commonly found in worship services of nearly every denomination, some even non-Christian. Bach himself anticipated this by his practice of recomposing secular music for the sacred service by adding sacred text and by using organ preludes and fugues that had no explicit sacred semantic, before and after a liturgy. In sum, Bach's style has come to represent so fine a sacred semantic in the modern sensibility that almost any composition of his is admissable in church today.

That style was well out of fashion by the time of his death in 1750 and so, except for a small number of keyboard works used for teaching purposes and very rare revivals of isolated movements, his music went underground and much of it was lost. A modicum of interest was maintained by connoisseurs such as the *Berliner Gewandhaus*, but the great bulk of Bach's music remained unknown for nearly a century. Felix Mendelssohn's partial revival of the *St. Matthew Passion* in 1829 in Berlin sparked a more general interest, and by 1850 the *Bachgesellschaft* (Bach Society) was founded to publish a complete edition, finished in 1897. Performers and editors of those days routinely interpreted "historical" music according to Romantic tastes so that the sizes of choruses and orchestras would be far beyond anything Bach had in mind, to say nothing of added dynamics, changed orchestrations, and other "improvements."

About the same time, however, a more "scientific" historicism in certain musicians began to question such liberal adaptations. Interest in manuscripts, contemporary theorists, original instruments, and other sources grew ever more intense, until the mid-20th century saw the emergence of ensembles that tried to recreate "authentic" performances such as Bach himself might have known. While the most egregious of 19th-century abuses certainly required remedy, Bach's own common practice of transcribing and adapting his own works for other musical media suggests that his art accommodates a wide variety of interpretations. The universal and enduring qualities that has made Bach's music the most studied all over the world seem to arise from the complex relations and coordinations, often very abstract, that he has built into the notes themselves.

BACH, WILHELM FRIEDEMANN (22 November 1710, Weimar, Saxony [modern Germany]–1 July 1784, Berlin). Son of **Johann Sebastian Bach,** he became **organist** at St. Sophia's Church in Dresden on 1 August 1733 and stayed until April 1746, when he became organist at the Liebfrauenkirche in Halle, a more prestigious and better paid position. He left in May 1764 over various conflicts and was not able to secure another permanent post. A renowned organ virtuoso, he composed more than 100 works, including sonatas, **fugues**, **fantasias**, and **choral preludes**. Twenty-one **cantatas**, two **masses**, and about a dozen other sacred vocal works also survive.

BAQQASHOT. Jewish vigil service performed after midnight on Friday from Sukkot to Passover, consisting of a standard repertory of heterogenous *piyyutim* (**hymns**) sung **antiphonally**. The practice developed in Aleppo in the mid-19th century but may have roots in Jewish mysticism, particularly the Zohar and Safed kabbalists.

BAREKHU. "Bless you," a **chanted** summons to prayer opening a Jewish service. The melody changes to reflect the season and following prayers. **Melismatic** elaboration of single syllables accompanies silent recitation of a **congregational** response.

BASSO CONTINUO. See CONTINUO.

BAY PSALM BOOK. The first book printed (Boston, 1640) in the American colonies. It provides **metrical psalms**, text only, with suggested tunes to fit to them.

BEETHOVEN, LUDWIG VAN (baptized 17 December 1770, Bonn–26 March 1827, Vienna). Renowned chiefly for his supreme mastery of **instrumental** genres—symphony, concerto, sonata, and string quartet—Beethoven only composed four explicitly sacred works: the **oratorio** *Christus am Oelberge* ("Christ on the Mount of Olives," 1803), the **Mass** in C major (1807), a wedding song, and the massive *Missa Solemnis* in D major (1819–1823). The two masses are often heard in concert, very rarely in liturgy.

BELSHAZZAR'S FEAST. An **English oratorio** composed by Sir William Walton (1902–1983) on a libretto by Sir Osbert Sitwell drawing from Isaiah 39, Daniel 5, Revelation 18, and **Psalms** 81 and 137. It premiered at the Leeds Festival in 1931. The score calls for baritone solo, eight-voice choir, and large symphony orchestra and takes about 37 minutes to perform. *See also* HANDEL, GEORGE FRIDERIC.

BENEDICAMUS DOMINO (**Lat. "Let us bless the Lord"**). Concluding **versicle** for the **divine offices** in the Roman Catholic rite (except that in **compline** it is followed by a **votive antiphon** to the Blessed Virgin Mary). The melodies for this **chant** were often used as **cantus firmi** in early **motets**.

BENEDICTUS. This word begins four **canticles** sung at **lauds** in various rites: the Canticle of David (1 Chronicles 29:10–13); the canticle from the Prayer of Azariah (a deuterocanonical book included by some traditions in the Book of Daniel, 3–22); the canticle of the three young men from the same Prayer of Azariah, 29–68; and the Canticle of Zachariah (St. Luke 1:68–79; *see* Appendix A for text).

The Canticle of Zachariah is an **ordinary** prayer at lauds in the Roman and Byzantine rites. In the **Gregorian** tradition, it is **chanted** as would a **psalm**, with framing **antiphons** and the corresponding tone, except that there is an **intonation** for each verse pair. **Polyphonic** settings are rare; in the special lauds that formed part of the **Tenebrae**, simple polyphonic settings in *falsobordone* can be found.

Benedictus also denotes the latter part of the Sanctus ordinary from the Roman Catholic **mass** (*see* Appendix A for text), which in polyphonic settings is often composed as a separate movement or *pars*. *See also* MORNING PRAYER; *ORTHRŌS*.

BEN-HAIM, PAUL (PAUL FRANKENBURGER) (5 July 1897, Munich–14 January 1984, Tel Aviv). Composer, pianist, conductor, he left Germany in 1933 with the Nazi takeover and moved to Tel Aviv. A long collaboration with folksinger Bracha Zephira (1910–1990) provided inspiration and material for his music, which includes *The Sweet Psalmist of Israel* (1957), *Kabbalai Shabbat* (1968), an **oratorio**, two **cantatas**, a **motet**, and three **psalms**, as well as secular compositions. Paralysis resulting from a car accident in 1972 in Munich severely curtailed his musical activities.

BERLIOZ, (LOUIS–) HECTOR (11 December 1803, La Côte–St-André, Isère, France–8 March 1869, Paris). Composer whose few sacred works, including the **mass** fragment "Resurrexit" (1824), a huge **Requiem** (1837), a **Te Deum** (1849), and the **oratorio** *L'Enfance du Christ* ("The Infancy of Christ," 1850–1854), occupy a singular place in the modern choral concert repertory owing to Berlioz' personal and inimitable Romanticism heard throughout the music.

BERNSTEIN, LEONARD (LOUIS) (25 August 1918, Lawrence, Mass.–14 October 1990, New York). Conductor and composer of concert music and Broadway shows, he composed two symphonies employing Jewish **chants** sung by choruses, the *Jeremiah Symphony* (1943) and the *Kaddish* Symphony (1963). He set **Psalms** 2, 23, 100, 108, 131, and 133 in the *Chichester Psalms* (1965) for solo, chorus, and orchestra. His *Mass* (1971) is not liturgical but is a multi-media theater piece.

BERTHIER, JACQUES (27 June 1923, Auxerre, France–27 June 1994, Paris). Organist of St. Ignace, **Paris** from 1960 until his death, he composed 11 **masses**, one **Requiem**, 300 **antiphons**, 220 **chants**, and other liturgical works. In 1955, he composed his first works for the **Taizé** community, *Office pour le Temps de Noël*, and became the principal composer of the **congregational** music sung there and around the world since 1975. *See also* GELINEAU, JOSEPH.

BHAJAN. Popular Hindu songs associated with *bhakti*, an attempt at personal union with God that spread by poet-singers from southern India in the sixth century, at first in reaction to Buddhism, as a kind of Hindu revival. The domination of Islam in the north from the 12th century on inspired another wave. **Tyāgarāja** composed *bhajan*, which are still widely sung today, at the turn of the 19th century.

Bhajan texts are in all vernacular languages and Sanskrit and may consist of repetitions and listings of various names of a deity (*japa*), as well as supplications and didactic themes. The purpose of the music is to convey the text clearly: the simple *tala* is four beats, and the melodies are composed on easily recognizable *rāgas*. Refrains and repeated phrases are common. A **responsorial** *pundarïkam*, a melody of only two pitches, marks the beginning and end of a *bhajan*.

Bhajan may be performed in a building exclusively for them, or they may be heard in a wide variety of places and rituals. Rituals order the *bhajan* according to local custom, beginning and ending with auspicious **mantras** or songs. **Drums** and cymbals are commonly used, as is the **harmonium**, to provide the melody and drone. *See also DHRUPHAD*; KIRTANA; *KRITI.*

BIBLICAL ACCENTS. System of 26 symbols attributed to Aaron Ben Asher (c. 900–c. 960) of Tiberias in the first half of the 10th century that indicates how to **chant** the Pentateuch properly from scrolls. They indicate prosodic stress, punctuation, and melodic patterns. *See also* CHIRONOMY; *HAZAN.*

BILLINGS, WILLIAM (7 October 1746, Boston–26 September 1800, Boston). Influential composer of early American sacred music, almost all written for unaccompanied choir of four voices. His pieces exploit three contrasting vocal textures: unison singing by one or more voices; "plain," whereby all four voices make chords in **homorhythm**; and **canonic "fuguing."** His harmonic language, while vigorous in harmonic rhythm, is untutored by European standards of the time, with unusual dissonances, parallelisms in voice-leading, and open fourths and fifths in the harmonies, particularly at cadences.

All but one of his publications are devoted exclusively to his own music. The first was *The New-England Psalm-Singer* (Boston, 1770), with frontispiece engraved by Paul Revere, the first collection printed in America containing only American music and only a single composer's work. His most popular songbook, *The Singing Master's Assistant* (Boston, 1778), went through four editions by the late 1780s and made him famous.

As Americans matured in their musical sophistication, Billings' music fell out of fashion. Interest in him revived with academic appreciation of American music in the 20th century, and certain works—*Shiloh, The Rose of Sharon*, and *David's Lamentation*—have become popular with choruses.

BINCHOIS, GILLES (c. 1400, Mons, Hainault [modern Belgium]–20 September 1460, Soignies, France). Composer mostly known today for his secular *chansons* for the Burgundian court (served c.1430–death), he also wrote sacred music in a comparatively conservative style: 12 single **mass ordinaries**, eight **mass pairs**, six **Magnificats**, and about 30 **motets**.

BINGEN, HILDEGARD VON. *See* HILDEGARD VON BINGEN.

BLISS, PHILIP P. (9 July 1838, Clearfield County, Pa.–29 December 1876, near Ashtabula, Oh.). Part of an evangelical preaching-singing team with D. W. Whittle, he composed over 300 **gospel songs**, some of which are printed in *Gospel Hymns and Sacred Songs* (1875), compiled by **Ira D. Sankey**.

BLOCH, ERNST (24 July 1880, Geneva–15 July 1959, Portland, Ore.). Composer who often expressed his Jewish heritage in his works, including *Israel Symphony* (1916), *Trois Poèmes Juifs* (1913), *Suite Hébraïque* (1953), and the especially popular *Schelomo* (1916) for cello and orchestra. *See also KOL NIDRE*; MILHAUD, DARIUS.

BLOW, JOHN (baptized 23 February 1649, Newark-on-Trent, Nottinghamshire, England–1 October 1708, London). Composer of more than 85 **anthems**, he was **organist** at Westminster Abbey from December 1668, a Gentleman of the **Chapel Royal** from 16 March 1674, and Master of the Children from 23 July. He also composed 10 Latin **motets** whose purpose is unknown and several Anglican **services**.

BOETHIUS, ANICIUS MANLIUS SEVERINUS (c. 480, Rome–c. 524). Philosopher and statesman, he wrote among many writings *De Institutione Musica*, which after the ninth-century Carolinigian renaissance became the most widely known work of music theory through the late Middle Ages. It is the only work to present Greek music theory comprehensively—**modal** theory, tetrachords, Pythagorean consonances and their mathematical underpinnings, monochord division—and thus underlies most subsequent medieval music theory.

BOOK OF SONGS. *See KITĀB AL-AGHĀNI.*

BOOKE OF COMMON PRAIER NOTED. Published by John Merbecke (**London**, 1550), the first musical settings of the Anglican rite, closely based on **Sarum chant**. After centuries of neglect, at least five editions were published between 1843 and 1853 as a result of the **Oxford Movement**.

BORNEFELD, HELMUT (14 December 1906, Stuttgart-Untertürk-heim, Germany–11 February 1990, Heidenheim). Choirmaster, **organist**. Together with Siegfried Reda he formed the *Heidenheim Arbeitstage für neue Kirchenmusik* (1946–1960) and composed Protestant church music in Germany after World War II by using techniques of Paul Hindemith, Belà Bartok, and Igor Stravinsky that had been banned during the war. His *Das Choralwerk* (1930–1960) is a collection of simple arrangements of Lutheran **chorales** organized by liturgical year. (at)

BORTNYANSKY, DMITRY STEPANOVICH (1751, Glukhov, Ukraine–10 October 1825, St. Petersburg). Music director and composer for the Russian imperial court chapel, his Italianate **polyphonic** choral works for the Russian Orthodox Church anticipated the more freely imaginative church music of **Alexander Gretchaninoff**, **Sergei Rachmaninoff**, and **Piotr Ilyich Tchaikovsky**, who edited his sacred works. (at)

BOURGEOIS, LOUIS. *See* GENEVAN PSALTER.

BOUZIGNAC, GUILLAUME (c. 1587, Saint-Nazaire-d'Aude near Narbonne, France–c. 1643, n.p.). He composed **motets** characterized by word painting and was one of the first French composers to use the Italian concertante style, including **oratorio**-like passages, notably in his **polychoral motets** and **masses**. (at)

BOYCE, WILLIAM (baptized 11 September 1711, London–7 February 1779, London). Student of **Maurice Greene** from about 1719, composer to the **Chapel Royal** from 1736, he compiled the three-volume *Cathedral Music* (1760–1773), an anthology of Anglican church music from **Thomas Tallis** to **William Croft** that remained in common use into the 20th century. He also composed about 70 **anthems**, a **burial service**, four **Te Deum**s, and a dozen **hymns** and other **chants**.

BRAHMS, JOHANNES (7 May 1833, Hamburg–3 April 1897, Vienna). Chiefly renowned for his symphonies, chamber music, piano works, and *Lieder*, Brahms also composed works for chorus, both accompanied (two **motets** for women's voices, two for mixed voices, and one "sacred song") and unaccompanied (seven motets, seven *Marienlieder*, and six sacred choruses). Most of these were composed for choral societies and exhibit Brahms' mastery of **canonic** techniques learned from extensive study of the *stile antico*. He also contributed substantially to the **organ** repertory: 11 **chorale preludes**, three preludes and **fugues**, and a single fugue. His best known sacred work, by far, is *A German Requiem*.

BRITTEN, BENJAMIN (22 November 1913, Lowestoft, England–4 December 1976, Aldeburgh). Composer, conductor, and pianist famous especially for **operas**, Britten wrote some 20 choral and solo vocal works on sacred themes, the best known of which are the **cantata** *A Ceremony of Carols* (1942), a *Missa Brevis* in D for boys' choir (1959), and the *War Requiem* (1962).

BROWNE, JOHN (fl. c. 1490). He contributed four **polyphonic Magnificats** and 11 **antiphons** to the **Eton Choirbook**. Only seven antiphons, for four, five, six, and eight voices, survive in complete form.

BRUCKNER, ANTON (4 September 1824, Ansfelden near Linz, Austria–11 October 1896, Vienna). Renowned symphonic composer, he was **organist** at Olomouc, near Linz, from 1855–1868 and then professor at the Vienna Conservatory and court organist in Vienna until his death. Over half of his eight **masses**, two **Requiems**, and three dozen shorter choral works were composed comparatively early, during his extraordinarily long period of study (through 1861). The Masses in D minor (1864) and F minor (1867) are large symphonic works, but the Mass in E minor (1866) responds, as do many of the later sacred compositions, to the ideals of the **Cecilian movement**. These are concise pieces employing **modal chants** or chantlike melodies and spare orchestration or none at all.

BRUMEL, ANTOINE (1460, Chartres?, France–after 1520, n.p.). *Maestro di cappella* at Ferrera (1506–1510), his fame equaled that of his contemporary **Josquin** in his lifetime. He wrote mostly sacred music, including **motets**, **Magnificats**, and 15 **masses** that appear frequently in theoretical works as exemplary of their time. His mass *Et Ecce Terrae Motus* is set for 12 voices. (at)

BUDDHIST CHANT. Chant of the sacred texts in monasteries. The language of chanting by Theravāda Buddhists is the obsolete Pāli. The original language of Mahāyāna Buddhists was Sanskrit, but that tradition allows chanting in vernaculars, including some anachronistic or mixed languages. Transmitted orally, the texts are doctrinal.

There is great variety in the chanting styles among sects of Buddhism. One general type, sutra chanting, is a virtual monotone, with occasional inflections at the beginnings or endings of phrases. Longer and shorter note durations usually accord with the long and short vowels of the text, although in some Tibetan chant a system of strong and weak accents is used instead.

A second style, *gāthā* or **hymn** style, occurs with poetical texts in strophes. These chants have wider melodic range, usually three to five, but sometimes seven notes, organized into **modal** patterns. There is a central tonic for recitation and traditional melodic motives with occasional **melismatic** ornamentation. *Gāthā* chanting is most often in unison, but may be heterophonic, **responsorial**, or even **polyphonic**.

Instruments are sometimes used to articulate liturgical chant and its ritual. Depending upon locality and sect, these may include **drums**, bells, and clappers most commonly, but also gongs, cymbals, and other percussion. In Vietnam, these can be used to construct as many as three polyrhythmic layers. *See also* YUSHAN.

BURIAL SERVICE. An Anglican **service** with musical settings of one or more of the following texts: *I am the Resurrection* (John 11:25); *I know that my Redeemer liveth* (Job 19:25); *We brought nothing* (1 Timothy 6:7); *Man that is born of woman* (Job 14:1); and *I heard a voice* (Revelation 14:13).

BUSNOYS, ANTOINE (BUSNOIS, DE BUSNES) (c. 1430, probably near Busnes, France–before 6 November 1492, Bruges). Known mostly for secular songs, he composed about 18 **motets** and other **polyphonic** liturgical works. One of his two **masses** uses the tune *L'homme armé* as a **cantus firmus**, perhaps the first of 40 such by **Guillaume Du Fay**, **Josquin Desprez**, and other leading composers of his generation.

BUXHEIMER ORGELBUCH. Significant early collection of **pipe organ** repertory, dating from the third quarter of the 15th century and containing about 250 compositions: German, French, and Italian secular songs and liturgical pieces (e.g., **Magnificat**) and free **preludes**, probably of south German origin.

BUXTEHUDE, DIETRICH (c. 1637, Helsingborg?, (modern) Sweden–9 May 1707, Lübeck, Germany). The most influential **organist** in the generation before **Johann Sebastian Bach**, he was appointed organist at the St. Mary's Church in Lübeck, one of the most important church musicians in north Germany, on 11 April 1668 and remained there until his death. For organ, he composed three self-standing **fugues**, three well-known **ostinatos** (chaconnes), eight **canzonas**, five **toccatas**, and 20 "**preludia**" that almost always contain extended fugues along with improvisatory music. He also left 48 **chorale preludes** and **fantasias** for organ and about 113 sacred vocal works on Latin and German texts, most in the form of **chorale** settings and **sacred concertos**. Buxtehude is credited as one of the first to take full advantage of the north German organ's timbral capabilities, particularly in the pedal writing. *See also ABENDMUSIK.*

BYRD, WILLIAM (1543, Lincoln ?, England–4 July 1623, Stondon Massey, Essex). Great master of high Renaissance **polyphony**, he was appointed **Organist** and Master of the Choristers at Lincoln Cathedral from 25 March 1563, Gentleman of the **Chapel Royal** from February 1570, joint organist from December 1572 with **Thomas Tallis**, with whom he published his first Latin **motets**, the *Cantiones* of 1575.

Although a Roman Catholic, he composed more than 65 English **anthems**; in later years, he composed mostly for the Catholic rites, an act that demanded discretion. His most famous works today, the Latin **masses** for three voices (c. 1592–1593), four voices (c. 1593–1594), and five voices (c. 1595), he printed in limited editions without title pages. They exhibit a consummate mastery of contrapuntal technique and make no use of **cantus firmus, paraphrase,** or **parody** technique, but are freely composed, unusual for the time. After 1590, he undertook the immense project of setting an entire liturgical cycle of mass **propers** for feast days, the *Gradualia*. Byrd also composed six **fantasies** and five **preludes** and other liturgical pieces for keyboard and a significant amount of secular vocal and **instrumental** music. He exercised an enormous influence on English music; among his students were **Thomas Morley** and **Thomas Tomkins,** and possibly **Thomas Weelkes** and John Bull.

BYZANTINE CHANT. Chant of the Eastern Orthodox Church, the Uniate Church of the Byzantine Rite, and other ecclesial descendants of the eastern Roman empire. An estimated 15,000 manuscripts of the chant survive, although only about 10 percent are written in a musical notation that is decipherable. The earliest such books date from the 10th century. The notation indicates the direction and sizes of intervals, not absolute pitches in pitch space, as well as rhythmic, dynamic, and articulation nuances of great subtlety. The most commonly used liturgical chants are written in comparatively late sources since their vital oral tradition required no record.

Psalm chanting has much in common with **Gregorian chant,** with intonations, reciting tones, and cadences organized according to the eight **modes** (*oktoēchos*), although cadences are always four-note patterns regardless of textural accent, which some believe to be closer to the Jewish practice. The **"divine songs"** of *prokeimenon* and **Alleluia** sung at the **divine liturgy (mass)** are florid for solo performance, like their Gregorian counterparts.

Byzantine chant distinguishes itself from Western chants in the vast number of **hymns** permitted in both the divine liturgy and the **divine office.** Published sources alone account for 60,000; many more lie in manuscripts, the earliest of which is the *Propologion* from before the 10th century. The principal hymn forms are ***kontakion, kanon,*** and ***sticheron.*** Collections are called ***heirmologion.***

A highly embellished and florid chanting style, the ***kalophonic,*** arises in the 12th century, and in the 13th its sources are numerous, especially for **ordinary** chants. Hymn books of the 13th century became specialized; *Psaltikon* contained elaborate melodies for soloists while *Asmatikon* contained simpler ones for chorus. The earliest evidence for the characteristic *ison* or sung drone that accompanies Byzantine chant in many Orthodox churches dates from perhaps 1400. *See also* ASMATIKON; CHEROUBIKON; CHRYSANTHUS OF MADYTUS; CYRIL, ST.; *EKPHONESIS*; *KATISMA*; NINE CANTICLES; PSALM TONE; *PSALTIKON*; *TRISAGION.*

– C –

CABEZON, ANTONIO DE (c. 1510, near Burgos, Castrillio de Matajudíos, Spain–26 March 1566, Madrid). A blind **organist** who served the royal family from 1528, he composed about 275 works, including **hymns**, organ **versets**, and 29 *tientos* for four to six voices. Previously an improvisational form akin to the early **toccata**, Cabezon's *tientos*, published in 1557 and by his son in 1578, resemble the **ricercar** in their imitative use of **Gregorian** melodies, sometimes employed as a **cantus firmus**, and so were appropriate for liturgy.

CALDARA, ANTONIO (1671?, Venice–28 December 1736, Vienna). Prolific composer of **operas** and church music, including 43 **oratorios**, mostly composed for the Ruspoli family in **Rome**, 30 **masses** and many shorter works, including some in *stile antico* for the Viennese court.

CALVIN, JEAN (10 July 1509, Noyon, France–27 May 1564, Geneva). Founder of the Reformed Protestant traditions, he restricted liturgical music to **congregational** singing of **psalms** and a few **canticles**. The **hymnals** published under his supervision, from 1539 to 1562, include **monophonic** settings of vernacular, **metrical psalms** translated by himself, the great poet Clément Marot (c. 1497–1544) and Théodore de Beze (1519–1605). The most influential of these was the 1562 **Genevan Psalter**.

CAMP-MEETING SONG. *See* SPIRITUAL.

CAMPRA, ANDRE (baptized 4 December 1660, Aix-en-Provence, France–Versailles, 29 June 1744). *Maitre de musique* at St. Etienne

Toulouse from June 1683 until January 1694 and then at Notre Dame de **Paris** from 21 June 1694 to 13 October 1700, he was most renowned as an **opera** composer. He has left two **masses** (one a **Requiem**), 25 *grand motets*, and at least 35 other **motets**.

CANON. Composition, or section of a composition, in which voices proceed in strict **imitation**. The canon is classified by the interval between the first notes of the leading and following voices, e.g., "canon at the fifth." In a mensuration canon, the voices sing identical melodies but move at different speeds. Canon may be heard in Roman Catholic **polyphony** from the 13th century but became a mainstay of composition in the late 15th. *See also* BACH, JOHANN SEBASTIAN; JOSQUIN DESPREZ; OCKEGHEM, JOHANNES.

CANONICAL HOURS. *See* DIVINE OFFICE.

CANTATA. Refers to a great body of secular vocal music arising in Italy during the third decade of the 17th century as one of the many responses to the invention of **opera**. Secular cantatas set lyrical or dramatic texts for one or two voices and **continuo** that often emulate a single scene or speech from an opera. They may be as short as a single **aria**, although they usually are composed in several alternations of **recitative** and aria. Thousands were composed in Italy during the 17th century and were imitated in Germany and France in the 18th century, mostly as court entertainment.

The sacred genre "cantata" refers instead to a **Lutheran** tradition of setting Biblical texts in German for liturgy. The term "Kantate" is not found in German sources before 1700 and seems to have largely arisen from a 19th-century appellation for **Johann Sebastian Bach**'s church music and then to its antecedents. These went by various names: "concerto," "motetto," "psalmo," etc. The cantata grew out of the Lutheran *Evangelienmotette* (**Gospel motet**), which offered a musical interpretation of a Gospel pericope for the day, sung after the Gospel's **chanting** and preceding the sermon. Scoring could be as small as a solo voice and continuo or as large as full chorus and small orchestra, with all manner of intermediary scorings. Important developments from 1650–1700 include the addition of non-Biblical strophic poetry, increasing **metric** distinction between aria and recitative texture, and the importation of **chorales** traditionally sung by the **congregation** before the Gospel for structural and symbolic purposes.

In 1700, **Erdmann Neumeister** published *Geistliche Cantaten statt einer Kirchen-Music* ("Sacred Cantatas in Place of Liturgical Music"), which offered verses in recitative and da capo aria in the Italian manner, "madrigal" texts, perhaps for devotional use. He followed up with cycles in 1711 and 1714 incorporating Biblical and chorale texts into such operatic verses to make the "reform" cantata texts for which he became famous, although this combination was anticipated by Duke Ernst Ludwig of Meinigen by 1704. Five of Neumeister's texts were set by J. S. Bach. Unless based on explicit chorales, the arias and recitatives from such cantatas are musically indistinguishable from opera movements.

The Bach corpus of about 200 extant church cantatas (of supposedly 300 composed) is the central repertory of the genre, composed largely in two furious periods of activity from 1713–1716 in Weimar and from 1723–1729 in Leipzig. Most were composed for particular liturgies. The writing for the chorus and vocal soloists is the most technically demanding in church music before the 19th century.

Bach's promotion to *Konzertmeister* of the Weimar court in 1714 required of him a monthly cantata. He composed these to librettos written mostly by Salomo Franck according to the Neumeister pattern. The scoring and the pattern of movements vary widely.

The Leipzig cantatas most commonly call for a four-voice choir and four-part string ensemble, continuo, and a variety of obbligato **instruments** and vocal soloists. Bach's Obituary states that he composed "five annual cycles of church pieces for all the Sundays and holy days, running from the first Sunday after Trinity to Trinity Sunday." These should amount to 300 works, but only the first two cycles (1723–1725) are fairly complete. A typical pattern of movements for a Leipzig cantata would be:

Chorus (biblical text)—Recitative—Aria—Recitative—Aria—Chorale.

Insertions of additional movements were made if the text demanded them. For the second annual cycle Bach composed "**chorale cantatas**" almost exclusively. These make explicit use of a chorale melody, chosen for the particular feast, as a **cantus firmus** in the opening chorus, in the concluding movement as a simple **hymn**-like setting, and occasionally in the inner movements. The texts for the inner movements could be paraphrases of the traditional chorale text. The chorale cantata seems to be Bach's own invention; use of chorale melodies in cantatas by contemporaries was exceptional.

About 16 secular cantatas by Bach are extant. He composed these for civic events, princely birthdays, and occasionally as public entertainments.

Production of church cantatas continued apace in the years after Bach, but the cantata's privileged position as the musical centerpiece of Lutheran liturgy declined in the second half of the 18th century owing to increasing secularization in society, to the decline of the Italian *opera seria* with its strict alternation of recitative and *da capo* aria, and to the revival of simple chorale singing and older kinds of liturgical music. It was an anachronism by 1800, and thereafter the term "cantata" can be considered a marginally sacred genre only when, as in **Edward Elgar**'s *Sancta Civitas* (1926), the text is sacred. Such cantatas in any case took on the form of short concert **oratorios**, almost never intended for worship but rather for the concert hall.

CANTICLE. Christian term for sacred song whose text is Biblical but is not one of the **psalms**. The "Canticle of Moses" (Exodus 15:1–19), the **Hymn** of the Three Children (Daniel 3:57–88) and some others were used in Jewish temple and synagogue rites in ancient times. In **Byzantine** rites the **Nine Canticles** are sung in the morning prayer of the **divine office** (*orthrōs*). In the Roman Catholic office the New Testament canticles (*Cantica majora*) include the **Benedictus** at **lauds**, the **Magnificat** at **vespers**, and the **Nunc Dimittis** at **compline** (*see* Appendix A for texts). Other canticles occupied the place of one of the psalms at lauds and **matins**.

In the **Gregorian** tradition, canticles are sung in the same manner as psalms, usually with framing **antiphons** proper to the feast and with the verses sung in pairs **responsorially** or **antiphonally**. The **psalm tones** for the Benedictus and Magnificat are more elaborate, particularly in that each verse pair begins with the **intonation**, not just the first pair as in **psalmody**.

CANTIGAS DE SANTA MARÍA. Illustrated collection of over 400 songs (*cantigas*) about the Blessed Virgin Mary compiled circa 1270–1290 under the direction of King Alfonso El Sabio. The poems are in Portuguese-Galician of varying **meters** and lengths, although most have refrains, and are generally miracle stories, except that every tenth song is a **hymn** to the Virgin. Transcriptions of the square (non-**mensural**) musical notation are inevitably controversial.

CANTILENA. See DU FAY, GUILLAUME.

CANTILLATION. Method of **chanting** a sacred reading to an oral tradition formula that accounts for the accents of the text. *See also* BIBLICAL ACCENTS; BUDDHIST CHANT; CHIRONOMY; *SĀMAVEDIC* CHANT; *TAJWĪD.*

CANTIONAL. Simple, four-voice **homophonic** arrangement of a **chorale**, with the chorale melody in the soprano voice, not the tenor as had been traditional with **polyphonic** German *Lieder.* The earliest collection is Lucas Osiander's *Fünftzig geistliche Lieder und Psalmen* (Nuremburg, 1586).

Also, as *kancionál,* the Czech term for a book of sacred songs deriving from a tradition of **congregational** singing arising during Hussite influence in the 15th century, whence it passed to the Bohemian Brethren, who in turn brought the tradition to America.

CANTOR. Leader of **congregational** singing in liturgy. Also, the soloist(s) who sings the verses in a **chanted responsory**, or alternating verses in a **responsorial** performance of a chanted **psalm**, or the incipit (beginning) of any chant. In early **polyphony**, the term referred to the singer of the **cantus firmus** as opposed to the **discantor** who sang the counterpoint.

In Germany, after the Reformation the cantor (*Kantor*) of a large city church was a highly esteemed personage, in charge of all the liturgical music, the musical training of the youth, and often of their general education as well as of important civic musical events. *See also* BACH, JOHANN SEBASTIAN; *HAZAN.*

CANTUS FIRMUS (Lat. "fixed chant"). Compositional technique whereby the composer takes a preexisting melody, usually from the traditional repertories of **Gregorian** or medieval **chant, Lutheran chorales**, etc., and sets it in long durations (determined by him) while composing original **counterpoint** to accompany it. The technique originated in the **melismatic organum** of southern France in the 12th century and in the **discant** organum of the so-called Notre Dame school (c. 1160–c. 1225). The voice singing the traditional chant melody, called "tenor" from the Latin *tenere* "to hold," already has the comparatively long durations and the repetitions of the melody that would come to mark the classic technique. Repeating, often **isorhythmic** tenors were the foundation of virtually all **motets** and **polyphonic masses** until the turn of the 16th century when structural **imitation** and polyphonic **parody** replaced the cantus firmus. Throughout this period, the tenor voice was the most common location of the cantus firmus, but it might wander among the upper voices in some pieces. In Baroque compositions, it may be found in any voice.

The virtues of the technique are its repetition, its sustained tones, and its origin in tradition.

Its repetition allows a texture of fast rhythm to be extended for far longer duration than it could have otherwise sustained, an essential advantage in medieval polyphony. Repetition also unifies the composition perceptually while allowing creativity and change in the added contrapuntal voices. Composers often increased the speed of the repetitions in carefully chosen symbolic proportions (e.g., the motet *Nuper rosarum flores* of **Guillaume Du Fay**).

The sustained quality of the cantus firmus produces a subtle musical tension based on the disparate speeds in the texture. The composition cannot end until the voices match up. For this reason, when the cantus firmus repeats at proportional speeds it is almost always a faster proportion, never slower, in order to facilitate the matching.

The use of a traditional, known melody instantly assures a semantic reference for all those who know it. For this reason, **Josquin Despres** employs a chant from the **Requiem** mass in his famous *Nymphes des Bois*, the lament on the death of **Johannes Ockeghem** (c. 1497). **Chorale cantatas** and **chorale preludes** from the **Lutheran** tradition take advantage of the same principle. **Ludwig van Beethoven** uses a chant melody in the Credo of his *Missa Solemnis* in 1823, when few would have recognized it, because by then the sound of one slow voice against a fast texture was so singular that it had become, like choral **fugues**, part of the sacred semantic.

CANTUS FIRMUS MASS. A **polyphonic** setting of the Roman Catholic **mass ordinary** prayers using the same **cantus firmus** as the compositional basis for each one, thus creating a unified five-movement mass cycle. (An English setting may omit the Kyrie, leaving it to be **chanted** because its text had been **troped**.) The cantus firmus may also refer to a particular feast or event for which the mass was composed; its source is usually given after the Latin word for mass, *Missa*, in the title of the work. The earliest examples, dating from the 1420s or early 1430s in England or northern France, are the *Missa Alma Redemptoris Mater* attributed to **Leonel Power** and the *Missa Rex Seculorum* attributed to **John Dunstable**. The technique dominated mass composition in the 15th century and gave way to **paraphrase** and **parody** techniques, without disappearing entirely, in the 16th. In England, it remained vital until the Reformation.

The entire cantus firmus might be distributed over the three text sections of the Kyrie or repeated several times for the longer texts. In **Guillaume Du Fay**'s *Missa Se La Face Ay Pale*, one of the first to use a secular cantus firmus, both Gloria and Credo sound the melody three times in quickening durational proportions of 3:2:1, as in an **isorhythmic motet**. The melody might also be inverted, transposed, or sung in retrograde.

CANZONA. Composition, modeled on the **Parisian** chanson, which was sometimes used as a **prelude** or **verset** in Christian liturgies in Italy and German-speaking countries. Canzonas range from mere transcriptions of French songs early in the 16th century to embellishments thereof to entirely original compositions late in the century. The latter are usually **imitative**, often marked by typical long-short-short rhythms in the **subject**, played by a four-voiced instrumental consort or **pipe organ**. *See also* FRESCOBALDI, GIROLAMO; GABRIELLI, GIOVANNI.

CARISSIMI, GIACOMO (18 April 1605, Marino near Rome–12 January 1674, Rome). Composer credited with significant development of the **operatic** style in Italian sacred music, particularly in the genre of Latin **oratorio**, of which he composed 14, *Jephte* being the most famous. There are also 100 **motets**, and a few *stile antico* **masses**. He worked in Tivoli (1627) and Assisi (1628–1629) and by 15 December 1629 was appointed *maestro di cappella* of the Collegio Germanico in Rome, where he remained until his death.

CAROL. A popular song, nearly always strophic, often with refrain (burden), sung to celebrate Christmas and its related feasts. Much less frequently, a carol may celebrate other Christian themes, such as Christ's **passion**.

Although carols, until recently, were rarely sung in liturgy, they may have originated in the late Middle Ages as Christmastide substitutes for the *Benedicamus Domino* **versicle** that concludes Roman Catholic **divine offices**. Translated into vernacular languages, they entered the popular repertory. Many medieval carols were preserved in the English collection *Piae Cantiones* ("Pious Songs") of 1582.

In England, Parliament abolished the feast of Christmas from 1644 to 1660, and carol singing declined until the **Oxford movement** and other such reforms in the 19th century promoted its revival. The first modern *Collection of Christmas Carols* was published by Davies Gilbert in 1822, while new compositions, in the form of **congregational hymns**, appeared in the influential *Christmas Carols New and Old* (1871) of Rev. H. R. Bramley. This rise in status culminated in the *Oxford Book of Carols* of 1928.

In the 20th century, carols may stand in for **antiphons** and hymns in Christmas liturgies, and particularly popular is the service of lessons and carols, in which Bible readings alternate with carols, which replace the traditional **psalms**. Invented in 1880 for Truro cathedral, the service is commonly associated with King's College, Cambridge. *See also NOËL; WECHSELGESANG.*

CASTELNUOVO-TEDESCO, MARIO (3 April 1895, Florence–16 March 1968, Los Angeles). Wrote Jewish liturgical works including *Kol Nidre* (1944), the **cantatas** *Naomi and Ruth* (1947) and *The Queen of Sheba* (1953), the biblical **oratorios** *Ruth* (1949), *Jonah* (1957), and *Esther* (1962), and a Sacred Synagogue Service (1943). Some secular works display Jewish influence, e.g., the Second Violin Concerto, entitled *The Prophets* (1938). (at)

CAZZATI, MAURIZIO (c. 1620, Lucera, Italy (near Reggio Emilia)–1677, Mantua). Composer and *maestro di cappella* at San Petronio in Bologna (1657–1671), he introduced trumpets and other **instruments** into liturgy and attracted highly skilled **instrumentalists** to San Petronio. (at)

CECILIAN MOVEMENT. Name for various efforts, beginning in the late 18th century, especially in Germany, Austria, France, the Netherlands, Italy, and later in the United States, to recover the ancient traditions of Roman Catholic church music for modern liturgical use. It was in part a reaction to **operatic** and other secular techniques used in sacred composition from the early 17th century on, but a more specific stimulus was a 1749 edict of Pope Benedict XIV, *Annus qui*, that summarized many of the controversies regarding liturgical music and, while expressing a preference for unaccompanied **chant**, excluded neither **polyphony** nor diverse **instrumental** accompaniment categorically. In response, *Caecilien-Bündnisse* ("Cecilian groups") attempted in Germany to promote *a cappella* choral singing through the study and revival of **Giovanni da Palestrina**'s music and **chant** and through new compositions based on those traditions. In 1869, **Franz Xaver Witt** founded the *Allgemeiner Deutscher Cäcilien-Verein* ("General German Cecilian Society") for the purpose of providing practical resources to parishes large and small. This group was recognized by Pope Pius IX in 1870 and was imitated in many European and American nations. The movement never reconciled the conflict between composing in an anachronistic *stile antico* and the 19th-century ideals of artistic innovation, and efforts to publish usable new works brought forth a great number of mediocrities. With its zeal fading in the early 20th century, the movement's longest lasting effects may have been in founding educational publications for liturgical music and in promoting good choirs and **congregational** singing. *See also* LITURGICAL MOVEMENT; OXFORD MOVEMENT; *TRA LE SOLLECITUDINI.*

CENTO CONCERTI ECCLESIASTICI **(It. "100 Sacred Concertos").** The title of Ludovico Viadana's Op.12 (1602), the first published collection of sacred music to include a figured basso **continuo**. The concertos are pragmatically designed, so that with the continuo they may be sung by one, two, three, or four voices without distortion of the text. For this reason the **meter** is strong; these are not sacred **recitatives** in **operatic** style. *See also* SACRED SYMPHONY.

CENTONIZATION. Coined in 1934, the term describes the composition of medieval **chant** melodies as a process of combining pre-existing melodic motives or formulae.

CHACONNE. *See* OSTINATO.

CHANDOS ANTHEMS. Set of 11 **verse anthems** and one **Te Deum** composed for James Brydges, later Duke of Chandos, by **George Frideric Handel** in 1717–1718 while he was in residence at Brydges' Cannons estate in Edgeware, England. The scoring is for woodwinds, strings, three- or four-voiced choir, and soloists.

CHANSON SPIRITUELLE (Fr. "Spiritual song"). Devotional song, often created by combining a sacred poem with a popular melody, found in both Protestant and Roman Catholic French homes in the 16th and 17th centuries. *See also CONTRAFACTUM; LAUDA; MADRIGALE SPIRITUALE; VILLANCICO.*

CHANT. Vocal music of religious rites the world over. Chant connotes the sacred more consistently than any other kind of music. Although certain traditions may not hold to all of them, common characteristics of chant include: texts drawn from ancient sacred writing or holy books; singing in unison or octaves; singing without **instrumental** accompaniment; melodic formulae (**centonization**); melodies of highly restricted melodic range, even monotones; and non-**metric** rhythm. Although some traditions provide for modern translations in chant, most liturgical chant is sung in ancient languages: Arabic, Aramaic, Armenian, Coptic, Ethiopic, Georgian, Greek, Hebrew, Latin, Old Slavonic, Sanskrit, and Syriac are the most important. *See also* AMBROSIAN CHANT; BUDDHIST CHANT; BYZANTINE CHANT; CANTILLATION; CANTOR; COPTIC CHANT; GALLICAN CHANT; GREGORIAN CHANT; *HAZAN*; MOZARABIC CHANT; *SĀMAVEDIC* CHANT; SYRIAN CHANT; *TAJWĪD*; *ZEMA*; *ZNAMENNĪY RASPEV*.

CHAPEL ROYAL. Private chapel attached to the English court, and home of one of the foremost vocal ensembles of Europe until the 18th century. The Chapel Royal choir originated as a group of administrator clerks temporarily assigned to sing at English royal liturgies. By the late 13th century, a permanent *capella regis* was established. By 1360, membership had grown to 16 men and four children; by the mid-15th century it was 36 and 10, a liturgical choir of highly skilled, well-paid singers that likely encouraged the high standards of composition of the time. Royal patronage continued through the Elizabethan period, while music in outlying parishes languished under Puritan influence. Abolished during the Commonwealth, it recovered much of its stature under Charles II (after 1660), who augmented its vocal and **instrumental** resources with a band of 24 violins in imitation of the court of France. **Henry Purcell** was its last outstanding composer. Under the Hanoverians and the general secularization of English society, the Chapel Royal declined as a musical institution, although it survives to the present. *See also* BYRD, WILLIAM; GIBBONS, ORLANDO.

CHARLEMAGNE. *See* GREGORIAN CHANT.

CHARPENTIER, MARC-ANTOINE (1645–1650, Paris–24 February 1704, Paris). Student of **Giacomo Carissimi** and composer of 11 **masses**, 56 **antiphons**, 10 **Magnificat** settings, 55 **responsories**, 83 **psalm** settings, 170 **motets**, 35 **oratorios**, and other assorted sacred works. He provided sacred music for the Duchess of Guise until 1688, for various Jesuit churches of Paris, and for the prestigious Sainte-Chapelle, where he was appointed music director on 28 June 1698 and remained until his death. Charpentier's Baroque style has an astonishing variety of orchestrations within each genre, an often brilliant mixture of Italian and French traits, including impressive movements for chorus. *See also* LALANDE, MICHEL-RICHARD.

CHEROUBIKON **(Gk. "Cherubic Hymn").** The **ordinary chant** for the **Byzantine** offertory of the **divine liturgy**. Text: "We who mystically represent the cherubim." There are three alternate texts for high feasts.

CHERUBINI, LUIGI (Carlo Zenobio Salvatore, 14 September 1760, Florence–15 March 1842, Paris). Director of the Paris Conservatory (1821–1841), he began composing professional sacred music late in his career. His **Mass** in F (1809) was well received, and he followed it with seven more masses between 1811 and 1825 in a deliberately conservative style. It is the critical consensus that his famous **Requiems** in C minor (1817) and D minor (1836, written for his own death), are his most outstanding works. *See also* CECILIAN MOVEMENT. (at)

CHESNOKOV, PAVEL (24 October 1877, Voskresensk, Russia–14 March 1944, Moscow). Choral conductor who composed around 400 choral works for Russian Orthodox liturgy, one third based on **chant**. He also wrote *The Choir and How to Direct It* (1940), Russia's first theoretical book on choral conducting. (at)

CHIRONOMY. Use of the hands to indicate rise and fall of melodic direction in Biblical **cantillation**, used in teaching and in certain Jewish communities in Baghdad and Yemen at least through the 19th century. *See also* BIBLICAL ACCENTS; CHANT; GLYKYS, JOANNES; *HAZAN.*

CHOIRBOOK FORMAT. A musical manuscript, often very large, designed to be set on a stand so that the whole choir could sing **polyphony** from it at once. The soprano part appears on the top left-hand page above the tenor. The alto appears on the top right-hand page above the bass.

CHORALE. Borrowed from the German, where it connotes sacred singing, in English it refers more precisely to **Lutheran congregational** vernacular **hymns** and their four-voice harmonizations.

Martin Luther enthusiastically promoted the chorale as a central element in Lutheran liturgy in the belief that worshippers should participate in the proclamation of the Word of God. He contributed both texts and melodies to the first Lutheran collections that appeared in Wittenberg in 1524: *Etlich Christlich lider*, known as the "Achtliederbuch"; *Erfurter Enchiridion*; and he wrote the foreword to **Johann Walther**'s *Wittenberger Geystliches Gesangk Buchlein*. The steady stream of new publications throughout the 16th century shows how fervently congregations welcomed this kind of liturgical music.

Luther's adaptation of the Latin liturgy, the *Deutsche Messe* of 1526, began to substitute chorales in German for traditional **ordinary** prayers. Eventually, a typical German **mass** might replace the Gloria by *Allein Gott in der Höh sei Ehr*; the Credo by *Wir glauben all an einen Gott*; the Sanctus by *Jesaja dem Propheten das geschah*; the Agnus Dei by *Christe, du Lamm Gottes*. (The last three are all Luther's own.) The Greek of the Kyrie remained but could have a German **trope** such as *Kyrie, Gott Vater in Ewigkeit*. A chorale sung between the Epistle and the Gospel, the *Gradual-lied*, eventually became the thematic chorale for the service. Others might be used in place of Latin **propers** as the occasion demanded.

Some early chorales are simply ancient Latin hymns whose melodies were **metricized** and adapted to German translations of the original. Luther's own *Nun komm, der Heiden Heiland* comes from *Veni redemptor gentium*. Other chorales derived from old German traditions of sacred folksong, including pilgrim songs, Crusader songs, *Geisslerlieder* (penitential songs), and 15th-century devotional songs, often with mixed German and Latin (macaronic text), typically associated with popular feasts such as Christmas. Others are *contrafacta*, with an entirely new text applied to a secular song. Still others have entirely original tunes and texts.

Since chorales were widely used in schools as well as liturgy, both tunes and texts became very well known. By the late 16th century, the repertory was sufficiently large and inculturated so as to supply an inexhaustible resource of material for new compositional forms, just as the Latin **chant** repertory underlay the flowering of **polyphony**: **chorale motet**, **choral mass**, **chorale cantata**, and much of the great repertory of **organ preludes** stemmed from this popular sacred music. In such guises, the chorale melody might be sung or played out in long durations with surrounding free melody, as was the ancient **cantus firmus**, or it might serve as the **subject** of **imitative counterpoint**, with each chorale phrase initiating a new section. Chorale melodies long associated with particular feasts could amplify or specify the semantics of a composition, as when **Johann Sebastian Bach** implants *O Lamm Gottes unschuldig* as a cantus firmus in the midst of the opening chorus from the **St. Matthew Passion**. *See also* CANTIONAL; *CHANSON SPIRITUELLE*; *LAUDA*.

CHORALE CANTATA. German church **cantata** based in music and text on a **Lutheran chorale** melody, in several self-contained movements. In its strict sense, no text foreign to the chorale is used, and a chorale cantata *per omnes versus* sets all its strophes, with the same melody in varying musical textures as the melodic foundation for each movement (e.g., Cantata BWV 4 of **Johann Sebastian Bach**). More loosely, the term includes those cantatas that make explicit use of a chorale melody in at least one movement.

CHORALE FANTASIA. A **fantasia** based upon a **chorale** melody. Important early examples appear in **Samuel Scheidt**'s *Tabulatura Nova* of 1624.

CHORALE MASS. Setting of the Kyrie and Gloria texts (Greek and Latin) using **Lutheran chorale** melodies in **counterpoint** for Lutheran **masses**, flourishing in the second half of the17th century until the early 18th century in central Germany.

CHORALE MOTET. Vocal **polyphonic** composition based exclusively on the text and melody of a **Lutheran chorale**, in one through-composed movement or several short ones, dating from the end of the 16th century. Typically, each phrase of the melody serves as a point of **imitation**. **Instruments** may double the vocal parts. Most were composed during the first two decades of the 17th century, after which the genre merged with the **sacred concerto** and **chorale cantata**. *See also* MOTET; PRAETORIUS, MICHAEL.

CHORALE PARTITA. A set of variations on a **chorale** melody for **organ**, originating in the latter half of the 17th century in northern Germany. Often the number of variations corresponds to the number of verses in a chorale text.

CHORALE PRELUDE. An **organ** composition that prepared the congregation to sing a **Lutheran chorale** by using it as the principal thematic material. Such pieces were commonly improvised from the late 16th century onward, but composers also made and collected formal compositions based on well-known chorales for use throughout the liturgical year, such as the *Orgelbüchlein* of **Johann Sebastian Bach**. In modern times, it functions much more often as a **prelude** to the entire liturgy, and its chorale may or may not be sung within that liturgy, although it usually refers to the liturgical theme or season in some way.

The most common ways of using the chorale melody are: as a **cantus firmus**, in durations much longer than the surrounding texture, most often in the soprano voice (e.g., *Der Tage, der ist so freudenreich*, BWV 605); as an ornamented version that blends the melody into the texture by adopting the same rhythmic motives (e.g., *Nun komm, der Heiden Heiland*, BWV 599); by using each melodic phrase to construct a fughetta (e.g., *Komm, Heiliger Geist*, BV 652); as a **canon** (e.g., *Gottes Sohn ist kommen*, BWV 600). Many of Bach's works combine these methods.

Composers' interest in chorale preludes declined along with liturgical music generally in the late 18th century. In the 20th century, however, the genre has revived somewhat, and preludes upon **hymn** tunes of all Christian traditions abound in publishers catalogs. Among the more renowned American composers of hymn preludes are Michael Burkhardt (1957–), Charles Callahan (1951–), Wilbur Held (1914–), and Paul Manz (1919–).

CHORALIS CONSTANTINUS. Monumental collection of **polyphonic propers** for 99 **masses** for liturgical feasts throughout the year, composed almost entirely by **Heinrich Isaac** and completed by his student **Ludwig Senfl** for the court of Emperor Maximilian I (vols. 1, 3) and the Cathedral at **Constance** (vol. 2). Volume 1 was first published in Nuremburg in 1550 and volumes 2 and 3 in 1555.

CHORALITER. To sing as a **chant**, without measured notes or **meter**.

CHOURMOUZIOS THE ARCHIVIST (c. 1770, Chalki, Greece– 1840, Chalki). Composer of festal **tropes**, **psalms**, six Great **Doxologies**, Cherubic **hymns**, and communions, he is renowned for his 34 volumes attempting to transcribe the entire repertory of **Byzantine chant** into the reformed musical notation of **Chrystanthos of Ma-**

dytos, with the help of Gregorios the Protopsaltes (c. 1778–1821). His realizations of the **kalaphonic** chants, highly **melismatic**, have stirred arguments about their authenticity among scholars.

CHRISTMAS CONCERTO. A concerto intended to accompany Eucharistic adoration on Christmas Eve, originating in late-17th-century Italy. The Italian "concerto grosso" is an **instrumental** composition in several movements for large ensemble, typically strings with **continuo**, which contained a number of soloists, typically two violins and violoncello. To make it appropriate for a Christmas liturgy, composers included a "pastorale" movement, with 6/8 or 12/8 time signature that included drone effects in the bass and melodies in rocking parallel thirds and sixths in the high instruments. This texture recalled a peasant custom of providing bagpipe and woodwind music for re-enactments of the shepherds adoring the Christ child at the manger (St. Luke, Ch. 2). The *pastorale ad libitum* in Arcangelo Corelli's (1653–1713) famous Op. 6, No. 8 (about 1690, pub. 1714), is the last movement, so that it may be omitted when the concerto is performed apart from Christmas. Other Christmas concertos include Giuseppe Torelli's Op. 8, No. 6, Francesco Manfredini's (1680–1748) Op. 3, No. 12, and Pietro Antonio Locatelli's (1695–1764) Op. 1, No. 8. *See also* KUHNAU, JOHANN; OPERA.

CHRISTMAS ORATORIO, JOHANN SEBASTIAN BACH, BWV 248. The most famous of **Bach**'s three **oratorios**, it is actually a set of six self-contained church **cantatas** linked by the birth narratives from the St. Luke and St. Matthew Gospels running through them all. Bach performed them during the six festival days of the Christmas season of 1734–1735: Christmas Day, St. Steven's Day and Holy Innocents (26 and 27 December), Feast of the Circumcision (1 January), Sunday (2 January), and Epiphany (6 January).

The text is set much as in Bach's **passions**. The Gospel text is sung to tenor **recitative**, with speeches by the shepherds or another group given to through-composed "madrigal" choruses. Solo ariosos and **arias** comment upon the events. Each cantata begins with a substantial chorus introducing the day's theme, except the second in which a sublime pastoral *sinfonia* sets the scene instead and concludes with an often highly elaborated summary **chorale**.

Most of the concerted movements in the Christmas Oratorio are **parodies** of secular cantatas composed for the Elector of Saxony in 1733 and 1734. Each cantata has a different scoring, reflecting the theme of the day, so that for example the second day, setting the shepherd narrative, eschews the festival brass and requires only the "pastoral" colors of flutes, oboes d'amore, oboes da caccia, strings, and **continuo**. Performing the entire set requires in addition three trumpets, two horns, and timpani, and about two hours time. The choral parts, as in most of Bach's works, are challenging.

CHRISTMAS ORATORIO, HEINRICH SCHÜTZ (*Historia der freuden- und gnadenreichen Geburth Gottes und Marien Sohnes, Jesu Christi*, SWV 435). The most frequently performed of the **oratorios** of **Heinrich Schütz**, first heard on Christmas Day at the Elector of Saxony's court chapel in Dresden in 1660. The German libretto is a compilation of the birth narratives from the Gospels of St. Luke and St. Matthew. The narration is sung to **recitative** in the tenor range. Schütz composed the speaking roles of the Angel (soprano), Herod (bass), the shepherds (soprano, mezzo, alto), the Magi (three basses), and Herod's counselors (two tenors, two basses) as seven concerted pieces, mostly in strict **meter**, called *intermedii*. All of them, along with an introductory and a concluding chorus and most of the recitative, are in F major. The **instrumentation** of each *intermedium* varies to reflect the character singing. The work calls for two violins, two "violettas," one viola, one cello or viola da gamba, two recorders, two trumpets, two trombones, bassoon, and **continuo** and requires about 40 minutes to perform. The most recent modern critical editions are edited by Günther Graulich for the Stuttgarter Schütz-Ausgabe (1998) and Neil Jenkins for Novello (2000).

CHRYSANTHOS OF MADYTUS (c. 1770, Madytus, northwestern Turkey–1846, Bursa, Turkey). Byzantine theorist. Working with **Chourmouzios the Archivist** and Gregorios the Protopsaltes (c. 1778–1821), he wrote *Theōretikon mega tēs mousikēs* ("Great Theoretical Book on Music"), which simplified the neumatic notation of **Byzantine chant**, which had grown extremely complex over the centuries, with a kind of solfege and a reduction of the traditional eight **modes** into three species: diatonic, chromatic, and enharmonic. This

Reformed or "Chrysanthine" notation is today the system of the Greek Orthodox Church. *See also* GUIDO D'AREZZO; *OK-TOĒCHOS*.

CHRYSAPHES, MANUEL (fl. c. 1440–1463, Constantinople). More compositions of **Byzantine kalophonic chant** by him appear in post mid-15th-century sources than of any other composer. He also wrote *Peri tōn entheōroumenōn tē psaltikē technē kai hōn phronous kakōs tines peri autōn* ("On the Theory of the Art of Chanting and on Certain Erroneous Views That Some Hold About It"), which provides much information about the changes in the Byzantine tradition during the 14th and 15th centuries and criticizes singers who were content to sing a simple melody without ornamentation. *See also AKOLOUTHIAI*; KOUKOUZELES, JOHANNES.

CHURCH SLAVONIC. Liturgical language of many Eastern Christian Orthodox Churches (e.g., Russian). Slavic peoples who accepted Christianity from **Byzantine** missionaries translated the liturgies into Old Slavonic, using an alphabet dating from the ninth century attributed to **St. Cyril** of Thessalonika. In the 10th century, a new alphabet (Cyrillic) appeared in Bulgaria. After the 11th century, the written liturgical language became known as Church Slavonic (also known as Old Bulgarian), of which there may be variants in the liturgies of national churches. *See also* GLAGOLITIC MASS.

CHURCH SONATA. An **instrumental** composition in several movements or sections, dating from the 17th or early 18th century, that might be used to substitute for **organ versets** in a Roman Catholic **mass**. The traditional term *sonata da chiesa* appears only infrequently in contemporary sources; any ensemble sonata using **imitation** and other suitable sacred idioms might be so used. Although the movement pattern of slow-fast-slow-fast was once thought to be the defining feature, the sources show a wide variety of orders.

CLASSICAL POLYPHONY. *See STILE ANTICO*.

CLAUSULA (pl. CLAUSULAE). Section of a Notre Dame **organum** composed in **discant**, which can replace a section of previously composed **melismatic** organum (*organum purum*).

CLAVIER-ÜBUNG III. Johann Sebastian Bach's 1739 publication of his own selected **organ** works. The collection begins with a massive five-voiced **Praeludium** in E-flat major and ends with the "St. Anne" **Fugue**, also for five voices in the same key. In between are two settings of the three-section **Lutheran Kyrie chorale** (six movements in all), three of the **Gloria** *Allein Gott in der Höh sei Ehr*, and two each of the "catechism chorales": *Dies sind die heilgen zehen Gebot, Wir glauben all an einen Gott, Vater unser in Himmelreich, Christ unser Herr, Aus tiefer Not*, and *Jesus Christus unser Heiland*. Each pair has one setting for manuals only, one with obbligato pedal. The settings exhibit all manners of treating the chorale melodies: **cantus firmus** in all registers, fugal treatments, and all varieties of **counterpoint**. Four "duetti" (small pieces for two voices) follow before the concluding fugue.

CLEMENS NON PAPA (c. 1510, probably Ieper, Belgium?–1555 or 1556, Dixmuiden, near Ieper). Prolific composer of 15 **masses** and over 230 **motets**, he set many of the 159 **psalms** and **canticles** from the *Souterliedekens* psalm collection to three-voice **polyphony**.

COLOR. Pitch sequence in the **tenor** of an **isorhythmic motet**. *See also TALEA.*

COMMUNION. *See* MASS.

COMMUNION SERVICE. *See* HOLY COMMUNION.

COMPLINE. The major hour of the **divine office** of the Roman Catholic rite sung before retiring for the night. A **chanted** compline begins with a **versicle** followed by three or four **psalms** (4, 31, 91, 134), each framed by the same **antiphon** (usually *Miserere mihi*). Then follows a **hymn** (*Te lucis ante terminum*), short Biblical reading ("capitulum") and a short **responsory**. Next comes the **Canticle** of Simeon, **Nunc Dimittis** (*see* Appendix A for text). Spoken prayers ("Our Father," the Apostles' Creed) may follow. The concluding versicle ***Benedicamus Domino*** is followed by one of the Marian **votive antiphons**. Compline is distinct from the other major hours because it has few **proper** chants; antiphons change only according to the day of the week, and the same weekly set is sung throughout the year. *See also* GREGORIAN CHANT; VESPERS.

CONCERT SPIRITUEL. See PARIS.

CONDUCTUS. Christian paraliturgical compositions dating from the 12th and 13th centuries from Europe, **monophonic** or **polyphonic**, that show a wide variety of texts and musical forms. Their liturgical function, if any, remains obscure, although in *The Play of Daniel*, they are processional songs. The *conductus simplex* is **homorhythmic** with syllabic text-setting; the embellished form includes interpolated **melismatic** passages.

CONGREGATIONAL SINGING. Singing by lay congregants in a worship service. Most major religious traditions have some form, but the practice varies widely. At one extreme is a **Buddhist** burial service, which is sung entirely by the priest, and at the other might be an American revival where everyone present sings every **praise chorus**. Many traditions combine the professional singing of a **cantor** or priest and congregational singing.

The principal constraints on congregational singing are technical: the music must be simple enough for musically untrained members of a culture, the great majority, to learn quickly and execute, especially in cultures where printed matter is not traditional. Refrains with simple texts, strophic forms, and other repetitive forms are common strategies. Direct settings of sacred writings such as the Bible, the Vedas, the Qur'ān, etc., are generally too complex. As one solution, ancient Jewish **psalmody** employed brief **responsorial** interpolations such as *Hallelujah* sung by the congregation within a **psalm chanted** by the soloist. More common are **metric** paraphrases of sacred texts or original **hymns**. *See also BHAJAN*; CHORALE; DESCANT; *DHIKR*; GOSPEL SONG; *KIRTANA*; *LEKHA DODI*; *LAUDE*; LINING OUT; *NIGGUN*; *PIYYUT*; *QAWWALI*; RESPONSORY; SONGS OF THE *HAJJ*; SPIRITUAL; TONGUE-SINGING; *ZEMIROT*.

CONSTANCE SONGBOOK (Constance, 1540). The most influential of Swiss Reform songbooks, actually the third edition of precedents published in Zurich (1st ed. 1533–34; 2nd ed. not later than 1537), compiled by poets Ambrosius Blaurer and Johannes Zwick, containing 67 **metrical psalms**, and 83 other songs, some for domestic use only. There are only 71 different melodies. Zwick's preface contradicts the reform ideals of **Huldrych Zwingli**, who incorporated no singing in his liturgy.

CONSTITUTION ON THE SACRED LITURGY. Central document on liturgical theology and practice promulgated by the **Second Vatican Council** on 4 December 1963. Articles 112–121 contain the norms for liturgical music, which, in general, express strong preference for **Gregorian chant**, the **pipe organ**, and other features of the Roman Catholic tradition but also provide for alternatives, particularly in "certain parts of the world" (119), and emphasize the "active participation of the people" whenever possible (113, 114, 121). In practice since the late 1960s, however, popular and indigenous musics have almost entirely replaced chant and other traditional idioms in most places, and the true natures and purposes of "sacred music" and "active participation" continue to be disputed among reformers and traditionalists.

CONTEMPORARY CHRISTIAN MUSIC. Umbrella term for American Christian songs composed and performed in various rock styles from the 1970s onward. Larry Norman's (1947–) recording *Upon This Rock* (Impact, 1969) is considered to be the earliest exemplar. The genre is controversial among American Christians. Recent stars include Steven Curtis Chapman (1962–) and Amy Grant (1960–). *See also* GOSPEL SONG; PRAISE CHORUS.

CONTINUO. Ensemble of at least one melodic bass **instrument** and one chord-playing instrument (usually **organ** in sacred music) that provides the harmonic progressions and structure in Baroque compositions. Beginning as an efficient and simple frame for **operatic** monody around 1600, the continuo became so customary that Baroque scores call for it even when a large ensemble provides all the necessary harmonic information. It fell out of use in the late 18th century when slower harmonic rhythms in periodic phrases made its power of harmonic articulation unnecessary.

CONTRAFACTUM (Lat. "counterfeit"). The practice of fitting an existing vocal work with a new text. In the Middle Ages this occurred frequently with the establishment of new feasts or simply the composition of new **sequence** or **hymnodic** poetry. After the 15th century, the term almost always indicates the replacement of a secular text by a sacred one in order to create a piece suitable for devotion or liturgy. Such *contrafacta* are common in *laude*, spiritual songs of all types, and early Protestant **chorales** and **hymns**. *See also* AMALARIUS OF METZ; *LAHAN*; PARODY.

COPTIC CHANT. Chant sung in the Orthodox Coptic Rite of Egypt and, in simplified form, in the Coptic Catholic Church. Languages sung include the original Greek, Coptic (a remnant of ancient Egyptian), and Arabic. Liturgies of the Eucharist, lasting from three to six hours, and of the **divine office** are chanted. The repertory has come down through history via oral transmission. Modern studies suggest that the melodic formulae remain remarkably unchanged through time and place.

CORI SPEZZATI (It. "split choirs"). A kind of **antiphony** by which independent melodies of a single **polyphonic** composition are distributed among two or more distinct choirs that often sing at considerable distance from each other in a church. Unlike antiphonal **psalmody** or *alternatim*, this **polychoral** music frequently overlaps one choir with another and at climactic moments calls for all choirs to sing together. All sorts of Latin texts—**mass ordinaries, sequences, psalms,** and generic **motet** texts—might be set to polychoral texture. The choirs may or may not be equivalent in range and vocal assignment, and evidence from northern Italian churches in the late 16th century indicates that one or more of the choirs may have been **instrumental**, affording an even greater contrast of timbre.

Tradition associates the practice with St. Mark's Basilica in **Venice** because of its widely separate choral galleries, each with its own **organ**, because of the eight *psalmi spezzati* of **Adrian Willaert** of 1550, and especially because of the spectacular works of **Andrea** and **Giovanni Gabrieli**, Claudio Merulo (1533–1604), Giovanni Croce (1557–1609), and others composing there in the last quarter of the 16th century. However, firm evidence of polychoral music in other northern Italian cities is earlier: from Treviso in 1521; from Ferrara in 1529; from Bergamo in 1536. Dominique Phinot (c. 1510–c. 1555), published five motets for two equal four-voiced choirs in 1548 in Lyons, which were often reprinted in German anthologies in the next two decades. Although a second organist was appointed in 1490, the first hard evidence of polychoral performance at St. Mark's is 1574.

By then the practice also appears in the works of **Orlandus Lassus** in Munich, where both Gabrielis probably learned the art, **Giovanni da Palestrina** in **Rome**, and **Tomas Luis di Victoria** in Spain, whence it was exported to Latin America. The **Lutheran** composers Hieronymous and **Michael Praetorius**, **Johann Hermann Schein**, **Samuel Scheidt**, and **Heinrich Schütz** continued the tradition into the 17th century as it faded elsewhere, using German as well as Latin texts. Vestiges of the technique appear in certain choral works of **Johann Sebastian Bach**, especially the motets, and in certain of the English **oratorios** of **George Frideric Handel**.

CORONATION ANTHEMS. Set of four **anthems** composed by **George Frideric Handel** and performed on 11 October 1727 for the coronation of King George II. Scored for large five- to seven-voice chorus, woodwinds, trumpets, timpani, and strings, they introduced to the English public the weight of choral sound associated with Handel's later **oratorios**.

COUNCIL OF TRENT. The 19th Ecumenical Council of the Roman Catholic Church (Trent, northern Italy, 13 December 1545–4 December 1563). Decrees specific to liturgical music were issued from sessions 22–24 (September 1562–November 1563) and provided that liturgical music should make words easy to understand and that no "lascivious or impure" elements of secular music should intrude. Abolishing **polyphony** in favor of **chant** may have been discussed but was not legislated. The practical results of the Council included a revised breviary (liturgical book for the **divine office**, 1568) and a revised missal (1570), obligatory in all dioceses unless proof of local practices older than 200 years could be shown. These publications, in effect, eliminated all **troped mass ordinaries** and all but four **sequences** accumulated since the late Middle Ages. On 25 October 1577 Pope Gregory XIII commissioned a new Roman gradual, which appeared in 1614. This so-called **Medicean** chant probably reflects 17th-century chant practice, including revised liturgical texts and melodies to conform to humanistic taste. A number of composers, including **Giovanni da Palestrina**, used inventive **homorhythmic** textures in polyphony to clarify diction to follow the Council's wishes, although this effort weakened with distance from Rome. Nevertheless, the coincident invention of radically new **operatic** textures at the close of the 16th century helped to define consciously the church style, the *stile antico*, by rejecting traditional **counterpoint**.

COUNTERPOINT (adj. CONTRAPUNTAL). A **polyphonic** texture of more or less equally salient voices. *See also* HOMOPHONY; HOMORHYTHM; IMITATION; MONOPHONY.

COUPERIN, FRANÇOIS (10 November 1668, Paris–11 September 1733). Preeminent composer of keyboard music in France. He began his music career as an **organist** at St. Gervais (1685–death), then at Chapelle Royale (1693). He published *42 Pièces d'orgue* (1690) contained in two **organ masses** that are recognized as among the greatest examples of the genre. He also composed some 40 **motets**. (at)

COYSSARD, MICHEL (1547, Besse-en-Chandesse, France–1623, Lyons). Jesuit who translated into French popular **hymns** and **canticles** (e.g., *Paraphrases des Hymnes et Cantiques Spirituelz* 1592), and Latin liturgical texts such as the **Credo**, *Pange lingua* and *Stabat mater*. He defended the use of the vernacular in religious songs. (at)

THE CREATION (DIE SCHÖPFUNG). One of the most frequently performed **oratorios**, composed by **Franz Joseph Haydn** during all of 1797 and part of 1798 (semi-private premiere at the Palais Schwarzenberg in **Vienna** in April) to a libretto based (by Lindley) on John Milton's *Paradise Lost* and adapted and translated into German by Baron Gottfried van Swieten. It is scored for full classical orchestra, four-voiced chorus and soprano, tenor, and bass soloists. Its three parts require about one and three-quarters hours to perform. In English-speaking locales, the work is often performed in one of several translations. **Recitative** sets the seven-day creation story from Genesis, while commentary, often from **Psalms**, is sung with **arias** and

choruses, a grand **Handelian** chorus marking the end of each day.
See also THE SEASONS.

CREDO. *See* MASS; Appendix A for text.

**CRESTON, PAUL (born Giuseppe Guttoveggio, 10 October 1906,
New York–24 August 1985, San Diego).** He composed music for
the Roman Catholic liturgy including a **Requiem** (1938), *Missa Solemnis* (1949), *Missa "Adoro Te"* (1952), and *Missa "Cum Jubilo"*
(1968), as well as a Christmas **oratorio** called *Isaiah's Vision* (1962).
(at)

**CROFT, WILLIAM (baptized 30 December 1678, Nether Etting-
ton, Warwicks–14 August 1727, Bath).** Composer and Master of
Children at the **Chapel Royal** and **organist** at Westminster Abbey,
he broke ground by publishing in score form a two-volume collection, *Musica Sacra* (1724). His numerous **anthems** were among the
first English compositions to employ the late-Baroque continental
techniques. Several of his **hymn** tunes are still in use including "St.
Anne" ("O God, Our Help in Ages Past"). (at)

**CRÜGER, JOHANN NEPOMUNK (9 April 1598, Gross-Breesen,
near Guben, Lower Lusatia–23 February 1662, Berlin). Cantor**
at St. Nicholas Church (1622–death), he composed **Lutheran chorales** including *Nun danket alle Gott, Jesu meine Freude*, and
Schmücke dich o liebe Seele. Crüger compiled and arranged several
chorale collections, the most influential of which is *Praxis Pietatis
Melica* (1647), the first to set chorale melodies solely with a figured
bass for domestic use. The publication was reprinted 45 times before
1736. (at)

**CYRIL, ST. (826, Thessalonika–14 February 869, Rome) AND
METHODIUS (c. 815, Thessalonika–6 April 885, Stare Mesto
(Velehrad), Moravia (modern Czech Republic).** Brothers and **Byz-
antine** missionaries to Moravia instructed to teach in the vernacular.
In compliance, Cyril invented the **Glagolitic** alphabet from which
Church Slavonic is derived. The two also translated the Scriptures
and liturgical **hymns**. (at)

– D –

DAVID, JOHANN NEPOMUK (30 November 1895, Eferding, Austria–22 December 1977, Stuttgart, Germany). Organist who composed **motets, masses**, mostly for four-voiced chorus *a cappella,* and *Das Choralwerk* for organ—21 volumes of **chorale** settings (1932–1973).

DE LA RUE, PIERRE. *See* LA RUE, PIERRE DE.

DELLO JOIO, NORMAN (24 January 1913, New York). Composer, **organist**, and educator at many American institutions, he wrote three **masses**, four dramatic works, and other works for chorus based on Roman Catholic liturgy, hagiography, or the **psalms**. Quotations from **Gregorian chant** and references to other liturgical styles figure heavily in his music.

DEMESTVENNY. Highly elaborate Russian Orthodox **chant** used for solemn feasts; derivative of *kalaphonic* chant, heard today only in the congregations of "Old Believers." *See also ZNAMENNĪY RASPEV.*

DESCANT. A countermelody sung, usually by a segment of the choir, mainly above the principal melody of the **hymn** sung by the **congregation**.

DESPREZ, JOSQUIN. *See* JOSQUIN DESPREZ.

DEUS IN ADJUTORIUM **(Lat. "God come to my assistance," Psalm 70).** **Versicle** that opens all the **divine offices** of the Roman Catholic rite with the exception of **matins**, where it follows directly on other opening prayers. The lesser **doxology** (*Gloria patri . . .*) follows.

DHIKR **(Arab. "remembrance").** Islamic mystical (Sufi) ritual involving formulaic repetition, usually of the name of God (Allāh), "God is he," or something similar. The rituals, often lasting several hours, may also include **chanting** the Qur'ān, **hymns,** and ecstatic dancing, depending upon the particular dervish (ascetic) community. A frame **drum** may be used. Shï'ite Sufis, however, have abandoned or forbidden such music since the 16th century.

DHRUPAD. Considered the oldest and purest genre of Hindustani (North Indian) vocal composition, it sets two or four rhymed verses, usually on religious themes. A *tāla* from a specific set is used; any *rāga* may be used. The *dhrupad* is introduced by an *ālāp* and then sung in an austere manner with minimal ornamentation by one or two male singers to the accompaniment of the drone *tambürä* and a barrel **drum** called *pakhāvaj*. The genre developed in Gwalior and was promoted by **Tānsen** in the mid-16th century.

DIE SIEBEN LETZTEN WORTE UNSERES ERLÖSERS AM KREUZE. See THE SEVEN LAST WORDS OF OUR SAVIOUR FROM THE CROSS.

DIES IRAE (Lat. "Day of wrath"). Sequence sung at a **Requiem mass**, one of four liturgical sequences retained after the **Council of Trent**.

DIGITAL ORGAN. A keyboard **instrument** that may simulate the **pipe organ** in timbre and operation, whose tones are generated from large stores of computer samples of actual pipe organs, scaled through the pitch range, and projected through loudspeakers. The Allen Organ Co. demonstrated the first digital organ in 1971. The principal limitations on how closely the timbre approximates that of a pipe organ are the rate of sampling and the speaker technology. Advances in computer processing technology have enabled the storage of accurate wave envelopes, pipe release effects, sound environments, and other irregularities of actual pipe sound, so that the digital organ surpasses the **electronic organ** in its approximation of pipe organ timbre. *See also* ORGAN.

D'INDY, (PAUL MARIE THÉODORE) VINCENT (27 March 1851, Paris–2 December 1931). With Charles Bordes (1863–1909) and Alexandre Guilmant (1837–1911), he founded the **Schola Cantorum** of Paris (1894). Originally specializing in the study of plainchant and the **Palestrina** style, the school became a general conservatory in 1900. He harmonized 24 **Gregorian chants**, the *Pentecosten* (1919). (at)

DISCANT. Technique of **organum** composition by which all voices, including the *vox principalis* singing the original **chant** melody, move at comparable speed in triple **meter**.

Discant is also an improvised **polyphony** described by 14th-century English theorists. They describe a **homorhythmic** texture based on consonant intervals among voices with a strong preference for contrary motion. *See also* FABURDEN; *FALSOBORDONE*; *MAGNUS LIBER ORGANI*; PEROTINUS.

DISTLER, HUGO (24 June 1908, Nuremberg, Germany–1 November 1942, Berlin). **Organist** and composer active in the revival of traditional **Lutheran** music and in the restoration of Baroque organ-building techniques. His major sacred works include a Christmas **oratorio** (*Die Weihnachtsgeschichte*, 1933) and collections of four-voiced **motets** modeled on those of **Heinrich Schütz** (*Geistliche Chormusik*, 1934–1936, 1941).

DIVINE LITURGY. Name of the **Byzantine** Eucharistic rite analogous to the Roman Catholic **mass**. There are three: the Liturgy of St. Basil and the Liturgy of St. John Chrysostom, nearly identical except for the **chants** of the anaphora (consecration), and the Liturgy of the Presanctified sung during Lent. This last has no anaphora and contains the famous *Hesperinos hymn Phōs hilaron*.

The order of service for the Liturgies of St. Basil and St. John Chrysostom is as follows (all chants are **proper** unless noted as **ordinary**):

- Three **antiphons** or *typika*, common **psalms** with the hymn *Ho monogenēs huios*;
- Ordinary: *Eisodikon* from Psalm 94 for the procession of the lectionary;
- **Troparion** and the proem of a **kontakion**;
- Ordinary: *Eis polla ta etē* for the entrance of the celebrant;
- **Trisagion** (one of several versions);

- Ordinary: *Psalmos tō Dauid* with a proper **reponsorial** *Prokeimenon* preceding the Epistle reading;
- Ordinary: *Allēlouia psalmos tō Dauid* with a proper **responsorial Alleluia** preceding the Gospel reading;
- Ordinary: *Hosoi katechoumenoi proelethete*, dismissing the cathechumens;
- **Cheroubikon** (one of several versions);
- **Creed**;
- Chants of the anaphora, including *Hagios, hagios, hagios* analogous to the Roman **Sanctus**;
- Chants for **communion** (*koinōnikon*);
- Ordinary post-communion hymn *Plērōthētō to stoma hēmōn*;
- Ordinary benediction *Eie to onoma Kyriou* from Psalm 112;
- Ordinary post-communion hymn *Eidomen to phōs to alēthinon* and possibly other hymns.

See also HOLY COMMUNION.

DIVINE OFFICE. Cycle of monastic liturgies sung at particular times each day. In the Benedictine rule there are eight, called "hours," thus the common expression "liturgy of the hours." The four major hours are **matins** (sometimes called vigils) during the night, **lauds** at daybreak, **vespers** in the evening, and **compline** before retiring. The four **minor hours** are prime, terce, sext, and none, named for the hours of daylight.

Other religious orders may observe a different pattern. In 1972 a reform of the divine office subsequent to the **Second Vatican Council** relaxed the regimen by substituting an Office of Readings for matins, eliminating prime, and offering a choice among terce, sext, and none. *See also* BYZANTINE CHANT; GREGORIAN CHANT; *HESPERINOS*; *ORTHRÖS*; SYRIAN CHANT.

DIVINE SONGS (Greek: *ta theia asmata*). Byzantine **hymns** sung during the Liturgy of the Catechumens. They include the *prokeimenon*, to be sung before the reading from St. Paul, and the **Alleluia**, sung before the Gospel. *See also ASMATIKON*; DIVINE LITURGY; *PSALTIKON*.

DORSEY, THOMAS A. (1899, Villa Rica, Georgia–23 January 1993, Chicago). "The father of gospel music," renowned performer and composer of **gospel songs**. After a successful career in blues with Ma Rainey, Dorsey devoted the rest of his career to the promotion of gospel music. He founded the Thomas A. Dorsey Publishing Company in 1931 and composed over 500 songs, including "Precious Lord, Take My Hand" (1932).

DOXA EN UPSISTOIS THEO **(Gr. "Glory to God in the highest").** A Byzantine morning **hymn** text of the pre-Constantinian period, source of the Western *Gloria*, known as the "major **doxology**."

DOXOLOGY. Christian formula of divine praise. The are many examples in both the Old and New Testaments. The most familiar ones for musical contexts include the "greater doxology," which is the Gloria of the Roman Catholic **mass**, and the "lesser doxology" adapted from St. Matthew's Gospel 28: 19 that concludes the **chanting** of every **psalm** and the *Deus in adjutorium* in the **divine office** (*see* Appendix A for texts).

In the **Byzantine** tradition, which does not use the terms "greater" and "lesser," a doxology is heard many times in the **divine liturgy** (mass): at the beginning, after the **hymn** *Ho Monogenēs Huios*, the **litany**, the *Cheroubikon*, the anaphora, and the Lord's Prayer.

In Protestant churches, the doxology may refer to a self-contained hymn that offers divine praise such as "Praise God from whom all blessings flow." Single hymn verses, usually the last of a set, often invoking the Trinity, may also be doxological. *See also TE DEUM.*

DRUM. Drums play in the sacred musics of Hinduism, Buddhism, the Chinese religions, shamanism, many African religions, and the religions of American Indians. They generally do not play in the most traditional sacred musics of Judaism, Christianity, and Islam, although they have appeared in Christian **gospel** music, **praise choruses**, and other types based on popular idioms of the 20th century, and in Muslim lands drums have escorted prominent personages on their pilgrimages to Mecca (*atabl al-hajj*, "pilgrim's drum"), and have accompanied sacred dance in Sufism.

The Hindu god Siva is often identified in iconography with the *damaru*, a drum shaped like an hour-glass which he plays to accompany his dancing. In music, drumming is an essential component of traditional Karnatic and Hindustani music, almost all of which has religious connotations if not strictly liturgical, since the drum articulates tempo and the **talā**, the fundamental rhythmic pattern of the song. A barrel drum held horizontally and played with both hands, the *mrdangam*, produces a variety of sounds by combining different hand strokes (full hand, half hand, forefinger, etc.) with qualities of damping with the other hand. Another important drum is the Hindustani *tablā*, which has a small wooden barrel drum on the right side and a small kettledrum on the left.

"Sounding the drum of the Dharma" is an expression for the proclamation of Buddhist teaching. In Buddhist ritual, drums may date from the time of the Buddha himself (died c. 480 B. C.) and drum notation dates from the mid-eighth century A. D. The type of drum played varies widely with the particular sect or caste of the player. The music played ranges from auspicious beat patterns to five-fold offerings of praise to the accompaniment of singing, dancing, and meditation.

In Tibet, Bon ceremonies require the drum (*mga*).

In China, drums participate in the system of *pa yin* ("eight sounds"), by which the materials the drums are made of coordinate with seasons of the year and points of the compass. In practice they play in the orchestra for Confucian ceremonial music (**ya-yüeh**).

In Indonesia, frame drums may accompany poems praising Muhammad, especially the *Burda* and the **Mawlīd**.

In the shamanism of Inner Mongolia and North Asia, the drum is considered to be a living spirit that aids the shaman in motivating other spirits or in transporting him on spiritual journeys to the other worlds. It may even be the object of life-cycle rituals, such as birth and death ceremonies.

Africa owns a vast diversity of religious drumming. In some tribes, drumming and sacred rituals may be so closely wedded that they share the same word, or in others, drumming may have no role in worship whatsoever. Drums may stay on the periphery of ritual, or take center stage as spirits as in shamanist traditions. They come in every size and shape. The well-known "talking drums" of the Ewe and Yoruba may transmit prayers and messages to the spirit world.

Drums may also symbolize concepts of sacral leadership in some traditions, and as such may not even be played. On the other hand, there is a great deal of music for drums alone, often used to summon the spirits.

Ritual drumming of American Indians parallels that of Asian shamans in many respects and accompanies almost all sacred song. A simple frame drum beaten with one stick is often used. The **peyote songs** of the Native American Church, however, employ a drum containing water, which allows tuning and creates a characteristic reverberation caused by the water flowing inside. *See also DHIKR*; INSTRUMENTS, USE OF; TIBETAN CHANT.

DU'Ā. "Supplication," the formula of praise to Allah **chanted** at mosques on Friday services and festivals. Melodies may range from simple chants to ornate compositions, particularly in Turkey.

DU FAY, GUILLAUME (?5 August 1397, Beersel, near Brussels–27 November, 1474, Cambrai, France). Du Fay's compositions include seven complete **masses**, including one **plenary**, the *Missa Sancti Jacobi* (before 1440), and 35 mass **ordinary** movements, 15 settings of various mass **propers**, three **Magnificats**, two settings of *Benedicamus Domino*, 16 **polyphonic antiphons**, 25 polyphonic **hymns**, 24 **motets**, and over 30 **plainchant** melodies.

Earliest documents place him at Cambrai Cathedral in the summer of 1409 as a chorister. He probably attended the Council of Constance (1414–1418). In summer 1420, he entered the service of Carlo Malatesta da Rimini. In 1424 and 1425 he may have been a *petit vicaire* at Laon Cathedral. He was in Bologna by February 1426, having joined the household of Cardinal Louis Aleman. He next joined the papal chapel in **Rome** by October 1428 and remained there until July 1433. From at least 1 February 1434 he served the Duke of Savoy as *maistre de chapelle*. By July 1435 Du Fay had returned to the papal chapel, then in Florence. On 9 September 1436, Pope Eugenius IV granted him a canonicate at Cambrai, and Du Fay was officially received as canon there on 12 November 1436. By 6 July 1439 he had entered the service of the Duke of Burgundy but by December had taken up residence at Cambrai, where he remained until March 1450. He returned to Savoy from 1452 to 1458 as *magister* *capellae*. He moved back to Cambrai as canon in October 1458 and remained there until his death.

Du Fay composed almost all his polyphony by adding third and fourth voices to a fundamental duet of **tenor** and cantus (soprano) voices, a premise which flowers into a wide variety of textures and genres. The motets fall into two large groups: cantilenas, freely composed treatments of **chant** melodies quite unique in the 15th century; and the more traditional **isorhythmic** motets, including the renowned *Nuper Rosarum Flores* (1436). The mass ordinaries are not united cyclically by a common tenor until 1450, when Du Fay composed *Missa Se La Face Ay Pale* on the tenor of one of his own songs, one of the earliest examples of a secular melody used in a **cantus firmus mass**. The *Missa Ave Regina Caelorum* (c. 1464) parodies to the extent of quoting his own motet, and appears to be Du Fay's valedictory summary of compositional techniques for masses. *See also* TRENT CODICES.

DU MONTE (DE THEIR), HENRI (y) (1610, Villers-L'Evêque, near Liège–8 May 1684, Paris). Organist at St. Paul's, Paris (1643–death), composer for Chapelle Royale (1672–1683). His *grands motets* standardized the distribution of **instrumental** and vocal parts for this genre. (at)

DUNSTABLE, JOHN (c. 1390, England–24 December 1453). Composer who is most frequently cited in continental music theory as the one responsible for bringing the "English sound" to European **polyphony**, that is, a texture governed by a strict syntax of consonance and dissonance treatment and greatly simplified rhythmic patterns as compared to the French polyphony of the late 14th century. He is also credited, along with **Leonel Power**, with the earliest **cantus firmus mass**, the *Missa Rex Seculorum* (c. 1420s–1430s), although the attribution is not certain. Besides one other cyclic **mass**, there are 22 single mass **ordinary** movements, 15 **isorhythmic motets**, and 27 other settings of Latin texts.

DUPRÉ, MARCEL (3 May 1886, Rouen, France–30 May 1971, Meudon). World-famous **organist**, he established his reputation in 1920 by performing the first complete cycle of organ works of **Jo-**

hann Sebastian Bach ever given at the Paris Conservatoire. He succeeded Charles-Marie Widor at St. Sulpice in 1934. Some of his amazing improvisations there became part of a large corpus of organ publications: ricercars, preludes and fugues, toccatas, organ symphonies, chorales, and many other quasi-liturgical works. He also composed an oratorio La France au Calvaire ("France at Calvary," 1954) and a half dozen motets.

DURUFLÉ, MAURICE (11 January 1902, Louviers, France–16 June 1986, Louveciennes). Organist, composer, professor of harmony at the Paris Conservatoire (1943–1969), he is best known for his Requiem Op. 9 (1947) which decorates Gregorian chants with modernist modal harmonies. He has also published a small number of motets and the mass "Cum Jubilo" (1966).

DVORÁK, ANTONÍN (8 September 1841, Nelahozeves near Kralupy [modern Czech Republic]–1 May 1904, Prague). Composer chiefly of concert music, he wrote a few symphonic sacred pieces including: a Stabat Mater (op. 58, 1877), the oratorio Svatá (St.) Ludmila (op. 71, 1886), a Mass in D (op. 86, 1887, orchestrated 1893), a Requiem (op. 89, 1890), and a Te Deum (op. 103, 1892). Almost all were intended for concert, not liturgical performance.

DYKES, JOHN BACCHUS (10 March 1823, Kingston-upon-Hull–22 January 1876, Ticehurst, Sussex). Composer of hymn tunes. Sixty of these were included in the first edition of Hymns Ancient and Modern (1861), including Nicaea ("Holy, Holy, Holy"), Hollingside ("Jesu, Lover of My Soul"), Horbury ("Nearer My God to Thee"), St. Cross ("O Come and Mourn"), and St. Cuthbert ("Our Blest Redeemer"). (at)

– E –

EBEN, PETR (22 January 1929, Žamberk, Czech). Composer who wrote Missa Adventus et Quadrasisimae (1950) expressing "the fight of our citizens for their faith and freedom, the fight of the church for her existence," the Prague Te Deum (1989) in thanks for the Velvet

Revolution, and simpler works written to encourage **congregational** participation (e.g., *Trouvere Mass* [1968], *Missa cum Populo* [1982]). (at)

EGERIA (Etheria) (fl. late 4th century). A pilgrim from Spain or Gaul, her diary of her visit to the Near East 381–384, surviving in a single 11th-century copy, provides one of the best early accounts of Christian liturgy and liturgical music of the **Jerusalem rite**.

EKPHONESIS. Type of **Byzantine chanting** used for liturgical readings of the Bible, thought to be midway between speech and song. *Ekphonetic* notation gives a pair of signs for each phrase of text, which remind the **cantor** of the pitch and formula to be sung. Such notation is found in sources dating from the ninth to the 14th centuries, but remains indecipherable. *See also* CANTILLATION; CHANT; *TAJWĪD*.

ELECTRONIC ORGAN. A keyboard **instrument** designed to simulate the **pipe organ** in respect of timbre, **polyphonic** facility, and sustaining power but whose tones are synthesized electronically and projected through loudspeakers. Laurens Hammond founded the Hammond Instrument Co. of Chicago in 1929, but the first instrument designed for church was built in 1930 by Armand Givelet and Eduard Coupleaux of France. In 1937 Jerome Markowitz (1917–1991), founder of the Allen Organ Co., patented the stable valve oscillator. A bank of 12 such oscillators, one for each pitch class, became the standard technology before the advent of the **digital organ.** Outputs are manipulated and combined with one another electronically to produce the range of pitch and timbre required. The principal advantage over the pipe organ is lower cost and maintenance, especially since the introduction of transistors in 1958; the principal disadvantage has been an artificial sounding timbre. It is extremely difficult to make an electronic device reproduce the irregularities of the pipe sound wave that give it particular character and, in any case, the quality is dependent upon an electronic speaker in a single location. *See also* ORGAN.

ELGAR, EDWARD (SIR) (2 June 1857, Broadheath near Worcester, England–23 February 1934, Worcester). Primarily a composer of concert music, Elgar also wrote about two dozen **motets, hymns, anthems,** and other liturgical works, and three **oratorios:** the widely admired *The Dream of Gerontius* (1900) on the theme of death and final judgment, and the diptych *The Apostles* (1903) and *The Kingdom* (1906; a third in the series, *The Last Judgment,* was left incomplete), based on Biblical texts selected by Elgar.

ELIJAH **(German:** *ELIAS***).** The most famous **oratorio** of **Felix Mendelssohn** (Op. 70) to a libretto of his own, mostly compiled from 1 Kings, **Psalms,** and other Old Testament books. Mendelssohn contemplated the oratorio Elijah over a long period after the success of his oratorio *St. Paul* (*Paulus*), and a commission from the Birmingham (England) Music Festival stimulated its completion. Mendelssohn conducted the premiere on 26 August 1846. The original setting was in German, but Mendelssohn, working with William Bartholomew, provided an English version. The better known revision of the score was premiered in **London** on 16 April 1847. The work calls for large symphony orchestra, four-voice chorus (subdivided in nos. 11, 36), a bass soloist for the substantial part of Elijah, and boy soprano, soprano, contralto, and tenor soloists for minor roles. It requires a little over two hours to perform.

ELMORE, ROBERT HALL (2 January 1913, Ramapatnam, India–22 September 1985, Ardmore, Pennsylvania). American professor and **organist,** he composed *Psalm* of Redemption, *Three Psalms, Reconciliation, Doxology* (all 1958) and *God is Ascended* (1974). He worked Moravian **hymn** tunes into much of his **organ** and vocal music. (at)

ENGLISH ORATORIO. *See* HANDEL, GEORGE FRIDERIC; ORATORIO.

EPISTLE SONATA. An **instrumental** composition of a single sonata-form movement played at a Roman Catholic **mass** after the intonation of the Epistle, the portion of one of St. Paul's letters preceding the Gospel reading. The Epistle sonata therefore occupied the place formerly held by the **sequence. Wolfgang Amadeus Mozart** composed the most famous set, 17 pieces written for the Salzburg Cathedral between 1772 and 1780, which call for **organ** and various other combinations of instruments.

ETHERIA. *See* EGERIA.

ETON CHOIRBOOK. The most important late-15th-century source of English church music. Compiled around 1504–1505, the choirbook contains music by three overlapping generations of composers. Many are known to us from other contemporaneous sources, but some are obscure figures whose only surviving works appear in this source. It is the main source for works by **John Browne**, William Cornysh, Richard Davy, and Walter Lambe and is a significant source for works by **Robert Fayrfax**.

The manuscript contains **polyphonic** settings of **votive antiphons** and **Magnificats**. With one exception, the texts are in honor of the Virgin Mary. The book was compiled for use at Eton College, a royal foundation established in 1440 by King Henry VI. The book survives incomplete, but an index dating from the time of the manuscript's compilation provides information about the full contents of the source. Even in its fragmentary state, however, the choirbook is far more complete than most late 15th-century manuscripts of English sacred music. *See also* MOTET; OLD HALL MANUSCRIPT; *STABAT MATER DOLOROSA*. (Noël Bisson)

EVANS, DAVID (6 February 1874, Resolven, Glamorganshire, Wales–17 May 1948, Rhosllannerchrugog, near Wrexham). Composed **hymn** tunes including *Charterhouse*, *Erfyniad*, *Ton-Mân*, and *Lucerna Laudoniae*. His harmonizations of many traditional tunes are found in *The Hymnal 1982*, and the *Pilgrim Hymnal*. (at)

EVENING PRAYER (EVENSONG). Anglican conflation of the Roman Catholic **divine offices** of **vespers** and **compline**. Musical settings may include **Magnificat**, *Cantate Domino* (**Psalm** 98), **Nunc Dimittis**, and *Deus Misereatur* (Psalm 67) with English texts despite the Latin referents. The Alternative Services Series II (revised, 1971) provides alternative **canticles**. *See also* ANTHEM; GREAT SERVICE; MORNING PRAYER; SHORT SERVICE; VERSE SERVICE.

– F –

FABURDEN. A technique of improvising three-voiced **homorhythmic polyphony** described circa 1430 in England. One singer takes a traditional **chant** melody. Another sings the same melody a perfect fourth above. The third, the "faburdener," sings either a third or a perfect fifth below the chant. The result is a series of open fifth chords, mandatory at the beginning and end, and first-inversion triads.

In 16th-century England faburden referred to a melody composed in **counterpoint** to a traditional chant, which was then discarded. *See also* DISCANT; *FALSOBORDONE*; FAUXBOURDON.

FALSOBORDONE. A means of harmonizing **psalm tones** with **homophonic** chords in root position, it is reminiscent of, but historically not derivative of **fauxbourdon**. It seems to have grown up in Spain (as *fabordón*) and Italy in the 1480s with the addition and embellishment of cadences in psalm tones. The vocal parts were written out, although *ad libitum* embellishments were not uncommon.

In the late 16th century the texture became detached from psalm tones and could be heard in **toccatas**, early Baroque **sacred concertos**, and even in large compositions such as the *Dixit dominus* of **Claudio Monteverdi**'s *Vespers of 1610* or the famous *Miserere* of Gregorio Allegri. As its use waned on the Continent, it flourished in 19th-century England as **Anglican chant**.

FANTASIA. Free composition for lute, keyboard, or ensemble characterized by improvisatory as well as highly organized **imitative** passages originating in the mid-16th century and flourishing until the early 18th. It is generally a secular genre, but when composed over a **Gregorian** cantus firmus or **Lutheran chorale** and played on the **organ**, a fantasia might have been used as a **prelude** or **verset** in Christian liturgies.

FAURÉ, GABRIEL (12 May 1845, Pamiers, Ariège, France–4 November 1824, Paris). Master of French art song who composed about a dozen **motets**, mostly for solo voices and **organ**, one *Messe* *basse* ("low **mass**"), and a **Requiem,** by far his most famous sacred work.

FAUXBOURDON. An unwritten melody sung a perfect fourth below the **chant** melody, which is sung by the top voice in three-voiced **textures.** The third voice, the tenor, is written out, usually **homorhythmic** with the chant, by the composer. The convention appears in 15th-century continental **polyphony.** *See also* DISCANT; FABURDEN; *FALSOBORDONE.*

FAYRFAX, ROBERT (23 April 1464, Deeping Gate, Lincolnshire, England–24 October 1521, St. Albans, Hertshire). A Gentleman of the **Chapel Royal** from 6 December 1497, he composed six **cantus firmus masses,** two **Magnificats,** and 10 **motets,** all for five voices except two motets for four, the largest surviving *oeuvre* of his generation. *See also* ETON CHOIRBOOK.

FERIAL. Liturgical term for weekdays without a feast or commemoration. **Polyphonic masses ordinaries** without Gloria and Credo may be entitled "De Feria."

FINALIS. The central, or tonic, pitch of a church **mode.** The final note of a Latin **chant.**

FIORI MUSICALI **(It. "Musical Flowers").** A set of three **organ masses** of **Girolamo Frescobaldi (Venice,** 1635). The three cycles of **organ versets** for Sunday **mass,** for Mass of the Apostles, and for Mass of the Virgin offer all the typical organ genres and idioms of the time—**toccatas, fantasias, canzonas, ricercars,** etc.—except works explicitly based on popular tunes (saving the two concluding capriccios).

FLOWER, ELIZABETH "ELIZA" (19 April 1803, Harlow, England–12 December 1846, London). She wrote tunes to the **hymn** texts of her sister, Sarah Flower Adams, "Darkness Clouded Calvary" and "Nearer, my God, to Thee." Sixty-three of her **hymn tunes** were published in W. J. Fox's *Hymns and Anthems* (1840–1841). (at)

FOLK MASS. American term for a Roman Catholic **mass** whose music is composed in idioms related to popular and folk traditions. An early example is *20th-Century Folk Mass*, composed by Geoffrey Beaumont (later Fr. Gerard Beaumont) in 1956. As at the **Taizé** community, this movement wished to encourage **congregational** singing through a more familiar and accessible musical idiom.

After the **Second Vatican Council** loosened regulations on liturgical music in 1963, the number of "folk choirs" in the United States increased rapidly, as did the music for them to sing, which included some **ordinary** settings but many more original texts that replaced the traditional **propers** with congregational songs, nearly always accompanied by guitars and sometimes other **instruments**.

In the 1960s, these songs adopted the solo styles of the folk revival, then current in American pop. Thereafter, folk choirs' music approximated more and more the **praise choruses** of the evangelical Protestant churches. *See also* GOSPEL SONG; HOVHANESS (CHAKMAKJIAN), ALAN; *MISA CRIOLLA*; SPIRITUAL.

FRANCK, CÉSAR (10 December 1822, Liège–8 November 1890, Paris). A superb **organist** who made lasting contributions to the secular concert repertory, Franck published 11 collections of organ works, some very large. The *Six Pièces* of 1868, compared by **Franz Liszt** to the music of **Johann Sebastian Bach**, derive from his prodigious improvisations after services. He also composed two grand **oratorios**, *Ruth* (1843–1846) and *Les Béatitudes* (1869–1879), five **cantatas**, two **masses**, 16 **motets**, and five **offertories**.

FRANCO CODEX. Collection of 16 **polyphonic Magnificats**, two for each of the **psalm tones**, set by Hernando Franco (1532–1585), *maestro di capilla* of the **Mexico City** Cathedral. The pair for tone III is missing.

FREEDOM'S LYRE (1840). "Or, **Psalms**, **Hymns**, and Sacred Songs for the Slave and His Friends," the best known of the anti-slavery hymnals inspired by William Lloyd Garrison and published between 1834 and 1856. Compiled by Edwin F. Hatfield, clergyman and hymnologist, *Freedom's Lyre* contains 291 hymns, **metrical psalms**, and **doxologies** (texts only) devoted to anti-slavery themes.

FRESCOBALDI, GIROLAMO (baptized mid-September 1583, Ferrara–1 March 1643, Rome). Composer of three dozen **motets** in both *stile antico* and Baroque styles, and two **masses**, he is renowned chiefly for his keyboard works and great influence on **organ** playing well into the 18th century.

He was elected organist of the Cappella Giulia in Rome in 1608 and assumed his position on 29 October. In November 1628, he became organist to Grand Duke Ferdinando II of Tuscany but returned to the Cappella Giulia under the patronage of the Barberini family in April 1634. In his last years he played regularly for the **Oratorio** del Crocifisso during Lent.

The first major composer to concentrate on **instrumental** music, Frescobaldi composed more than 125 works in every keyboard genre of his time, some of which were useful in liturgy: **toccatas, fantasias, canzonas, ricercars,** which exhibited the **imitative** art of Franco-Flemish **counterpoint.** The only publication explicitly for liturgy was his late collection *Fiori Musicali* (1635).

FUGING TUNE. An English or American **hymn** or **metrical psalm** characterized by structural **imitation** in at least one section. Typically, a quatrain would have its first two lines set in block chords, moving to a cadence. The third line would be set with imitation, and the fourth would return to **homophony.** The third and fourth lines would often repeat.

Fuging tunes originated in English parish churches in the middle of the 18th century. James Lyons published some of these in *Urania* (Philadelphia, 1761), the first American tunebook to contain them. *See also* BILLINGS, WILLIAM; *SACRED HARP.*

FUGUE. A composition or a significant, self-contained portion of a larger composition, based entirely on **imitation.** The **subject** is announced unaccompanied:

Most commonly, a single subject and its countersubject provide all the motivic material for the entire fugue; occasionally fugues may have multiple subjects (double fugue, etc.). A two-voice texture, the minimum, is rare; three and four voices are most common; five and six occasionally occur, especially in vocal music. Fugues are significant for sacred music in two ways: as a means of constructing choral numbers in **masses, oratorios, cantatas, motets,** etc.; and as **organ** repertory which may have a peripheral function, as **prelude** or **postlude** music, in Christian liturgy.

The Latin word *fuga* ("flee") has been associated since the early 15th century with imitative composition in various genres: popular song, round, catch, **canon,** motet, **fantasia, ricercar, canzona.** But while some of those terms could include other textures, *fuga* came to be associated exclusively with imitative texture by the 17th century. In modern usage it generally applies to music dating from the late 17th century or later.

There is no traditional form for fugues, but there are many conventional terms (see figure 2). An *exposition* of the fugue presents a complete subject, or *entry*, in any voice, whereas an *episode* works with material derived from the exposition. A *stretto* (It. "tightened") is an exposition in which the entries are overlapped more quickly than originally.

The acknowledged master of the keyboard fugue, and in particular those for organ that might have been heard in church, is **Johann Sebastian Bach.** His cantatas, **passions,** masses, and motets also contain many choral fugal movements, but in this application of fugal technique he is joined in mastery, although of a more dramatic, less religious kind, by his contemporary **George Frideric Handel,** whose **English oratorios** inspired many choral fugues of **Franz Joseph Haydn** and those of later composers of **oratorios.** In fact, after the 18th century the choral fugue was an essential component of the sa-

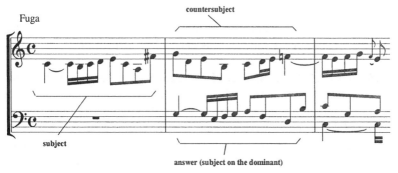

Figure 2.   Fuga from BWV 547, mm. 1–3.

cred musical semantic; no serious sacred oratorio or mass could do without one.

FULL ANTHEM. An **anthem** composed for chorus, without vocal solos.

FULL SERVICE. A complete setting of the Anglican **Morning Prayer**, **Holy Communion**, and **Evening Prayer services**, united by a common key or **mode**. *See also* GREAT SERVICE; SHORT SERVICE; VERSE SERVICE.

FUX, JOHANN JOSEF (1660, Styria, Austria–13 February 1741, Vienna). *Kapellmeister* at the imperial court in Vienna (1715–death). His theory book, *Gradus ad Parnassum*, summarizing the *stile antico* of classical **polyphony**, became a standard text for traditional church composition until the 20th century. He composed over 600 works including 14 **oratorios** and about 80 **masses**. (at)

– G –

GABRIELI, ANDREA (1510, Venice–late 1586, Venice). Composer who contributed to the rising reputation of Venice as a musical center in the late 16th century, particularly in ceremonial sacred music for feasts, including compositions for *cori spezzati* and **instrumental canzonas**, **ricercars**, and **toccatas**. In 1562, he met **Orlandus Lassus** at Frankfurt and possibly studied with him for the two years following. In 1566, he won the competition for one of two **organ** positions at St. Mark's in Venice. Later he was influential as a teacher; one of his students was his nephew **Giovanni**.

GABRIELI, GIOVANNI (c. 1553–1556, Venice–August, 1612, Venice). Composer most associated with the spectacular Venetian school of composition, owing to his brilliant deployment of both **instrumental** and vocal forces in compositions for *cori spezzati*. He studied with his uncle **Andrea** and then with **Orlandus Lassus** in Munich from 1575 to (probably) 1579. He substituted for **Claudio Merulo** as **organist** at St. Mark's and won a permanent post there on 1 January 1585. After Andrea's death, Giovanni supervised the collection and publication of his works and assumed the role of principal composer at St. Mark's. His own major publications are the *Sacrae Symphoniae* (1597 and 1615). His more than 100 **motets** and **mass** movements are almost all for *cori spezzati* of two or three choirs. He also composed **canzonas**, sonatas, **ricercars**, **fantasias**, and **toccatas** for instruments as well as a significant repertory of early organ music.

GAITHER, WILLIAM J. (BILL) (28 March 1936, Alexandria, Ind.). Best-known composer of **praise choruses**, including "Because He Lives" and "He Touched Me."

GALLICAN CHANT. Chant sung in Christian churches in the Frankish kingdom before the Carolingian order to unify liturgies in the empire by imposing the Roman rite along with its **Gregorian chant**. No Gallican chant book has survived; the small repertory is known through individual surviving chants in other traditions and identified by textual and musical features, the most noticeable of which is perhaps the use of two different recitation tones for the two halves of a **psalm** verse.

GARCIA, JOSÉ MAURICIO NUNES (22 September 1767, Rio de Janiero–18 April 1830, Rio de Janeiro). Ordained a Roman Catholic priest on 3 March 1792, he was appointed *mestre de capela* of Rio de Janeiro Cathedral, the highest post in the city, and then to the same title for the royal chapel of Prince Dom João VI in 1808. He conducted the Brazilian premiere of **Wolfgang Amadeus Mozart**'s **Requiem**. He composed more than 400 works, mostly sacred music for four-voiced chorus with accompaniment, including 32 **masses** (19 surviving, seven of which set the complete **ordinary**) and four **Requiems**, music for Holy Week, five **polyphonic sequences**, and many polyphonies for the **divine office**.

GĀTHĀ. See BUDDHIST CHANT.

GAUNTLETT, HENRY JOHN (9 July 1805, Wellington, Shropshire–21 February 1876, London). Virtuoso **organist** at St.

Olave's, Southwark (1827–1846), he helped to bring large Germanic organs to England and aided William Hill in designing organs with a C compass, larger pedal range, and more stops. He also wrote **hymn tunes** and compiled **hymnals** (e.g., *Congregational Psalmist*, 1856). (at)

GELINEAU, JOSEPH (31 October 1920, Champs-sur-Layon, Maine et Loire, France). Jesuit priest since 1951 and liturgical scholar, his most influential compositions are four sets of **psalms** and **canticles** dating 1953–1963 which attempt to imitate in French the original poetic structure. These provided a model for the **responsorial psalm** in the Roman Catholic **mass** since 1970.

As liturgist he argued in *Chant et Musique dans le Culte Chrétien* (1962) that the chief value of liturgical music was in its ability to perform a ritual function and that the great body of traditional Catholic music, too complex for the **congregation**, had to be replaced by simpler **chants**. In 1985, however, he regretted the commonness of much new liturgical music and the preponderance of strophic songs to the exclusion of Biblical chants. *See also* LITURGICAL MOVEMENT; SECOND VATICAN COUNCIL; TAIZÉ.

GENEVAN PSALTER (1562). Also known as the Huguenot Psalter, the most influential **hymnal** supervised by **Jean Calvin**, preceded by earlier versions in 1539, 1542, 1543, and 1551. The texts are **metrical psalms** translated into French by Calvin, Clément Marot (c. 1497–1544), and Théodore de Beze (1519–1605). The chief composers involved were Louis Bourgeois (c. 1510–after 1560) and an unidentified "Maître Pierre." The simple, mostly conjunct melodies, adapted from Latin **chants**, folk tunes, and even **Lutheran chorales**, set the **psalms** syllabically with only minims and semiminims (half and quarter notes), with phrase endings marked by longer notes. These proved to be popular and memorable: by 1565, 63 editions had been printed. It became the standard source for psalm singing in the French-speaking world, and **polyphonic** versions composed by **Claude Goudimel** from 1551 to 1564 and then by **Claude Le Jeune**, published posthumously in 1601, were widely disseminated for domestic use. A German edition of Goudimel's versions issued by Ambrosius Lobwasser (Leipzig, 1573) allowed the Calvinist repertory to intermix with the Lutheran, resulting in a partial fusing of the traditions in the 17th century.

GERMAN REQUIEM, A (*Ein Deutches Requiem*). Composed by **Johannes Brahms** and a favorite of choral societies. The work is a non-liturgical German **Requiem** in seven movements, scored for solo soprano and baritone, four-voiced chorus, and symphony orchestra augmented by bass tuba, contrabassoon, harps, and **organ**. It requires about 45 minutes to perform.

An outline for a German Requiem among Robert Schumann's effects may have inspired Brahms to begin the project in the late 1850s. He assembled texts emphasizing the hope of redemption from the **Lutheran** Bible, chiefly the **psalms**, Old Testament prophets, and New Testament letters. The first three movements were performed on 1 December 1867 by the *Gesellschaft der Musikfreunde* in **Vienna**, and all seven on 18 February 1869 at the *Gewandhaus* in **Leipzig**. *See also* SCHUBERT, FRANZ.

GIBBONS, ORLANDO (1583, Oxford–5 June 1625, Canterbury). Composer, member of the **Chapel Royal**, probably from 1603. An **organist** by profession, he made significant and very popular contributions to the Anglican repertory: 40 **anthems**, a **short service**, a **second service**, three **psalms**, and two **Te Deums**.

GINASTERA, ALBERTO (11 April 1916, Buenos Aires–25 June 1983, Geneva). Composer of concert music who nonetheless scored a success with a monumental modernist **passion** using **Gregorian chant**, the *Turbae ad passionem gregorianam* (1974) for large chorus, boy's choir, orchestra, and soloists.

GĪTA-GOVINDA. Hindu epic poem about the love of Radha and Krishna, composed by Jayadeva in Sanskrit in the 12th century. Divided into 12 chapters of 24 *prabandha*, each containing groups of eight couplets (*ashtapadi*) and other **metric** types. After each stanza there is a refrain (*dhruvā*), which is musically distinct yet completes the sense of the stanza. The manuscript sources specify a *rāga* and a *tāla* for each of the 24 songs, but local preferences often replace them. The *Gīta-Govinda* is the primary source of texts for popular

Hindu songs, the *bhajan*, and the poetic conventions are those of classical Hindustani and Karnatak music.

GLAGOLITIC MASS (*Msa glagoljskaja*). Symphonic setting of a **mass ordinary** in **Church Slavonic** by Leos Janácek (3 July 1854, Hukvaldy, Moravia–12 August 1928, Moravská Ostrava). "Glagolitic" is one of the two scripts used for the Old Church Slavonic introduced by the ninth-century missionaries Sts. **Cyril** and **Methodius**. The **Cecilian movement** in Moravia encouraged its study in the 19th century, but Janácek, an agnostic, wanted to set the ordinary chiefly as a nationalistic expression, not as a liturgical composition. He used a carefully edited text in Cyrillic script, despite the title, as only a few scholars could read Glagolitic.

The Glagolitic Mass premiered on 5 December 1927 in Brno. Last-minute changes by the composer and subsequent editions to the text and music make Universal Edition's first published version of April 1928 controversial. It appears that Janácek intended a concert performance to comprise nine movements: an opening **instrumental** "*Intrada*," a second instrumental "*Úvod*" (introduction), the five ordinary texts "*Gospodi pomiluj*" (Lord, have mercy), "*Slava*" (Glory), "*Veruju*" (I believe), "*Svet*" (Holy), "*Agnece Bozij*" (Lamb of God), an organ solo, and lastly a repetition of "*Intrada*." The score calls for four vocal soloists (SATB), an organ soloist, a large chorus, symphony orchestra, and requires about 45 minutes to perform. *See also* HANUŠ, JAN.

GLAREAN, HEINRICH (June 1488, Mollis–28 March 1563, Freiburg). In 1547, Glarean published the *Dodecachordon*, which updated the theory of eight church **modes** by adding four additional modes which adumbrate the modern major and minor scales.

GLORIA. *See* MASS; Appendix A for text.

GLORIA IN D, ANTONIO VIVALDI, RV 589 (1708). Well-known setting of the Gloria, an **ordinary** prayer of the Roman Catholic **mass**. The scoring calls for two soprano soloists and one alto, a four-voiced choir, and an orchestra of two flutes, oboe, oboe d'amore, bassoon, three trumpets, timpani, **organ**, and **continuo**. Vivaldi composed the Gloria in the manner of a "Neapolitan" or **cantata** mass, with the text segmented into 12 self-contained movements, all together requiring about one half hour to perform. The solo **arias** are in the **operatic** style of the high Baroque; the choral textures range from solemn **homophony** to a concluding double **fugue**.

GLYKYS, JOANNES (fl. late 13th century). Along with **Johannes Koukouzeles**, he developed the elaborate **Byzantine kalophonic chant**. Known as the "teacher of teachers," a manual of Byzantine **chironomy** is attributed to him, as is a didactic chant, *Ison oligon oxeia*, which, in manner analogous to the system of **Guido d'Arezzo**, demonstrates chant formulas in the eight **modes**. *See also AKOLOU-THIAI.*

GOMBERT, NICOLAS (c. 1495, southern Flanders–c. 1560, n. p.). Pupil of **Josquin Desprez**, cleric, and unofficial court composer for Emperor Charles V, he wrote **parody masses** (10 have survived in complete form), over 160 **motets** (one fourth Marian compositions), and eight **Magnificat** settings, one in each church **mode**. He was highly regarded as a master of **imitation**, and **Claudio Monteverdi** parodied Gombert's motet *In Illo Tempore* to exhibit his own **contrapuntal** mastery in his *Missa In Illo Tempore* (1610). (at)

GÓRECKI, HENRYK MIKOLAI (6 December 1933, Czernica near Rybnik, Poland). Known for symphonic compositions, he has also composed a large repertory of unaccompanied sacred choral music using Polish folk tunes and traditional Roman Catholic melodies in the 1980s. His accompanied **psalms** *Beatus Vir* Op. 38 and *Miserere* Op. 44 both played a role in the tumultuous Polish politics of that decade.

GOSPEL MOTET. *See SPRUCHMOTETTE.*

GOSPEL SONG. American religious song type that sprang from urban revivalism after the Civil War. The term appears in a printed collection of **Philip P. Bliss**: *Gospel Songs, A Choice Collection of Hymns and Tunes, New and Old, for Gospel Meetings, Sunday School* (1874). Such meetings consisted of preaching followed by gospel songs intended to heighten religious fervor; Dwight L. Moody (1837–1899) and **Ira D. Sankey** formed the first of many such teams in 1873. The format continues to the present, often broadcast by "televangelists."

The music of gospel is rooted in older American **hymnody**, and southern **congregations** continue to sing "gospel" songs that originated in the **shape-note** books and periodicals. But the religious movements, including Pentecostals and the African American Holiness and Sanctified movements, have eagerly adopted elements of contemporary popular music—circus quicksteps, sentimental ballads, ragtime rhythms, blues harmonies, country **instruments**, etc.—so that "gospel" musical language is eclectic and changes rapidly with popular tastes. In recent decades, congregants at revival meetings often listen to gospel songs performed by famous soloists, small ensembles, or choirs, and in other respects gospel has become thoroughly commercialized, so that the sacred quality of modern gospel is no longer musical but depends upon lyrics and context.

The African American tradition of gospel music ("black gospel") is quite distinct. After the Civil War, segregated urban congregations had meager means to print collections, so that their gospel songs traditionally have the hallmarks of an oral tradition: call-and-response patterns, endlessly repeated ecstatic refrains, and improvised ornamentation suited to the simple song structures. Charles Price Jones published his *Jesus Only No. 1* only in 1899. After World War II, recordings of black gospel stars such as **Thomas A. Dorsey** and Mahalia Jackson (1911–1972) popularized the tradition so that the black gospel is the main referent of the term "gospel" today. *See also* PETERSON, JOHN WILLARD; SPIRITUAL; TINDLEY, CHARLES A.

GOUDIMEL, CLAUDE (Besançon, France, c. 1510–Lyons, 27 August 1572). Publisher and composer of five **masses**, 10 **motets**, and three **Magnificats**, Goudimel's greatest influence on sacred music is through his **metrical psalm** settings, particularly his **polyphonic** settings of the **Genevan Psalter** melodies. These are simple **homorhythmic** settings with the Genevan melody in the tenor, occasionally the soprano.

GOUNOD, CHARLES (18 June 1818, Paris–18 October 1893, St. Cloud). Opera composer who also contributed 16 **masses**, over 50 motets, four **oratorios**, three sacred **cantatas**, and many other sacred songs. His earliest and latest masses attempt a sacred semantic through an austere texture and **chant**-like rhythms. His most famous work is the *Messe Solonnelle de Ste. Cécile* (1855), which is more operatic.

GRADUAL. Liturgical book containing the chants for singing the **mass**. Also, one of the **mass propers**.

GRADUALIA. Composed by **William Byrd**, a two-volume cycle of 109 **polyphonic** Latin **mass propers** for major feasts, possibly for the household of Sir John Petrie, leader of an outlawed Roman Catholic community in Essex, England. Book I was published in 1605, but anti-Catholic reaction to the Gunpowder Plot forced its withdrawal. Book II was published in 1607, and both volumes were reprinted in 1610.

GRANDI, ALESSANDRO (c. 1577, n.p.–1630, Bergamo, Italy). *Maestro di cappella* at the cathedral of Ferrara (1615–1617), singer (1617) and then second *maestro* under **Claudio Monteverdi** at St. Mark's, **Venice** (1620–1627), and *maestro di cappella* of Santa Maria Maggiore, Bergamo (1627–death). Grandi excelled in the **concertato** style, and his sacred monodies are exceptional in that they include obbligato **instrumental** accompaniment. He published six volumes of **motets** and several **masses** and **polyphonic psalms**. (at)

GRAND MOTET. Type of **motet** associated with the courts of Kings Louis XIII and XIV. Nicolas Formé, *sous-maitre* of Louis XIII, directed an ensemble of two five-voiced choirs, one chiefly of soloists and the other, larger, weighted to the lower registers. This tradition was continued by **Henri Du Monte** with 20 *grands motets* composed from c. 1663–1683, followed by 12 works of Jean Baptiste Lully, 24 of Pierre Robert, 77 by **Michel Lalande**, and over 85 by **Marc-Antoine Charpentier**. After 1725, some of these were heard publicly at the Concert Spirituel in **Paris**.

The *grand motet* usually sets a Latin **psalm** text, dividing the verses into vocal solos, small choruses, and large choruses. In the works composed after 1660, orchestral *symphonies* articulate the musical structure, and the vocal distributions vary more. *See also* VERSE ANTHEM.

GREAT SERVICE. An Anglican **service** composed with complex **contrapuntal** texture for as many as eight voices. A "First Service of 4, 5, 6 and 7 Parts" of Robert Parsons uses texts from the first edition of the *Booke of Common Praire* (1549) and probably dates c. 1550. *See also* BYRD, WILLIAM; EVENING PRAYER; HOLY COMMUNION; MORNING PRAYER; SHORT SERVICE; VERSE SERVICE.

GREENE, MAURICE (12 August 1696, London–1 December 1755, London). Organist at St. Paul's Cathedral, London, from March 1718, he composed 14 **full anthems**, 44 **verse anthems**, and 22 solo **anthems**, all with **continuo** in the high Baroque idiom, and 23 "orchestral anthems" as well as seven **Te Deums** and a **Service** in C.

GREGORIAN CHANT. Repertory of **chant** most closely associated with liturgies of the Roman Catholic Church. In Richard Crocker's strict definition, this repertory includes about 600 **propers** for the **mass** whose earliest sources date from about 900 and originate in northern Europe. Other scholars would include propers for the **divine office** whose sources are slightly later. Common usage also includes **ordinary** chants for the mass composed later still, and even more casual usage would include medieval **tropes** and **sequences**, neo-Gallican chants of the 17th century, and any piece published in books authorized by the Vatican such as the *Liber Usualis*. The name Gregorian comes from a Carolingian attribution of the chant, no longer credited, to **Pope St. Gregory the Great**, who is depicted in medieval iconography writing music dictated to him by a dove representing the Holy Spirit.

Ninth-century documents report that Gregorian chant came from **Rome** when the Carolingian monarchs Pepin I (ruled 741–768) and Charlemagne (ruled 768–814) ordered the liturgies of their kingdom to conform to those of the Eternal City. The few surviving chant books from Rome itself, however, dating from the 11th century, record many of the same texts as the northern sources but different melodies, now known as Old Roman chant, and so there is considerable uncertainty as to whether the northern chant is really Roman, or whether the northern authorities merely wished it to be known as such, whether the Old Roman chant evolved greatly in the intervening two centuries, etc.

Tenth-century sources show a steady accretion to the Gregorian repertory. First the propers of the divine office appear shortly after those for the mass (the Hartker **Antiphoner**, c. 1000). Then come multiple settings for the ordinaries, then tropes and sequences. Feasts newly added to the liturgical calendar required their own proper chants. The style of later chants naturally evolved and responded to other musical developments, above all **polyphony**, which began by adding simultaneous melodies at a fixed harmonic interval above or below the chant. As the originating tradition became ever more distant, verbal accents were made to conform with contemporary tastes, **melismas** were removed, and the rhythm acquired a **meter** in performance. A number of French dioceses created entirely new chants near the close of the 17th century, known as neo-Gallican chants, some of which remain popular members of the "Gregorian" repertory today.

In 1837 **Prosper Guéranger** became abbot of the Benedictine monastery of St. Pierre at Solesmes, France, which he established as a center for the recovery of both the music and the performance tradition of Gregorian chant. His monks collected and copied ancient manuscripts from all over Europe. **Dom Joseph Pothier** (1835–1923) adapted an easily legible square notation from 14th-century manuscripts, and a modern edition of the mass propers, *Liber Gradualis*, was published in 1883. While the pitches of the melodies seemed settled, their rhythmic quality was not. Finding a uniform length for each note unpalatable, Dom André Mocquereau (1849–1930) devised a system of three rhythmic signs that he believed recaptured the chant's subtlety: the dot to double a duration, the episema to lengthen it by an unspecified amount less than double, and the ictus to indicate a stress. Fiercely controverted among scholars, this "Solesmes method" nevertheless spread through recordings and new editions that included Mocquereau's signs, including the *Liber Usualis*, first published in 1896, the most widely used chant book in history. It also inspired a concerted effort to teach chanting in parishes and schools from about 1920 to 1960.

The words of the oldest Gregorian chants are almost always sentences taken from the Bible, usually the psalter. (Entire **psalms** were sung to chanting formulas called **psalm tones**.) Chants for the divine office included **hymns** of medieval poetry. Ordinary texts for the mass came from a variety of Biblical and other sources (*see* MASS). Later medieval chants such as tropes and sequences could be **litanies** or devotional poetry.

Gregorian chant plays an essential part in the history of Western music if only because the Carolingian imposition of liturgical uniformity led to the invention of a musical notation. The earliest chant books with musical notation (St. Gall Codex 359 and Laon MS 239, both c. 900) record staffless neumes (notes) that indicate melodic direction but not precise intervals. Neumes on staves date from c. 1000. Scholars have speculated recently that the staffless neumes recorded a local performance of the rhythm, given that the melodies were already known by heart through oral tradition. Following the lead of Dom Eugène Cardine, Rupert Fischer and Marie-Claire Bellocq collated the notations of St. Gall and Laon with modern square notation in the *Graduale Triplex* (1979). *See also* CECILIAN MOVEMENT; COUNCIL OF TRENT; GUIDO D'AREZZO; MEDICEAN CHANT; *TRA LE SOLLECITUDINI.*

GREGORY THE GREAT, (POPE) (ST.) (c. 540, Rome–12 March 604, Rome). Pope from 590, St. Gregory reformed the liturgy by importing certain **Byzantine** practices such as singing the **Kyrie** and **Alleluias** outside the Easter season. He may have founded or reorganized the Roman **Schola Cantorum**. A preface in an eighth-century **chant** book from Monza names Gregory as the composer of the music. Pope Leo IV (847–855) referred to *Gregoriana carmina* in a letter making this kind of chant, now "Gregorian," compulsory. *See also* GREGORIAN CHANT.

GRETCHANINOFF, ALEXANDER TIKHONOVICH (25 October 1864, Moscow–3 January 1956, New York City). Composer who diverged from the Russian Orthodox tradition by his irregular use of **chant** and occasional **instrumental** accompaniment. His *Missa Oecumenica* (1944) sets the Latin **mass** text and includes Orthodox, Roman Catholic, and non-Christian elements. *See also ZNA-MENNĪY RASPEV.* (at)

GROUND. *See* OSTINATO.

GUÉRANGER, DOM PROSPER (4 April 1805, Sablé-sur-Sarthe, France–30 January 1875, Solesmes). He purchased the deserted priory of St. Pierre at Solesmes in 1837 and established the Benedictine monastery that became the center for restoring Roman liturgy and **Gregorian chant**. Guéranger's own research and writings formulated principles of manuscript correlation by which Gregorian melodies were reconstructed, expressed in his book *Les Mélodies Grégoriennes* (Tournai, 1880). *See also* CECILIAN MOVEMENT.

GUERRERO, FRANCISCO (4 October ? 1528, Seville–8 November 1599, Seville). Composer of **masses** (2 vols.), **motets** (2 vols.), **psalms** (1 vol.), **vespers** (1 vol.), two **passions**, and 61 *canciones y villanescas espirituales*, he was associate *maestro di capilla* (1551–1574), then *maestro* (until death) at the Cathedral of Seville. While occupying this post he traveled widely to **Rome, Venice, Jerusalem**, and all over Spain. Owing to his functional harmonies and straightforward textures, he was a favorite composer in cathedrals into the 18th century.

GUIDO D'AREZZO (c. 995–after 1033). The most famous music theorist of the late Middle Ages, he was active in Arezzo, Italy from 1025, with a visit to **Rome** probably about 1028 at the behest of Pope John XIX, who had heard of his teaching methods.

In his treatise *Aliae Regulae* (c. 1020–1025) Guido proposes using a system of lines to express the pitch height of neumes (notes) more precisely than the old practice of using staffless neumes. He used two lines, one yellow to represent C and one red for F, because below those pitches occur the troublesome half-steps.

In his *Epistola de Ignoto Cantu* (c. 1028, before 1033) Guido introduces his method of sight-singing by which a student abstracts pitch relations, relating them to the familiar **hymn** to St. John *Ut queant laxis*. Its first phrase begins with the syllable *ut* on the pitch C, the second phrase with the syllable *re-* (from *resonare*) on D, and so on until the familiar solfege pattern *ut re mi fa so la* is associated with locations in cognitive pitch space.

These two innovations utterly revolutionized the use of musical notation in Europe and allowed the learning of newly composed music far faster than the rote methods which they replaced. In short, they underlie the entire **polyphonic** tradition of the west.

In his *Micrologus* (1026–1032), the second most widely copied treatise on music after *De Institutione Musica* of **Boethius**, Guido discusses **modes**, polyphony, and the rhythmic relations in **chant**.

– H –

HAGGADAH. Book of rituals, prayers, songs, and stories about the Exodus of the Israelites from Egypt, compiled from c. 200 to c. 1500, used for the Passover Seder service. The introductory portion is a mnemonic of 15 words that begin specific rituals. These have acquired various folk song settings and **cantillations**. The texts following the introduction are chanted to particular *Steiger* (**modes**), according to both local and international traditions. *See also* SIDDUR.

HALLELUYAH (HALLELUJAH) (Heb. "Praise the Lord"). It occurs 23 times in the **Psalter** and is used as an acclamation in the Jewish Temple. *See also* ALLELUIA.

HAMMERSCHMIDT, ANDREAS (1611 or 1612, Brüx, Bohemia–29 October 1675, Zittau, Germany). Organist at St. Peter's, Freiburg (1634–1639), and St. John's, Zittau (1639–death). He published more than 400 sacred vocal works in 14 collections including five volumes of *Musicalische Andachten* ("Musical Devotions," published between 1639–1653) containing **motets** and *madrigale spirituale*. Included in the preface to volume five is a commendatory poem written by **Heinrich Schütz**. (at)

HANDEL, GEORGE FRIDERIC (23 February 1685, Halle, Saxony, Germany–14 April 1759, London). With **Johann Sebastian Bach**, one of the supreme composers of the high Baroque, Handel was not by profession a church composer. He did write a number of

anthems and smaller sacred works and invented the English **orato-rio**, a hybrid of sacred and secular elements that assures his renown in sacred music, particularly through a single work of that genre, *Messiah*.

While Handel enjoyed the occasional patronage of the great families of Florence and Rome during his sojourn in Italy (1706–1710), and of English nobility and royalty (along with pensions) after his permanent move to London in 1712, he made his living chiefly by composing **operas** for a paying public and thus was one of the first major composers to liberate himself from both court and church. Between 1711 and 1741 he composed about 40 Italian *opere serie* based on historical and mythological plots for small companies of professional singers, usually Italian.

It is simplistic to say that Handel invented the English oratorio as a way to save his theatrical career after the foreign *opera seria* would no longer sell to the London public, as the table on page 83 shows an overlap of over 20 years between his first oratorio and last opera, and yet there is some truth to this traditional view. He did suffer both competition with a rival opera company and the public's growing indifference to any opera production through the mid-1730s, and although he was slow to give up the Italian opera, persisting until 1741 with *Imeneo* and *Deidemia*, both of which failed, he attempted no more after *Messiah*. The relative success of his new English-language genre convinced him of his new livelihood.

The transition was not difficult. Handel's English oratorio is not far from Italian *opera seria*. The essential musico-dramatic conventions of **recitative** and **aria** remain. The plots are still mythological and historical, except that the history is almost always sacred, with sources predominantly in the Old Testament. The **instrumental** effects, textures, and genres within the work are the same. The language shifts from Italian to English. All of Handel's powers as a musical dramatist won from decades of operatic experience could apply directly. The one substantial change, and the hallmark of Handel's adaptation, is the addition of a chorus that at times comments and moralizes on the action in the manner of a Greek chorus, and at other times participates in it. An early acquaintance with Racine's Biblical tragedies *Esther* and *Athalie*, sources for two of Handel's earliest essays in the form, may have given him the inspiration to exploit the great English tradition of choral singing in this way.

Seven of the 24 oratorios listed have classical literature as the text sources. The remaining 17, being sacred dramas designed for the commercial theater, occupy a strange border zone in the sacred repertory. Except for *Israel in Egypt*, composed like a grand anthem on the **Canticle** of Moses (Exodus 15), and the unique, contemplative *Messiah*, the dramas in Handel's oratorios are entirely human and, like Greek tragedies, demand little in the way of belief to make sense. On the other hand, the grandeur of their choral praises of God and the virtues of their Biblical heroes can certainly edify a faith already present.

Handel's sacred music, apart from the oratorios, consists of nine concerted **motets** written in Italy, one sacred Italian oratorio *La Resurrezione* (1708), one **passion** on the widely set libretto of Barthold Heinrich Brockes (1716), 11 anthems composed for the Duke of **Chandos** (1717–1718), four "**Coronation**" anthems (1727), five settings of **Te Deum**, including the famous *Utrecht* (1713) and *Dettingen* (1743), and 12 other occasional anthems. Many of these are richly scored in the Baroque manner and may occupy up to 45 minutes in performance.

HANUŠ, JAN (2 May 1915, Prague). He used electronic, aleatoric, serial, and *Sprechstimme* techniques in setting the **oratorio** *Ecce Homo* (1977–1978), translated Old **Church Slavonic mass** texts into modern Czech in *Mse Hlaholska* (**Glagolitic Mass**, 1986), and published a collection of 10 works, *Opus Spirituale Pro Juventute* (1969–1977), including **motets**, **passions** according to Sts. Matthew and John, and a Christmas musical drama, all meant to instruct children. (at)

HARMONIUM (REED ORGAN). A keyboard **instrument**, popular from the mid-19th to mid-20th centuries, that produces tones by forcing air over freely vibrating metal tongues (reeds). There are two general types, compression and suction, describing how the bellows, operated by treadles, draw air. Pitch range is five octaves and ranks, usually eight, are typically divided into bass and treble. Gabriel Joseph Grenié (1756–1837) is credited with the construction of the first

Handel's English Oratorios

English Oratorio	First Performance	Librettists and Sources
Acis and Galatea	May 1718	John Gay et al. after Ovid
Esther	1718?	Alexander Pope and John Arbuthnot after Racine after the Book of Esther
Deborah	17 March 1733	Samuel Humphreys after Judges 5
Athalia	10 July 1733	Humphreys after Racine after 2 Kings and 2 Chronicles
Alexander's Feast	19 February 1736	After John Dryden
Saul	16 January 1739	Charles Jennens after 1 Samuel and 2 Samuel
Israel in Egypt	4 April 1739	Exodus
Messiah	13 April 1742	Compiled by Jennens from Old and New Testament
Samson	18 Feburary 1743	Newburgh Hamilton after Milton after Judges 14–16
Semele	10 February 1744	William Congreve after Ovid
Joseph and his Brethren	2 March 1744	James Miller after Genesis 41–44
Hercules	5 January 1745	Thomas Broughton after Ovid, Metamorphoses 9, and Sophocles Trachiniae
Belshazzar	27 March 1745	Jennens after Daniel 5, Jeremiah, Isaiah, Herodotus, and Xenophon
Occasional Oratorio	14 February 1746	Hamilton after Milton and Spenser
Judas Maccabaeus	1 April 1747	Thomas Morell after 1 Maccabees and Josephus
Joshua	9 March 1748	Morell?
Alexander Balus	23 March 1748	Morell after 1 Maccabees
Susanna	10 February 1749	Anonymous after Apocrypha
Solomon	17 March 1749	Anonymous after 2 Chronicles, 1 Kings 5, and Josephus
Theodora	16 March 1750	Morell after Robert Boyle: The Martyrdom of Theodora and Didymus
The Choice of Hercules	1 March 1751	Robert Lowth: The Judgment of Hercules (adapted)
Jephtha	26 February 1752	Morell after Judges 11 and George Buchanan: Jephtes sive Votum
The Triumph of Time and Truth	11 March 1757	Morell after Pamphili Il trionfo del Tempo

working instrument, which he called *"orgue expressif."* "Harmonium" comes from the instrument of four ranks of Alexandre François Debain (1809–1877) patented in 1842.

Harmoniums were common domestic instruments and an inexpensive substitute for the **pipe organ** in small churches in Europe. **César Franck**, Louis Vierne, **Max Reger**, and many other composers for pipe organ composed serious music specifically for the harmonium in the late 19th and early 20th centuries. The colonial powers exported it in large numbers to Africa and especially India, where it came to be used commonly in Hindu *bhajan*.

HASSLER, HANS LEO (baptized 26 October 1564, Nuremburg–8 June 1612, Frankfurt). One of the first German musicians to journey to Italy to complete his training (**Venice** 1583–1584), he spread Italian methods beyond the Alps. He composed 11 **masses**, including two for *cori spezzati*, about 120 **motets**, and about 75 **chorale** settings and other German-language sacred works.

HAYDN, FRANZ JOSEPH (31 March 1732, Rohrau, Austria–31 May 1809, Vienna). Known as the "father of the symphony" and "father of the string quartet," Haydn also made important contributions to the sacred repertory that survive mainly in the concert repertory of choral societies: 15 **masses**, 24 **motets,** and six **oratorios**.

The best known of the earlier masses is the *Cäcilienmesse* (1766), a "Neapolitan" or "**cantata**" mass that breaks the texts into self-contained movements. His last six masses were composed at the request of his patron, Nikolaus Eszterháza (the younger), whose family Haydn served for most of his career, to celebrate the name day of the Princess Maria Hermenegild on 8 September. All have entered the repertory:

- Mass in C major (*Paukenmesse*; *Missa in Tempore Belli*, 1796)
- Mass in B-flat major (*Heiligmesse*, 1796, performed 1797)
- Mass in D minor ("Lord Nelson Mass," 1798)
- Mass in B-flat major (*Theresienmesse*, 1799)
- Mass in B-flat major (*Schöpfungsmesse*, 1801)
- Mass in B-flat major (*Harmoniemesse*, 1802)

These are symphonic masses scored usually for four vocal soloists, four-voiced choir, and symphony orchestra, and last about 45 minutes. Haydn composed each of the **ordinary** prayers as a continuous movement, the shorter ones in sonata style. The longer ones have changes of tempo and texture to express the text and articulate structure.

The Creation is among the most frequently sung of all oratorios; *The Seasons* is also frequently performed, and *The Seven Last Words of Our Saviour from the Cross* less so.

HAYDN, JOHANN MICHAEL (baptized 14 September 1737, Rohrau, Austria–10 August 1806, Salzburg). Concertmaster (1763–death) and **organist** at Trinity Church (1777–death), he succeeded **Wolfgang Amadeus Mozart** as organist of the cathedral in Salzburg (1781–death). Haydn's sacred works comply with the reforms of **Joseph II**: he wrote some 100 *a cappella* Latin **offertories** and **graduals** to replace concerted ones. He edited a German **hymnal** (*Der heilige Gesang zum Gottesdienste in der römisch-katholischen Kirche*, 1790) and wrote eight **masses** in German, presumably to satisfy reformers' desires for vernacular in the services. He also wrote 38 Latin masses and numerous other sacred works. (at)

HAZAN **(pl.** *HAZANIM***). Cantor** of Jewish liturgies. Originally a sexton, the office dates from about 650, coinciding with the rise of *piyyutim* for **congregational** singing with a soloist. A professional appointed by the community, the *hazan* acted as liturgical leader as well as poet and teacher in the community. Until *siddur* were printed in 1486, the *hazan* possessed the single manuscript copy for a synagogue, and the congregation followed his singing by rote. Because rabbis often considered popular *piyyutim* liturgically superfluous, *hazanim* were often at odds with them, particularly from the 16th century on, when the *hazan*'s improvisations (*hazanut*) came under fierce attack.

HEILLER, ANTON (15 September 1923, Vienna–25 March 1979, Vienna). World-renowned **organist** and improviser, he composed **polyphony** with **Gregorian chant**–like melodies while modernist in harmony: eight **masses**, two German masses, two unaccompanied

motets, two **cantatas**, the **oratorio** *Tentatio Jesu* (1952), and more than a dozen works for **organ**.

HEIRMOLOGION. Liturgical book of the **Byzantine chant** containing the first strophes for the **Nine Canticles** for the **divine office** of *orthrōs*. A mnemonic resource, the book would be used by singers to remind themselves of the melody for each ode, which would then be repeated for all the *troparia* (strophes). The earliest heirmologion with musical notation dates from the mid-10th century.

***HESPERINOS* (Gk. "Evening").** The principal evening **divine office** in the **Byzantine** rite. It became distinct from the **Roman** rite **vespers** by the sixth century. It consists of two main parts: *prooimaikos*, an excerpt of **Psalm** 103 with a **doxology**; and a *katisma*. *See also* ORTHRŌS.

HILDEGARD VON BINGEN (1098, Bermersheim near Alzey, Germany–17 September 1179, Rupertsberg near Bingen). Benedictine Abbess from 1152, natural scientist, and composer, Hildegard composed 77 original **chants** on her own texts that describe visions that had visited her since the age of five. These chants are known as *Symphonia armonie celestium revelationum* in modern editions and include **sequences**, **antiphons**, and elaborate **responsories**. She also composed a **liturgical drama**, *Ordo virtutum*, containing 82 more chants.

HISTORIA. German-language musical setting of a Bible story, most commonly the birth, **passion**, resurrection, or ascension of Christ, used in a **Lutheran** liturgy. In the 16th and first half of the 17th century, the sung text was strictly scriptural: a Gospel sung to a recitation tone for narration and for individual speaking roles, to **polyphony** for group responses. Later techniques from Italian **opera** appeared—**recitative**, **aria**, **continuo** accompaniment—and also non-Biblical commentary, particularly in passions. *See also* BACH, JOHANN SEBASTIAN; CARISSIMI, GIACOMO; CHARPENTIER, MARC-ANTOINE; ORATORIO; SCHÜTZ, HEINRICH.

HODDINOTT, ALUN (11 August 1929, Bargoed, Wales). Lecturer and then professor at University College, Cardiff (1959–1987). Hoddinott wrote **cantatas** *Dives and Lazarus* (1965), *The Tree of Life* (1971), and *St. Paul at Malta* (1971), **anthems** and **motets** such as *Puer Natus* (1972), and *Sinfonia Fidei* ("Symphony of Faith," 1977), a three-movement setting of medieval Latin text for soloists, chorus and orchestra. (at)

HOLMBOE, VAGN (20 December 1909, Horsens, Jutland–1 September 1996, Ramløse, Nordsjælland/Nordseeland). Professor at the Royal Danish Conservatory of Music, Copenhagen (1955–1965), he wrote a series of six-part *a cappella* **motets** called *Liber Canticorum* (includes *Expectavimus Pacem*, 1951–1952; *Benedicamus Domino*, 1952; *Dedique Cor Meum*, 1953; *Beatus Vir*, 1968; *Hominis Dies*, 1984; *Laudate Dominum*, 1984). (at)

HOLST, GUSTAV (21 September 1874, Cheltenham–25 May 1934, London). Music teacher at St. Paul's Girls' School (1905–death), his study of Sanskrit and the Hindu religion led him to translate and set four groups of *Choral Hymns from the Rig Veda* (1908–1912). His **opera** *Savitri* (1908) was founded on an episode from the *Mahabharata. See also GĪTA-GOVINDA; SĀMAVEDIC* CHANT. (at)

HOLY COMMUNION. The Anglican Eucharistic liturgy, including musical settings of the Kyrie, Gloria, Creed, Sanctus, **Benedictus**, and Agnus Dei with English texts despite the Latin referents held over from the Roman Catholic **mass**. The earliest sources of Anglican part music contain complete settings of the **service**, but in the Elizabethan period it began to be shortened to include only Kyrie, Gloria, and Creed. Musical interest in the Communion service declined steadily until the **Oxford Movement** in the mid-19th century. Thereafter, many new settings were composed, including commissions for **Ralph Vaughn Williams**, **Benjamin Britten**, and others of high reputation, and settings of the Latins texts also became accepted. *See also* DIVINE LITURGY; EVENING PRAYER; MORNING PRAYER; SHORT SERVICE; VERSE SERVICE.

HOMOPHONY. Polyphonic texture of one salient **voice** (melody) and one or more other accompanimental voices.

HOMORHYTHMIC. Polyphonic texture in which all **voices** have identical rhythmic patterns.

HONEGGER, ARTHUR (10 March 1892, Le Havre–27 November 1955, Paris). One of *"Les Six,"* a group of composers who included **Darius Milhaud** and **Arthur Honegger,** he is noted for his five **oratorios**, particularly *Le Roi David* ("King David," 1921), his most frequently performed piece, which employs Asian sonorities, **Lutheran chorales**, and **polyphonic** techniques. *Jeanne d'Arc au Bûcher* ("Joan of Arc at the Stake," 1934–1935), another oratorio, uses **Gregorian chant** and various folk idioms in a score for five speakers, five soloists, mixed choir, children's choir, and symphony orchestra. (at)

HOSHA'NOT. See LITANY.

HOVHANESS (CHAKMAKJIAN), ALAN (8 March 1911, Somerville, Mass.–21 June, 2000, Seattle). Prolific composer of over 400 works. Most of his vocal music is sacred and includes *Missa Brevis* (1935), a **Magnificat** (1958) that is among the first vocal works to use aleatoric techniques, and practical works for liturgy including *The Way of Jesus* (a **folk mass**, 1974), and *A Simple Mass* (1975) as well as numerous **anthems** and **motets**. He applied his studies in Eastern folk music (including Armenian, Indian, Japanese, Korean, and others) to his secular works. For example, the flute concerto, *Elibirs* (1944), uses Hindu *rāgas*. (at)

HOWELLS, HERBERT (NORMAN) (17 October 1892, Lydney, Gloucestershire–23 February 1983, Oxford). Organist and professor at the Royal College of Music (from 1920), he succeeded Gustav Holst as music teacher at St. Paul's Girls' School in 1932, serving there 1932–1962. From 1950–1964, he was King Edward VII Professor of Music at University of **London**. He composed many **anthems**, **motets**, and settings of **canticles** including *Hymnus Paradisi* (which includes portions of a **Requiem** for his nine-year-old son composed after his son's death but not released for performance until 1950), *Missa Sabrinensis* (1954), *An English Mass,* and a *Stabat Mater* (1963). (at)

HURD, DAVID (27 January 1950, Brooklyn). Concert **organist**, music director of the Church of the Holy Apostles in Manhattan, and professor of church music at the General Theological Seminary, New York. He has written many **hymn tunes** including *Mighty Savior*, *Andújar*, *Julion*, *Tucker*, and others that appear in several hymnals including the Episcopalian *The Hymnal 1982* for which he served as an editor. (at)

HYDRAULIS. *See* PIPE ORGAN.

HYMN. A devotional song. The term, of obscure Greek origin, refers to repertories in every major religion that have the following characteristics:

- Texts are sacred but non-scriptural strophic poetry.
- The melodies, through elements of repetition, periodic phrasing, and **meter**, have strongly patterned structures that make them easy to learn and remember.
- The songs have popular roots; often they arise outside of authorized liturgies and then grow into some liturgical role.

These features are not present in all repertories translated as "hymns," but taken together they form a cluster concept that can set this sacred music apart from other types.

Hymn traditions almost always prefer poetic texts. These are very often highly structured, with isosyllabic lines, uniform strophes, and regular meter. This means that hymn texts are not often taken from sacred writings, since the Bible, the Qur'ān, and the Vedas are for the most part prose. The **Buddhist** *gāthā* **chant** may be an exception.

The **psalms**, a collection of sacred poetry from the Bible that occupies a central position in both Jewish and Christian liturgies from ancient times to the present, would seem to be a major exception to the non-liturgical quality of hymns. However, historically the Jewish and Christian traditions have distinguished between **psalmody** and **hymnody**, the term "hymn" being reserved for other non-Biblical texts. The structures of Latin hymns and chanted psalms in the **Gregorian** tradition, for example, are completely different, particularly since the hymns have lines of uniform length. The distinction was reinforced in the 16th century when **Calvinist** Protestants insisted that only **metrical psalms**, and not hymns, could be sung in their worship services, though the two might be musically indistinguishable. But **Isaac Watts** blurred the distinction in the early 18th century with his psalm paraphrases that quickly found their way into many hymnals of Congregationalists, Methodists, and finally Anglicans and other major Christian denominations by the late 19th century. In this recent Western Christian context, "hymn" denotes a type of musical setting more than a type of text.

The music of hymn traditions is typically less complex than liturgical chant and has strong elements of repetition. Such an element may be as simple as a refrain in Hindu *bhajan* sung by the **congregation** between more complex solo passages, but the overwhelming preference is for songs in strophic form by which the same melody repeats for each strophe of poetry, creating a mutually reinforcing poetic-melodic structure. Such strophic hymns would include the later Jewish *piyyutim*, the Byzantine *kanon*, the Japanese (Buddhist) *wasan*, and various Christian forms, including the Latin hymn, the **Lutheran chorale**, Anglican hymns, and hymns of the reformed churches. The later Byzantine *kontakion* and the Islamic *qawwali* elaborate their strophic forms with introductory music.

The most ancient hymn traditions are **monophonic**. The hymn repertory of the Western world was significantly expanded with the addition of newly composed melodies to traditional hymn melodies to create the **polyphonic** hymn, beginning with improvised polyphony such as **faburden** and growing to large composed collections for **vespers** in the 15th century. Hymns of the Protestant Reformation were also sung monophonically at first, but quickly appeared in simple harmonized versions for all the major Protestant churches by the end of the 16th century. The development and application of modern functional harmony about that time regularized and intensified the metric properties of the **hymn tunes** by articulating not only whole phrases but strong/weak relationships within the phrases, i.e., measures, sometimes to the extent that the tunes themselves had to be altered. (Compare, for example, the modern version of "A Mighty Fortress Is Our God" with Martin **Luther**'s original tune "*Ein' Feste Burg.*") In virtually all Western churches today a four-voiced harmonization of every hymn is expected.

One principal effect of the poetic text and comparatively simple music is to make hymns relatively easy to learn and memorize, one indicator of the popular origins of many hymns. Every pattern of regular accent, every rhyme, and the periodic melodies offer bountiful cues for the memory. The conception of hymns as a popular sacred music raises a number of historical issues: the inclusion of hymns in authorized liturgy; the reception of hymns by professional liturgical musicians; the propriety of *contrafacta*; the practicalities of congregational singing; and evangelization.

Historically, especially in the older religious traditions, hymnody has often begun outside authorized liturgy. In strict Islam, hymns have never been included. In other traditions, hymns might gradually become accepted enough to win some role within the liturgy. Until the 1960s, Latin hymns in the Catholic tradition were regularly used only in the **divine office**, not the **mass**, and *laude* were limited to popular processions outside the churches. Only in the **Byzantine** rites do hymns occupy an honored place in liturgy from early on. One explanation for this exclusion might be that hymns, arising from an apparently natural human disposition to sing in praise of the Divine, collide with the equally profound awe for sacred writings—the Bible, the Qur'ān, etc.—which become the principal sources for liturgical prayer. These are complex texts, rarely poetic, and cannot directly be turned into hymns. Any liturgical tradition remaining close to its sacred writings will naturally resist hymnody.

A second reason is that the music to which sacred writings are traditionally set is usually very complex and difficult. Highly trained liturgical musicians naturally regard their art as exalted and often the only proper means of addressing the Divine. Hymn melodies, often arising from popular culture, might easily be considered unworthy of liturgy.

They might also bring with them the taint of secular culture and the corrupt world, as when Sephardic Jews of the Iberian peninsula adapted *piyyutim* texts to popular Arabic melodies. This practice of *contrafactum* is common in many hymn traditions, which is why the hymn text, usually identified by opening words, must be distinguished from the **hymn tune**, identified with a proper name. In medieval Latin hymn collections a text may appear with many different melodic settings. The earliest important Protestant hymn collections, the ***Wittenberger Geystliche Gesangk Buchleyn*** (1524) and the **Genevan Psalter** (1562) adapt new texts to folk melodies. Later hymnals specify the poetic meter of a text, so that one may be easily substituted for another using the same melody. But *contrafactum* necessarily raises the problem of a semantic conflict between the secular melody and the sacred text. For this reason, the practice of *Qirā'a Bi'l-Alhān*, singing verses of the Qur'ān to popular melodies, was condemned by juridical understandings of Islam, and despite their basis in Talmudic and Midrashic writings, Maimonides opposed including *piyyutim* in Jewish liturgy.

The liturgical antipathy toward hymnody was broken in Western Christianity in the 16th century by **Martin Luther**, founder of the Protestant Reformation. Luther's emphasis on the priesthood of all believers, along with his faith in the salutary spiritual effects of sacred music, naturally brought congregational singing into the heart of the liturgy and the chorale, the Lutheran form of hymnody, was the logical vehicle. When chorales came to be harmonized in four voices in **cantional** style toward the end of the century, they solved the paradox of simplicity and worthiness that had bedeviled other kinds of hymnody. The main melody, in the top voice, is simple enough for any congregation to learn, along with its poetic and vernacular text, while the other three independent voices provide a rapid harmonic rhythm and a **contrapuntal** texture complex enough to satisfy the most learned musician. These compositions epitomize what modern Christians mean when they use the term "hymn." Later hymnodies, particularly in the reformed churches, are obviously derivative of the Lutheran synthesis but dilute its quality by employing a much slower harmonic rhythm (one change / four to eight beats vs. one change / one to two beats) and accompanying voices that are hardly independent but merely shadow the main melody.

Luther's ideal of congregational participation was ratified at first by the great popularity and proliferating collections of chorales in the 16th century, then by the collapse of resistance to hymn singing in the reformed and eventually Anglican churches (one result of the **Oxford movement**), and finally in Roman Catholicism by the **Second Vatican Council**, which in the 1962 **Constitution on the Sacred Liturgy** encouraged "active participation" of Catholic congregations through music.

Some historians believe that chorale singing was one of the most effective means of spreading Luther's doctrines to the common people, and indeed hymnody has been an important tool of evangelization in many traditions. The Hindu preacher Puranda Dasa (1484–1564) composed *kirtana* on the simpler *rāgas* to inspire religious revival and they succeeded in some Hindu sects as congregational songs. American revivalists have similarly used the hymnodies known better as **spirituals**, **gospel songs**, and **praise choruses**. *See also KATISMA*; *MADĪH*; *MADRASHA*; *QALA*; SYRIAN CHANT.

HYMNODY. The practice of singing **hymns**. *See also* PSALMODY.

HYMNS ANCIENT AND MODERN. Extremely influential hymnal resulting from the **Oxford movement**, compiled by more that 200 Anglican clergy, and first published in 1861. The hymnal brings together excellent examples of the major Christian **hymn** traditions: Latin **plainsongs**, German **chorales**, and contemporary Victorian hymns. Outselling all rivals, its music was adopted by Welsh Methodists, Scottish Presbyterians, and American **Lutherans**, and finally by English and American Catholic hymnals of the last half century.

HYMNS AND SPIRITUAL SONGS (**London, 1707**). The first **hymnal** of **Isaac Watts**, extremely popular with both white and African American **congregations** in colonial America.

HYMN TUNE. The melody of a **hymn**, as distinct from an accompanying text, title, first line, or harmonization, and identified by an italicized or capitalized name that often reflects something of the tune's origin. "Proper" tunes have a fixed text; "common" tunes are applied to other texts in the same **meter**. *See also CONTRAFACTUM.*

HYPAKOAI. **Byzantine chant** divided between choir and soloist in the manner of a Western **responsory**. Different melodic settings of the same text may appear in a *psaltikon* (for a soloist) and in an *asmāti-kon* (for a choir).

– I –

IMITATION. A **contrapuntal** texture featuring a single motive (subject), i.e., a melody overlapping with itself. If the following voice (answer) copies the intervals of the leading voice precisely, it is strict imitation, even if the starting pitch of the subject is different (in which case the description specifies the intervallic distance from the original pitch, e.g., strict imitation at the fifth); if all intervals are not precisely copied, it is free imitation. If the answer is deformed merely to reinforce the overall key, it is called a tonal answer. *See also* FUGUE.

IMPROPERIA. *See* REPROACHES.

IN NOMINE. Singular and exclusively English form of **instrumental polyphony**, whereby the **Sarum antiphon** *Gloria tibi Trinitas* is used as a **cantus firmus**, following **John Taverner**'s use of it in his four-voiced setting of the **Benedictus** from his six-voice *Missa Gloria tibi Trinitas*. The second section, setting the words *in nomine Domini*, became detached and widely circulated. Over 150 *In nomines* down to **Henry Purcell** were inspired by this Tavener excerpt.

INSTRUMENTS, BIBLICAL. The following instruments have been identified in the Old Testament: percussion: bells, cymbals, *mena'ane'im* ("sistrum," metal rattle), and *tof* ("tympanum" or "tambourine"); winds: *halil* ("pipe" or "shawm"), *keren* ("horn"), *mashrokita* ("pipe" or "flute"), **shofar**, and trumpet; strings: *asor* ("ten-stringed" zither), *katros* ("lyre" or "guitar"), **kinnor**, *nebel* ("lyre" likely the same as *kinnor*), *psanterin* ("dulcimer" or "psaltery"), and *sabkha* (triangular harp).

INSTRUMENTS, USE OF. Because sacred music is so closely associated with sacred texts, it is primarily a vocal music the world over. Attitudes toward the use of instruments vary widely with religion and within sects of religions.

Some traditions exclude instruments completely and intentionally because instruments are too closely associated with the secular world, have unseemly connotations, or simply because religious authorities and the faithful believe that the human voice is given to man to praise the divine. These would include most kinds of traditional **chant** but also traditional Jewish *piyyutim*, many kinds of Roman Catholic **polyphony**, and **psalmody** of the reformed Protestant churches. Despite the widespread mention of instruments in the **Psalter** and elsewhere in the Bible, Jewish authorities forbad the use of STET instruments in worship after the destruction of the Temple in A. D. 70 as a sign of mourning. It is thought that early Christian liturgy, which took much from Jewish ritual, also avoided instruments in order to distinguish its music from that of pagan rites. The call to prayer (*'adhān*) and chanting of the Qu'rān (*tajwīd*) in traditional Islam have always been strictly vocal.

Some types of sacred music, usually less complex and more popular, may employ instruments if they are conveniently available to support the singing, but they are perfectly integral without them. Lutheran and other Protestant **hymnody** typically uses a **pipe organ** accompaniment, and American **gospel songs** and **spirituals** use a piano. In some areas, **Buddhist chant** may be articulated by bells or clappers. Islamic *qawwali* may be introduced and accompanied by a **harmonium**.

Other kinds of sacred music have traditionally used specific instruments, to the exclusion of others, so that those instruments have acquired sacred connotations for the culture. In Western Christianity, the pipe organ would be the example *par excellence*. In African and North American Indian rituals, specific **drums** would have such roles.

Since 1600, Western Jewish and Christian sacred music has increasingly adopted the instruments, along with their techniques and idioms, of the secular world. Organ accompaniment to Jewish liturgical chant, concerted **cantatas** in **Lutheran** churches, symphonic **masses** and **Requiems** in Catholic churches, and in the 20th-century the use of all manner of popular instruments in **praise choruses** and gospel music have all excited controversy among traditionalists and reformers within each religion. *See also A CAPPELLA*; *KAGURA*; LEWANDOWSKI, LOUIS; ORGAN.

INTONAZIONE. Brief, improvisatory composition for **pipe organ** that sets the pitch for a choral work to follow. **Andrea** and **Giovanni Gabrielli**'s *Intonati d'organo* (1593) is the first appearance of the term. *See also* TOCCATA.

INTROIT. *See* MASS.

IQAMĀ. See 'ADHĀN.

IRELAND, JOHN (13 August 1879, Bowdon, Cheshire, England–12 June 1962, Rock Mill, Washington, Sussex). Organist, choirmaster of St. Luke's, Chelsea (1904–1926) and teacher of composition at the Royal College of Music (1923–1939), he is known for settings of the Anglican **service** and for his **anthem**, *Greater Love Hath No Man*, (1912, orchestrated 1922). (at)

ISAAC, HEINRICH (c. 1450, Flanders–26 March 1517, Florence). Prolific composer who served the court of Lorenzo the Magnificent in Florence from 1485–1494, then joined the chapel of Emperor Maximilian I in 1496, traveled widely, and returned to Florence in 1512 where he remained until his death. He wrote 36 **masses** and over 50 **motets** in addition to the **polyphonic propers** in the collection *Choralis Constantinus*.

ISABELLA LEONARDA (6 September 1620, Novara, Italy–25 February 1704, Novara). Ursuline contemplative from 1636 who composed more than 200 sacred works in every contemporary genre: **masses, motets, sacred concertos**.

ISORHYTHM. Compositional technique, common in early **motets**, by which a melody or melodic fragment from a traditional Christian **chant** is repeated in both its original pattern of pitches (*color*) and a pattern of durations created by the composer (*talea*). Isorhythm seems to have originated in late 12th-century **discant clausulae** attributed to **Perotinus**. Because the chant melody in clausulae moved quickly along with the new melodies, its repetition was required to give the composition sufficient length. *See also MESSE DE NOSTRE DAME; NUPER ROSARUM FLORES.*

ISRAEL IN EGYPT. An **English oratorio** composed by **George Frideric Handel** between 1 October and 1 November 1739. The libretto, probably by Charles Jennens (1700–1773), Handel's *Messiah* librettist, sets the Exodus story in two parts, the second of which is the text of the **Canticle** of Moses (Exodus 15:1–21) with adaptations. The music is scored for strings, oboes, bassoons, trumpets, trombones, timpani, six vocal soloists, and double four-voiced choir and requires about one and one-half hours to perform. The work is remarkable among Handel's oratorios for its close adherence to the Biblical text, its contemplative as opposed to narrative libretto, its frequent borrowings from 17th-century sacred works, and its preponderance of choral numbers.

IVES, CHARLES (20 October 1874, Danbury, Connecticut–19 May 1954, New York). Early experimenter in modernist composition. Ives' nine **psalm** settings (between 1893–1897, Psalm 90 reworked in 1924) explored polytonality, whole tone harmony, and close dissonance. Much of his secular concert music quotes and refers to traditional American **hymn tunes**. (at)

– J –

JANACEK, LEOS. *See* GLAGOLITIC MASS.

JEPHTE. Famous Latin **oratorio** of **Giacomo Carissimi** composed before 1650 in **Rome**. The libretto, drawn from Judges 11: 28–38, tells the story of Jepthe, the Israelite general who vows to God to sacrifice the first living being he meets in exchange for victory over his enemy, only to encounter his only daughter first after the battle. The work minimally requires six vocal soloists (SSSATB), a six-voiced chorus (SSSATB), and **continuo**, although other **instruments** such as strings might be added. It requires about 25 minutes to perform. A critical score edited by Adelchi Amisano was published by Ricordi in 1977.

JERUSALEM. The ancient capital of Judea and of the modern state of Israel began developing into a center of sacred music when King David established the First Temple about 1000 B. C. As described in 1 Chronicles 15, 16, 23, and 25, by about 970 B. C. there were 288 active musicians employed, including singers, string players, trumpeters, and cymbal players. Only the first two groups performed during liturgy.

After the Babylonian exile, music for the Second Temple flourished again by about 450 B. C. (Nehemiah 27). The Roman destruction of Jerusalem in A. D. 70 not only ended this long tradition but occasioned a ban on the use of **instruments** in Jewish liturgy as a sign of mourning, a tradition still observed in orthodox sects but which was relaxed by many European synagogues in the 18th and 19th centuries.

As a Christian patriarchate, the city was the source of some of the most ancient musical traditions of the Jerusalem rite, including certain **Alleluias** and the *trisagion*.

Today, the most ancient traditions are maintained in the Armenian Orthodox church and monastery of St. James, the Ethiopian Orthodox church, and the Greek Orthodox church. *See also* ANTIPHONY; BIBLICAL ACCENTS; BYZANTINE CHANT; *KINNOR;* SHOFAR; SYRIAN CHANT.

JERUSALEM RITE. Most influential of the local liturgical traditions in the first centuries of Christianity, owing to transmission by the many pilgrims who visited the Holy Land, until the region fell under Muslim rule in the seventh century. *See also* BYZANTINE CHANT; EGERIA; JERUSALEM.

JOHANSSON, BENGT (2 October 1914, Helsinki–22 June 1989, Visuvesi). A teacher at the Sibelius Academy from 1960, his compositions are chiefly sacred choral works including **Requiem** (1967), *Stabat Mater* (1953), *Missa* Sacra (1960), and *Missa a 4 Voci* (1969). (at)

JOHN OF DAMASCUS (JOHANNES CHRYSORRHOAS, ST.) (c. 700, Damascus–754, Jerusalem). Composer of **Byzantine** *kanones* and traditionally credited with the sytematization of the *oktoēchos* and the improvement of musical notation.

JOSEPH II, EMPEROR (13 March 1741, Vienna–20 February 1790, Vienna). He initiated reforms in the Roman Catholic liturgy, restricting the use of **instruments** to **solemn masses** on Sundays and high feasts and limiting the time a movement might take. However, he encouraged **congregational** singing in the vernacular. (at)

JOSQUIN DESPREZ (c. 1440, Picardy, France–27 August 1521, Condé-sur-Escaut). Great composer whose 18 extant **masses** and over 100 extant **motets** brought the 15th-century *cantus firmus* techniques to perfection and at the same time established with consummate mastery the techniques of structural **imitation** that grounded the sacred music of the entire 16th century and beyond.

Although he was the most famous composer of his day, details of his life and the chronology of his works are obscure. The earliest record comes from the cathedral at Milan, listing him as an adult singer of **polyphony** in August 1459. In January 1473, he moved to the chapel of Milanese Duke Galeazzo Maria Sforza, where he remained until December 1476. Thereafter, documentary evidence is spotty until he entered the papal chapel in **Rome** in 1489. He left that service before 1500, showed up at the French court of Louis XII from 1501–1502, became *maestro di cappella* for Duke Ercole I d'Este of Ferrara from April 1503–April 1504, and finally retired to the Cathedral of Notre Dame at Condé-sur-Escaut. Throughout most of his career, he commanded the highest salaries for musicians of his time.

Josquin's masses explore virtually every **contrapuntal** technique of the Renaissance: the traditional tenor cantus firmus (*Missa Gaudeamus*), the secular cantus firmus (*Missa L'ami Baudichon*), the transposing cantus firmus (*Missa L'homme Armé Super Voces Musicales*), the acrostic cantus firmus (*Missa Hercules Dux Ferrarie*), the **parody** mass (*Missa Mater Patris*, from the motet by **Antoine Brumel**), the **paraphrase mass** (*Missa Pange Lingua*), and **mensuration canon** (*Missa L'homme Armé Super Voces Musicales*). The Agnus Dei of the *Missa L'homme Armé Sexti Toni* summarizes his mastery: the popular tune appears in long notes moving forward and backward in two voices simultaneously, while the other four voices construct two canons.

Josquin's motets also show enormous variety of technique and texture, ranging from **melismatic** duets reminiscent of **Guillaume Du Fay** (*Alma Redemptoris Mater / Ave Regina Celorum*) to simple but harmonically profound **homophonies** (*Tu solus*) to every kind of imitative scheme (*Ave Maria . . . virgo serena*). Settings may be concise, or monumental works of several *partes* (*Miserere mei, Deus*). The motets have the advantage over the masses of textual variety and expressive resource. Josquin takes both semantic and structural aspects of every text into account in his settings.

Difficult to capture are the harmonic and rhythmic properties of his music. Despite the strictures of imitation, the timing of the vocal entrances and above all the triadic progressions of the counterpoint seem absolutely free and truly profound.

The direct influence of Josquin lasted a generation or two after his death when his music was widely circulated in print and manuscript. But the indirect influence, chiefly through the demonstration by him and his colleagues **Johannes Ockeghem**, **Jean Mouton**, **Pierre de la Rue**, **Nicholas Gombert**, and others, of the musical effectiveness of imitative technique lasts through the present day. *See also* BYRD, WILLIAM; LASSUS, ORLANDUS; OCKEGHEM, JOHANNES; PALESTRINA, GIOVANNI DA; VICTORIA, TOMÁS LUIS DE.

JOUBERT, JOHN (20 March 1927, Cape Town, South Africa). He composed **anthems** and **canticles** for the Anglican **service**, and his *O Lorde, the Maker of Al Thing* (1952) won the Novello Anthem Competition. His large-scale works include a **cantata**, *The Martyrdom of St. Alban* (1969), and an **oratorio**, *The Raising of Lazarus* (1971). (at)

JUBILATE. First word, "rejoice," in the Latin (Vulgate) translation of **Psalm** 100. The 1552 version of the Book of Common Prayer allows this psalm to be substituted for the **Benedictus canticle** in **Morning Prayer**, and as such was set **polyphonically** by **William Byrd** and **Henry Purcell** among other composers.

JUBILUS. See ALLELUIA.

– K –

KADDISH **(Heb. "Sanctification").** Refers to a **doxological** text in Hebrew and Aramaic sung to articulate the sections of a Jewish liturgy. By 1200, it had become associated with mourning. There are 13 traditional melodic settings, used for different liturgical contexts, not including settings for particularly solemn feast days and a **Missi-**

nai setting. The textual version is independent of the melody used. (*See* Appendix B for text). *See also* BERNSTEIN, LEONARD.

KAGURA (**Jap. "God music"**). Refers to Shinto songs and dances. Ceremonial music documented in sources dating from the eighth century falls into eight categories: the generic *kagura* songs; "Eastern entertainment" containing dances; night duty songs; *Yamato* songs (named for the traditional first clan of Japan); funeral songs; palace guard songs; field songs used in agricultural ceremonies; and "big songs" performed before festival days.

Kagura, sung in sustained, formal manner, begin with a solo singer who may be joined by a unison chorus. All singers are male. The song may be accompanied by **instruments**; the *wagon*, a six-stringed zither, and a light clapper, the *shakubyōshi*, are the most common.

The *kagura* sung in large shrines may be danced by female attendants, *miko*. These formal dances are called *mikomai*.

Kagura are heard today at major shrines at Shinto festivals and in the imperial palace in November and December. The reduced *kagura* cycle on such occasions is 12 songs, broken into five groups articulated by instrumental pieces and dances, the whole lasting about seven hours.

KALOPHONIC CHANT. Elaboration of the traditional **Byzantine chants**, characterized by verbal and motivic repetition and performed by expert *maistores* from the 14th and 15th centuries until the 19th century, when **Chrysanthos of Madytus** simplified the repertory. *See also* KORONOES, XENOS; KOUKOUZELES, JOHANNES; *PSALTIKON.*

KANON (**pl. KANONES**). Byzantine **hymn** form derivative of Biblical **canticles** dating from the end of the seventh century. A *kanon* consists of nine odes, each of which contains its own melodic pattern (*hirmus*) setting six to nine stanzas (*troparia*) of identical form. The *kanon* replaced the singing of the **Nine Canticles** in the morning **divine office** (*Orthrōs*), and therefore each of its odes must refer in its poetry to the original scriptural source, even though its principal object of praise—Christ, the Theotokos, a saint—may differ from that of the source.

Originally, *kanones* were composed only for Lent, then Eastertide, and finally to celebrate all the feasts of the year. The earliest musical notation dates from the 10th century, and their melodies are thought to be more florid than those of the **kontakion**. *See also HEIRMOLOGION*.

KAPELLMEISTER. *See MAESTRO DI CAPPELLA.*

KATISMA (pl. KATISMATA). In the **Byzantine** tradition, a division of the **psalter**, one of 20. The *katisma* is divided into three *staseis*, or groups of **psalms** sung continuously in succession. The **hymn** sung at the conclusion of each group is also called *katisma*.

KAYSER, LEIF (13 June 1919, Copenhagen–15 June 2001, Mindeord). Chaplain and **organist** at St. Ansgar (1949–1964), possibly the most prolific Danish composer of **organ** music in the 20th century, he wrote primarily sacred music after he became a Roman Catholic priest (1949). His Christmas **oratorio**, **Te Deum**, several **masses**, and numerous **motets** are written in a conservative style influenced by **Gregorian chant**. Other more modernist works include *Three Psalms* (1952), the Masses Op.10 and Op.15 (1952, 1954), and *Stabat Mater* (1970).

KERLE, JACOBUS DE (1531 or 1532, Ypres, Flanders–7 January 1591, Prague). *Maestro di capella* at Orvieto (1555), and court chaplain for Emperor Rudolf II from 1583 until his death). Cardinal Otto Truchsess von Waldburg, whom Kerle served at intervals throughout his life, commissioned the *Preces Speciales* (1561–1562) for the **Council of Trent**: a blessing, a prayer for the success of the Council, for the reconciliation of the Christian Church, and for the end of religious wars, concluding with the **doxology** and **Kyrie**. The Council's admiration for the clarity of diction possibly influenced the future of **polyphonic** church music. Kerle's other sacred works include many **masses**, **motets**, **Magnificats** and **psalms**. (at)

KERLL, JOHANN KASPAR (9 April 1672, Adorf, Saxony, modern Germany–13 February 1693, Munich). *Kappellmeister* of the court at Munich (1656–1673), then **organist** at St. Stephen's in **Vienna** (1674–1677) and at the imperial court (1677–death). His *Delectus Sacrarum Cantionum* (1669) is an important collection of **sacred concertos**. (at)

KIEVAN CHANT. Variant of *znamenniy raspev* dating from the 17th-century characterized by formulaic repetition.

KINNOR. The **instrument** most revered by the Jews, as David and the Levites were players. Its earliest mention is Genesis 4:21. The precise structure of the *kinnor* is disputed, but it seems to be a lyre-like instrument of 3 to 22 strings played with the hand by sweeping or plucking or with a plectrum. The translation in the King James Bible and many other sources as "harp" is now considered erroneous but obviously influenced iconography and the image of the harp as an angelic or celestial instrument. *Kinnor* means "violin" in modern Hebrew.

KIRTANA **(Sanskrit, "praising").** Karnatic (South Indian) devotional songs dating from the 14th to 16th centuries. Puranda Dasa (1484–1564), "father of Karnatic music," composed them as a means of popularizing his preaching. *Kirtana* usually employ the simpler *rāgas*, and in some Hindu sects they are **congregational** songs.

KITĀB AL-AGHĀNI **(BOOK OF SONGS).** One of the most famous works in Arab literature, a 21-volume compendium of poems from pre-Islamic times to the ninth century compiled by Abū'l-Faradj al-Isfahāni (897, Persia–967, Baghdad). The melody of each poem is classified by its melodic and rhythmic **mode** and its origin.

KODALY, ZOLTAN (16 December 1882, Kecskemét, Hungary–6 March 1967, Budapest). Specializing in choral works influenced by Hungarian folk idioms, he composed the **oratorio** *Psalmus Hungaricus* (1923), which brought him international recognition, and the unaccompanied *Jézus és a kufárok* (*Jesus and the Traders*, 1934) as well as the Budavári **Te Deum** (1936), a *Missa brevis* (1948), and other **carol** and **psalm** settings.

KOL NIDRE (Heb. "All vows"). Refers to the **Missinai** melody **chanted** as a prologue to Yom Kippur. Although commonly associated with the Spanish Inquisition, the chant was introduced by R. Yehudai Gaon of Sura in the eighth century. Famous settings include those of Max Bruch (for cello and orchestra, 1881) and **Arnold Schönberg** (for speaker, chorus, and orchestra, 1938).

KONTAKION **(pl. *Kontakia*).** Byzantine **hymn** form of homiletic character dating from the early sixth century. A *kontakion* begins with an introductory *prooemium* of a single stanza (two to three in later hymns), ending with a refrain (*ephynmium*). Then begins the *kontakion* proper, 18 to 40 stanzas (*troparia*) of identical melodic pattern (*hirmus*), composed in the same **mode** as the *prooemium* and ending with the same refrain. The *kontakion* stanzas begin with initials that make an acrostic spelling the name of the text's author (*melodes*), or the saint commemorated, or, as in the case of the famous *Akathistos* **hymn**, the alphabet.

After the seventh century a new hymn form of *kanon* began to replace the *kontakion*; in modern liturgy only a small number of stanzas of the latter remain in use. *See also HEIRMOLOGION.*

KORONOES, XENOS (fl. c. 1325–1350). Second **cantor** (*lampadarios*) and possibly first cantor (*prōtopsaltēs*) at Hagia Sophia in Constantinople, he composed **Byzantine chants** in **kalophonic** style that appear in most *akolouthai* manuscripts from the late 15th century on.

KOUKOUZELES, JOHANNES (ST.) (c. 1280, Dyrrachium [now Durrēs, Albania–c.1360–75, Mount Athos) Known as *angelophōnos* ("angel voice") and the second most revered source of **Byzantine chant** after St. John Damascene, he retired to a hermitage on Mt. Athos while at the peak of his fame as a composer and singer of **Byzantine kalophonic chant** for the imperial court in Constantinople.

His chants are preserved mostly in the *akolouthiai* manuscripts and are credited with being among the first to expand upon the traditional melodies by adding more disjunct motion and embellishment in an expanded range.

KRENEK, ERNST (23 August 1900, Vienna–23 December 1991, Palm Springs, Florida). He taught at Vassar College (1939–1942) and Hamline University (1942–1947) and became an American citizen in 1945. In the United States, he experimented with serialism, using a principle of row rotation in *Lamentatio Jeremiae Prophetae* (1941). He wrote seven **masses** including four with **propers** (e.g., *Proprium Missae Trinitatis*, 1966–1967) and about 15 **motets**. (at)

KRITI **(Sans. "a creation").** Karnatic (South Indian) devotional songs, descended from *kirtana* but distinguished from them by comparatively elaborate musical settings. The texts may be prose or poetry, in Sanskrit, Tamil, or Telugu, but *kriti* are often performed as **instrumental** solos. The melodies may employ esoteric as well as commonly known *rāgas* and are usually composed in three sections: *pallavi, anupallavi,* and *charnam.* The village of Tiruvarur in Tamil Nadu produced three of India's most famous composers of *kriti*: **Tyāgarāja**, Syāma 'Sastri (1762–1827), and Muttuswāmi Dīkshitar (1776–1835).

KUHNAU (KUHN), JOHANN (6 April 1660, Geising, Germany–5 June 1722, Leipzig). He preceded **Johann Sebastian Bach** as **organist** (from 1684) and **cantor** (from 1701) at St. Thomas Church, Leipzig. Kuhnau is best known for keyboard works, especially his unique *Biblische Historien* (Biblical Sonatas, 1700): six programmatic sonatas, each based upon an Old Testament scene. (at)

KYRIALE. A collection of **chants** setting the **ordinary** prayers of the Roman Catholic **mass**. The earliest examples date from the 10th century and include **tropes**.

KYRIE. *See* MASS; Appendix A for text.

– L –

LADY MASS. **Votive mass** for the Blessed Virgin Mary usually sung on Saturdays in certain monastic and parochial traditions, often in a particular "Lady Chapel." *La Messe de Nostre Dame* by **Guillaume**

de Machaut may be the first **polyphonic** example. The popularity of this liturgy in 16th-century **London** occasioned an expansion of musical resources, including new **portative organs**, in parish churches.

LAHAN. (**Heb., Arab.** "**Tune**" or "**mode**"). Sephardic practice of fitting a modal pattern to a text, which is marked *be-lahan* "to be sung to the tune of . . ." *See also CONTRAFACTUM.*

LALANDE, MICHEL-RICHARD (15 December 1657, Paris–18 June 1726, Versailles). Composer best known for his 77 *grands motets*, although he composed about 50 other sacred works. He worked in several Paris churches and then held important posts at the court of Louis XIV at Versailles: *compositeur de la musique de la chambre* from January 1685 to March 1718 and *surintendant de la musique de la chambre* from January 1689 to November 1719. His motets combine **Gregorian cantus firmus** with the latest textures from Italian **opera** and continued to be heard in France throughout the 18th century. *See also* CHARPENTIER, MARC-ANTOINE; COUPERIN, FRANÇOIS; DU MONT, HENRI; LULLY, JEAN-BAPTISTE.

LANGLAIS, JEAN (15 February 1907, La Fontenelle, France–8 May 1991, Paris). **Organist**, composer, and conductor who promoted the music of **Josquin Desprez** and **Giovanni da Palestrina** early in the 20th century. He composed four **masses** and many works for **organ**. One quarter of his work uses **Gregorian chants**.

LA RUE, PIERRE DE (c. 1452, Tournai ?, France–20 November 1518, Kortrijk, Belgium). Court composer to the Hapsburg-Burgundian court from November 1492. He composed at least 30 **masses**, including ones for all of the most important Marian feasts, Christmas, and Easter, and one of the earliest **polyphonic Requiems**. The *Missa Ave Sanctissima Maria*, the first wholly **canonic** setting, could also be the earliest mass for six voices. A complete cycle of polyphonic **Magnificats** is probably also the first such composed.

LASSUS, ORLANDUS (ORLANDO DI LASSO) (1530 or 1532, Mons [modern Belgium]–14 June 1594, Munich). Composer of about 60 **masses**, four **passions**, 101 **Magnificats**, over 500 **motets**, in addition to all manner of secular vocal works in many languages, Lassus was *princeps musicorum*, the most internationally famous composer of his age. He joined the service of the Gonzaga family of Mantua while they traveled through the Low Countries in summer 1544. He next joined the household of Constatino Castrioto (c. 1550?) of Naples, and then was appointed *maestro di cappella* at St. John Lateran in **Rome** in 1553. In 1555, he visited Antwerp and published there his first motets, for four voices. The next year he published motets for five and six voices and accepted an invitation to join the court of Duke Albrecht V of Bavaria in Munich, where he remained until his death despite many offers throughout his remaining years. He became *maestro di cappella* in 1563. His duties included providing music for a morning service and probably **vespers**, accounting for the large number of *alternatim* Magnificat settings. He also supervised the education of choirboys, and it is possible that he taught **Andrea** (c. 1562) and **Giovanni Gabrieli** (1570s). Emperor Maximilian II granted him a patent of nobility in 1571 and Pope Gregory XIII made him a Knight of the Golden Spur in 1574.

In sheer numbers of publications and reprints, he outstripped every other composer of his time and his music was admired well into the 17th century, after which Lassus suffered the oblivion that obscured all high Renaissance composers save **Giovanni da Palestrina**. His **contrapuntal** technique was as accomplished as Palestrina's, but his harmonic vocabulary in sacred music is more liberal. To express a text, an art for which Lassus was most famous, he did not hesitate to use the chromatic inflections of secular music, although his textures and rhythm rarely betrayed the sacred idiom.

LAUDA. **(It. "praise," pl.** *laude).* A non-liturgical, devotional, **monophonic** song sung to Italian texts by migrant penitents, originating in the latter half of the 13th century as a response to plagues and devastations of war. **Polyphonic** *laude* developed late in the 15th century, were published by **Ottaviano Petrucci** of **Venice**, and enjoyed popularity in the Venetian religious confraternities (*scuole grandi*) and also in the *Congregazione dell'***Oratorio** founded by St. Philip Neri (1515–1595) in **Rome.** *See also CHANSON SPIRITUEL; MADRIGALE SPIRITUALE; VILLANCICO.*

LAUDS. The major hour of the **divine office** of the Roman Catholic rite sung about sunrise. A **chanted** lauds is close in form to **vespers**, except that an Old Testament **canticle** replaces the fourth **psalm**, and the Canticle of Zacharia, **Benedictus**, replaces the **Magnificat** (*see* Appendix A for text). The psalms are often chosen for themes of praise. *See also* GREGORIAN CHANT; *ORTHRŌS*.

LECTIONARY. Christian liturgical book indicating the readings and **psalms** to be used for each day of the liturgical year. Probably the first written lectionary was that of the **Jerusalem** rite in the fifth century.

LEGRENZI, GIOVANNI (baptized 12 August 1626, Clusone near Bergamo, Italy–27 May 1690, Venice). Elected *maestro di capella* at St. Mark's basilica in Venice, he may have taught **Antonio Vivaldi**, **Antonio Caldara**, and **Antonio Lotti**. He composed seven **oratorios**, 10 publications of **motets**, **sacred concertos**, and other sacred works, and two other surviving **masses**.

LEIGHTON, KENNETH (2 October 1929, Wakefield, England–24 August 1988, Edinburgh, Scotland). He taught composition at the Universities of Leeds (1953–1955), Edinburgh (1955–1968), and Oxford (1968–1988), and composed seven **masses** for various combinations of soloists, chorus, and **organ** and many other **anthems**, **canticles**, and **motets**.

LEIPZIG. Located in the German province of Saxony, the city prospered from trade from the 12th century and became an important intellectual center through the growing prestige of the University of Leipzig (founded 1409).

Gregorian chant, sponsored by the town council, was regularly performed in as many as five churches: the St. Nicholas (founded 1160), the St. Thomas (1212), the St. Paul's (1229, destroyed 1968), the New Church (1235, bombed in World War II, destroyed 1950), and the St. Peter's (1213, destroyed 1886) located outside the city walls. With the introduction of **polyphony**, St. Thomas took pride of place among them, and the Thomaskantor became a city officer in 1539 when Leipzig turned to **Lutheranism**. He was responsible for all the liturgical music in the city, and ranked third in the school for boys. Prominent occupants include **Georg Rhaw** (served 1518–1520), Sethus Calvisus (1594–1615), **Johann Hermann Schein** (1616–1630), **Johann Kuhnau** (1701–1722), and **Johann Sebastian Bach** (1723–1750).

Many Lutheran **chorale** books were published in Leipzig. In the 18th and 19th centuries, the important publishers Breitkopf & Härtel (1719) and C. F. Peters (1800) were founded there.

Sacred music declined in Leipzig in the latter half of the 18th century, as it did throughout Europe, but Leipzig played an important role in its 19th-century revival through organizations such as the Leipzig *Gewandhaus* Orchestra (founded 1781) and the *Singakademie* (1802), which, under the direction of **Felix Mendelssohn** and others, revived many of Bach's choral works. In 1859, the *Riedel'-scher Verein* performed the first known complete **Mass in B Minor**.

LEISE. A stanza in a Germanic language used as a refrain in **litanies** and devotional singing in the late Middle Ages. The name may derive from the last syllables of *Kyrie* eleison. The earliest known example dates from the ninth century.

LE JEUNE, CLAUDE (CLAUDIN) (c. 1528, Valenciennes, France–25 September 1600, Paris). Composer of French-language **psalms** for Huguenot worship in *vers mesurés*, which coordinates long and short syllables with minims (half notes) and semiminims (quarter notes), according to classical theory. His psalm settings in three to six voices, published 1601, employ the melodies of the **Genevan Psalter** in a variety of textures and went through many editions in Paris, **London**, Geneva, Amsterdam, and Leiden until the early 18th century.

LEKHA DODI **(Heb. "Come, my friend").** Famous Jewish **hymn** text adapted from the Song of Songs 7:12 and composed by Kabbalist Rabbi Solomon Alkabetz (1505–1584), who signed the text with an acrostic formed from the beginning of each stanza. Sung at the climactic moment of the *kabbalat shabbat* ("welcoming the Sabbath") service established by 16th-century kabbalists, it was widely adopted by many different kinds of Jewish **congregations**, sung by *hazanim* (**cantors**), and set to music by synagogue composers. *See also KON-TAKION.*

LEONINUS (LEONIN fl. c. 1160–1190, Paris). One of two compos-ers, along with **Perotinus**, named by an anonymous source as associ-ated with the cathedral of Notre Dame in Paris and compilers of the *Magnus Liber Organi*, an important source of early Roman Catholic **polyphony**.

LEWANDOWSKI, LOUIS (3 April 1821, Wreschen, Germany?–3 February, 1894, Berlin). Composer who introduced idioms of 19th-century Romanticism into synagogue liturgical music in Berlin, in-cluding music for four-voiced choir and **organ**. His most influential compositions are *Kol Rinnah* (1871) for Sabbath, festivals, and High Holy Days, and *Todah Wesimrah* (1876–1882), and two-volume compilation of works for four-part choir, solo, and **congregation** em-bracing the entire liturgical year.

LIBER USUALIS. Collection of **chant** first published by the abbey of St. Pierre at Solesmes in 1896. It contains, in the modern chant nota-tion adapted by Dom Joseph Pothier (1835–1923), music for the most important liturgies of the Roman Catholic Church including: mass **propers** and **ordinaries**, **vespers** and **compline** for Sundays and feast days; prime, terce, sext, and none for feasts of the first and second class; **matins** for Christmas, Easter, Pentecost, and Corpus Christi; **lauds** for feasts of the first class; liturgies for Holy Week; and various **litanies**.

Designed for practical use more than scholarly reference, the book does not identify the various provenances or ages of the individual chants. Nevertheless, its page numbers are commonly used to iden-tify a particular chant. *See also ANTIPHONALE;* CECILIAN MOVEMENT; COUNCIL OF TRENT; GREGORIAN CHANT; GUÉRANGER, DOM PROSPER; *KYRIALE.*

LIMA. The capital of Peru became an important center for Roman Catholic music in European styles soon after its founding in 1535 by Francisco Pizzaro. In 1583, the Third Lima Council required mis-sionaries to give musical instruction to indigenous Amerindians so that by 1622 the music of one settlement, Santiago del Cercado, was compared favorably to that of cathedrals in Spain. *Maestros di capilla* such as **Tomás De Torrejón Y Velasco** in Lima commanded a choir school, all liturgical performances, and a choral library, which he augmented with his own compositions. Sacred music of high quality might also be heard in the 17th-century convents of Encarnación or Concepción.

LINING OUT. Practice of **congregational** singing whereby the **precentor** (song leader) sings one or two lines of the **hymn** or **psalm**, quite slowly, which then the congregation repeats, often with melodic elaboration. The precentor proceeds to the next one or two-line segment, the congregation repeats it, and so forth for the entire text. The earliest documentary evidence of the practice is in *A directory for the publicke worship of God throughout the three kingdoms of England, Scotland and Ireland* (London, 1644), an English Puritan book. In America, the Dutch Reformed Church of New York ordered *voorzanger* to "tune the psalm" for the congregation in 1645. It was adopted in many colonial churches by the early 18th century, and since then it is associated with African American congregations. Today it may be found in Gaelic areas of Scotland and in some Baptist congregations in the American south.

LISZT, FRANZ (FERENC) (22 October 1811, Raiding near Sopron, Hungary–31 July 1886, Bayreuth, Germany). Perhaps the greatest pianist of all time, Liszt was uncommonly interested in sacred music, theorizing in his 1834 essay *Über die zukünftige Kirchenmusik* ("On the future of church music") of something that would unite "the theater and the Church on a colossal scale." When visited by Claude Debussy (1862–1918) in Rome in 1885, Liszt advised him to visit Santa Maria dell'Anima to hear the music of **Giovanni da Palestrina** and **Orlandus Lassus**.

Lizst composed 13 **organ** works, the most important of which are the **Fantasy** and **Fugue** on *Ad nos, ad salutarem undam* (1850) and the **Prelude** and Fugue on B-A-C-H (1855). He composed five **oratorios** and **cantatas**, *Die Legende von der heiligen Elisabeth* ("The Legend of Saint Elizabeth," 1857–1862) and *Christus* (1862–1867), a Christmas oratorio, being the most famous. He also wrote five **masses**, about 30 **motets**, and about 50 other short liturgical works.

LITANY. Form of **responsorial** prayer in which the leader makes varying invocations, which are answered with a consistent refrain:

> Holy Mary, Mother of God . . .   Pray for us.
> Saint Michael . . .   Pray for us.
> Saints Peter and Paul . . .   Pray for us.
> Etc.

The simple, short, and extremely repetitious responses and the variable list of invocations make litanies especially appropriate for processions. The total length is regulated by the time taken for the procession to complete its route.

The litanic form appears in the Old Testament (e.g., the song of the three children, Daniel 3: 57–88). The Jewish *selihot*, for Yom Kippur and other fast days, and *hosha'not* for the Feast of Tabernacles, are litanies.

The fourth-century *Apostolic Constitutions* notes a litany with the response *Kyrie* eleison at the Eucharist, and **Egeria** reports a similar form for **vespers**. In the **Ambrosian** rite, a litany replaced the Gloria during Lent. In fifth-century Gaul (France), litanies were sung in petition of local needs, a practice that spread to England by the seventh century and **Rome** by the eighth.

In the Roman rite, the Kyrie was probably once a litany that was shortened into the nine-fold form by Pope St. **Gregory the Great**, and the **Agnus Dei** was routinely extended by **troping** into a litany to cover the ritual of fraction. Litanies of saints (as above) occur in the **Byzantine** rites by the sixth century; the earliest notated version in the West is 11th century. Litanies specific to individual saints, such as the Litany of Loreto, appear late in the 12th century.

An anthology of **polyphonic** litanies, *Thesaurus Litaniae*, was published in Munich in 1596 and contains works of **Giovanni da Palestrina**, **Orlandus Lassus**, and **Tomás Luis de Victoria** as well as German composers. Polyphonic litanies could be sung in *alternatim*, with the **cantor** answered by the choir, often in *falsobordone*. Settings for *cori spezzati* also take advantage of the responsorial form. The 17th century saw this tradition peak, with 600 polyphonic litanies published, the Litany of Loreto being the most frequent text. **Wolfgang Amadeus Mozart** set it twice (1771, 1774) along with two others (1772, 1776).

LITURGICAL DRAMA. Chanted **monophony** that **tropes** a liturgical **chant** into a dialogue form. The earliest surviving (**Winchester Tropers**, c. 996 and St. Martial of Limoges, 11th century) and most widespread are *Quem queritis* tropes of the **Introit** for Easter and Christmas **masses**. Such tropes might be transplanted to other liturgical positions, however, such as after the third **responsory** of **matins** of Easter, *Dum transisset sabbatum*. The dramas might also be augmented by other **antiphons**, **sequences**, **hymns** and even extra-liturgical chants such as laments (*planctus*). Such elaborations for Easter, called *Vistatio sepulchri* account for over 400 of the surviving dramas.

Even when elaboration distances the dramas from their original liturgical contexts, their music retains their liturgical character. This repertory has nothing to do with the invention of **opera** at the end of the 16th century, nor with the **passion**.

LITURGICAL MOVEMENT. General term for efforts to renew and reinvigorate liturgy, primarily in Roman Catholicism but also in some Protestant traditions, by encouraging the active participation of **congregants**, restoring the communal sense of the Eucharist, eliminating rituals no longer understood, emphasizing the liturgical year, and by many other means. Although there was some interest in liturgical reform in 18th-century France, the most prominent campaigner was **Prosper Guéranger**, who also founded the Abbey of St. Pierre at Solesmes, where he and his colleagues did research to recover **Gregorian chant**. His attention to liturgy spurred a great wave of interest in historical liturgy, ancient texts, and liturgical reform that has not yet abated. The place and quality of sacred music in practical liturgy remains a central issue. *See also* CECILIAN MOVEMENT; OXFORD MOVEMENT; WITT, FRANZ XAVER.

LITURGY OF THE HOURS. *See* DIVINE OFFICE.

LONDON. The capital city of England was home to most of the leading institutions of sacred music in the British Isles. While **chant**

could be heard in most any parish church up through the Dissolution, **polyphony** appeared in St. Paul's Cathedral about 1230 and the Westminster Customary (c. 1260) describes its performance in three voices at Westminster Abbey. The Abbey claimed the services of many masters through the centuries, including **Orlando Gibbons, John Blow, Henry Purcell**, and **William Croft**. In 1739, **John Wesley** established the Foundery Chapel and introduced the Methodist **hymn**. In 1856, **Henry John Gauntlett** published *The Congregational Psalmist* under the auspices of the Union Chapel.

Outside the churches, London's theaters and concert halls sponsored extra-liturgical **oratorios** and **cantatas** of **George Frideric Handel, Franz Joseph Haydn, Felix Mendelssohn, Edward Elgar**, and others. *See also* CHAPEL ROYAL; LADY MASS; VAUGHN WILLIAMS, RALPH.

LÓPEZ CAPILLAS, FRANCISCO (c. 1605, Mexico City–18 January 1674, Mexico City). Organist at the Puebla Cathedral under **Juan Gutiérrez de Padilla** from December 1641 and *maestro de capilla* from April 1654, he composed eight **masses** and many **motets** in the *stile antico* using **polychoral, parody**, and complex **contrapuntal** techniques.

LOTTI, ANTONIO (1766, Hanover, Germany–5 January 1740, Venice). Composer and teacher, first **organist** at St. Mark's in Venice from 1704 to 1736 and then *maestro di cappella* until his death. His many **masses** and **motets** may combine traits of **chant**, *stile antico*, and **opera**, and remained in repertory through the 18th century.

LOVY (LOWY), ISRAEL (1773, Danzig–1832, Paris). Cantor and composer who introduced four-voiced liturgical music of his own composition to synagogue liturgy in Paris beginning in 1822.

LOW MASS. A Roman Catholic **mass** without singing.

LULLY, JEAN-BAPTISTE (29 November 1632, Florence–22 March 1687, Paris). Renowned for fusing Italian **opera** techniques with French choral traditions to produce the *tragédie lyrique* for the royal court of Louis XIV, his 12 *grands motets* also exploited **homo-**

phonic choral textures and orchestral interludes to famous effect. The *Miserere* of 1663, one of the first *grands motets* to open with a five-voiced **instrumental** introduction, was particularly revered. He also composed 10 *petits motets*, in three voices with **continuo**, devoted to the Virgin Mary and the Blessed Sacrament.

LUTHER, MARTIN (10 November 1483, Eisleben, Germany–18 February 1546, Eisleben). Founder of the Lutheran church, which initiated the Protestant Reformation, in a series of events beginning with the nailing of Ninety-Five Theses to the door of the Schlosskirche at Wittenberg on 31 October 1517 and culminating with the presentation of the Augsburg Confession to Emperor Charles V on 25 June 1530.

Luther's reform was primarily theological, not liturgical, and at first did nothing to abolish the Latin language or Catholic musical traditions, which he admired, being a trained singer, flutist, and lutenist. Unlike **Huldrych Zwingli** or **Jean Calvin**, Luther believed music to be essential to liturgy. His first liturgical reform, the *Formula Missae* of 1523, provides for traditional Latin **chant** throughout. But ultimately much more influential was his second reform, the *Deutsche Messe* ("German **mass**") of 1526, intended for smaller and less cultivated **congregations**. In the meantime, he had been heavily involved in the publication of the first Lutheran **chorales** (1524), which replaced many **ordinary** and **proper** Latin prayers in the *Deutsche Messe*. These, along with **metrical** settings of the most important **psalms**, became the *Kernlieder*, the core **hymn** repertory of Lutheran liturgy. Some of these are Luther's own compositions; Friedrich Blume ascribes 36 chorales "with certainty to the Reformer."

LUTHERAN MASS. *See MISSA BREVIS.*

L'VOV, ALEKSEY FYODOROVICH (5 June, 1798, Tallinn, Estonia–28 December 1879, Kaunas, Lithuania). A professional engineer, he was director of the Russian imperial court chapel choir from 1837 and composed about three dozen *kheruvimskiye pesni* (Orthodox communion **hymns**) and a Latin ***Stabat mater*** (1851) that nonetheless imitated the *znamennïy* chant. He also composed the Russian national **anthem** *Bozhe, tsarya khrani* ("God Save the Tsar," 1833).

– M –

MACHAUT, GUILLAUME DE (c. 1300–before November 1377, Reims?). Highly respected poet who traveled widely as secretary to King John of Bohemia from about 1323 until John's death at the battle of Crécy on 26 August 1346. Documents thereafter locate him intermittently at Reims, where he was canon. He composed mostly secular music, much of it setting his own poetry. Three of the late **motets** (nos. 21–23) can be considered sacred owing to their texts, but by far his most historically significant sacred work is the *Messe de Nostre Dame*.

MADĪH. Islamic songs praising Allah or the Prophet, occasionally heard within the mosque, often sung by itinerant singers, one of the more famous being Hajj El-Mahi (c.1780–1870) of Sudan, composer of 330 songs. *See also KIRTANA; QĪRA.*

MADRASHA. Type of strophic **hymn** sung in the Syrian Orthodox and Assyrian (Nestorian) Church tradition, attributed to St. Ephrem Syrus (d. 373), of no specific liturgical function. Each melody may have several different texts. *See also* BYZANTINE CHANT; *CONTRA-FACTUM; KANON;* SYRIAN CHANT.

MADRIGALE SPIRITUALE. **Polyphonic** setting of an Italian devotional text for unaccompanied voices, usually not strophic. *Vergine Sacra* of Sebastiano Festa, published in 1526, is an early example. Thereafter, its development paralleled that of its much more famous secular counterpart, with contributions from most major madrigal composers, including some **contrafacta**. Generally they were sung by small groups of well-educated amateurs, particularly clerics, but they were also known in the early **oratorio** devotions late in 16th-century **Rome**. *See also LAUDA;* SCHEIN, JOHANN HERMANN; *VILLANCICO.*

MAESTRO DI CAPPELLA (It. "Chapel master"; Fr. *maître de chappelle*; Ger. *Kapellmeister*; Sp. *maestro di capilla*). The musician, usually a composer, in charge of all musical activities at an important musical establishment (not always technically a chapel). Important posts were at the Sistine Chapel in **Rome**, St. Mark's in **Venice**, and the *Hofkappelle* in **Vienna**, the cathedrals of Seville and Toledo, as well as several in New Spain. The German term acquires a somewhat pejorative tone by the 19th century.

MAGNIFICAT. One of the three Gospel **canticles** for the major **divine offices** of the Roman Catholic liturgy. The Magnificat (St. Luke 1: 46–55; see Appendix A for text), known as the Canticle of Mary, is sung near the conclusion of **vespers**.

In the **Gregorian** tradition, the Magnificat is **chanted** much like a **psalm**. It is introduced by an ornate **antiphon** proper for the day, sung by the entire **schola**. Then follow the verses of the Magnificat itself, chanted in pairs either **responsorially** or **antiphonally**, with the concluding **doxology** (*see* Appendix A) appended to the Gospel passage. The antiphon is repeated by the full schola. The Magnificat, however, has chanting tones for each **mode** that are distinct from the **psalm tones**, and while a psalm tone begins with an incipit melody that links the antiphon to the first verse only, the Magnificat begins every verse pair with the incipit.

Because of its liturgical eminence as the climactic moment of daily vespers, the Magnificat was the Latin text most commonly set to **polyphony** during the Renaissance after the **mass**. Composers set it numerous times to accommodate the various modes; **Giovanni da Palestrina** has 30 settings, **Orlandus Lassus** more than 100.

The type of polyphonic setting varied with liturgical practice. A minority are through composed works like **motets**. Others preserve the pairing of the verses and use one of the Magnificat tones as a *cantus firmus*. Most common in the 15th and 16th centuries was the *alternatim* setting, by which half the verses, usually the odd numbers, would be chanted and the other half would be sung in polyphony.

Baroque composers continued to distinguish the verse pairs with strong cadences at the end of each one. Later, as in the "Neapolitan" mass settings, each pair became a short **aria** with distinct **instrumen-**

tal accompaniment. The **Magnificat** of **Johann Sebastian Bach** is the best example of this type.

Thereafter, the verse distinctions were lost in through-composed musical settings, and composers in the later 18th and 19th centuries mostly ignored the genre, probably because of liturgical constraints. Some composers turned to **oratorio** type settings: Magnificats for chorus and orchestra by Lennox Berkeley (1968) and **Krzysztof Penderecki** (1974) are examples. The promotion of vernacular languages after the **Second Vatican Council** (1962–1965) encouraged some commercial settings. *See also BENEDICTUS.*

MAGNIFICAT, JOHANN SEBASTIAN BACH, BWV 243. The most famous setting of this text and one of the most popular choral works of **Johann Sebastian Bach**. There are two versions, both in autograph, of essentially the same work with minor variants. The earlier, in E-flat major (BWV 243a) originally had four **Lutheran** Christmas **chorales** interpolated into its Latin text. The later, more familiar version in D major has no such chorales, thus making it appropriate for any festival **vespers**. The first performance took place in **Leipzig** during the Christmas Day vespers, 1723.

Bach sets each of the 10 verses of the **Magnificat** and the two verses of the **doxology** as a short, self-contained movement in the manner of a "Neapolitan" **mass**. He scored it for five vocal soloists (SSATB), five-voiced choir, and an orchestra of two flutes, oboe and oboe d'amore, bassoon, timpani, strings, and **continuo**. A performance requires about half an hour.

MAGNUS LIBER ORGANI **(Lat. "Great Book of Organum").** Collection of **organum** associated with the cathedral of Notre Dame in **Paris** and believed to have been composed between 1160 and 1225. No manuscript with the title exists; the collection has been reconstructed on the basis of later collections containing the repertory described by a 13th-century English student known as Anonymous IV, who cites **Leoninus** and **Perotinus** as the principal composers. This reconstruction contains 35 **responsories** and 12 settings of the *Benedicamus Domino* for the **divine office**, and 20 Graduals and 40 **Alleluias** for the **mass**. There are also 500 *clausulae* that may be substituted for portions of the **melismatic** organum with the same text. In most cases, the **polyphony** is intended to be sung in alternation with traditional **chant**, which completes a **respond** or supplies a verse. *See also ALTERNATIM.*

MAHARIL. *See* MOLIN, JACOB.

MANTRA. Word, syllable, or even a single letter that becomes the object of Buddhist meditation by constant repetition in a kind of **chant**. The Japanese writer Kukai recognized five types: resonant recitation, by which the meditator sings into a shell so that his voice streams out; lotus recitation, by which his voice may be heard only by himself; *vajra*, with the tongue striking against closed lips and teeth; *samadhi*, recitation totally within the spirit; and light recitation, whereby the meditator imagines light streaming from his mouth. *See also* BUDDHIST CHANT.

MARCELLO, BENEDETTO (24 June or 24 July 1686, Venice–24 July 1739, Brescia, Italy). Nobleman who composed nine **masses**, two sacred **oratorios**, and about 30 miscellaneous sacred works, his fame rose chiefly from his 50 **psalm** settings, admired through the late 19th century as models of **contrapuntal** writing and sacred music style. Sixteen of them quote Hebrew and Greek **psalmody**.

MARIAN ANTIPHON. **Votive antiphon** in praise of the Virgin Mary sung at the end of **compline**.

MARTIN, FRANK (15 September 1890, Geneva–21 November 1974, Naarden, The Netherlands). He composed an unaccompanied **mass** for eight-voiced **split choir** (1922) and a few other small sacred works before coming to public attention with *Et in Terra Pax* (1945), an **oratorio** for five soloists, eight-voiced split choir, and orchestra commissioned for the moment when World War II ended. He followed this with *Golgotha* (1948), a kind of **passion** for five soloists, choir, and orchestra. Other major works include the *Pseaumes de Genève* ("Genevan **Psalms**, 1958), an **oratorio** *Pilate* (1964), and a **Requiem** (1973) for four soloists, chorus, and orchestra.

MASON, LOWELL (8 January 1792, Medfield, Mass.–11 August 1872, Orange, N. J.). Hymnologist and influential educator whose collections, arrangements, and original compositions of **hymns** based on European models and sources competed directly with the less learned **shape-note** hymns and **gospel** tunes. He worked chiefly in Savannah, Georgia, from 1813, where he opened North America's first Sunday school for black children in 1826, in Boston from 1827 to 1851, and finally in New York. His *The Boston Handel and Haydn Society Collection of Church Music* appeared in 1822 and ran to 22 editions by 1858. Three of his best known **hymn tune**s are *Antioch* ("Joy to the World"), *Bethany* ("Nearer My God to Thee"), and *Hamburg* ("When I Survey the Wondrous Cross").

MASS. The Roman Catholic name for the celebration of the Eucharist; **Lutheran**, Anglican, Orthodox, and other traditions refer to essentially similar liturgies with some variant of "the Holy Eucharist, "**Holy Communion**," or "the **divine liturgy**." Also, a musical setting or performance of all the texts of such a Eucharistic celebration. Also, a musical setting of the **ordinary** prayers of the Roman liturgy in Greek and Latin languages: Kyrie, Gloria, Credo, Sanctus/Benedictus, Agnus Dei, and in early examples, Ite Missa Est.

The form of the mass—the particular texts and actions that compose it—has evolved more or less continuously and gradually since early Christian times, but also on occasion rapidly, as after the **Council of Trent** (1545–1563) and after the **Second Vatican Council** (1962–1965). Local traditions, such as the **Ambrosian** of Milan, may have variant forms. Historians have traditionally distinguished between two broad classes of included texts: the **propers**, which are prayers chosen to commemorate a particular feast, and the ordinaries, The prayers that occur at every mass regardless of the feast day. The table lists a typical solemn mass form.

The sources of the texts are various. The Introit, Gradual, **Alleluia**, Offertory, and Communion are believed by some to have at one time introduced the **chanting** of complete **psalms** to simple formulas. Later, the psalms were truncated to a single verse framed by an **antiphon** that referred explicitly or obliquely to the proper feast. If the liturgical action were prolonged, more psalm verses and antiphons could be added *ad libitum*. The Kyrie antedates Christianity and was often used as a response in the **litany** of saints. The Gloria is a prose **hymn** stemming from the proclamation of the angels in the Gospel

Proper	Ordinary	Function	Performance mode
Introit		Entrance procession	Schola/cantores
	Kyrie	Supplication	Schola
	Gloria	Praise	Schola
Collect		Opening prayer	Celebrant
Epistle		Scripture lesson	Celebrant or deacon
Gradual		Psalm response	Schola / cantores
Alleluia or Tract (Lent)		Invoke Gospel	Schola / cantores
Gospel		Scripture lesson	Celebrant
	Credo	Proclamation of faith	Schola
Offertory		Procession of gifts	Schola
Preface		Praise	Celebrant
	Sanctus	"Holy, holy, holy"	Schola
	Eucharistic prayer		[Priest–spoken quietly]
	Pater Noster	"Our Father"	Celebrant
	Agnus Dei	Supplication	Schola
Communion		Distribution of the Sacrament	Schola
	Ite Missa Est	Dismissal	Celebrant / Schola

of St. Luke (2:14). There is a Greek version from the fifth century; the oldest Latin text dates from the seventh. The Credo, a relatively late addition to the ordinary, was composed by Patriarch Paulinus of Aquileia (d. 802) after the proclamation of the Council of Nicea (325). The Sanctus quotes both Old and New Testaments (Isaiah 6:3; Revelation 4:8). The Agnus Dei derives from John the Baptist's salutation to Christ (John 1:29) and is also thought to have originated in a litany. Finally, the Ite Missa Est ("Go, you are sent"), from which the word "mass" comes, is a simple exhortation to the people at the point of dismissal.

In the **Gregorian** tradition of the late Middle Ages, performance of the chants depended upon the particular part of the mass in question and its function. Those executed by the celebrant, brief prayers for the occasion, and the readings from Scripture were chanted on a single pitch (*recto tono*) or on simple lectionary formulas. (The Ite Missa Est could be more ornate; its response came from the **schola**.) Everything else was sung by the schola of trained singers and could therefore be quite elaborate, though in varying degrees. The chants on the short ordinary prayers Kyrie and Agnus Dei had threefold invocations on "Kyrie eleison," "Christe eleison," and "Agnus Dei" and so encouraged repetition of the melodies. The other ordinary prayers were generally more through-composed, although melodic formulas could recur, especially when cued by a verbal repetition such as "Osanna" in the Sanctus/Benedictus pair. Most difficult of all were the Graduals, Tracts, Alleluias, Offertories, and Communions. These propers have short texts extended melodically by very elaborate **melismas** of great subtlety. In the other cases, there were processions to accompany, and the Sanctus/Benedictus could be longer than its text warranted because the celebrant could begin the Eucharistic prayer as the schola continued to chant.

The canonical texts were often **troped** with additional words and sometimes music, particularly the repetitive Kyrie and Agnus Dei and the highly melismatic Alleluia. In the late Middle Ages, an additional piece called a **sequence** was often inserted. By the 15th century, so many compositions, texts, and local saints' propers had accrued to the mass, often displacing the traditional prayers and Scripture readings, that the Council of Trent (1545–1563) issued two decrees that reformed the liturgy, chiefly by pruning the accretions of recent centuries. The reformed missal appeared in 1570, and printing made possible a dissemination throughout the Catholic world that ensured a unity of liturgical practice previously unknown. Only places where distinctive traditions could be traced back 200 years were permitted to continue them.

The next dramatic reform was authorized by the **Second Vatican Council** (1962–1965). The **Constitution on the Sacred Liturgy** promotes the continued preeminence of Gregorian chant, classical **polyphony**, and the Latin language, but also allows the vernacular and other appropriate music and emphasizes **congregational** singing. Nevertheless, the revised *Ordo cantus missae* and *Graduale romanum* (1974) provide the traditional chants, along with new rubrics for the celebrant to chant the prayer over the gifts and the entire Eucharistic prayer. These publications have not seen widespread use, perhaps because the chants traditionally assigned to the schola were too difficult for congregations, and because of the quick adoption of vernacular languages after 1965.

The mass dominates the early history of music because it was the object of so much early polyphony, the distinguishing feature of the western tradition. Polyphonic mass propers and ordinaries come from the earliest sources (*Musica enchiriadis*, c. 900; the **Winchester Troper**, 11th century; St. Martial and Codex Calixtinus, 12th century; *Magnus Liber Organi*, c. 1170) and are featured in every stage of the development of polyphonic technique. Often the texts are troped and the chants melismatic, suggesting that polyphony was reserved for high feasts. In 14th-century France, manuscripts began to collect polyphonic settings of the ordinary prayers all together to be sung as a unified liturgy. From this point, polyphonic composition of propers declines abruptly, presumably because such works may be heard only on certain feasts of the year whereas ordinaries may be sung at every mass. The first so-called "mass cycle" to be composed by a single composer as a liturgical (not musical) unity was *La Messe de Nostre Dame* of **Guillaume de Machaut**, about 1350.

Composers in the next two centuries discovered various musical means of uniting the separate movements of a mass cycle. The earliest was the **cantus firmus** mass, in which a repeating tenor melody sung to relatively long note durations recurred in all the movements. The melody was usually taken from a traditional chant proper that might relate to a particular performance occasion. The earliest surviving cantus firmus masses, dating from the early 15th century are the *Missa Rex Secolorum* attributed to **John Dunstable** and the *Missa Alma Redemptoris Mater* attributed to Lionel Power. Two masses by **Guillaume Du Fay** of about 1450, *Missa Se La Face Ay Pale* and *Missa L'Homme Armé*, take as cantus firmus popular tunes rather than traditional propers and in the following generations such secular borrowings become common. Du Fay and his contemporaries tightened the unity of their masses by quoting a "head motive" at the beginning of each movement.

The idea of linking a new composition with a traditional melody through the *cantus firmus* was logically extended by the thoroughgoing **imitative** technique of **Josquin Desprez** and the generation around the turn of the 16th century. With all four voices imitating one another, the borrowed chant is heard throughout the choir and in every movement. Josquin's *Missa Pange Lingua* (c. 1515?) is a sublime textbook example of this "**paraphrase mass.**"

Borrowing a melody from an imitative **motet** for a mass using the same technique meant borrowing essentially the whole texture. Thus

Josquin's *Missa Mater Patris* is based on a three-voice motet of **Antoine Brumel**, *Mater Patris*. The "**parody mass**" was the logical conclusion of the premise of taking preexisting material as a means to unify the mass cycle. As composers more frequently took as their models erotic madrigals and secular tunes, the Council of Trent banned "seductive and impure" melodies in polyphonic masses, and insisted on the clarity of words in imitative texture. **Giovanni da Palestrina**'s *Missa Papae Marcelli* is a legendary albeit chronologically dubious response to this reform, and an example of a mass without any borrowing, not at all uncommon in the 16th century; often such masses are called *Missa Sine Nomine*.

The invention of **opera** at the turn of the 17th century forced a bifurcation in sacred music composition. Palestrina's disciples around **Rome** canonized his style and made it a kind of classical language, the *stile antico*, which embodied an intrinsic sacred semantic distinguished from the new secular music. At the same time, in other localities new mass compositions began to absorb, slowly, the dramatic ideals and textures of opera: solo singers, contrasting textures, **instruments**. All of these can be heard in the *cori spezzati* repertory associated with **Venice**. The remainder of the century witnessed a bewildering variety and mixture of styles in mass composition, from the strictest *stile antico* to the most operatic **cantata** mass in the "Neapolitan" style. This type segmented the mass texts, especially the longer ordinaries of the Gloria and Credo, into separate movements for chorus or soloists. The greatest exemplar is the **Mass in B minor** (1733–1749) of **Johann Sebastian Bach**.

The huge dimensions of Bach's masterpiece ignore the practicalities of liturgy, and the works of his successors, while mostly composed for actual liturgical occasions, are rarely heard in liturgies today. Instead, they are favorites of choral societies singing in concert halls, accompanied by full orchestras. Some of the more famous of these "symphonic masses" are:

> **Mozart**, "Coronation Mass," K.317 (1780)
> Mass in C minor, K. 427 (1783, incomplete)
> **Haydn**, *Missa in Tempore Belli*, (1796)
> *Heiligmesse*, (1797)
> *Nelson* Mass, (1798)

Theresienmesse, (1799)
Schöpfungsmesse, (1800)
Harmoniemesse, (1801)
Beethoven, Mass in C (1807)
Missa Solemnis in D (1823)
Schubert, Masses in G (1815) and A-flat (1823)
Rossini, *Petite Messe Solennelle* (1864)
Bruckner, Masses in D minor (1864) and F minor (1868)
Janacek, **Glagolitic Mass** (1927)
Duruflé, *Messe "Cum Jubilo"* (1966)

The tradition of composing masses branched radically in the 20th century. Some composers have written with deliberate anachronism in order to evoke the *stile antico* with its ascetic sacred semantic: **Ralph Vaughan Williams'** Mass in G minor (1921), **Edmund Rubbra**'s *Missa Cantuariensis* (1945) and *Missa in Honorem Sancti dominici* (1949), and **Benjamin Britten**'s *Missa Brevis* for boys' voices and organ (1959) are examples. So, to a lesser extent, is **Igor Stravinsky**'s Mass for chorus, soloists, and 10 winds (1948). Others experimented with artificial musical languages in vogue: **Anton Heiller**'s *Missa Super Modos Duodecimales* (1960) is a serial work.

Still others tried to incorporate popular idioms, with the intent of either inviting the congregation to be part of the performance, such as **Jean Langlais**'s *Messe Solennelle 'Salve Regina"* (1947) for chorus, brass, **organ**, and congregation, or of simply making the music more appealing to all classes of churchgoers, such as Ariel Ramirez's *Misa Criolla*, based on Argentine folk idioms. The Second Vatican Council's allowance for local idioms in exceptional circumstances has been widely interpreted as a mandate to make liturgical music as simple as possible so that amateurs can compose and perform it. When parishes adopt such a policy, the result is often indistinguishable from the commercial musical language of television and radio.

MASS IN B MINOR. Composed by **Johann Sebastian Bach**, the Mass in B minor (BWV 232) is one of the largest and most outstanding concerted settings of the Roman Catholic **mass ordinary** in the entire Western tradition. Scored for five-voice chorus, vocal soloists, strings, flutes, oboes, bassoons, trumpets, timpani, and **continuo**, the work consists of 27 movements and requires about two hours to perform.

Bach did not compose the mass all at once. He wrote the Sanctus in 1724 for the Christmas liturgy at St. Thomas **Lutheran** church in **Leipzig**, where he was **cantor**. The Kyrie (three movements) and Gloria (nine movements) were sent in 1733 to petition Friedrich August II, Elector of Saxony, for an honorary court title. (A mass consisting only of the first two Latin ordinary prayers was common Lutheran practice.) In the late 1740s, Bach completed the mass by adding the movements of the Credo, Osanna, and Agnus Dei, mostly **parodies** of previously composed movements dating as far back as 1712. Since no performance of the entire mass in Bach's lifetime is known, some critics believe it to be a "speculative" composition, a retrospective summary of what he judged to be his life's best work.

The Mass in B minor exhibits a great range of compositional form and color, from the intimate Benedictus **aria** for solo flute, tenor, and **continuo** to tremendous festal choruses requiring every instrument. Much of Bach's revising seems to have been directed at integrating the individual movements into large-scale compositions, particularly in the case of the Gloria and Credo. He removed or truncated many of the articulating ritornellos so that one movement demands the next, and in fact Bach indicates many links explicitly in the score. The work is both an encyclopedia and tour-de-force of compositional technique: *cantus firmus*, strict **canon**, **ostinato** bass, *stile antico*, and chromatic fantasy merely head the list of devices displayed. Virtuoso solos for every instrument lend great timbral variety and the difficulty of all the vocal parts make the Mass in B minor one of the most challenging of choral projects.

Despite the interest of his son Carl Philipp Emanuel Bach (1714–1788), **Franz Joseph Haydn**, and **Ludwig van Beethoven**, the first complete performance did not occur until 1859 in Leipzig, owing perhaps to the lack of a suitable performing edition. The most recent critical edition, edited by Christoph Wolff, was issued by C. F. Peters in 1994. The Mass has been a touchstone of authentic historical performance practice and its attendant controversies over the last half-century.

MASS IN TIME OF WAR. *See* HAYDN, FRANZ JOSEPH.

MASS PAIRS. Two **polyphonic mass ordinaries**, usually the Gloria-Credo or the Sanctus-Agnus Dei, that seem to be intended, from their clefs, **mensuration** signs, **finalis**, number of voices, and common motives, for a single liturgy. Precursors of the **cantus firmus mass** cycle, they date from the early 15th century. *See also MESSE DE NOSTRE DAME.*

MATHIAS, WILLIAM (1 November 1934, Whitland, Carmarthenshire, Wales–29 July 1992, Menai Bridge, Anglesey). In the latter half of his career, he composed a significant number of sacred works for chorus: **psalm** settings, **cantatas**, **canticles**, and **anthems**, sometimes employing non-canonical texts, such as his large *Lux Aeterna* (1982), a kind of **Requiem troped** with writings from St. John of the Cross.

MATINS. The major hour of the **divine office** of the Roman Catholic rite sung after midnight. It is the longest and most elaborate of all the hours. The **chanting** begins with the **versicle** *Deus in adjutorium*, followed by the invitatory (**psalm** verse), followed by Psalm 95 with its **proper antiphon**, and then a **hymn**.

Next follow three nocturnes of responses and readings. Each nocturne consists of three psalms with proper antiphons, then three lessons—one Biblical, one patristic, one homiletic—each followed by a great **responsory**. The third nocturne is followed by the **canticle** *Te Deum* laudamus, another versicle, prayer, and the concluding versicle *Benedicamus Domino*.

On ferial days, the matins service is reduced to one nocturne. *See also* GREGORIAN CHANT; *ORTHRŌS*; VESPERS.

MAUNDER, JOHN HENRY (21 February 1858, London–25 January 1920, Brighton). Composer whose **anthems**, combining imagination with technical restraint, remained popular in parish churches well into the 20th century. He also wrote two popular **oratorios**, *The Martyrs* (1894) and *From Olivet to Calvary* (1904).

MAWLĪD **(Arab. "birthday;" Turkish:** *MEVLIT***).** Refers to the celebration of the Prophet's birthday, common since the ninth century, or of local saints' days, and to Islamic songs and epics composed for attendant festivals. Techniques can range from simple **chanted** recitation in rural areas to sophisticated associations of **mode** (*maqā-māt*) with particular texts. In 1409, Sūleyman Celibi composed the "Way to Salvation," which spread through the Ottoman Empire and is now known as "the *Mevlit*." In Alexandria, "The Prophet's Cloak" is recited weekly at the tomb of Sharaf al-Din al-Būsīrī (d. 1298). In Iraq, believers sing an Arabic text by Ja'far al-Barzanjī (d.1765).

The celebrations themselves may be very large with many musical performances simultaneously. The *mawlīd* in Cairo, commemorating the Prophet's grandson Hossein, lasts several weeks. *See also SAMA; TA'ZIYE.*

MECCA. *See* SONGS OF THE *HAJJ*.

MEDICEAN CHANT. Refers to the Roman **Gradual** and **Antiphonal** published by the Medicean press in **Rome** in 1614 under the direction of Felice Anerio (c. 1560–1614) and Franceso Soriano (c. 1548–1621) that revised texts and melodies of older **chant** books in the wake of the **Council of Trent**. Pope Gregory XIII charged the composer-editors on 25 October 1577 with "revising, purging, correcting, and reforming" the existing chant books, but it is possible that the new edition merely codified contemporary practices. It became the principal source for the Ratisbon (Regensburg) edition of **chant** (1870) promoted by the **Cecilian** reformers in Germany. This was replaced as the standard modern edition of **Gregorian chant** by the *Editio Vaticana*, the work of the Benedictines at **Solesmes**, at the end of the century.

MELISMA (adj.: melismatic). In singing, especially **chant**, the prolongation of a single syllable over many notes in a melody. *See also* ALLELUIA; GREGORIAN CHANT.

MENDELSSOHN, ARNOLD (26 December 1855, Racibórz, Poland–19 February 1933, Darmstadt). Organist who promoted the revival of **Lutheran** sacred music, particularly that of **Heinrich Schütz** and **Johann Sebastian Bach**, and composed a **German**

mass for eight voices, 14 German **motets** for the liturgical year, and some **cantatas**.

MENDELSSOHN, FELIX (3 February 1809, Hamburg–4 November 1847, Leipzig). Renowned conductor and composer of symphonic, piano, and chamber works, Mendelssohn also composed nearly 30 sacred **motets**, **psalms**, and **canticles**, in German and in Latin, with orchestral accompaniment, and another three dozen shorter works more modestly scored. This collection remains neglected. Better known are works for **organ**: six sonatas, three **preludes** and **fugues**, and two dozen smaller works. He also completed two **oratorios**, *St. Paul* (*Paulus*, 1834–1836) and *Elijah* (*Elias*, 1846), which remain in the choral concert repertory.

Mendelssohn was one of the very first to champion the music of the past, affecting the appreciation of sacred music in Europe more materially than through his own music. He almost singlehandedly inaugurated the revival of interest in the music of **Johann Sebastian Bach** when he organized and conducted what was thought to be an impossible work, the **St. Matthew Passion**, by the Berlin *Singakademie* on 11 March 1829, and he similarly ignited the German fascination with **George Frideric Handel** with a performance in Düsseldorf of *Israel in Egypt* on 26 May 1833, followed up in later years by other Handel oratorios, all in Mendelssohn's own arrangements.

MENSURAL NOTATION. Refers to Western notation developed in the late 13th century that represented the duration ("measure") of a pitch by the shape of the neume (note).

MERULO, CLAUDIO (8 April 1533, Correggio, Italy–4 May 1604, Parma). Appointed **organist** at Brescia Cathedral on 21 October 1556, he then defeated **Andrea Gabrieli** to become second organist at St. Mark's in **Venice**. He served the court of Parma, probably in 1584 and became organist at the cathedral in 1591, holding both posts until his death. Honored with knighthood and renowned as the greatest organist of his age, he left two **organ masses**, eight sets of **versets**, one set of organ **ricercars**, two of **toccatas**, three of **canzonas**, as well as a significant body of vocal music: four books of **motets** and two of **masses**.

MESSE DE NOSTRE DAME. Composed by **Guillaume de Machaut**, this is the first surviving **polyphonic mass** cycle, that is, a polyphonic setting of the mass **ordinaries** apparently conceived as a unified musical structure and intended to be sung as one liturgy. It was composed almost certainly between 1350 and 1372, likely in the early 1360s. The traditionally cited occasion—the coronation of Charles V at the Cathedral at Reims on 19 May 1364—has no documentary support but cannot be ruled out. The traditional **chants** used by Machaut as tenor melodies all have connections to the Virgin Mary, and it is possible that Machaut wrote the work to be sung at Saturday masses in her honor at the Reims Cathedral, a local tradition.

The shorter ordinary texts—Kyrie, Sanctus, Agnus Dei, and Ite Missa Est—Machaut sets in the texture of **isorhythmic motets**, with isorhythmic elements sometimes extending to all voices. The longer texts—Gloria and Credo—are set in **homorhythmic** texture and divided into clear sections articulated by cadence patterns according to the structure of the texts. The "Amen" sections of these prayers are isorhythmic.

Machaut composed the mass for four voices, and a performance requires about a half hour, depending on which liturgical elements are included. How many singers should sing each part and whether **instruments** should double them are disputed matters. *See also* LADY MASS.

MESSIAEN, OLIVIER (10 December 1908, Avignon, France–27 April 1992, Clichy, Hauts-de-Seine). Composer, teacher, and **organist** of world renown, Messiaen wrote little explicitly liturgical music—an unpublished **mass** dates from 1933 and an **organ mass** from 1951—but a high proportion of his music owes its inspiration to Christian theology and aims to project its mystical aspects, e.g., *Le Banquet Céleste* ("The Celestial Banquet," organ, 1928); *L'Ascension: Majesté du Christ Demandant Sa Gloire à Son Père* ("The Ascension: the majesty of Christ demanding His Glory from His Father," for orchestra, 1933); *Et Expecto Resurrectionem Mortuorum* ("And I await the resurrection of the dead," for woodwinds, brass, and percussion, 1964); *Trois Petites Liturgies de la Présence Divine* ("Three small liturgies of the Divine Presence," 1945, text by

Messiaen); and *Vingt Regards sur l'Enfant Jesus*, ("Twenty Contemplations on the Infant Jesus," for piano, 1945). His idiosyncratic rhythms are influenced by those of **Igor Stravinsky**, Claude Debussy (1862–1918), ancient Greek **meters**, and an extensive study of Hindu *tālas*.

MESSIAH. An **oratorio** of **George Frideric Handel**, composed from 22 August to 12 September (orchestrated by 14 September) 1741, first performed for a charity concert in Dublin on 13 April 1742, *Messiah* is likely the most famous large piece of music set to English text. Its original version is scored for strings, **continuo**, trumpets, timpani, four vocal soloists (SATB), and four-voice choir (in "Lift Up Ye Heads," five). Handel added oboes, bassoons, and possibly horns as doublings for the **London** performances (1743), and altered some of the **arias**, including the vocal solo assignments. The work requires about two and one-half hours to perform.

Messiah is a singular work even within Handel's English oratorios, themselves singular in their midway position between the sacred and secular worlds of art music. The London advertisements termed the work "A New Sacred Oratorio" to ward off charges of profaning a sacred subject in the theater. But while almost all his other English oratorios are close to **opera** in aesthetic, having directed plots motivated by named characters singing arias and **recitatives**, *Messiah* is contemplative and abstract. The vocal soloists are anonymous voices, and while there is no doubt that Christ is the subject, the events and ultimate significance of his life, but for a snippet from St. Luke's Gospel, are alluded to without explicit description. Prophecies from the Old Testament dominate the libretto.

The libretto was compiled from the King James Bible, with minimal changes, by Handel's collaborator Charles Jennens (1700–1773) and is in three parts. The first features the traditional messianic prophecies of Isaiah (7, 9, 40, and 60), Malachi and Zechariah, and the shepherd scene from the birth narrative of St. Luke's Gospel. The second part describes the passion and resurrection obliquely through the "suffering servant" passages of Isaiah (53) and excerpts from the **Psalms** and Romans. (The tradition of the audience standing for the concluding "**Hallelujah**" chorus because King George II once did is founded on a dubious anecdote in a letter written 37 years after the first London performance.) The final part covers the general resurrection through 1 Corinthians and Revelation. There are also contributions from Job, Lamentations, and the Gospel of St. John scattered throughout.

Messiah was revived for London in 1745 and again in 1749, beginning a series of performances for the Foundling Hospital that occurred annually until Handel's death in 1759 and thereafter until 1777. The full score was published in 1767 (London), allowing more frequent local performances throughout the country. The 'Commemoration of Handel' at Westminster Abbey in 1784 may have had as many as 500 performers, anticipating a practice, maintained by the growth of amateur choral societies in the 19th century, of using forces far larger than Handel would ever have imagined. Such performances naturally required massive reinforcements of **instruments** and entire reorchestrations. **Wolfgang Amadeus Mozart** performed his own such arrangement in 1789. With growing appreciation of Baroque performance practices in the 20th century, recent professional performances and recordings have returned to a scale that Handel might have recognized. Thus, the performance history of *Messiah* mirrors changing historiographical and aesthetic attitudes about Western classics.

Indeed, *Messiah* governed Handel's very reputation as a composer for more than a century after his death, since, along with *Judas Maccabeus* and *Israel in Egypt*, it was virtually the only work of his in the repertory and was performed constantly. The brilliant choruses with sacred text and the famously brief period of composition understandably built an image of Handelian spiritual inspiration foreign to his character. Since the mid-20th century, the image has been filled out. He always worked rapidly; after completing *Messiah* and taking a week off, he completed *Samson* by 29 October. Growing familiarity with other, classically oriented oratorios, the 40 operas, and a wealth of instrumental music has somewhat restored to *Messiah* its peculiar hybrid quality of sacred art as entertainment.

METER. The consistent pattern of accented and unaccented beats, which themselves must occur at consistent time intervals. The strength of metric perception depends upon how regular in time are the phenomenal accents and the qualitative difference between accented and unaccented beats. **Chant**, lacking regular beats and patterns of accent, is nearly always non-metric, one of its defining qualities.

In **hymnody**, meter refers to the count of syllables in each line in conjunction with a prosodic description, usually iambic or trochaic. The most common for four-line stanzas, all iambic, are the Short Meter (6.6.8.6.), the Common Meter (8.6.8.6.) and the Long Meter (8.8.8.8.). A modern hymnal will have a metrical index to facilitate the matching of **hymn** texts with alternative melodies. *See also CONTRAFACTUM*; METRICAL PSALMS.

METHODIUS (ST.). *See* CYRIL (ST).

METRICAL PSALMS. A rhymed vernacular translation of a **psalm** sung to music with a regular pattern of beats (**meter**). Because the poetry of the Hebrew psalms has neither rhyme nor meter, but rather depends on semantic parallelisms between verse pairs, singing complete psalms before the 16th century had traditionally been the province of trained singers, **cantors** or choirs. When Protestantism insisted on a singing **congregation** and, in its Reformed and Puritan churches, on the psalms as the only appropriate texts to be sung, the metrical psalms provided, at first, simple tunes and strong memory cues in its meter and a familiar language so that the musically untutored might sing them.

Versified psalms at first appeared without explicit musical settings. Two of the earliest influential sets are by Clément Marot in France (1532) and Thomas Sternhold in his *Certayne Psalmes Drawen into Englishe Metre* (c. 1549). But Sternhold's psalms were likely meant to be sung to popular tunes, and Marot's were similarly set in the three editions of the **Genevan Psalter**. Both became mainstays of Reformed traditions. Robert Crowley also published a *Psalter* in 1549 whose **homorhythmic** harmonizations suggest the English liturgical practice of **faburden**. **Polyphonic** versions of the Genevan melodies and Sternhold's psalms (harmonized by John Day, 1563) soon followed. Eventually the line between metrical **psalmody** and **hymn** blurred as the translation of psalms became a rhymed, metrical paraphrase, as in **Isaac Watts'** *The Psalms of David* (1719). *See also BAY PSALM BOOK*; CALVIN, JEAN; LINING OUT.

MEXICO CITY. After Hernan Cortes conquered the city in 1521, the Indian people assimilated very rapidly the idioms of the sacred music brought by the Franciscans, Dominicans, and Augustinians to their new churches. Ten years later a **polyphonic** choir of Indian singers won the praise of Bishop Juan de Zumárraga and by 1539 the cathedral boasted a *maestro de capilla*, Juan Xuárez, and an **organist**, Antonio Ramos. In 1556, an Augustinian *Ordinarium* of **chant** appeared—the first music book printed in the new world.

Polyphony continued to flourish in the city throughout the 16th and 17th centuries, supported by paid choirs and an ever growing choral library that included European works as well as new ones composed by the *maestros*. The cathedral had an **instrumental** ensemble of brass and woodwinds by the end of the 16th century, to which later were added harps and strings. *See also* FRANCO CODEX; PADILLA, JUAN GUTIÉRREZ DE; LOPEZ CAPILLAS FRANCISCO.

MIGOT, GEORGES (27 February 1891, Paris–5 January 1976, Levallois near Paris). Intellectual, poet, and painter, he composed six **oratorios** on the life of Christ (1936–1955), *La* **Passion** (1942), an unaccompanied **Requiem** (1953), and about 65 other choral works.

MILHAUD, DARIUS (4 September 1892, Aix-en-Provence, France–22 June 1974, Geneva). A prolific composer of secular works, Milhaud nevertheless wrote some works exhibiting his Jewish heritage, in particular: *Poèmes Juifs* (1916), *Liturgie Comtadine* (1933), and *Service Sacré* (1947).

MINOR HOURS. Prime (6 a.m.), Terce (9 a.m.), Sext (noon), and None (3 p.m.) of the **divine office** follow the same format: opening **versicle** *Deus in adjutorium*, **hymn**, three **psalms**, each framed by the same **antiphon**, a Biblical chapter followed by a short **responsory**, and the concluding versicle *Benedicamus Domino*. Only the responsory is **proper**. *See also* COMPLINE; GREGORIAN CHANT; LAUDS; MATINS; VESPERS.

MISA CRIOLLA **(Sp. "Native mass").** Setting of the **ordinary** prayers of the Roman Catholic mass in Latin composed by Ariel Ramirez

(1921–), completed in 1964. While faithful to the traditional liturgical forms of the *stile antico*, Ramirez incorporates a variety of Latin American folk idioms: *vidala* and *bauala* rhythms in the Kyrie; a *carnavalito* dance in the Gloria; an insistent *chacerera trunca* rhythm in the Credo; the Bolivian *carnaval cochabambino* in the Sanctus; and the *estile pampeano* in the Agnus Dei.

The original scoring requires a four-voiced mixed choir, a tenor soloist, piano or harpsichord, *bombo* (type of percussion), guitar, double bass, *charango* (Andean snare), *quena* (Inca flute), and *siku* (Andean pipe). The work requires 20 minutes to perform. *See also* FOLK MASS; SECOND VATICAN COUNCIL.

MISERERE. A setting of **Psalm** 51 by Gregorio Allegri (1582–1652), it was for centuries the most celebrated piece in the repertory of the papal choir in **Rome**. Allegri composed it in 1638, and thereafter its transmission was forbidden, but **Wolfgang Amadeus Mozart** supposedly wrote it out in 1770 after two hearings, and the historian Charles Burney (1726–1814) was given a copy in Milan the same year. Modern editions derive from 19th-century sources.

Burney opined that it is the performance of the work in the near total darkness of **Tenebrae** services rather than the music itself that impressed, and indeed the work is merely an *alternatim* setting in *falsobordone*, whereby a verse **chanted** in loud monotone is answered by another verse sung by one choir in four voices or another choir in five. The final verse is sung by the combined choirs in nine voices. The simplicity is enlivened by largely oral traditions of embellishment.

The work requires nearly 15 minutes to perform. *See also A CAPPELLA; CORI SPEZZATI.*

MISERERE MEI, DEUS. Monumental five-voiced **motet** of **Josquin Desprez** probably composed for Holy Week services of 1504 at the chapel of Duke Ercole d'Este of Ferrara. The text is **Psalm** 51 (Vulgate 50), subdivided into three *partes* of the motet. Josquin sets the words *Miserere mei, Deus* ("Have mercy on me, O God") to a monotonic *cantus firmus* that he invented after the manner of a **psalm tone**. This cantus firmus recurs periodically through the singing of the psalm, like an **antiphon**, except that the pitch of its monotone changes, falling through the eight tones of the Phrygian (E) **mode** in the first *pars*, rising back up the octave in the second, and falling down a perfect fifth to A, the tonal center of the work, in the climactic last section. The piece is thus a unique and ingenious application of cantus firmus and **imitative** technique. It lasts about 15 minutes. *See also* TENEBRAE.

***MISSA* (Lat. "mass").** Identifies a composition as a **polyphonic** mass. What follows specifies it, usually by naming the **mode** or pre-existing music on which the mass is based, e.g., *Missa L'Homme Armé* ("Mass on the song *L'Homme Armé*").

***MISSA BREVIS* (Lat. "Short mass").** A **polyphonic** setting of mass **ordinaries** of short duration. This might be achieved by setting the texts syllabically, or by having different parts of longer prayers sung simultaneously by different voices in the choir.

In 17th- and 18th-century **Lutheran** contexts, *missa brevis* indicates a setting of the Kyrie (in Greek) and Gloria (in Latin). Five such settings, including the first version of the **Mass in B Minor**, were composed by **Johann Sebastian Bach**.

***MISSA L'HOMME ARMÉ*.** Title of over 40 **polyphonic masses** using a popular song "The Armed Man" as a *cantus firmus*. The earliest is a matter of dispute: candidates composed by **Guillaume Du Fay**, **Johannes Ockeghem**, and **Antoine Busnoys** all date from the mid-15th-century. Composers of *Missa L'Homme Armé* make up an honors list of the Renaissance: **Jacob Obrecht**, **Josquin Desprez** (two), **Antoine Brumel**, Loyset Compère (c. 1450–1518), **Pierre De La Rue** (two), **Crostóbal De Morales** (two), **Francisco Guerrero**, and **Giovanni da Palestrina** (two) among many others.

No two *L'Homme Armé* masses use precisely the same tune, which suggests that the tune comes from oral tradition. There is no general explanation of its widespread use in polyphony. *See also* CANTUS FIRMUS MASS; COUNCIL OF TRENT.

***MISSA PANGE LINGUA*.** A late and possibly the last **mass** (after 1514 ?) of **Josquin Desprez**, it is a superb example of the **paraphrase mass** whereby the borrowed **hymn** melody *Pange lingua* *gloriosi* appears throughout the mass **ordinaries** in all four voices at different times in the new technique of **structural imitation**. Fifteen early 16th-century sources attest to its fame. A recent critical edition has been edited by Thomas Warburton for the University of North Carolina Press, 1977. The piece requires about one half hour to sing.

MISSA PAPAE MARCELLI (Lat. "Mass of Pope Marcellus"). The most famous of **Giovanni da Palestrina**'s 104 masses, published in 1567. Its link with the three-week pontificate of Pope Marcellus II (died 1 May 1555) is obscure, as is its date of composition. Pope Marcellus did summon his singers on Good Friday, 1555, and encouraged them to make the words of the liturgy clearly understood. That is also one of the most specific wishes of the **Council of Trent**, but there is no hard evidence to support the legend that a hearing of the *Missa Papae Marcelli* convinced the council delegates to forbear abolishing **polyphony** from Catholic liturgy, although it may have been heard on 28 April 1565 by a post-concillar commission deliberating on liturgical music. The mass is remarkable for its textural clarity and diction. At times, voices enter in mid-sentence so that their syllables coincide with previously entered voices.

Most of the mass calls for six voices; a few sections require five or four, and the concluding Agnus Dei requires seven. It lasts about 30 minutes.

MISSA PROLATIONUM. Four-voiced **mass** of **Johannes Ockeghem** constructed as a series of **canons** progressing from the unison to the octave in which the four voices sing the same melody at different speeds. *Prolationum* (Lat. "prolation") refers to the ratio of durations between two kinds of written note, the semibreve and the minim. The mass requires a bit over half an hour to sing.

MISSA SOLEMNIS (Lat. "Solemn mass," also known as "high mass"). Roman Catholic liturgical books specify that the solemn mass is to be considered the norm. No prayers are omitted, and almost all are sung, as well as the readings. In sacred music of the last three centuries, *missa solemnis* may indicate an especially lengthy or elaborate setting of the five **ordinary** prayers.

MISSA SOLEMNIS, **LUDWIG VAN BEETHOVEN.** Scored for soprano, alto, tenor, and bass soloists, large four-voiced choir, and a symphony orchestra augmented by contrabassoon and **organ,** Beethoven's is one of the largest-scale settings of the **mass ordinary.** Each of the five prayers is a continuous movement, albeit with changes of texture and tempo. The solo parts and the choral parts are very demanding, particularly in range, and there is an extended violin solo in the Benedictus. The work requires about 75 minutes to perform.

Beethoven began work on the *Missa Solemnis* in April or May 1819, intending it for the grand installation as Archbishop of Olmütz of his longtime patron Archduke Rudolph of Austria at the Cologne Cathedral. But he did not finish the first version until the end of 1822, long after the installation, and added trombone parts and revised the Kyrie, Credo, and Agnus Dei significantly in 1823. The mass was first performed as a concert piece, in the *Kärntnerthor Theater* in **Vienna** on 7 May 1823, and included only the Kyrie, Credo, and Agnus Dei. The first liturgical performance celebrated the 400th anniversary of the University of Freiburg in Breisgau on 4 August 1857. Today it is rarely heard outside the concert hall.

Without attempting a revival of the *stile antico*, Beethoven did make earnest efforts to imbue the *Missa Solemnis* with some sense of the sacred. One hears these most easily in the enormous **fugal** sections that conclude both Gloria and Credo, the frequently **homorhythmic** declamations, and in the *a cappella* announcement of "Et resurrexit." At the same time he sacrifices none of the complex harmonic relations that fill all his late major works.

A recent critical edition has been edited by Norbert Gertsch for G. Henle Verlag (2000).

MISSINAI **MELODIES.** Set of Ashkenazic **chants** originating in the Rhineland from the 12th to 14th centuries, a time of persecution of Jews there. The name "from Sinai" indicates the great veneration accorded these melodies. They are sung on the most solemn feasts of Rosh Hashanah, Yom Kippur, and the Three Festivals on the following *keva* texts: *Tefillah,* **Shema, Barekhu,** *Alenu, Kedushah,* and **Kaddish.** They also set certain common prayers otherwise not sung, including *Kol Nidre.* The great majority have little or no **meter;** those that have meter are settings of strophic texts from the mid-16th century or later.

MODE. From the Latin *modus* ("manner"), mode may denote, depending on the context: the classification of a **chant** according to its pitch range (*ambitus*) and final pitch (**finalis**); a scale for composition and improvisation, distinguished from other modes not by pitch collection (as different keys are) but by its tonic and the pattern of intervals made by the scale degrees; the distinction between Western major and minor scales, e.g., "the minor mode." Or a model for melodic improvisation (**Byzantine *oktoēchos***, Indian *rāga*, Chinese *tyao*, Arabic *maqam*, Persian *dastgah*, Japanese *choshi*).

The traditional classification of **Gregorian chants** into one of eight "church modes" is an adaptation by Carolingian musicians of the **Byzantine** system of eight *oktoēchos* transmitted to the west during the eighth century. Thus the use of Greek ordinals (*proteus*, etc.) to classify the modes by finalis and Greek names for individual modes deriving from melodic *ambitus*. The Arabic numerals in figure 3 are found in modern chant books.

The finalis of a chant determines whether its mode is *proteus*, *deuterius*, *tritus*, or *tetrardus*. Whether it is authentic or plagal depends upon the *ambitus* of the whole melody. Since the oldest Gregorian chants have an *ambitus* of one octave or less, they usually fit quite easily into an authentic mode if the finalis is among the lowest pitches, or into a plagal mode if the finalis is in the middle range.

Medieval theorists tried to classify and explain a chant repertory that already existed, and while the fit is remarkably good, inevitably there are chants that find no easy modal classification. Chants of the later Middle Ages often move through an ambitus of a twelfth or more, making the authentic/plagal classification tenuous. The common use in some modes (especially *proteus* and *tritus*) of the "soft B" or B-flat makes the pitch collection an increasingly important attribute of the mode. Much medieval modal theory concerns itself with reconciling such problems.

Heinrich Glarean added four additional modes to the traditional eight in his *Dodechachordon* (1547) to account for **polyphony** composed on tonal centers C and A. Gioseffo Zarlino (1517–1590) offered a different synthesis based on the **Guidonian** hexachords in his

The Eight Church Modes

Figure 3. Breves indicate the finalis. Whole notes indicate the dominant, which was taken as the tenor, or reciting pitch in the psalm tones.

Le Istitutioni Harmoniche (1558). Preference for the Glarean versus the Zarlino numeration varied by locality.

The most practical application of modal theory to Latin chant is in **psalmody**. Every **psalm** sung in the **divine office** is introduced and followed by a **proper antiphon**, and the mode of this antiphon determines that of the psalm. By specifying the reciting tone, range, and melodic cadence and finalis, this use of the mode concept approximates the "manner of singing" or melodic modeling that predominates in the modal concepts of other cultures.

The *Steiger* in the music of Eastern European Jewry, for example, are not scales but melodic formulas for chanting associated with its function as a beginning, middle, or ending, and also with the mood of the moment. In figure 4, the names are taken from the prayers with which the *Steiger* are most commonly identified. In *Die Tonarten des traditionellen Synagogen-Gesanges* (**Vienna**, 1886), Joseph Singer (1841–1911) systematized these traditional prayer modes.

Other systems of the Middle East and South Asia emphasize such melodic models of improvisation with more and less important pitches; the Persian *dastghah* or Arabic *maqam* are examples. North Indian (Hindustani) *rägas* tend to reflect the melodic shapes that arise from improvisations, as well as principal pitches and kinds of ornamentation, while South Indian (Karnatak) *rägas* are more like scales in concept. All of these systems have important semantic associations with moods, times of day, seasons, therapies, and cosmologies in varying degree. *See also LAHAN;* MUSICA FICTA.

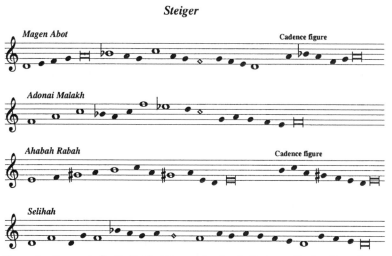

Steiger

Figure 4. Breves indicate finals. Diamond notes indicate co-*finals,* alternate cadence points for interior sections or phrases. Whole notes indicate principal melodic tones; black noteheads indicate ornamental melodic tones.

MOLIN (MÖLLN, MOELLIN), JACOB (c. 1365, Mainz–1427, Mainz?). Also known as "Maharil," rabbinic authority who standardized the practices of **chanting** in Ashkenazic liturgy, including the *Missinai* melodies. His usages were compiled about 1450 and printed as *Minhagim Sefer Maharil* in 1556.

MONK, WILLIAM HENRY (16 March 1823, London–18 March 1889, London). Hymnist, **organist**, choirmaster, and **Tractarian** who promoted high musical standards for Anglican parishes, he edited *Hymns Ancient and Modern*.

MONOPHONY (adj. MONOPHONIC). A musical texture of a single voice, one pitch at a time. By definition, all such music is unharmonized. Men and women or boys singing in octaves is usually considered monophonic. *See also* CHANT; COUNTERPOINT; HOMOPHONY; POLYPHONY.

MONTEVERDI, CLAUDIO (15 May 1567, Cremona, Italy–29 November 1643, Venice). Composer whose madrigals and **operas** established the aesthetic integrity of the early Baroque style in the early 17th century, Monteverdi's sacred music, consisting of some 145 Latin **motets**, 17 Italian *madrigali spirituali*, three **masses**, and the **Vespers of 1610**, has received less attention despite its superb quality only because the musical culture of Europe in general was moving away from sacred music. It was published chiefly in three collections: the 1610 print containing the Vespers, the *Missa In illo tempore*, and the **Magnificat** for six voices; the large collection *Selva Morale e Spirituale* of 1641; and a posthumous collection of 1650, as well as in anthologies that appeared throughout his professional career.

Many of the motets exploit the monodic and concertante idioms of opera, and are thus typical of early Baroque trends in Italian and German sacred music. At the same time, Monteverdi seemed anxious to show that he also commanded the *stile antico* approved by the **Council of Trent**. All three masses are exemplars, and along with the *Missa In illo tempore* he took the trouble to print separately the 10 **subjects** of **Nicholas Gombert**'s motet **parodied** in his own music. The Vespers of 1610 is unique in 17th-century sacred music because it synthesizes all available idioms sacred and secular in a single monumental composition.

Because he had to provide new music for important festivals during his long tenure (1613–1643) as *maestro di capella* at St. Mark's Basilica in **Venice**, it is thought that much of his sacred music must be lost.

MORALES, CROSTÓBAL DE (c.1500, Seville–between 4 and 7 September 1553, probably Marchéna). One of the best known composers of sacred music in his time, both in Europe and Mexico, his 21 **masses**, two **Requiems**, six **Magnificats** *alternatim*, and 90 **motets** preserved their reputation into the 18th century. He was *maestro di capilla* at Avila Cathedral (1526–1528), then Plasencia (1528-1531) before entering the papal choir in **Rome** (1535–1540; then 1541–1545). He returned to Spain as *maestro di capilla* at Toledo Cathedral (1545–1547), with the Duke of Arcos in Marchéna (1548–1551), and finally at Málaga Cathedral (1551–1553).

MORLEY, THOMAS (1557 or 1558, Norwich, England–early October 1602, London). Composer, he studied with **William Byrd** and composed four Anglican **services** (first, **second**, **short**, and **burial**), 19 **anthems**, seven English **psalm** settings, and 14 Latin **motets**, all of which maintain a distinctly sacred style as compared to his more famous English madrigals. He was **organist** at Norwich Cathedral (1583–1587), organist at St. Paul's in **London** (from 1588) and a Gentleman of the **Chapel Royal** from 24 July 1592.

MORNING PRAYER (MATINS). Anglican conflation of the Roman Catholic **offices** of **lauds** and **matins**. Musical settings may include *Venite* (**Psalm** 95), **Te Deum**, *Benedicite* (Daniel 3), *Benedictus*, and *Jubilate Deo* (Psalm 100) with English texts despite the Latin referents. John Day's *Certaine Notes* (**London**, 1565) is the earliest source that orders its music into discrete **services**, the music for **Communion** coming between that for **Morning Prayer** and **Evening Prayer**. From the Elizabethan period on, Morning and Evening Prayer assumed ever greater liturgical prominence at the expense of the Communion Service.

The Alternative Services Series II (1968, revised 1971) allows a

wide variety of **canticles** to be sung. *See also* ANTHEM; GREAT
SERVICE; SHORT SERVICE; VERSE SERVICE.

MOSCOW. The capital of Russia was the principal center for Russian
Orthodox sacred music. Tsar Ivan III established the *gosudarevī pevchiye d'yaki* (ruler's singing clerks) after 1472 to sing at court functions and all important religious services. Its members outranked
those of the *patriarshiye pevchiye d'yaki i podd'yaki* (patriarchal
singing clerks and sub-clerks), an older body, but the two choirs became the center of advanced music education, performance, and
manuscript production.

Two developments in the 17th century changed the character of
Orthodox music materially: the reform of the ecclesiastical **chant**
and its *kryukovaya* notation system, carried out by Aleksandr Meze-
nets and Ivan Shaydur; and the introduction of *partesnoye peniye*
(**polyphonic** singing), promoted by Nikolay Diletsky and Vasily
Titov. *See also* ZNAMENNĪY RASPEV.

MOTET. A **polyphonic** composition for unaccompanied choir setting
a Latin sacred, often Biblical text. This is the most common connotation, but motets may have **instruments**, solo voices, and texts in
other languages in certain historical contexts.

Motets originated in France in the early 13th century when the
upper voices of **discant clausulae** were given texts that **troped** the
original liturgical text. Or, such pieces were simply composed with
new texts, sometimes in French; the sources do not indicate a clear
chronology. In any case, the 13th-century motet consisted of a repeating traditional **chant** melody called the tenor, whose sometimes
isorhythmic duration pattern was determined by the composer, a
newly composed **counterpoint** with a new text, called the *motetus*,
and often another new melody with yet a different text, called the
triplum. With the resources of the new rhythmic notation of the *Ars
Nova* in the 14th century, the independence of melodies and texts
became so extreme as to seem at times hardly belonging to the same
composition. This type persisted until the early 15th century, having
spread to Italy and England.

The 15th century witnessed a number of fundamental changes that
produced the archetype of the common understanding of motet. First,

perhaps as a delayed response to a decree issued by Pope John XXII from Avignon in 1324 against elaborate polyphony or perhaps as a response to English polyphony heard during the Hundred Years War, the texture became much simpler and developed a more strictly consonant harmonic syntax based on triadic sonorities. Second, the number of voices in a conventional motet texture became four, with the chant melody, now known as the **cantus firmus**, generally found in the third voice. Four-voiced texture balanced the needs of free melody with the requirements of a triadic harmony, and the new contratenor or bass voice provided acoustical support for the triads. Third, the four voices all sang a single text, although seldom **homorhythmically**; the mixed texts and languages of the 14th century disappeared. Fourth, in the last quarter of the century the **imitation** of **Josquin Desprez** provided an alternative structure to the cantus firmus, which at one stroke allowed all the other voices access to the chant used in the motet and thereby unified the entire texture. Alternatively, it made possible the composition of imitative motets without reference to any preexisting melody. The combination of the two techniques could create truly monumental works such as Josquin's *Miserere Mei, Deus*.

Sixteenth-century motets represent the epitome of what is variously called "classical polyphony," "high Renaissance polyphony," and the "*stile antico*." Josquin and his colleagues **Jacob Obrecht**, **Jean Mouton** and others had developed both the musical language and the formal procedures based on imitation in paired voices that their successors built upon and elaborated. **Adrian Willaert** and **Nicolas Gombert** composed with imitation less formulaic, and the great generation of **Giovanni da Palestrina**, **Orlandus Lassus**, **William Byrd**, and **Tomas Luis de Victoria**, each in his own way, dominated the second half of the century in both number and quality of motets. By this time, four-voiced texture was considered somewhat antiquated. In England, the **Eton Choirbook** preserves works for up to 10 voices in non-imitative texture. On the continent five and six voices in contrasting imitative and homorhythmic textures were preferred, and experiments with *cori spezzati*, or split-choir texture, began in the 1520s.

The liturgical function of the motet is quite vague from the beginnings. The logical supposition for motets setting texts from the **di-**

vine office is that they would substitute for traditional chants in those liturgies, and this would explain the large number of **Marian antiphon** motets, which could always be sung at **compline**. Sixteenth-century diaries from the Sistine Chapel, however, show that motets were sung at the Offertory, Elevation, the distribution of communion, or the conclusion of a **mass**, regardless of its text. Motets could be heard in the private chapels of the nobility, as private devotions, and might also be a form of spiritual entertainment. One of the best known music prints of the 16th century, Willaert's *Musica Nova* (**Venice**, 1559), is a collection of motets and secular Italian madrigals.

The invention of **opera** in 1597 made permanent the fissure between sacred and secular musical languages that had been deepening throughout the 16th century and split motet composition into two paths. Composers, particularly those working near **Rome**, could follow the legendary Palestrina and uphold the fixed ideals of the *stile antico* and the *a cappella* sound, or they could write "motets" with the new operatic textures. Contemporary terminology becomes confused and imprecise at this juncture; "motet" in the 17th century might refer to any vocal composition associated with liturgy, while the settings of sacred texts in operatic manner might be called "concerted motets," "**sacred concertos**," or "**sacred symphonies.**" In these works, beginning with Ludovico Viadana's *Cento Concerti Ecclesiastici* ("One Hundred Church Concertos") in 1602, and followed by many publications of **Claudio Monteverdi, Alessandro Grandi, Heinrich Schütz,** and others, solo voices and instruments combine to make a complete harmonic texture. The ensemble might be as simple as one singer and **continuo**, or as elaborate as double or triple choir with a large instrumental group. Late 17th-century motets, such as those of **Alessandro Scarlatti**, become like spiritual operas in their use of **recitative** and *da capo* **aria**. In general, semantic referents such as traditional chant melodies are abandoned, although German **Lutheran** composers wrote **chorale motets** using their own traditional melodies as cantus fermi. Some Baroque motets, such as those of **Antonio Lotti** and Schütz (*Cantiones Sacrae*, 1625 and *Geistliche Chormusik*, 1648) combine traditional *stile antico* textures with secular harmonic effects. This strain culminates in the six motets of **Johann Sebastian Bach**.

French composers did not adapt operatic techniques until the approximately 100 motets of **Guillaume Bouzignac** in the 1630s. Thereafter they readily assumed secular elements, culminating late in the century in the *grand motet* at the court of Versailles and the *petit motet* composed for less ostentatious circumstances such as convents. These genres continued to follow the secular trends until the French Revolution.

As secular musical languages seemed less and less appropriate for liturgy and the gap between them and the *stile antico* grew enormous, composers naturally lost interest in motet composition, the only exceptions being those mostly French composers who were inspired by the **Cecilian Movement**, such as **Charles Gounod**, **Camille Saint-Saëns**, and **Gabriel Fauré**, or others such as **Anton Bruckner** and **Franz Liszt** who had a particular devotion to church music and who could employ **modal** harmonies and other sacred sounds while maintaining some originality. The encyclical *Tra le sollecitudini* of Pope Pius X (1903) exalted the "Classical Polyphony" of Palestrina but discouraged motet composition in contemporary idioms. Motets of the last 250 years are rarely heard in liturgy but some, such as **Wolfgang Amadeus Mozart**'s *Ave Verum Corpus*, have become favorites of choral societies.

MOTETTI MISSALES. **Motets** organized in cycles of as many as eight motets unified by **mode** and **mensuration** scheme designed to substitute for **ordinary** and **proper** prayers of the Roman Catholic rite in the diocese of Milan. The genre flourished in the last quarter of the 15th century.

MOTU PROPRIO (1903). *See TRA LE SOLLECITUDINI.*

MOUTON, JEAN (before 1460, Haut-Wignes near Samer, Pas-de-Calais, France–30 October 1522, St. Quentin). Roman Catholic priest and composer of 18 **masses**, 116 **motets**, and eight **Magnificats**, and teacher of **Adrian Willaert**, the earliest record (1477) is as a singing teacher in Nesle (Somme). He entered the service of Queen Anne of Brittany sometime after 1502 and served the royal court for the rest of his life. Mouton's masses and motets exhibit most of the

contrapuntal techniques current at the turn of the 16th century: **cantus firmus**, **canon**, **paraphrase** and **parody**.

MOZARABIC CHANT. Chant sung in the Iberian peninsula during the period of Muslim rule, although documents suggest that it originated before their invasion in 711. It was supplanted by the **Gregorian chant** of the Roman Catholic rite with the fall of Toledo in 1085; Mozarabic chant and liturgy were officially suppressed. Cardinal Jiménez de Cisneros published a missal in 1500 based on manuscripts preserved in Toledo, and this rite may be heard in the Toledo Cathedral today. But the music represents a 16th-century compilation of oral tradition; the only Mozarabic chant sources with precise pitch notation date from the 16th century, with one small exception, and therefore the ancient melodies remain indecipherable.

MOZART, WOLFGANG AMADEUS (27 January 1756, Salzburg, Austria–5 December 1791, Vienna). Renowned chiefly for his consummate mastery of every kind of secular music of the late 18th century, Mozart's contribution to the sacred repertory, while clearly secondary, is hardly insignificant: his eight **masses**, nine *missae breves*, two Kyrie movements, four **litanies**, two **vespers**, two **oratorios**, six **cantatas**, 17 "**Epistle sonatas**," four **litanies** and about 24 **motets** represent over a tenth of the Köchel catalog listing his works. Most of these were composed as a youth in the service of the archbishops of Salzburg, whom he served with his father from 1769 until his dismissal on 9 June 1781. The better known late works were usually composed for individual commissions, with the notable exception of the C minor mass K. 427 (January 1783, incomplete), written for personal reasons that remain obscure.

Mozart composed his sacred music in an unabashed secular idiom of the late 18th century with full orchestrations and **operatic** vocal writing. Choral movements present an occasional **fugue** as a signal of their original liturgical purpose. Today this music is mostly heard in the concert hall. The best known works include an early three-movement motet *Exultate, jubilate* K. 165 (1773), the "Coronation" Mass K. 317 (1779), the C minor mass, the motet *Ave Verum Corpus* K. 618 (1791), and the **Requiem** mass K. 626 (1791). *See also MESSIAH.*

MUEZZIN. Person who **chants** the 'adhān, or Islamic call to prayer. The first was an Abyssinian slave and early convert named Bilāl. Later, some large mosques employed as many as 20, and in the Ottoman empire they banded into guilds. Once commanding great respect, their role in modern times has diminished owing to the use of recorded 'adhān. *See also TEMCIT.*

MUSICA FICTA **(Lat. "false music").** The performance practice of adding accidentals to written diatonic pitches, chiefly in medieval, Renaissance, and early Baroque music. The specifics of the tradition are inconsistent in both musical and theoretical sources of those times, and thus the practice is highly controverted today. In a critically edited modern score of an early work, a note "signed" with an accidental next to it on the staff indicates that the accidental appeared so in an original source; if the accidental appears above the staff, usually in small type, it did not appear in the source at all. Rather, it is an editor's suggestion for *musica ficta*, based on considerations of harmonic consonance, **mode**, and voice-leading, among other things.

– N –

NAJARA, ISRAEL (c. 1555, Safed, modern Israel–c. 1628, Gaza). Poet and *hazan*, first to publish a *diwan* (song collection) in 1587, which contained 108 of his own poems with the intention of attracting Jewish youth away from secular songs. His most famous **hymn**, printed on prayer books and sung the world over, is the Aramaic *Yah Ribbon Alam* ("God of the World"). *See also PIYYUT.*

NĀLĀYIRATIVVIYAPPIRAPANTAM. Great collection of **hymn** texts dedicated to the Hindu deity Vishnu, assembled c. 1000. Their language is Tamil. The hymns may be sung in temples or in private devotions. The tunes conform to Karnatic *rāgas*. *See also GĪTA-GOVINDA; TĒVĀRAM.*

NANINO, GIOVANNI MARIA (1543 or 1544, Tivoli, Italy–11 March 1607, Rome). With **Giovanni da Palestrina**, with whom he may have studied in the 1560s, he was the most influential musician in Rome of his time and taught Felice Anerio (c. 1560–1614), Gregorio Allegri (1582–1652), and others who maintained the tradition of classical **polyphony** into the 17th century. *See also MISERERE.*

NAYLOR, BERNARD (22 November 1907, Cambridge–20 May 1986, Keswick, Cumbria, England). Composer of unaccompanied **motets** and **canticles**, one *Missa Sine Credo*, and the orchestrated **cantatas** *The Annunciation According to Saint Luke* (1949), *King Solomon's* Prayer (1953), and *The Resurrection According to Saint Matthew* (1965).

NEAPOLITAN MASS. *See* MASS.

NELSON MASS. *See* HAYDN, FRANZ JOSEPH.

NEO-GALLICAN CHANT. *See* GREGORIAN CHANT.

NEUMEISTER, ERDMANN (12 May 1671, Weissenfels, Germany–18 August 1756, Hamburg). Poet and theologian, he wrote nine cycles of church **cantata** texts for all Sundays and many feasts of the **Lutheran** liturgical year. His second such cycle legitimized the alternation of **aria** and **recitative**, as in Italian **opera**, for Lutheran Church cantatas. **Johann Sebastian Bach** drew on the fourth cycle for his Cantatas BWV 18, 24, 28, 59 and 61.

NICHOLSON, SIR SYDNEY (9 February 1875, London–30 May 1947, Ashford, Kent). **Organist** of Westminster Abbey who left in 1928 to found the School of English Church Music, later called the Royal School of Church Music, where organists, choirmasters, and clergy might study to improve the standards of parish music. *See also* OXFORD MOVEMENT.

NIGGUN **(pl.** *NIGGUNIM***).** Vocal music of the Hassids, who from their foundation by Rabbi Israel Baal Shem Tov (1700–1760) considered singing an important spiritual aid. Ecstatic and often spontaneous, originating in 18th- and 19th-century Poland and Ukraine, *niggunim* most often have no text, although there may be a brief phrase repeated incessantly. The melody may be popular, or freely invented; likewise a march-like or waltz **meter** may obtain, or the music may be heavily ornamented **chant**.

Also, Jewish melody type or model, suitable for **contrafacta**.

NINE CANTICLES. Also know as "The Nine Odes," a set of Biblical poems sung in the **Byzantine** morning **office** (*Orthrōs*), perhaps as early as the sixth century. They are: 1) the canticle of Moses (Ex. 15: 1–19); 2) the death canticle of Moses (Deut. 32: 1–43); 3) the canticle of Hannah (1 Sam. 2: 1–10); 4) the canticle of Habakkuk (Hab. 3: 2–19); 5) the canticle of Isaiah (Isa. 26: 29–19); 6) the canticle of Jonah (Jonah 2: 3–10); 7) the canticle of Azariah (Dan. 3: 26–45, 52–56); 8) the song of the three children (Dan. 3: 57–88); 9) the canticles of Mary, the Theotokos, and Zacharia (Lk. 1: 46–55, 68–79; *see* Appendix A). Since the late Middle Ages the second has not been sung except during Lent.

NOËL. French term for Christmas **carol**, with French text, often made by mating a new sacred text to a traditional folk melody. Also, a composition for **pipe organ** based on one of these songs. *See also CONTRAFACTUM; WECHSELGESANG.*

NOTKER OF ST. GALL. *See* SEQUENCE.

NUNC DIMITTIS. One of the three Gospel **canticles** for the major **divine offices** of the Roman Catholic liturgy, known as the Canticle of Simeon (St. Luke 2: 29–32; *see* Appendix A for text), sung at **compline** in the Roman rite and at **Evening prayer** in the Anglican rite. In the **Gregorian** tradition, it is **chanted** as would be a **psalm**, with framing **antiphons** (the same weekly set is used throughout the year) and the corresponding tone. **Polyphonic** settings are rare in the Roman rite but not at all uncommon in the Anglican tradition.

NUPER ROSARUM FLORES. Renowned four-voiced **motet** of **Guillaume Du Fay**, composed for the reconsecration of Santa Maria del Fiore (Duomo) in Florence on 25 March 1436, with Pope Eugene IV in attendance. The motet treats its borrowed **chant** melody, the **Introit** *Terribilis est locus iste*, in expanded **isorhythm**. Each **talea** of the motet begins with a free duet in the upper voices, followed by the full four-voiced texture that includes two tenor voices singing the Introit a perfect fifth apart in a free **canon**. The entire motet includes four presentations of the **cantus firmus** (plus a concluding "Amen") in durational proportions of 6:4:2:3, unusual in that they do not become progressively faster as was customary in isorhythmic motets. Explanations include a correspondence to the architectural proportions of Filippo Brunelleschi's famous dome and a reference to a biblical tradition about the ratio of the Temple of Solomon.

– O –

OBRECHT, JACOB (22 November 1457 or 1458, Bergen op Zoom? Netherlands–1505 Ferrara). Priest and highly regarded composer of 29 **masses** (27 extant, almost all **cantus firmus** masses) and about 28 **motets**. A difficult personality, he occupied various posts at Utrecht, Bruges, Antwerp, Cambrai, and Bergen op Zoom with a leave from August 1487 to June 1488 to visit the court of Duke Ercole I d'Este at Ferrara. He undertook a second journey there in 1504. Though comparatively young, contemporaries routinely compared him to **John Dunstable, Guillaume Du Fay, Johannes Ockeghem**, and **Antoine Busnoys**.

OCKEGHEM, JOHANNES (after 1410, Saint-Ghislain, Hainaut–6 February 1497, Tours ?, France). Eminent composer of 13 extant **masses**, nine **motets**, and the earliest surviving **polyphonic Requiem**, Ockeghem was regarded by contemporaries as the premier **contrapuntalist** of his generation. The earliest record lists him as a singer at Notre Dame in Antwerp on 24 June 1443. From 1452, he served the French royal court. His death was lamented in a celebrated work of **Josquin Desprez**, the song motet *Nymphes des Bois*.

OFFERTORY. *See* MASS.

OFFICE. *See* DIVINE OFFICE.

OKTOĒCHOS. **Byzantine** system of eight **modes**, possibly originating in monasteries around eighth-century **Jerusalem**. As in the Western modes, there are four authentic (higher) and four plagal (lower) modes, with *finales* on D, E, F, and G. The Byzantine system differs in use: a single mode is employed for all **chanting** for the week Sunday to Sunday, when it is succeeded by the next mode, until the cycle is completed through eight weeks, at which point it recommences. *See also* JOHN OF DAMASCUS; SYRIAN CHANT.

OKTOĒCHOS OF SEVERUS. Ancient Byzantine collection of non-Biblical **hymn** texts for the liturgical year, dating from the early sixth century.

OLD HALL MANUSCRIPT. Containing 147 sacred works (40 **Glorias**, 35 **Credos**, 27 **Sanctus**, 19 **Agnus Dei**, 11 **motets**, and 15 **discants**) composed between 1370 and 1420, all but two by English composers, it is the earliest large source with named attributions in the Western tradition, with **Lionel Power** having the most. The complete absence of **Kyrie** movements remains a puzzle. *See* ETON CHOIRBOOK.

OLD ROMAN CHANT. *See* GREGORIAN CHANT.

OPERA. *"Dramma per musica,"* as early practitioners called it, a drama told through music. The invention of opera in Florence at the end of the 16th century is one of the great turning points in the history of Western music because it changed the culture's conception of music from an art of contemplation, in sacred music, or lyrical expression, as in secular song, to one of drama and dramatic action.

The invention affected sacred music in important ways. First, it provided with its new musical syntax a radical alternative to the prevailing sacred style of classical **polyphony**, thus delimiting the sacred character of the latter as no previous genre had ever done, especially in Catholic countries. After opera, two musical languages, each with its own purpose, divided European composition. Second, it attracted talented composers away from the church and into the theater by offering the first music that could be marketed on a scale sufficient to provide an independent living, with artistic challenges and goals on the same level as the grandest liturgy. Third, operatic principles and syntax generated new, para- or extra-liturgical sacred genera such as the **oratorio**, *grand motet*, and church **cantata**, and eventually infected the traditional forms: **masses, psalms, responsories**, all composed in operatic style.

ORATORIO. A sacred drama set to music, whose appearance at the turn of the 17th century coincides with the invention of **opera** and whose aesthetics and conventions closely parallel that genre. At first heard in prayer halls of certain **Roman** churches (oratories), oratorios soon joined the opera in aristocratic salons, theaters, and concert halls but utilized no staging or scenery. **Instrumental** accompaniment ranges from **continuo** alone to large orchestral forces. A chorus for both commentary and character portrayal (e.g., the people of Israel), is typical, particularly of oratorios after 1700, perhaps the most distinctive element of the genre. Vocal soloists sing individual character roles. The plots are most often adaptations of Bible stories, particularly Old Testament stories and hagiographies, with librettos of moral or allegorical character a distinct minority.

The name derives from the *Congregazione dell'Oratorio*, a religious order founded by St. Philip Neri (1515–1595) dedicated to renewal of contemplative prayer for the laity, whose oratory services were animated by *laude* and other sacred music. In 1600, the oratory at the Chiesa Nuova in Rome saw the first performance of Emilio Cavalieri's (c. 1550–1602) *Rappresentazione di Anima et di Corpo*, a dialogue between the Spirit and the Body set to **recitative**, with intermittent choruses. The same kind of work is Pietro Della Valle's (1586–1652) *Oratorio della Purificazione* of 1640, the first instance of the term applied to a piece of music. In the first half of the 17th century, however, traditional **contrapuntal** music (*stile antico*) continued to set oratorios along with the newer recitative texture. In the second half, the music resembled opera and **cantata** closely, with recitative and **aria** alternation as the basic scheme. Texts were in Italian (*oratorio volgare*) or Latin (*oratorio latino*). Italian poetry was typically 350–400 lines and required from one and one-half to two hours to perform. Latin librettos were usually prose, often excerpted from the Vulgate Bible, and a narrator (*testo*) often took the role of evangelist. **Giacomo Carissimi** wrote 13 influential Latin works that included a significant choral role, but choruses are rare in the 20 or so extant oratorios of his much younger colleague **Alessandro Scarlatti**, replaced by an occasional *coro*, an ensemble of the vocal soloists.

In France, however, Carissimi's student, **Marc-Antoine Charpentier**, composer of 35 oratorios, sometimes called *histoires sacrées*, in French and Latin, expanded the number of choruses and employed them as commentators and dramatic agents.

In German-speaking lands, sacred dramas or *historiae* were usually liturgical with strictly Biblical librettos (e.g., **Christmas Oratorio of Heinrich Schütz**) and often provoked controversy when performed in theaters. In England, **George Frideric Handel** managed to overcome such objections with his English oratorio. Handel's personal amalgam of Italian operatic conventions, the English language, and the English cathedral choir tradition, and his international reputation, particularly through *Messiah*, provided the model for oratorio composition that remained more or less consistent through an age of expanding orchestras and choruses and changing musical languages until the present.

Some of the more frequently performed oratorios after Handel are:

Franz Joseph Haydn, *Die Schöpfung* ("**The Creation**," 1798)
Haydn, *Die Jahreszeiten* ("**The Seasons**," 1801)
Felix Mendelssohn, *Paulus* ("**St. Paul**," 1836)
Mendelssohn, *Elias* ("**Elijah**," 1846)
Hector Berlioz, *L'Enfance du Christ* ("The Childhood of Christ," 1854)
Camille Saint-Saëns, *Oratorio de Noël* (1858)
Franz Liszt, *Christus* (1862–67)
Antonin Dvorák, *St. Ludmilla* (1886)
Edward Elgar, *The Dream of Gerontius* (1900)
Claude Debussy, *Le Martyre de St. Sébastien* ("The Martyrdom of St. Sebastian, 1911)
Arthur Honegger, *Le Roi David* ("King David," 1921)
Ralph Vaughn Williams, *Sancta Civitas* ("The Holy City," 1923–1925)
William Walton, ***Belshazzar's Feast*** (1931)
Michael Tippett, *A Child of Our Time* (1941)
Krzysztof Penderecki, *Paradise Lost* (1971)
John Tavener, *Lamentations and Praises* (2001)

See also PASSION.

ORBÁN, GYÖRGY (12 July 1947, Tirgu Mures, Romania). Composer of nine **masses** for vocal soloists, chorus, and various **instrumental** forces (No. 7 is unaccompanied). He also has written three **oratorios**: *Regina Martyrum* (1993), *Rorate Coeli* (1993), and a Christmas oratorio (1998); and one **passion** (1998).

ORDINARY. Refers to those prayers that are sung every day unchanged throughout the liturgical year, e.g., Kyrie, as opposed to **propers**. *See* MASS.

ORGAN. The most important traditional **instrument** in Christian music, also known in some kinds of non-Orthodox Jewish music, and the Hindu ***bhajan***, the term refers to a family of keyboard instruments derivative of the **pipe organ**. Members of one branch of the family produce sound by forcing air through a set of scaled vibrators activated by the keyboard: pipes of different lengths, materials, and shapes in pipe organs, **portatives**, and **positives**; vibrating metal tongues of different lengths in **harmoniums** and **regals**. Members of a second branch attempt to imitate the sound of a pipe organ by producing sound through loudspeakers controlled either by oscillators of varying frequencies as in the early 20th-century **electronic organ**, or by sound samples stored in computers as in the late 20th-century **digital organ**.

"Organ" therefore will denote different instruments depending upon the context. Discussions of historical repertory (e.g., "the organ music of **Johann Sebastian Bach**"), refer almost certainly and exclusively to pipe organ, but in a performance of an **oratorio** it could well be the positive, and reference to "the organ" in a modern church could denote a pipe organ, a positive, an electronic organ, or a digital organ.

As the sole instrument admitted to Christian liturgies since the 10th century, the organ has by far the largest and most varied repertory of sacred instrumental music, and has in those centuries acquired an incomparable connotation of the sacred for Western culture. Nevertheless, the tradition of organ playing has declined noticeably in the last half of the 20th century owing to the use of popular styles in the **gospel songs** and **praise choruses** common in Evangelical Protestantism throughout the century and in **folk masses** in Roman Catholicism since the **Second Vatican Council**.

ORGANIST. A principal authority in the musical establishment of a church or cathedral. In small parishes, the organist not only is the sole player of the **organ** but has charge of all liturgical music including directing the choir or **schola**. Historically, this holds true of many large churches in northern Europe, while in Italy and Spain the organist was usually subordinate to the *maestro di cappella*. In any case, the cathedral organist was almost always a highly trained composer and improviser as well as expert player.

ORGAN MASS. A principal practice of *alternatim* by which **organ versets** substitute for **chanted** portions of the **ordinary** and **proper** prayers of the **mass** in alternation. The earliest versets are found in the Faenza Codex (Italy, c. 1400). In 1600, Pope Clement VII's *Caeremoniale Episcorporum* ("Bishops ceremonial") ratified this long-standing practice. At that time, the organ typically played 19 versets: five for the Kyrie, nine for the Gloria, two for the Sanctus, one for the Benedictus (entire text), and two for the Agnus Dei. The document also called for soft organ music during the Elevation (Consecration) and at the end of mass. The Credo could not be performed *alternatim* after the **Council of Trent**. The division of proper chants varied widely; the Offertory enjoyed particular freedom of treatment. In general, the relation of the versets with original chants grew ever more distant until the *Tra Le Sollecitudini* of Pope Pius X (1903) banned *alternatim* practice altogether. However, the tradition of organ improvisation during chanted masses continued in France, and **Olivier Messiaen** composed *Messe de la Pentecôte* in 1951.

Publications of organ masses peaked in the 17th century. Particularly important are **Girolamo Frescobaldi's** *Fiori Musicali* (1635), Antonio Croci's *Frutti musicali* (1642), Guillaume Gabriel Nivers' *2e Livre d'Orgue* (1667), Nicolas-Antoine Lebègue's *Second Livre D'Orgue* (1678?), André Raison's *Livre D'Orgue Contenant Cinque Messes* (1688), Nicolas de Grigny's *Premier Livre d'Orgue* (1699), and above all **François Couperin's** *Pièces d'Orgue Consistantes en Deux Messes* (1690).

ORGAN SONATA. Composition for **organ**, usually in several movements of contrasting tempo, patterned after secular **instrumental** sonatas. *See also* BACH, JOHANN SEBASTIAN; RHEINBERGER, JOSEPH.

ORGANUM. Earliest known type of Western **polyphony**. Anonymous treatises dating from the second half of the ninth century describe the addition of a new melody, the *vox organalis* ("organal voice") to a traditional Roman Catholic **chant** melody, the *vox principalis*. The new melody is a near copy of the chant but sung at the interval of a perfect octave, fourth, or fifth, note against note. Other intervals may be used to begin and end the organum on a unison. Early 12th-century sources indicate more melodic independence in the *vox organalis*, but always **homorhythmic**, note against note.

A decisive break for rhythmic independence of the combined melodies occurs in manuscripts associated with the Abbey of St. Martial, Limoges, Toulouse, and Narbonne in southern France, dating from the 12th century. For originally syllabic chants, they show a **melismatic** organum, a precursor of the **cantus firmus** technique, in which the traditional chant is sustained in long tones under a florid countermelody, and for originally melismatic chants another type, in which one, two, three, or four notes of the new melody sound against one (or sometimes more than one) note of the chant. Thirteenth-century theorists distinguished these as *organum purum* and **discant**.

Sources indicate advanced and prolific composition in polyphony associated with the cathedral of Notre Dame in **Paris** from the latter half of the 12th century. The melismatic *organa pura* attributed to **Leoninus** are rhapsodically long. **Clausulae** (discant organum) attributed to **Perotinus** employ as many as four voices. In the 13th century, the genre gives way to **motet** and **conductus**.

ORGELBÜCHLEIN **(Ger. "Little Organ Book").** Famous collection of **chorale preludes** composed by **Johann Sebastian Bach** almost certainly during his Weimar years, probably from 1713–1716. The collection is unfinished. The autograph indicates Bach's intention to provide 164 chorale preludes along the plan of a **Lutheran** hymnal, with 60 **proper hymns** preceding the 104 common ones. He finished 46. Their short length, one or two pages of score, made impractical the kind of setting in which each phrase of the chorale initiates a brief **fugue**, but all other types of chorale prelude are represented, the majority of the pieces presenting the tune unadorned in the highest voice. The pedal is obbligato in all of them, and there is a wide variety of texture and **contrapuntal** effect, including double **canons**. According to the title-page, Bach intended the collection to be played and studied by beginners, but many of the pieces are quite difficult by modern standards.

ORTHRŌS (Gk. "dawn"). The principal morning **divine office** in the **Byzantine** rite. Taking shape as early as the fifth century, monastics began to add the singing of *stichēra* and *kanon* in the sixth.

The parts of the *orthrōs* are: *troparia*; *hexapsalmos*, selections from six **psalms**; *Theos kyrios*; usually an excerpt of Psalm 117 with verse 27 used as a refrain; *polyeleos*, verses from Psalms 134–135; *amōmos*, Psalm 118; *anabathmoi*, three or four *troparia*; *prokeimenon*, a *responsorial* chant of selected psalm verses; *pentēkostos*, Psalm 50, sung **antiphonally** with concluding *stichēron* or *troparion* on important feasts; *kanōn*; *kontakion*; *exposteilarion*, a short chant; *hoi ainoi*, Psalms 148–150, sung on Sundays and feasts; *heōthinon*, an elaborate *stichëron* of 11 chants on Resurrection themes; *Doxa en hypsistois*, the major **doxology**; and *trisagion*.

OSIANDER, LUCAS. *See CANTIONAL.*

OSTINATO. A melody repeated exactly many times, usually in the bass, to provide harmonic structure particularly in **instrumental** works of the 17th and 18th centuries, some of which were heard as part of Christian liturgies, especially when they were for **pipe organ**. These melodies often derived from popular dances that gave them specific names for ostinato technique: chaconne, passacaglia, ground. *See also CANTUS FIRMUS.*

OXFORD BOOK OF CAROLS, THE (1928). Edited by Percy Dearmer, Martin Shaw, and **Ralph Vaughn Williams**, who contributed many excellent arrangements of the tunes, this collection of both traditional and modern **carols** dominated carol singing by choirs in the English-speaking world for most of the 20th century. It was superceded by *The New Oxford Book of Carols* (1992) edited by Hugh Keyte and Andrew Parrott.

OXFORD MOVEMENT. Also known as the Tractarians after the 90 *Tracts for the Times*, published between 1833 and 1841, a group of churchmen and scholars who sought to restore to the Anglican Church its theological and liturgical foundations, including its musical heritage. Under the influence of the movement, the **Holy Communion** service regained its liturgical preeminence, lost to other **services** since the early 17th century, the standards of both cathedral and English parish liturgical music rose, and a great deal of new liturgical music, both services and **anthems**, were published. *See also* CECILIAN MOVEMENT.

– P –

PACHELBEL, JOHANN (baptized 1 September 1653, Nuremberg, Germany–buried 9 March 1706, Nuremberg). He served as **organist** at the Pridigerkirche at Erfurt from 19 June 1678 to 15 August 1690. After two short-term positions in Würtemberg and Gotha, he was invited by his home city authorities in 1695 to be organist of St. Sebaldus at Nuremberg without the customary examination. He remained there until his death.

His compositions include 66 **chorale** settings of various types, including **chorale fugues** and **cantus firmus** settings, 11 **motets**, all but one for *cori spezzati*, 11 **sacred concertos**, 13 **Magnificats** and other **versicle**s for **vespers**, two **masses**, and 98 "Magnificat" fugues written for St. Sebaldus church. These fugues, constituting one of the most ambitious compilations before **Johann Sebastian Bach**, are so called not because they take the Magnificat tones as **subjects**, but because they give the choir the pitch for singing that vespers **canticle**.

PADILLA, JUAN GUTIÉRREZ DE (c. 1590, Málaga, Spain–c. 22 April 1664, Puebla, Mexico). *Maestro di capilla* at Jérez de la Frontera (1613–1616), Cádiz Cathedral (1616–1620), and Puebla Cathedral in Mexico (1629–death) where he established a first-rate choir and **instrumental** ensemble. He wrote some 50 sacred vocal works in *stile antico*, including works for *cori spezzati*, several **masses**, and many vernacular *villancicos* to be sung on church festival days. (at)

PALESTRINA, GIOVANNI PIERLUIGI DA (between 3 February 1525 and 2 February 1526, Palestrina near Rome–2 February 1594, Rome). Composer of 104 **masses**, at least 375 **motets**, 68 **polyphonic** offertories, 65 **hymn** settings, and 35 **Magnificats**, in addition to Lamentations, *madrigali spirituali*, and secular vocal works, his *oeuvre* is one of the largest of his time and came to represent the ideal style for Roman Catholic polyphony.

He is listed as a singer at Santa Maria Maggiore in Rome in October 1537. He took an **organist**'s position in a small church, San Agapito, in Palestrina, married Lucrezia Gori there on 12 June 1547, and then was suddenly appointed to lead the *Cappella Giulia* at the Vatican on 1 September 1551. He published his first book of masses in 1554. On 13 January 1555, Pope Julius III appointed him to the *Cappella Sistina*, but he was dismissed in September when rules against married members were strictly enforced under Pope Paul IV. The next month, he began a five-year tenure as *maestro di cappella* at St. John Lateran. After various short engagements, he returned to the *Cappella Giulia* in April 1571 for the remainder of his career, despite many offers from **Vienna**, Mantua, and elsewhere. He considered entering the priesthood after his wife died of the plague in 1580, but then married a fur merchant's widow and lived in relative security until his death.

In 1577, Palestrina and Annibale Zoilo were engaged by Pope Gregory XIII to revise the **chant** in the wake of the **Council of Trent**. He worked on the project, eventually known as the **Medicean chant**, only one year.

It is clear from wide citation by theorists and testimonials of other composers that Palestrina was esteemed as the greatest living composer in his own lifetime, challenged perhaps only by **Orlandus Lassus**. But unlike the great reputations of Lassus, **Josquin Desprez**, and most others, Palestrina's reputation did not wane with the succeeding centuries. Instead, he became an icon of "classical polyphony," or the *stile antico*, a musical language frozen in time, particularly after the invention of **opera** at the close of the 16th century.

His sincere efforts at intelligible diction in his polyphony and its association with the Council of Trent were exaggerated into legends early on, as when Agostino Agazzari wrote in 1607 that his *Missa Papae Marcelli* had convinced the council delegates not to abolish polyphony from Catholic liturgy. With such fame, it was natural that Palestrina should be the model for those who wished to learn the traditional **counterpoint** of the church: he is the teacher in **Johann Josef Fux**'s *Gradus ad Parnassum* (1725), the most influential such textbook for the 18th and 19th centuries. Giuseppe Baini (1775–1884) wrote the first Palestrina biography in 1828, and a complete edition of Palestrina's works was completed in 1903.

The modern historical view is that the "Palestrina style" was the common musical language for sacred music in the second half of the 16th century and practiced as such by all of Palestrina's colleagues, including the great Lassus, **William Byrd**, and **Tomas Luis di Victoria**. But his early canonization by church authorities and pedagogues was no accident. In its melodic and rhythmic syntax and rare chromaticism, his personal musical style is conservative, even for his own time, but without the slightest effect of constraint or rigidity. For example, Palestrina's **imitation**: it can be perfectly strict, and yet he designs the **subjects** so that they may enter at varied, unpredictable time intervals. In particular, his handling of **meter**, always present but subtle, allows his music a flowing, flexible movement that comes close to a true polyphonic chant.

PARAPHRASE MASS. A **polyphonic** setting of the Roman Catholic **mass ordinary** prayers that employs a preexisting melody, usually taken from **Gregorian** or medieval **chant**, in all voices as the **subject** of **imitative** passages. This technique became important in the last quarter of the 15th century when composers began to use structural **imitation** as their principal polyphonic technique. It allows all voices of the **texture** to share the same speed and melodic material, as compared to the older **cantus firmus** technique in which one voice, usually the tenor, moves at markedly slower speed with a distinct melody. A great exemplar of a paraphrase mass is **Josquin Desprez**'s *Missa Pange Lingua*.

PARIS. The capital of France became the center of innovation in Roman Catholic liturgical music from the mid-12th to the early 14th century, when the so-called school of Notre Dame produced the first large body of **polyphony** for the **mass** and **divine office**, the composers **Leoninus** and **Perotinus**, the first system of rhythmic notation, and the new genres of **organum** and both polyphonic and **monophonic conductus**. The cathedral acquired a **pipe organ** in 1332.

In the 15th and 16th centuries, the city, while not always at the cutting edge, remained an important locus for liturgical music. The chapel of King Francis I in the 1530s had three dozen adult singers plus boy singers distributed over two choirs, one for **chant** and one for polyphony. Another choir could be heard at the Sainte Chapelle at the same time.

In the 17th century Parisian liturgical music generally followed the wishes of the **Council of Trent**. The **organ** was the only **instrument** officially permitted, and by the 1660s the four-manual French organ was standardized. But by the 1680s, concerted liturgical music of **Marc-Antoine Charpentier** could be heard at the church of St. Louis, and Italian **operatic** influence was also strong at the chapel of the Théatins. Most churches provided only plainchant until the French Revolution, although from 1725–1790 the public could hear Baroque sacred music at the Concert Spirituel, a concert series founded by Anne Danican Philidor for that purpose. A new organ installed there in 1748 encouraged organ renditions of *Noëls*, the **Te Deum**, and other **canticles** that made the virtuosi popular.

Parisian sacred music recovered only very slowly after the revolution. In 1853, the Swiss Louis Niedermeyer (1802–1861) opened L'École Niedermeyer for the training of church musicians. **Camille Saint-Saëns** taught there, and **Gabriel Fauré** studied there. The installation of Aristide Cavaillé-Coll's (1811–1899) first organ at St. Denis in 1841 and the publication of **César Franck**'s *Six Pièces* (1860–1862) did much to revive organ playing. *See also* BERLIOZ, HECTOR; CHERUBINI, LUIGI; COUPERIN, FRANÇOIS; DUPRÉ, MARCEL; DURUFLÉ, MAURICE; LOWY, ISRAEL; LULLY, JEAN-BAPTISTE; RAMEAU, JEAN-PHILIPPE; VITRY, PHILLIPE DE; WIDOR, CHARLES-MARIE.

PARODY. Technique by which a composer employs a preexisting composition to create a new one, using its melodic ideas, **imitative**

patterns, harmonic structures, etc. to whatever extent he sees fit. The concept of borrowing music to begin a new piece is as old as Western music and exists in most other traditions in some form, but "parody" usually refers to the practice of reconfiguring a **polyphonic** composition, prevalent in the 16th–18th centuries. Two repertories of parody most frequently heard today are the **parody masses** of the 16th century and the works of **Johann Sebastian Bach**, who parodied his secular **cantatas** to create church cantatas with new texts and parodied both kinds to build such large works as the **Christmas Oratorio** and the **Mass in B Minor**.

Historians and critics who came of age with Romantic prejudices about artistic originality were once embarrassed when they realized the great extent to which Bach, **George Frideric Handel**, and other Baroque masters parodied their own works and those of others. More recently, studies have shown that parody usually demanded more effort from the composer than the creation of a new work from scratch. The large repertory of parody masses in particular shows intense reworking and filling out of models.

PARODY MASS. A **polyphonic** setting of the Roman Catholic **mass ordinary** prayers that employs a preexisting polyphonic composition, usually a **motet**, less often a secular French *chanson* or Italian madrigal, as a structural pattern and source of melodic motives in **imitation**. Although polyphonic models were quoted in mid-15th-century masses, the slow **cantus firmus** remained the structural frame; the true **parody** mass (also called "imitation mass") dates from the turn of the 16th century and remained an important technique in the *stile antico* masses from then on.

PARRY, HUBERT (SIR) (27 February 1848, Bournemouth, England–7 October 1918, Rustington, Sussex). As a charter Professor of Music at the Royal College of Music from 1883, he exercised great influence on British choral music. He contributed nine **anthems**, two **Magnificats**, four **Te Deums**, three sacred **oratorios** including *King Saul* (1884), *Judith* (1888), and *Job* (1892), and many **hymn** tunes and other **service** music. For **organ**, he wrote three large **fugues**, three **chorale fantasias**, and two sets of **chorale preludes**.

PARS (Lat. "part," pl. *PARTES*). A section of a **polyphonic motet**. Composers often divided lengthy texts into self-contained sections, which, in certain circumstances, may be performed apart from the other sections that make up the complete motet.

PÄRT, ARVO (11 September 1935, Paide, Estonia). While supporting himself with music for theater and film, Pärt first attracted great attention and political reprobation with *Credo* (1968) for chorus, orchestra, and piano. He then developed a new **homophonic** technique called *tintinnabuli*, in which bell-like static triads form the ground for a more prominent, usually **modal**, melodic figure. *Tintinnabuli* became the basis for his *St. John Passion* (1982) and for most of the later compositions for chorus or small vocal ensemble, most on Christian texts or themes. He left Estonia in 1980 and settled in West Berlin in 1982.

PASSACAGLIA. *See* OSTINATO.

PASSION. A setting of one of the four Gospel accounts of Christ's suffering and death on the cross. The genre sprang from a traditional practice of reading or **chanting** the passion accounts during Holy Week—St. Matthew on Palm Sunday, St. Luke on Wednesday, St. Mark on Thursday, St. John on Friday—and it retained its liturgical function until the late 18th century.

A distinct, even dramatic **mode** of chanting these particular Gospel excerpts may be discerned in ninth-century manuscripts written in *litterae significativae*, indicating differentiations of pitch, dynamics, and tempo. Recitation tones distinct from the normal **psalm tones** are known by the 12th century, the particular pitches varying by locality. The Dominican *Gros livre* (1254) is the earliest evidence of the various parts of narrator, Christ, *turba* (crowd), and other speaking roles divided among diverse singers. By the 15th century, the use of three singers became customary, although an entire *schola* might take on the *turba* role.

All of these performance modes were **monophonic**, preserving some quality of chanting the Scripture. Composers in the 15th century began to set some of the text **polyphonically**. If the narration is chanted, with polyphony being reserved for the *turba*, and one or more of the solo roles, including Christ, it is classified by scholars as a "**responsorial** passion" (also "choral passion," "dramatic passion"). If the entire text is polyphonic, it is a "through-composed" or "**motet** passion." The text could be truncated, or enlarged by combining texts from all four Gospels into a *summa passionis*. Frequently an introductory *exordium* and a final *conclusio* were added, both set to polyphony. Liturgical preferences in all these matters varied by region.

Despite **Martin Luther**'s reservations about performing the passion texts and compiled *summae*, the monophonic and polyphonic passion were widely practiced in Protestant Germany. Two German-language responsorial passions, St. Matthew and St. John, attributed to **Johann Walther**, Luther's most important musical collaborator, exercised great influence on the Lutheran passion until well into the 18th century.

The north German Hanseatic cities contributed the next innovation by modeling the passions after Italian **operatic** practices: Thomas Selle's (1599–1663) *St. Matthew Passion* of 1641 provides a **continuo** throughout the score as well as melodic **instruments** to accompany Christ and the narrator. **Heinrich Schütz** invented his own recitation tones having the character of **recitative** for his three passions, and others added instrumental sinfonias. The "**oratorio** passion" also added non-Biblical texts drawn from **hymns**, spiritual verse, and other sources that subdivided the Gospel into episodes. After the publication of **Erdmann Neumeister**'s operatic **cantata** texts after 1700, the recitation tones could be abandoned in favor of free recitative, with **arias** for the poetic texts. Reinhard Keiser's (1674–1739) *St. Mark Passion* (c. 1710), performed by **Johann Sebastian Bach** at Weimar, is such an oratorio passion, and could have provided the model for Bach's own *St. John* and *St. Matthew Passion*(s), which are the culmination of the genre and own permanent places in the choral concert repertory.

The early 18th century saw the conversion of the liturgical passion into secular form completed. In Protestant Germany, poets wrote passion texts that could replace the Biblical accounts: C. F. Hunold's *Der blutige und sterbende Jesus* ("Jesus, bloody and dying"), set by Keiser in 1704, omitted the narration altogether and B. H. Brockes's *Der für die Sünden der Welt gemarterte und sterbende Jesus* ("Jesus, martyred and dying for the sins of the world") use expressive para-phrase and became very popular, set by Keiser (1712), **Georg Phil-lipe Telemann** (1716), **Georg Frideric Handel** (1717), and Johann Mattheson (1718), among others. In Catholic **Vienna**, the *sepolcro* (passion stories) followed the opera completely, even to the point of staging a scene at Christ's tomb. Performances of the *sepolcro* took place only on Holy Thursday or Good Friday, thus retaining a link with the liturgical tradition.

In the latter half of the 18th century, however, the interest of the best composers in liturgical music declined, and so did the tradition itself. With few exceptions, vocal works composed around the pas-sion story—e.g., **Ludwig van Beethoven**'s *Christus am Ölberg* (1803), **Krzysztof Penderecki**'s *Passio et mors Domini nostri Jesu Christi secundum Lucam* (1965)—are concert oratorios and cantatas.

PATER NOSTER **(Lat. "Our Father").** The Latin version has settings by **Josquin Desprez**, **Giovanni da Palestrina**, and other classical **polyphonists**.

PAYTAN. Composer and performer of Jewish paraliturgical songs who works alongside the **cantor**. *See also HAZAN.*

PEDAL POINT. A sustained pitch, usually in the bass, around which other voices continue to move at the speed normal for the composi-tion. The term probably derives from the practice of **organists** impro-vising over a bass tone played on the pedal division, just before an oncoming cadence.

PEETERS, FLOR (4 July 1903, Tielen, Belgium–4 July 1986, Ant-werp). World renowned **organist** and teacher, he composed more than two dozen Latin **motets**, seven **masses**, and numerous **anthems** and other sacred choral works as well as a 24-volume set of *Hymn Preludes for the Liturgical Year* (Op. 100, 1959–1964) and preludes, **fugues**, elegies, **passacaglias**, **sonatas**, and other works for **organ** dating from 1923 to 1985. Since **Gregorian chant** influenced his music, he also published *A Practical Method for Plainchant Accom-paniment* (1943; English version, 1949). *See also FRANCK, CÉSAR.*

PELOQUIN, C. ALEXANDER (16 June 1918, Northbridge, Mass.–27 February 1997, Providence, R. I.). Composer of Roman Catholic liturgical music, about 150 works including the well-known "Gloria of the Bells," that embodied reforms following the **Second Vatican Council**, including **congregational** participation and English language. *See also* TAIZÉ.

PENDERECKI, KRZYSZTOF (23 November 1933, Debica, Poland). Composer and conductor of the avant-garde, he first achieved popular notice with his *St. Luke Passion* (1966). He directed the Kraków Academy of Music from 1972–1987 and has held many university residencies. His major contributions to sacred music include a **Dies Irae** (1967) in memory of the Auschwitz victims, *Utrenia* (1971) a sequel to the *Passion* incorporating aspects of **Byzantine** rites, an **oratorio**-like *Paradise Lost* (1978), another oratorio, *Seven Gates of Jerusalem* (1996), a Polish **Requiem** (1984, rev. 1993), and *Credo* (1998). He also composed many **psalms, canticles,** and other **versicles.**

PEPPING, ERNST (12 September 1901, Duisburg, Germany–1 February 1981, Berlin). Active in the revival of **Lutheran** music, he taught at the *Kirchenmusikschule* in Berlin-Spandau from 1934. He composed the *Spandauer Chorbuch* of 20 volumes of unaccompanied choral pieces for two to six voices (1934–1938), two **German masses** (1928, 1938), a St. Matthew **Passion** (1950), and many other **motets** and liturgical works, mostly in German. He also composed **organ chorale preludes** and partitas, many contained in the *Grosses Orgelbuch* (1939) and the *Kleines Orgelbuch* (1940).

PERGOLESI, GIOVANNI BATTISTA (4 January 1710, Jesi near Ancona, Italy–16 March 1736, Pozzuoli near Naples). Opera composer of meteoric fame who mixed contemporary Italian secular styles with elements of *stile antico* in two **masses,** eight **psalms** and **canticles,** and the *Stabat Mater* (1736) for solo soprano, solo alto, and strings, his most famous sacred work.

PEROTINUS (PEROTIN, fl. c. 1200, Paris). Composer of **discant** style **organum** and **conductus,** one of two composers, along with

Leoninus, named by an anonymous source as associated with the cathedral of Notre Dame in Paris. This source credits Perotinus with compiling, revising, and improving the *Magnus Liber Organi*, an important source of early Christian **polyphony**.

PERSICHETTI, VINCENT (6 June 1915, Philadelphia–14 August 1987, Philadelphia). Known chiefly for his abstract **instrumental** concert works, he also compiled and composed *Hymns* and *Responses for the Church Year* (Vol. I, 1955; Vol. II, 1987) with texts both modern and traditional, a **Magnificat** and **Nunc Dimittis** (1940), one **mass** (1960), a **Te Deum** (1963), a *Stabat mater* (1963), and a few settings of other Biblical texts.

PETER, JOHANN FRIEDRICH (19 May 1746, Heerendijk, the Netherlands–13 July 1813, Bethlehem, Pa.). Composer of the earliest chamber music in America, he also composed 105 concerted **anthems** for Moravian congregations, reputed to be among the best sacred compositions in America of their time.

PETERSON, JOHN WILLARD (1 November 1921, Lindsborg, Kan.). Composer of over 1,000 **gospel songs**, he also developed a type of church **cantata** in gospel idiom: *Night of Miracles, Born a King, No Greater Love, Carol of Christmas, Easter Song, Jesus Is Coming, King of Kings,* and *Down From His Glory* have become standard repertory in churches using gospel music.

PETRUCCI, OTTAVIANO DEI (18 June 1466, Fossombrone, Italy–7 May 1539, Venice). He received a privilege on 25 May 1498 for a method of printing polyphonic music, and became the first to print such sacred music in 1502, beginning with masses of Josquin Desprez and Antoine Brumel, followed by two volumes of motets.

PEYOTE SONGS. Principal sacred music of the Native American Church, which is the 20th-century descendant of an ancient religious cult of central Mexico associated with the practice of chewing the peyote cactus for hallucinogenic effect. The modern church has Christian themes and has supplanted older religious traditions and songs in many tribes in North America.

The songs are **monophonic**, as are virtually all songs of North American Indians, and frequently build phrases from a single rhythmic motive. The fast singing style seems distinct from most other known Indian singing. The syllables sung, while standardized, make no language and each tribe believes them to have come from some other. Accompaniment is provided by gourd rattles and a special water-filled **drum**.

PICANDER. *See* ST. MATTHEW PASSION.

PINKHAM, DANIEL (5 June 1923, Lynn, Mass.). After studying composition with Walter Piston, Paul Hindemith, **Arthur Honegger**, Nadia Boulanger, harpsichord with Wanda Landowska, and **organ** with E. Power Biggs, he became music director at King's Chapel in Boston in 1958 and joined the faculty at the New England Conservatory in 1959. He has composed many sacred works for choir with various accompaniments, including **psalms**, four **cantatas**, a **Requiem** (1963), a *Stabat mater* (1964), the *St. Mark Passion* (1965), and a sacred **opera** *The Passion of Judas* (1976). He has also composed many works for organ solo and organ with **instruments** obbligato.

PIPE ORGAN. Principal **instrument** of many Christian traditions. How an instrument associated with outdoor political and secular festivals of ancient **Rome** became the sole instrument allowed inside Christian churches by the 13th century remains mysterious, as does its liturgical function in the Middle Ages. Traditions associating organs with St. Cecilia date from the fifth century; the 15th-century historian Platina credits Pope Vitalian (ruled 657–672) with introducing it into the church; Patristic commentaries on the **psalms** may have promoted it (Psalm 150, Vulgate: *laudate eum in chordis et organo.* In any case, its privileged position in the Church encouraged a technical evolution that made it the most sophisticated of all machines by the 18th century and simultaneously cultivated the richest by far of all sacred instrumental repertories in the West.

The organ has three essential components: pipes, which sit upon a container of pressurized air ("windchest," supplied by a bellows), which is connected to a lever system or keyboard. The organ produces tones when the player depresses a key on the keyboard, which then opens one (or more) valve at the bass of a pipe(s), allowing the pressurized air to vibrate the column of air within the pipe(s). The number and arrangement of these components in each organ is unique. Organ building recognizes the particular needs of each church as well as national traditions and terminologies that have developed through history.

Most pipe organs found in churches today comprise three or four quite separate sets of pipes, windchests, and keyboards. Each of these *divisions* may be played alone or in combination with the others. The keyboards (manuals) are terraced together to allow simultaneous playing of the divisions, but the division pipes themselves may be separated widely in the church. (One division is played by the feet on a pedalboard below the manuals.) The English-language names for divisions are: *great*, the main division that characterizes the entire organ; *positive* or *choir*, containing lighter sounding (flute) pipes; *swell*, enclosed within a shuttercase that opens and closes during playing to regulate volume; and *pedal*, which has the largest pipes and therefore lowest pitches, the bass section of the organ.

Each division normally contains several (or many) *ranks*, sets of similarly constructed and therefore similarly sounding pipes. Ranks have one pipe for each key on that division's keyboard. The player activates a rank by pulling a *stop* near the manuals. The player may pull any combination of stops (**registration**) in the division, thus allowing a great variety of timbre from each division. *Couplers* combine ranks from separate divisions onto a single keyboard, creating even greater timbral possibilities.

Each rank's timbre is determined by the construction of its pipes. The two basic types are open cylinders (flues) and pipes fitted with flappers (reeds). Timbre may be further controlled by the pipe's diameter to length ratio (*scale*), its material (type of metal, or wood), and by tapering or closing the pipe.

Each pipe's pitch is determined by its length. The pitch range of a whole rank or stop is indicated by the length of its longest pipe. The standard is 8' ("eight foot"), the approximate length of the pipe producing C^2. All 8' stops produce their notes at concert pitch; 4' stops sound one octave higher, 2' two octaves, etc.; 16' stops sound one octave lower, 32' two octaves. *Mutation stops*, used to affect the timbre of other stops, include non-octave partials: a 2 2/3′ stop sounds one octave and a perfect fifth above concert pitch.

Evidence for instruments combining pipes, windchests, and key-boards dates from the third century B. C. One type, the *hydraulis*, controlled wind pressure with a reservoir of water. Greeks, Romans, and then Byzantines used organs entirely for secular political events or festivals and as a symbol of power. In 757, the Byzantines sent Pepin of the Franks a gift of such an instrument, and Charlemagne possibly also received one in 812. A Venetian priest named Georgius constructed a *hydraulis* at Aachen, the imperial court, in 826. Tenth-century records show that monasteries at Malmsbury, Ramsey, and Winchester (England) had organs. The *Diversarum Artium Schedule* of one monk Theophilus (fl. 1110–1140) describes some technical features but nothing about liturgical use. Two important later docu-ments tell more about construction: a treatise of Henri Arnaut de Zwolle, written in Dijon between 1436 and 1454, a detailed descrip-tion of several contemporary organs, and Arnolt Schlick's *Spiegel der Orgelmacher und Organisten* (The Mirror of Organmakers and Organists, Mainz, 1511), a manual of construction.

The 16th century saw many new kinds of stops, flutes and reeds being especially important, as well as steady growth in the technol-ogy and organization of divisional organs. From this enormous po-tential for different timbres developed national preferences and types. English organs, for example, had no pedal division until the 19th century, so even **George Frideric Handel**'s concertos could have no pedal part. The late 17th and 18th centuries represent the golden age of organ music and organ building; the technical achievements of Gottfried Silberman, Arp Schnitger, Christian Müller, and many oth-ers remain marvelous today. The 19th century saw the repertory of music become more international, owing especially to the revival of **Johann Sebastian Bach**'s music, and the instruments lost something of their national character as they were modified to play it.

At the same time technical advances made organs ever larger. The French builder Aristide Cavaillé-Coll (1811–1899), known as the creator of the French Romantic organ, perfected pneumatic levers by 1841 and made possible gradual changes of dynamics without arbi-trary changes in timbre by placing the most fundamental pipes in all the divisions and controlling swell boxes with pedals. Experiments with electric action occurred as early as 1826, and the electro-pneumatic action, by which the keyboard activates pipes by completing an electric circuit, was patented in 1868. In the 20th century, other devices became powered by electricity: swell shutters, bellows, couplers, etc. Players at keyboards could be far removed from pipes; while practical in large churches, such devices also removed the subtler aspects of sound production from the player's control. In 1921, Oscar Walcker and Wilibald Gurlitt built the Praetorius-Orgel in Freiburg, Germany according to a description of **Michael Praetorius**, a landmark in the movement to restore some of the building techniques and aesthetic principles of the golden age. Since then, many old organs have been restored, and historical research has motivated the new construction of historic national types of organ.

The privileged position of the pipe organ as the instrument exclusively, if at times tacitly, approved for liturgical use since the Middle Ages has over the centuries built up cultural associations between its characteristic sound and liturgy and thus accorded the organ a robust connotation of the sacred. The practice in recent centuries of permitting other instruments, even supplanting it entirely by the piano, guitar, or other ensembles in modern times, has perhaps weakened this connotation somewhat. Yet the **Second Vatican Council's Constitution on the Sacred Liturgy** (1963) singled out "the pipe organ . . . to be held in high esteem, for it is the traditional musical instrument which . . . powerfully lifts up man's mind to God." (120)

The vast pipe organ repertory grew out of the essential association responsible for this sacred semantic, that is, with liturgical singing. The most obviously liturgical pieces are those in which the organ supports or accompanies liturgical vocal music. A second class of composition uses the organ as a substitute for singing that still ties the instrument intimately to liturgy. In a third class, the organ supplements liturgical singing, at first as an appendage to liturgy, as in a **chorale prelude**, and then apart from it, eventually spawning organ compositions that are not explicitly liturgical, such as **fugues**, and finally to ones not sacred, such as sonatas.

The 11th-century terms for an early polyphonic composition, *organum* (pl. *organa*), and particularly the term for the added voice, *vox organalis*, suggest, but by no means prove, the participation of the pipe organ in medieval liturgical music, since the Latin *organum* has many meanings. In later **polyphony** and **motets**, it is not hard to imagine the organ sustaining the **chant** melody (**cantus firmus**) in long notes beneath a sung florid countermelody, or at least supporting the singer(s) assigned to the cantus firmus, but there is no documentary proof of this. Also possible are the doublings of vocal lines in Renaissance polyphony and the *ex tempore* harmonization of chant. The Baroque sacred vocal repertory of **sacred concertos, sacred symphonies**, *grand motets*, **anthems**, **cantatas**, and **figural masses** explicitly demands the organ as the principal supporting instrument, particularly as **continuo**. The most familiar supporting role of the organ in **congregational** singing developed sporadically in various Protestant churches. **Lutherans** at first sang **chorales** unaccompanied and only gradually introduced harmonized versions played on the organ. The English Puritans and more radical **Calvinists** tried to ban organs altogether in the 16th century, but polyphonic versions of their simple **psalmody** appeared in print by the end of that century, probably intended for organ accompaniment, and some form of **hymn** accompaniment occurs in many Reformed congregations today.

The Faenza Codex (Italy, c. 1400) contains the earliest *alternatim*, by which the organ substitutes for a portion of sung liturgical chant a polyphonic version that is not sung, an organ **verset**. The left hand plays the chant melody as a cantus firmus, while the right accompanies it with a florid **discant**. This practice of replacing a liturgical text by versets peaked in the French and Italian **organ masses** of the late 17th and early 18th centuries. It was banned by Pope Pius X in 1903 but persisted in Roman Catholic liturgies, especially in France, until the reforms of the Second Vatican Council.

A simple practical need of establishing the **mode** and starting pitch for a **schola** or choir seems to have given rise to a number of introductory organ *intonazioni*, **toccatas**, **voluntaries**, and **preludes** early in the 16th century. As such extra-liturgical instrumental works became accepted, it was only natural that the symbolic power of a well-known chant, chorale, or hymn would be harnessed in other kinds of organ music played before, after, and during the service: **ricercar**, chorale prelude, **fantasia**, etc. By the late 17th century, it is possible that **imitative** texture, reminiscent of Renaissance **motets** and masses, alone might justify an abstract fugue in church.

During the proliferation of these organ genres from the 16th through the 18th centuries, the preferences of nations and even fairly small regions—north Germany, central Germany, south Germany, for example—remained quite distinct, often due to sectarian differences as well as the types of organ available. *See also* PORTATIVE; POSITIVE.

PIYYUT (pl. *PIYYUTIM*). Liturgical **hymns** of the Jewish tradition. Originally written to enhance prayers, they eventually became detached as those prayers became more and more the province of the professional *hazan* (**cantor**) by the sixth century.

The classical *piyyut* flourished in Palestine from the sixth to 11th centuries, characterized by isosyllabic, non-rhyming texts based on the Talmud and Midrash. Some authorities, notably Maimonides, protested their introduction into the liturgy. The earliest notated *piyyutim* date from c. 1100. Another branch of *piyyutim* flourished in Spain from the 10th to 14th centuries, heavily influenced by the dominant Arabic culture. Here poets turned to Biblical sources and adopted rhymed and eventually strophic poetry. Some *piyyutim* are **contrafacta** of popular Arabic songs. In general, the melodies are **metric**, except those with strictly Biblical texts, in contrast to the classical *piyyutim*, which are believed to have been **chanted** in the manner of prayers.

Piyyutim may be sung by one or more soloists, by a chorus, or in some combination with the **congregation** contributing brief responses such as "Amen" or **Halleluya**. Traditionally, only men sing, but in modern Western communities women may also perform. *See also LEKHA DODI; PIZMON.*

PIZMON. Specific type of *piyyut* associated with penitential prayers. Strophic, with four lines maximum per stanza, the melodic is **metric**, often traditional, and there is a refrain for **congregational** response.

PLAINCHANT. Unaccompanied, **monophonic** song without **meter**. *See also* CHANT.

PLAINSONG. *See* CHANT; PLAINCHANT.

PLAY OF DANIEL. The name of two **liturgical dramas**. The earlier (12th century) has no music with its text and survives in a manuscript with the name Hilarius.

The later, accompanied by over 50 melodies that appear nowhere else, was composed by students of Beauvais in the 13th century. Concluding with the **hymn** *Nuntium vobis fero*, the single item identified with traditional liturgy, the Play of Daniel is actually a Christmas piece, using the Old Testament prophet of Daniel to prefigure Christ. The play contains a large number of **conductus**.

The play has 15 separate roles and requires about 45 minutes to sing.

PLENARY MASS. A setting of the Roman Catholic **mass** that includes both **ordinary** and proper prayers.

POINTING. *See* ANGLICAN CHANT.

POLYCHORAL MOTET. Motet composed for multiple choirs, or *cori spezzati*.

POLYCHORAL PSALM. Psalm set as a motet for multiple choirs, or *cori spezzati*.

POLYPHONY. The art of combining simultaneous melodies, the hallmark of Western music (excluding the non-melodic drones of some **Byzantine chant** and Hindu music). It is believed that polyphony originated as an improvisation technique, a means of solemnizing a traditional **monophonic** liturgical chant for great feasts. The earliest written evidence of such improvisations, called **organum**, dates from the ninth century. The earliest practical source is the later of the **Winchester tropers** (c. 1050).

For medieval theory, the principal technical problem of polyphony was the syntax of acoustic consonances and dissonances. The perfect octaves, fifths, and fourths were the preferred harmonic intervals; all others were restricted to occasional moments, and cadences were unison.

Such ideals were easily accomplished as long as the simultaneous melodies always moved together, with the added *vox organalis* shadowing the original *vox principalis*. Melodic independence such as contrary motion, whereby the melodies may move in opposite directions at the same time, complicated the matter and likely encouraged writing down the compositions. Some such appear in the second Winchester Troper. The St. Martial repertory, from 12th-century southern France, introduces a much greater complication, rhythmic independence. When the simultaneous melodies move at different speeds, the singers must know how long to hold pitches in order to coordinate the harmonic syntax.

Thus polyphony seems to have driven the invention of the rhythmic modes, the first system of rhythmic notation, based on grouping the notes and associated with the cathedral of Notre Dame and the composers **Leoninus** and **Perotinus** in **Paris** in the late 12th century. Rhythmic modes were replaced at the turn of the 14th century, as composers desired even greater melodic-rhythmic independence, by a system called *Ars Nova* ("the new art") based on the shapes of the notes, in essence the concept behind modern notation.

As centuries passed, polyphonic composition occupied more and more of the attention of the most talented Christian composers, who had comparatively few opportunities to create in the medium of monophonic chant. Roman Catholic authorities generally did not discourage new polyphonic **masses**, **motets**, and other settings of traditional liturgical texts. The more radical of the Protestant reformers, especially **Jean Calvin** and **Huldrych Zwingli**, condemned polyphony as a distracting artifice and insisted on a return to monophonic **psalmody** in the early 16th century. Nevertheless, simple kinds of polyphony had been restored to many reformed congregations by the century's end. Jewish music began to incorporate polyphony in the 17th century, as did the Russian Orthodox Church. In modern times, all serious composers of Western sacred music compose polyphony. *See also ZNAMENNĪY RASPEV.*

POPE MARCELLUS MASS. *See MISSA PAPAE MARCELLI.*

PORTATIVE. Easily portable **pipe organ**. The bellows is operated by the left hand and the keyboard by the right. Its depiction in medieval art suggests a role in sacred music, but there is no other documentary proof.

POSITIVE. A movable, independent **pipe organ**, but more substantial than a **portative**. Also, one of the divisions of a large pipe organ.

POSTLUDE. Organ composition to be played directly following a Christian church service.

POTHIER, DOM JOSEPH. *See* GREGORIAN CHANT.

POULENC, FRANCIS (7 January 1899, Paris–30 January 1963, Paris). A composer of diverse genera, he frequented intellectual circles of Paris beginning in the First World War, and was a member of *Les Six*, a group of composers that included **Darius Milhaud** and **Arthur Honegger**. He began to compose Roman Catholic sacred music regularly from 1936, including *Litanies* à la Vierge Noire, composed in the week following a visit to Notre Dame de Rocamadour in 1936, a **mass** (1938) and 15 **motets** for unaccompanied choir, a *Stabat mater* (1951), and a **Gloria** (1960).

POWER, LEONEL (c. 1375, Kent?, England–5 June 1445, Canterbury). Credited, along with **John Dunstable**, with the earliest **cantus firmus mass**, the *Missa Alma Redemptoris Mater* (c. 1420s–1430s), although the attribution is not certain. He was admitted to the fraternity of Christ Church in Canterbury on 14 May 1423. He composed three cyclic **masses**, four other pairs of mass **ordinaries**, 19 single mass movements, and about 16 **motets** and other sacred Latin settings, although there are many other works of disputed authorship that may be his. *See also* OLD HALL MANUSCRIPT.

PRAETORIUS (SCHULTHEISS), MICHAEL (15 February ? 1571, Creuzburg an der Werra near Eisenach, Germany–15 February 1621, Wolfenbüttel). Appointed **organist** to Duke Heinrich Julius of Brunswick-Wolfenbüttel in 1595, and court *Kapellmeister* in 1604. Except for the years 1613–1617 spent in Dresden serving the Elector Johann Georg, Praetorius remained in Wolfenbüttel until his death.

He composed over 1,000 sacred works, mostly based on **Lutheran chorales** or setting the Latin prayers of the Lutheran **mass**. Many of his settings are in common use today. In the first phase of composition, he published *Motectae et Psalmi* (1602), Latin **motets** that explored the *stile antico*. Next he systematically compiled and arranged all the Lutheran chorales required for the liturgical year in the nine-part *Musae Sionae* (1605–1610). He included **hymns** arranged for two to four choirs in *Urania* (1613), and **canons** are prominent in *Hymnodia Sionae* (1611), which also includes four **organ** pieces with **cantus firmus**. Last, he exploited the **operatic** elements newly imported from Italy in *Polyhymnia Caduceatrix* (1619). *See also CORI SPEZZATI*.

PRAISE CHORUS. American **congregational** songs first noted in the 1940s rooted in the Pentecostal and charismatic movements, characterized by simple periodic melodies and refrains and very slow harmonic rhythms suitable for guitar accompaniment. In recent decades, a "praise band" composed of piano, **drum** set, synthesizers, sequencers, and various melodic **instruments** may accompany praise songs in large churches, varying the orchestration from song to song. *See also* GAITHER, WILLIAM J.; GOSPEL SONG.

PRELUDE (PRELUDIO, PREAMBULUM). **Organ** composition to be played directly before the beginning of a Christian church service. If based upon a traditional liturgical melody, the piece might be more specifically termed **chorale prelude**, **ricercar**, **fantasia**, or **voluntary**, and give the tune's name. *See also* CANZONA.

The term also refers to the first of two paired movements of a composition, usually for organ, e.g., "Prelude and **Fugue** in a minor."

PROPER. Refers to those prayers that proclaim and reflect upon the feast of the day, e.g., **Introit**. *See also* DIVINE LITURGY; DIVINE OFFICE; HOLY COMMUNION; MASS; ORDINARY.

PROSA. See SEQUENCE; TROPE.

PROSULA. See SEQUENCE; TROPE.

PROULX, RICHARD (3 April 1937, St. Paul, Minn.). **Organist** and music director at the Cathedral of the Holy Name in Chicago, he contributed to and consulted for *The **Hymnal** 1982*, *New Yale Hymnal*,

Methodist Hymnal, Worship II & III, the *Mennonite Hymnal* and the *Presbyterian Hymnal*. He has composed 13 **masses**, many mass movements, and over 135 other sacred choral works as well as 30 pieces for **organ**.

PSALM. Poetic prayer, one of 150 contained in the Old Testament Book of Psalms. "Psalm" comes from the Greek *psallein*, "to sing accompanied"; the Hebrew name for the book is *Tehillim*, "praises." King David of Israel, says tradition, composed most of the poems and assembled the book; the Levites provided the singing and the music for them. Psalms are treasured by both Jews and Christians and occupy central places in their liturgical traditions.

Numeration of the psalms differs slightly among the traditions. The most common systems are shown in the table on p. 181.

PSALM MOTET. A **motet** whose text is a **psalm**.

PSALMODY. The practice of singing the **psalms**, greatly varied among the many Jewish and Christian traditions. Strictly speaking, the term would encompass many musical settings of partial psalm texts designated otherwise: **hymns**, **motets**, **anthems**, and **propers** of Eucharistic liturgies and the **divine offices** that contain single verses of psalms within larger structures. **Byzantine** rite churches rarely sing entire psalms, but combine parts of them with other sacred texts, *troparia*. More commonly "psalmody" refers to the sing-

Hebrew, Masoretic, and English Bible	Septuagint, Vulgate (Latin)
1–8	1–8
9, 10	9
11–113	10–112
114, 115	113
116 vv.1–9	114
116 vv.10–19	115
117–146	116–145
147 vv.1–11	146
147 vv.12–29	147
148–150	148–150

ing of complete psalms, which may be categorized broadly into **chanted** psalms (without **meter**) and **metrical psalms**.

In the Jewish Temple, professional singers, the Levites, chanted psalms to **instrumental** accompaniment. In synagogues, the music seems to have been simpler, and in any case instruments were banned after the destruction of the Temple in A. D. 70. In the course of morning, afternoon, and evening services, 50 psalms would be chanted each day. The Talmud implies three methods of chanting psalms: direct, in which each verse is sung by the soloist or choir without differentiation; **responsorial**, which alternates the **cantor** with the choir; and **antiphonal**, which alternates halves of the choir. Certain responsorial practices indicated in Talmudic literature might facilitate **congregational** participation: the repetition of each verse after the soloist, known as **lining out** when used in English-speaking Protestant communities in the 17th century; singing "**Hallelujah**" after each verse; the use of a congregational refrain from the first verse, or from an external text. This last method is reported also by **St. Augustine** among Christian congregations and has been revived for modern Roman Catholic **masses** since 1970. This responsorial psalm occurs between the first two Scripture readings, replacing the Gradual of the old rite.

Christian monastics also made psalmody central in liturgy. The Rule of **St. Benedict** prescribed the singing of the entire Psalter (150 psalms) each week through the eight daily liturgies of the **divine office**. In the **Gregorian** tradition, each psalm is preceded by a proper **antiphon** whose text refers to the feast or saint commemorated on that day and whose musical **mode** determines the specific **psalm tone** for the psalmody. At the psalm's conclusion, the **minor doxology** is sung to the same tone, thus further Christianizing the Old Testament psalm, and then the antiphon is repeated.

Chanted psalmody is nearly always **monophonic** since a simultaneity of independent melodies would require measured durations of notes, therefore converting the chanted psalm into a metrical psalm. An exception occurs in **Claudio Monteverdi**'s **Vespers of 1610**, in which a choir chants certain sub-phrases of Psalm 110 in harmony of up to five voices before ending the phrase in measured time. A similar, though much simpler, technique may be heard in **Anglican chant**. In modern Catholic liturgies, the antiphons are usually metric and harmonized with functional harmony in order to facilitate quick learning by the congregation. *See also* BYZANTINE CHANT; CANTICLE; GALLICAN CHANT; *KATISMA;* NINE CANTICLES; RESPONSORY; *STICHERON;* SYRIAN CHANT.

PSALM TONE. Melodic formula for **chanting** a **psalm**. In the **Gregorian** tradition, each psalm verse is split into halves (see figure 5).

The psalm begins with a rising melodic figure, the *intonation*, and then settles on a reciting tone, or *tenor*, on which is sung as many syllables as necessary to reach the end of the first half, when a cadential figure, the *mediant*, is sung. The second half begins immediately on the same tenor, again prolonging it to accommodate all the remaining syllables in the verse except those for the final cadence, the *termination*. (The *tonus peregrinus* uses a different pitch for the tenor of the second half.) Subsequent verses of the psalm are sung in the same way, except that the intonation is omitted after the first verse. Verses with many words may have an extra cadence, or *flex*, within the first half verse. Optional notes in the cadential figures are used to ensure that the textual accent falls in the right place.

The psalm itself is introduced and followed by the appropriate **antiphon**. The antiphon determines the **mode** being sung, usually by the range of its melody and the pitch of its last note. The mode then determines which of the many psalm tones will be used to sing the psalm text. The particular melodies of the intonation, the cadences, flex, and the pitch of the reciting tone are all determined, therefore, by the psalm tone and indirectly by the mode of the antiphon. Terminations may vary even within a single mode, in order to smooth the transition to the concluding antiphon. *See* ANTIPHON; BYZANTINE CHANT; DIVINE OFFICE; *OKTOĒCHOS.*

PSALTER. *See* PSALM.

Figure 5. A typical Latin plainchant psalm tone in mode 1.

PSALTIKON. Liturgical book of **Byzantine chant** compiled for the soloist as contrasted with the choir's *asmatikon.* **Responsorial** chants divided between soloist and choir will likewise be divided between the books; both are required for a complete performance. The *psaltikon* has **melismatic** chants quite distinct from those of the *asmatikon.* The earliest copies date from the 13th or 14th centuries. They contain *prokeimena* for both the **divine liturgy** and **divine office**, the verses for *troparia* and **Alleluias**, the *hypakoai, kontakia* for the liturgical year, and sometimes the complete *Akathistos* **Hymn.**

PURANDA DASA. *See KIRTANA.*

PURCELL, HENRY (10 September 1659?, London?–21 November 1695, London). Composer of 56 masterly **verse anthems**, 18 **full anthems** (all before 1682), four Latin **psalms**, 34 other sacred songs, a morning and evening **service**, and a few works for **organ**, he succeeded Matthew Locke (c. 1621–1677) as composer-in-ordinary for the violins at Westminster Abbey in 1677 and then **John Blow** as **organist** in 1679. He was appointed organist at the **Chapel Royal** in 1682. His sacred music fully assimilates the Italian and French Baroque influences, and Purcell is an acknowledged master of setting English text.

– Q –

QALA. Type of **hymn** sung **antiphonally** between complete **psalms** or psalm verses in the **Syrian divine office**. The earliest Syrian sources are ninth century. The musical form, *AABBCC . . .*, may include up to 50 strophes, may be truncated or extended according to circumstance, and the *qala* ends with an **Alleluia**. *See also* SYRIAN CHANT.

QAWWALI. Song setting Islamic mystical poetry in Farsi, Hindi, or Urdu. The *Qawwali* song begins with an improvisatory **prelude** played on a **harmonium**, followed by an introductory verse sung by a professional soloist (*qawwal*), which gives way to the song proper, a strophic setting of the poem alternating the soloist(s) with an entire chorus of *qawwals*, all accompanied by a barrel-shaped **drum**, the *dholak*. The drumming suggests the repetition of God's name and the whole ensemble is intended to arouse the mystical love and divine ecstasy that is the Sufi experience.

Some *qawalli* melodies are heard wherever the ritual is enacted in Persian and South Asian shrines. Others are restricted to particular shrines or rituals. Others may be composed by the *qawwals* who sing them. *See also DHIKR; SAMA; TA'ZIYE.*

QĪRA'A. **Cantillation** of the Qur'ān by a *qāri* (**cantor**), one of the two forms of compulsory mosque music. The language is Arabic. It may be done by a layperson in plain style (*muratta*), usually for private devotion, or in an embellished, learned style (*mujawwad*) by a highly trained professional, usually at a public event. *See also 'ADHĀN; QIRĀ'A BI'L-ALHĀ; TAJWĪD.*

QIRĀ'A BI'L-ALHĀN. **Chanting** of the Qur'ān to popular melodies, especially widespread from the ninth to the 12th centuries in the Arabic-speaking world and condemned by juridical understandings of Islam.

QIR'AT. Indo-Muslim liturgical music, sung in Arabic, including Koranic and liturgical texts.

– R –

RACHMANINOFF, SERGEI (1 April 1873, Oneg, Russia–28 March 1943, Beverly Hills, Ca.). *See* VESPERS (ALL-NIGHT VIGIL).

RĀGA. The manner of pitch organization, analogous with **mode** in Western music, in Indian classical music, both Hindstani and Karnatic, and also simpler Hindu songs (***bhajan, kirtana, kriti***). There are many hundreds of *rāgas*, some famous and easily recognized by knowledgeable listeners, other obscure, some ancient, others brand new. A particular *rāga* connotes a set of pitches to be used as a source of improvisation, but it equally connotes melodic patterns and characteristic ornamentations. *Rāgas* often have strong semantic associations with time of day, season, mood, and history or origin. *See also TĀLA.*

RAMEAU, JEAN-PHILIPPE (baptized 25 September 1683, Dijon, France–12 September 1764, Paris). Renowned for his harpsichord pieces and **operas**, and for his revolutionary theory of harmony, he was **organist** at churches in Clermont, Dijon, and Paris at various times from 1702 and contributed four *grands motets* to the sacred repertory.

RAMIREZ, ARIEL (4 September 1921, Santa Fe, Argentina). *See MISA CRIOLLA.*

RANK. *See* PIPE ORGAN.

READ, DANIEL (16 November 1757, Attleborough, Mass.–4 December 1836, New Haven, Conn.). Influential composer and publisher of American **psalmody**, including his own *The American Singing Book* (1875), source for many subsequent tunebooks. *See also* BILLINGS, WILLIAM.

RECITATIVE. Operatic composition originating in the late 16th century for solo singer harmonized by **instrumental** accompaniment with virtually no **meter** and whose speech rhythms and phrase structure are determined entirely by the text. Recitative allows characters in a music drama to exchange dialogue rapidly, to convey plot information efficiently, and to express mercurial changes of emotion. In sacred music, it retains these functions in **oratorios** and **passions**. In church **cantatas**, they may link concerted movements. *See also* ARIA; CONTINUO.

REDA, SIEGFRIED. *See* BORNEFELD, HELMUT.

REGALS. Table-top **organ** that produces tones by forcing air from attached bellows over one or more sets of beating metal tongues (reeds). Documentary evidence for regals dates from 1511. Used mostly for secular music, it was occasionally heard in north German churches in the 17th and 18th centuries. *See also* HARMONIUM; PIPE ORGAN.

REGER, MAX (19 March 1873, Brand near Bayreuth, Germany–11 May 1916, Leipzig). Known for his many chamber pieces, Reger, spurred perhaps by his friendship with **Arnold Mendelssohn**, also composed practical liturgical works for chorus, of which his **Psalm** 100 (1909, op. 106) is his best known, and about 30 publications for **organ** containing over 190 pieces, many based on **chorales** and most exploiting Baroque forms such as **fugue**. Some are intended for moderately skilled players, while others require a virtuoso **organist**.

REGINA COELI LAETARE. See VOTIVE ANTIPHON.

REGISTRATION. The selection of ranks on an **organ** that will sound for a particular composition. Before 1700 composers, with the exception of the French, rarely left specific registration instructions for their organ compositions, although there is a good deal of advice from theorists and organ builders as to the best combinations. Players therefore determine the timbre when they perform these works.

REPROACHES. Chant sung during the Veneration of the Cross at the liturgy for Good Friday in the Roman Catholic rite. The refrain, sung to a **Mode** 1 melody, is: *Popule meus, quid feci tibi? aut in quo contristavi te? responde mihi.* ("My people, what have I done to you? How have I ever grieved you? Answer me.")

In the greater Reproaches this refrain is interwoven with texts recalling events of divine salvation, and the whole is alternated with the *Trisagion*.

In the lesser Reproaches the refrain is alternated simply with paired statements chanted as a **psalm tone**, each pair contrasting an instance of God's kindness with man's perfidy.

REQUIEM. A setting of the Roman Catholic **mass** for the dead including both **ordinary** and **proper** prayers. The name is taken from the first piece sung in a traditional liturgy, the Introit *Requiem aeternam dona eis, Domine* ("Eternal rest grant to them, O Lord"). It could be sung on All Souls Day, November 2, and on the day of someone's burial as well as on funeral anniversaries and certain other commemorations.

The texts for a Requiem mass include:

Introit—*Requiem aeternam*
Kyrie
Gradual—*Requiem aeternam*
Tract—*Absolve, Domine*
Sequence—*Dies irae, dies illa*
Offertory—*Domine Jesu Christe*
Sanctus-Benedictus
Agnus Dei (altered)
Communion—*Lux aeterna luceat eis*

On solemn occasions the following could be sung during the committal rites:

Responsory—*Libera me, Domine*
Antiphon—*In Paradisum*

The will of **Guillaume Du Fay** (1474) requests that his Requiem be sung on the day after his funeral, but the work does not survive. The earliest extant **polyphonic** setting (late 15th century) is by **Johannes Ockeghem**, which sets only the Introit, Kyrie, and the alternative Gradual (*Si ambulem in medio umbrae mortis*) and Tract (*Sicut cervus*) allowed before the **Council of Trent**. In all, 41 Requiems composed before 1600 survive, including two by **Orlandus Lassus**, two by **Tomas Luis de Victoria**, and one by **Giovanni da Palestrina**. They show considerable variety in which texts were set polyphonically and which were **chanted**, and in general they are conservative in comparison to contemporary polyphonic mass ordinaries: no **parody** technique, little **imitative** texture, and a great reliance on **cantus firmus**.

After 1600, Requiem masses often adapted **operatic** and other secular idioms, as did other sacred genres. Often they were composed for specific commissions or occasions, as was **Giuseppe Verdi**'s **Requiem** (1874) for the great Italian writer Alessandro Manzoni (1785–1873). That work, like many others of the 19th and 20th centuries, calls for very large chorus, soloists, and symphony orchestra, making regular liturgical usage impossible. These works live on in the concert repertory of choral societies. Some of the most famous are the Requiems of **Wolfgang Amadeus Mozart** (1791), **Luigi Cherubini** (C minor, 1817), **Hector Berlioz** (1837), **Franz Liszt** (1867–1871), **Gabriel Fauré** (performed 1894), **Antonin Dvorák** (1890), and **Maurice Duruflé** (1947). *See also* GERMAN REQUIEM; *WAR REQUIEM.*

REQUIEM, HECTOR BERLIOZ, Op. 5. Composed to commemorate those killed in an attempt to assassinate French King Louis-Philippe on 28 July 1835, **Hector Berlioz'** *Grande Messe des Morts,* dated 29 June 1837, did not see its first performance, owing to a lapse of funding, until 5 December at *Les Invalides* to commemorate instead Count Charles of Demrémont. A patriotic more than liturgical work, the **Requiem** is famous for its "Tuba mirum" chorus from the *Dies Irae* **sequence,** scored for four brass choirs, four bass **drums,** 10 pairs of cymbals, and 16 timpani that accompany the symphony orchestra of more than 120. Berlioz' score calls for a six-voiced chorus of 210 and a tenor soloist. It requires about 85 minutes to perform.

REQUIEM, GABRIEL FAURÉ, Op. 48. Composed over a period of years beginning in late 1887, without commission, and first performed in concert on 17 May 1894, **Gabriel Fauré** scored his **Requiem** for soprano and baritone soloists, four-voiced chorus, and chamber orchestra including **organ** and harp, giving it a more intimate and traditionally sacred sound than many 19th-century sacred pieces. The violins play in unison while violas and cellos are *divisi,* creating a darker than usual timbre. At the request of his publisher he completed an arrangement for symphony orchestra in 1901. The choral parts are not difficult to learn, and the piece requires about 35 minutes to perform.

REQUIEM, WOLFGANG AMADEUS MOZART, K. 626. Composed in 1791 on a commission from a Count Walsegg and left unfinished, Wolfgang Amadeus Mozart's **Requiem mass** is certainly the most famous setting of the 18th century and a favorite concert work for chorus. It is scored for four soloists (soprano, alto, tenor, bass), four-voiced chorus, and symphony orchestra, and requires something under one hour to perform.

Mozart's autograph score gives us only a fully orchestrated **Introit** and vocal score with figured bass and indications of orchestration for the Kyrie and some parts of the **sequence**. Contributions to the score after his death were made by two of Mozart's students, Joseph Eybler (1765–1846), who orchestrated some movements, and Franz Xaver Süssmayr (1766–1803), who seems to have composed the Sanctus-Benedictus and filled out the rest. How much each man followed Mozart's instructions, if any existed, exactly what was written by each, as well as the merits of such contributions have long been controverted, and there are competing editions, although the Süssmayr completion published by Breitkopf and Härtel is the one traditionally performed.

REQUIEM (*Messa da Requiem*), **GIUSEPPE VERDI.** Composed as a personal tribute to the revered Italian writer Alessandro Manzoni (1785–1873), it premiered on the anniversary of his death, 22 May 1874, at the church of St. Mark's in Milan with **Giuseppe Verdi** himself conducting four soloists (soprano, alto, tenor, bass), a four-voiced chorus of 120 singers (subdivided into eight voices for the Sanctus), and an orchestra of 100 players including four horns, four trumpets, three trombones, an ophicleide, winds, percussion, and strings. A resounding success, the work immediately entered the choral concert repertory. Its performance forces and length (about 90 minutes) make it impractical for liturgy.

RESPOND. That part of a **responsory** sung by the choir. Also, any short choral response to a reading or prayer.

RESPONSORIAL. Method of **chanting** a **psalm**, by which a soloist (**cantor**) sings the opening verse, a choir sings the next verse, and so on in alternation. Other kinds of chant, notably **responsories**, may be performed responsorially. In such cases, the choir sings the framing **respond** and the cantor the verse(s).

RESPONSORY. This category of **chant** was first defined by Isidore of Seville (c. 559–636): "Responsories are so called because a chorus responds in consonance to a soloist" (New Grove, 15: 759). Responsories were sung especially at **matins**, where they take on a particularly luxurious form known as the great responsory, but also at **vespers** and at **mass** in the **Alleluia**. The simplest form is in three parts: the **respond** sung by the choir, the **psalm** verse sung by the **cantor**, and the *repetendum*, the last segment of the original respond, sung by the choir.

Reponsories are outnumbered in the repertory of Latin chant only by **antiphons**. The earliest source, the Hartker Antiphoner (c. 1000), contains 600 of them; the Worcester Antiphoner (13th century) almost 1,000. Responsories hold a proud place in the history of early **polyphony**, including settings in the *Magnus Liber Organi* (c. 1170).

Some scholars believe that responsories were originally simple, perhaps sung by the **congregation**, in alternation with an entire **psalm**. As the trained choir took over the singing, the responds became musically elaborate, and the psalm was reduced to a single verse. In the new Roman Catholic liturgy of 1969, the "**responsorial** psalm" approximates the supposed ancient practice.

RHAW, GEORG (1488, Eisfeld an der Were, Suhl, Thuringia, Germany–6 August 1548, Wittenberg). Musician and theorist, from 1518 to 1520 he was **cantor** at St. Thomas Church, preceding **Johann Sebastian Bach**, and also taught at the university in Leipzig. In 1523, he moved to Wittenberg and established that city as the publishing center for theological and musical documents of the newborn **Lutheran** reform, including an expanded edition of **Johann Walther**'s *Wittenberger Geystliches Gesangk Buchleyn* (1544).

RHEINBERGER, JOSEPH (17 March 1839, Vaduz, Liechtenstein-25 November 1901, Munich). Superb **organist** and influential teacher at the Munich Conservatory since 1859, he also completed 12 **masses** for various vocal combinations, mostly with **organ** accompaniment, a *Stabat Mater*, a **Requiem**, several **cantatas**, and 20 organ sonatas. Although circulated mostly among Roman Catholic churches, Rheinberger's sacred music is independent of the **Cecilian movement**'s influence.

RICERCAR (pl. It. *ricercari*). Keyboard composition that, when intended for **organ**, might have been used as a **prelude** or **verset** in Christian liturgies in Italy and German-speaking countries. One of the earliest important collections, Marc'Antonio Cavazzoni's (c. 1490–c. 1560) *Recerchari, motetti, canzoni* . . . (1523) contains two ricercars of improvisatory character. The term **toccata** replaced this type in the 17th century. Another type based on strict **imitation** appears in Girolamo Cavazzoni's (c. 1525–after 1577, son of Marc'Antonio) 1543 collection *Intavolatura cioe recercari* . . . and became the basis for the keyboard **fugue**. The master of the form is generally acknowledged to be **Girolamo Frescobaldi**, particularly in *Recercari et canzoni* (1615) and *Fiori musicali* (1635).

RIO DE JANIERO. *See* GARCIA, JOSÉ MAURICIO NUNES.

ROMANUS (ST.) (late fourth c., Emesa–c. 555, Constantinople). Believed by **Byzantine** hagiographers to be the originator of the *kontakion* **hymn** form, crediting him with 1,000 texts, although less than 100 have been authenticated.

ROME. The **Schola Cantorum** of the Lateran, the oldest Christian musical institution in Rome, has been traditionally attributed to Pope **St. Gregory the Great** (ruled 590–604) but possibly dates from the fourth century. Singers there received an excellent general education and musical training, and the Schola inspired a similar school at the Vatican and the ninth-century Carolingian effort to standardize liturgical **chant** in the empire.

When the papacy transferred to Avignon (1309–1377) the Schola vanished, but it was restored by Pope Eugene IV in 1443 and increased to 24 singers by Pope Sixtus IV (ruled 1471–1784). Eventually, the Vatican had two choirs: a new training choir founded by Pope Julius II, the *Cappella Giulia*, and the principal papal choir, now called the *Capella Sistina*. Other major basilicas in Rome established permanent choirs in the early 16th century, coincident with the golden age of Renaissance sacred **polyphony** associated with **Giovanni da Palestrina**.

The city also heard a great deal of popular religious music, including the *laude* of religious confraternities, *rappresentazioni* of the

passion story, and the earliest **oratorios** early in the 17th century at the churches of San Girolamo della Carità, Santa Maria in Vallicella, and the Oratorio del Crocifisso.

Thereafter, music of the theater and the secular world occupied the most talented composers, and the art of sacred music declined. The *Pontificio Istituto di Musica* was established by Pope Pius X in 1911 as part of his campaign to restore the ancient qualities of Roman Catholic sacred music. Despite this good intention, compositions and performance practices growing out of the **Cecilian movement**, such as accompanying **Gregorian chant** with 19th-century functional harmonies, have kept the papal choir from the front ranks of the world's sacred choirs.

ROSSI, SALOMONE (19 August 1570, Mantua–c. 1640, Mantua). Composer who first set ancient Jewish liturgical texts to **operatic** idioms. His collection *Ha-Shirim Asher Li'Shlomo* (1622) contains 33 works composed in the manner of Italian madrigals for three to eight voices. Attacked by orthodox Jews, they nevertheless encouraged many imitators in Italy, France, and the Netherlands.

RUBBRA, EDMUND (23 May 1901, Northampton, England–13 February 1986, Gerard's Cross). A Roman Catholic, he composed about 15 Latin **motets** and a dozen **anthems**, four **masses**, three **canticles**, and smaller works, both with and without **instruments**, many in a neo-medieval idiom.

RUSSIAN GREEK CHANT. Russian Orthodox **chant** of uncertain origins, dating from the 17th century and characterized by periodic phrases and strong **meter**, unusual for religious chants. *See also* KIEVAN CHANT; *ZNAMENNĪY RASPEV*.

RUTTER, JOHN (24 September 1945, London). Composer, conductor, and editor of choral music, he wrote a **Requiem** (1985), a **Gloria** (1974), and a **Magnificat** (1990), all for orchestra, soloists, and choir, now well-known in the United Kingdom and the United States, as well as some smaller scale **psalms** and **canticles**.

– S –

SACRED CONCERTO. A setting of a Christian text, usually Biblical, for voices and **instruments**, dating from the late 16th to mid-17th centuries in Italy and German-speaking lands. The earliest publication, which also contains secular works, is *Concerti di **Andrea**, et di **Gio**. **Gabrieli** (**Venice**, 1587).* Seventeenth-century collections adopted the textures and techniques of Italian **opera**, the sacred concertos of **Heinrich Schütz** (also called *Symphoniae Sacrae)* being among the greatest exemplars. The use of sacred concertos in worship would have paralleled that of **motets**. *See also CENTO CONCERTI ECCLESIASTICI;* DU MONTE, HENRI; MONTEVERDI, CLAUDIO; RECITATIVE; SACRED SYMPHONY; SCHEIN, JOHANN HERMANN.

SACRED HARP. Compiled by Benjamin Franklin White (1800–1879) and published in Hamilton, Georgia, and Philadelphia in 1844, the most famous and widely used of the "shape-note" tune books. Shape-notes help singers find the pitch of printed notes by employing four differently shaped noteheads to indicate the solmization syllable of the tetrachord (mi-fa-sol-la). The system originated in Philadelphia in 1801 and versions of it spread to the rural south and midwestern United States. *Sacred Harp* was revised in 1911, 1936, and 1991. It is still used today. *See also* BILLINGS, WILLIAM; GOSPEL SONG; HYMN; SPIRITUAL.

SACRED SYMPHONY (*Symphonia sacra***).** Term used synonymously with but less frequently than **sacred concerto** in early 17th century Italy and Germany. An important early collection is the 1597 *Sacrae Symphoniae* of **Giovanni Gabrieli**.

SAINT-SAËNS, (CHARLES) CAMILLE (9 October 1835, Paris–16 December 1921, Algiers). While known mostly for secular concert repertory, Saint-Saëns was a superb **organist** and held positions at various Paris churches from 1853–1876 and from 1861–1865 taught at the École Niedermeyer, founded to improve music in French churches. He contributed 13 publications of **organ** music, two **masses**, three **oratorios** in the **Handelian** tradition (*Oratorio de*

Noël, 1858; *Le Déluge* ("The Flood"), 1875; *The Promised Land*, 1913), two dozen **motets**, another 10 small works for chorus, and one sacred **opera**, *Samson et Dalila* (1877), which remains in the repertory.

SALAWATAN. A common form of Islamic devotional song found in Indonesia, performed by groups of men or women (not mixed) who may dance while sitting, kneeling, or standing as they sing, especially if **drums** provide accompaniment. Also known as *hadrah*, *rodat* in Java, *dikie rabano* in Sumatra, and *butabuh* in Lampung. *rabano* in Sumatra, and *butabuh* in Lampung.

SALVE REGINA. *See* VOTIVE ANTIPHON.

SAMA. In Islamic mysticism (Sufism), the ritual act of listening to music or dance, through which the listener hopes to achieve an ecstatic spiritual experience. *See also DHIKR; QAWWALI; TA'ZIYE.*

SĀMAVEDIC CHANT (Sans. "song of wisdom"). Singing of one of the four collections of ancient Hindu Vedic texts: the *Rig* veda, the *Yajur* veda, the *Sama* veda, and the *Atharva* veda, a late addition to the canon. About 90 percent of *Sämavedic* **chants** derive from the *Rig* vedas but have acquired a more precisely musical connotation (*sāman* meaning "music"). The principal collection is the *Sāmaveda Samhitā*, containing verses and their notated melodies (*sāmans*), although for many centuries the only transmission was oral. The oldest written source dates from the 11th century.

Chants are divided into sections (*parvans*) for breathing, indicated in the manuscripts by vertical strokes. Individual words may be repeated or otherwise altered in precisely specified ways to conform to the melodies. The melodies are of narrow melodic range, sometimes as small as a minor third, and are based on a tonal pitch set similar to the hypodorian **mode**.

SANCTUS. *See* MASS; Appendix A 4 for text.

SANKEY, IRA DAVID (28 August 1840, Edinburgh, Pa.–13 August 1908, New York City). Writer and compiler of **Gospel song** , he met prominent evangelist Dwight L. Moody (1837–1899) in 1870 and rose to prominence when the two conducted revival meetings in England from 1873–1875, Moody preaching and Sankey accompanying himself in solo singing on a portable **organ** and leading the **congregations**. He published *Sacred Songs and Solos* (1st ed. **London**, 1873) whose subsequent editions grew to 1200 songs, and six volumes of *Gospel Hymns and Sacred Songs* (1875–1891).

SARUM CHANT. Chant associated with the Sarum use of the Roman Catholic rite, originating in the secular chapter of the Cathedral Church at Salisbury, England, and spreading through the British isles from the 13th century until the Reformation. Most of the **proper** melodies match closely those of the Roman rite, i.e., **Gregorian chant** and its accretions. However, the expanse of the Salisbury Cathedral encouraged a number of elaborate and original processional chants. Much English **polyphony** uses texts and melodies of Sarum chant. *See also CONDUCTUS; IN NOMINE.*

SCARBOVA. See MISSINAI MELODIES.

SCARLATTI, ALESSANDRO (2 May 1660, Palermo, Sicily–22 October 1725, Naples). Active mainly in **Rome** (1672–1683, 1702–1708). Naples (1683–1702, 1708–1725), and **Venice** (1707), his sacred music, mostly composed in *stile antico*, has been greatly overshadowed by his **operas**. There are 10 extant complete **masses** (including one **Requiem**) and over 70 **motets** and other Latin settings, including two **Magnificats** and a *Stabat Mater*. The 25 extant **oratorios**, mostly commissioned for performance during Lent in Rome, are completely operatic in style.

SCHEIDT, SAMUEL (3 November 1587, Halle, Germany–24 March 1654, Halle). After studying with **Jan Pieterzoon Sweelinck** in Amsterdam, he returned to Halle in 1609 as court **organist** to the Margrave Christian Wilhelm, rising to *Kapellmeister* in late 1619 or early 1620. Scheidt suffered unemployment and other professional misfortune during the Thirty Years War but remained in Halle and resumed his official duties as *Kapellmeister* in 1638 for Duke August of Saxony. His most famous work is the three-volume collection of

57 **chorale preludes**, **fugues**, **canons** and other organ pieces in *Tabulatura Nova* of 1624. He harmonized 100 **chorales** in four voices in the *Görlitzer Tabulatur-Buch* of 1650. He also composed 176 **sacred concertos** published in four volumes (1631, 1634, 1635, 1640) and more than 80 other sacred vocal works, mostly in the Italian concerted style with **continuo**.

SCHEIN, JOHANN HERMANN (20 January 1586, Grünhain near Annaberg, Germany–19 November 1630, Leipzig). He was appointed *Kapellmeister* for the court of Duke Johann Ernst the Younger at Weimar beginning 21 May 1615, then summoned to try out to be **cantor** at St. Thomas Church in Leipzig on 21 May 1615. He was accepted, preceding **Johann Sebastian Bach** by a century, and finished his life there. His compositions include *Cymbalum Sionae* (1615), a collection of 30 Latin and German **motets**, *Opella Nova*, the first large publication of German **sacred concertos** with continuo (Part I, 1618, 31 works; Part II, 1626, 28 works), *Fontana Israel* (1623), 30 *madrigali spirituali*, and 130 **chorale** arrangements in *Cantional* (1627).

SCHOLA CANTORUM (Lat. "school of singers"). Roman Catholic term for church choir; or the ensemble responding to the soloists (*cantores*); or the **congregation** in various **responsorial** forms of liturgical music. *See also* D'INDY, VINCENT; GREGORY, POPE, ST.; ROME.

SCHÖNBERG, ARNOLD (13 September 1874, Vienna–13 July 1951, Los Angeles). The inventor of the serial method composed one liturgical work, a setting of *Kol nidre* (1938), unusable in traditional Jewish liturgies because Schönberg altered the text. He also composed an **oratorio**-like **opera**, *Moses und Aron* (1930–1932), on his own libretto loosely based on Exodus, a tone poem called *A Survivor from Warsaw* for male voices, narrator, and orchestra on a heroic Holocaust story (1947), again with his own text, and a setting of **Psalm** 130, *De Profundis* (1950, Hebrew text).

SCHROEDER, HERMANN (26 March 1904, Bernkastel, Germany–7 October 1984, Bad Orb). He incorporated aspects of medieval sacred music such as **fauxbourdon** and **modal** writing with modernist choral harmony to create an authentic idiom for mid-20th-century Roman Catholic liturgical music. He composed over 20 **masses**, mostly for mixed chorus, including two with German text, one **organ mass**, and one **Requiem** as well as a St. John and a St. Matthew **passion** and many **motets** and **canticles** in both Latin and German.

SCHUBERT, FRANZ (31 January 1797, Vienna–19 November 1828, Vienna). Primarily a composer of *Lieder*, symphonies, piano and chamber works, Schubert also composed about 30 short vocal works for the Roman Catholic liturgy, a "German **Requiem**," a German **mass**, and six Latin masses that are frequently performed in concert and occasionally in liturgies, particularly the second in G major (1815, D.167) and the last two in A-flat major (1819–1822, D.678) and E-flat major (1828, D.950). Schubert omitted some canonical phrases in all six masses, either for personal reasons or because that was the practice in Vienna. They are lightly scored symphonic masses in the tradition of **Wolfgang Amadeus Mozart** and **Franz Joseph Haydn,** lasting from about 25 minutes to one hour.

SCHÜTZ, HEINRICH (baptized 9 October 1585, Köstritz, Germany–6 November 1672, Dresden). The greatest German composer of the 17th century, his talent was spotted by the Landgrave Moritz, who took over Schütz's education in 1599 and sent him to **Venice** to study with **Giovanni Gabrieli** from 1609–1612. In 1615, he joined the court of the Elector of Saxony Johann Georg in Dresden and remained there for the rest of his life except for a short stay in Venice from 1627–1629 to study with **Claudio Monteverdi** and a sojourn with the Crown Prince Christian of Denmark from 1633–1635 to avoid the disastrous effects of the Thirty Years War.

Schütz's surviving works are almost entirely sacred and command all the various idioms that were available to sacred composers in the first half of the 17th century, although he rarely used **chorales**. His major publications fall into four categories. (The SWV *Schützwerkeverzeichnis* catalog numbers generally follow his publications, and so give a rough chronological order.)

Simple arrangements of **psalm** paraphrases by Cornelius Becker appeared as *Psalmen Davids* (1628, 90 works). **Motets** that approximate the *stile antico* in texture but are filled with chromaticisms and other expressive syntax from Italian madrigals were published as *Cantiones Sacrae* (1625, four voices and **continuo**, 41 works) and *Geistliche Chormusik* (1648, five voices and continuo, 29 works). Small-scale **sacred concertos** for solo voices and **instruments** were published as *Symphoniae Sacrae* (Part 1, 1629, 20 works; Part 2, 1647, 27 works) and *Kleine Geistliche Conzerte* (Part 1, 1636, 24 works; Part 2, 1639, 32 works). Large-scale sacred concertos employing solo voices, instruments, and *cori spezzati* on the Venetian model of Gabrieli appeared in *Psalmen Davids* (1619, 26 works) and *Symphonie Sacrae* (Part 3, 1650, 21 works).

Schütz also composed a funeral service, the *Musicalische Exequien* (1636), and three **passions** on St. Matthew, St. Luke, and St. John (all 1666) and three **oratorios**: on the resurrection (*Historia Auferstehung*, 1623), the Seven Last Words (c. 1650), and the **Christmas Oratorio** (1660).

SEASONS, THE (DIE JAHRESZEITEN). A frequently performed **oratorio** composed by **Franz Joseph Haydn** and premiered on 24 April 1801 at the Palais Schwarzenberg in **Vienna**. The libretto by Baron Gottfried van Swieten, very loosely based on J. Thomson's English poem, *The Seasons* (1726), reflects on providential changes in nature through the year. There are four parts; each "season" concludes with a **Handelian** chorus. The work is scored for full classical orchestra, four-voiced chorus, and soprano, tenor, and bass soloists. It requires about two and one-half hours to perform.

SECOND SERVICE. *See* VERSE SERVICE.

SECOND VATICAN COUNCIL. Twenty-first Ecumenical Council of the Roman Catholic Church (11 October 1962–8 December 1965, Rome) whose **Constitution on the Sacred Liturgy** (*Sacrosanctum Concilium*) became the basis for changes in the liturgy and in the practice of liturgical music from the late 1960s until the present.

SELIHOT. *See* LITANY.

SELLE, THOMAS (23 March 1599, Zörbig near Bitterfeld, Germany–2 July 1663, Hamburg). Educated at **Leipzig,** he made his career as **cantor** at various churches in northwest German, from 12 August 1641 at the Johanneum in Hamburg. His own catalog comprises 281 works, about 250 sacred settings of Latin and German texts. His St. John **Passion** (1641, rev. 1643) is the first to use **instrumental** interludes.

SEMICHOIR. *See* ANTIPHONY.

SENFL, LUDWIG (c. 1486, Basle?, Switzerland–between 2 December 1542 and 10 August 1543, Munich). A student of **Heinrich Issac,** he copied and completed the *Choralis Constantinus.* He brought out the first collection of **motets** printed in Germany in 1520, containing works of Isaac, **Josquin Desprez,** and himself. He directed the *Hofkapelle* in Munich from 1523 until his death. His compositions include 8 **masses,** a set of eight **Magnificats** (one for each **mode**), over 125 **motets, vespers** settings and other **polyphony,** much of which remained in use into the 17th century.

SEQUENCE. Latin **chant** sung regularly after the **Alleluia** of the **mass** from the ninth to 16th centuries. Liturgical reforms resulting from the **Council of Trent** (1545–1563) eliminated from the Roman Catholic rite more than 4,500 known works. These four sequences remained: *Victimae paschali laudes* for Easter, *Veni Sancte Spiritus* for Pentecost, *Lauda Sion* for Corpus Christi, and *Dies irae* for **Requiem** masses. One other, ***Stabat mater dolorosa***, was restored in 1727.

The earliest notated sources of sequences date from the 10th century and the origin of the genre is controverted. One monk, Notker Balbulus (c. 840–912), describes adding new Latin text to long **melismas** of **Alleluias** as an *aide-memoire.* Few sequences in the earliest sources, however, refer explicitly to Alleluia chants, and so scholars believe that sequences developed as a para-liturgical genre along with **Gregorian chant,** composers providing completely new words and music in most cases.

Sequences of the 11th and 12th centuries set poetic texts, often rhymed, as opposed to the *prosae* of the earliest examples. Many sequences follow a parallel construction in which the first and last musical phrases are heard once each, while all of the interior phrases are repeated: a bb cc dd . . . yy z. The majority of sequences, however, do not follow such strict parallelism. *See also* ADAM OF ST. VICTOR.

SERVICE. Anglican term referring to musical settings for one or more of the following liturgies: **Morning Prayer** (**matins**); **Evening Prayer** (Evensong); **Holy Communion**; the **Burial Service**. The elements of each service are united by their manner of composition—**short service**, **great service**, and **verse service**—and their **mode** or key. *See also* FULL SERVICE.

SEVEN LAST WORDS OF OUR SAVIOUR FROM THE CROSS (*Die sieben letzten Worte unseres Erlösers am Kreuze*, **1787**). Composition for symphony orchestra by **Franz Joseph Haydn** commissioned by the Bishop of Cadiz for an extraordinary Lenten liturgy invented a century earlier by a Jesuit priest, Alonso Messia Bedoya of Peru, in response to disastrous earthquakes of 1687. Haydn wrote an introduction, then seven more slow movements designed to allow reflection upon the pronouncement of one of the "words," utterances of Christ from the cross recorded in the gospels, and a sermon thereon delivered by the bishop. The work concludes with a fast movement representing the earthquake that occurred after Christ's death. The nine movements require from 45–80 minutes, depending on how many repeats are observed.

The work was so popular that Haydn arranged it for string quartet, probably the version most commonly heard today, and also authorized a piano version, both in 1787, the year of its first performance. In 1795–1796, Haydn collaborated with librettist Baron Gottfried van Swieten and transformed it into an **oratorio** for four soloists and four-voiced choir with expanded orchestration.

SHAPE-NOTE SINGING. *See SACRED HARP.*

SHEMA YISRAEL. "Hear, O Israel, " an essential prayer of Jewish liturgy and associated with martyrdom. The text consists of Deuteronomy 6:4–9 and 11:13–21; Numbers 15:37–41. (*See* Appendix B for text.) *See also* MILHAUD, DARIUS.

SHIRAH (Heb. "the Song"). Refers to the **chanting** of the **Canticle** of Moses (Exodus 15:1–18), part of the daily *shaharit* service of Jewish liturgy. Melodies vary by tradition and locality.

SHOFAR. Ritual "ram's horn" of Jewish Temple liturgies, and the only **instrument** allowed in synagogue liturgies after the Temple's destruction in A. D. 70. The Bible mentions the shofar 72 times, including **Psalm** 98. The shofar marks the coming of the new year (Rosh Hashana) and the end of the fast on Yom Kippur as well as other solemn moments. The timbre, intensity, and pitch of a shofar blast (*tekiot* or *kolot*) may vary, while the duration is specified by Jewish law.

SHŌMYŌ. Japanese term for singing and composing **Buddhist chants**. Because Buddhist chanting originated in India and afterward was transmitted to China and Japan, all three languages are heard. Chanted **hymns** in Pāli are called *bonsan*; in Chinese, *kansan*; in Japanese, **wasan**. Chants are also classified according to their functions: teaching (*kōshiki* and *rongi*), praise and lamentation (*sandan*), intercession (*kigan*), offering (*kuyō*), etc.; and according to **mode** and rhythm.

Kyoto has been home to the *shōmyō* tradition since the ninth century. Kūkai established Tōji as the center of the Shingon sect in 806 (later moved to Mt. Kōya south of Osaka), and Saichö made Enryakuji the center of the Tendai sect in 847. The chanting of Zen and Pure Land Buddhists developed strongly at Kamakura in the 13th and 14th centuries. Buddhist traditions in general declined sharply after the Mejii Restoration in 1868, but Yoshida Tsunezō (1872–1957) and Taki Dōnin (1890–1949) revived the Tendai chant while Yuga Kyōnyo (1847–1928) and Iwahara Taishin (1883–1965) revived the Shingon early in the 20th century. Today, an archive of *shōmyō* may be found at Ueno Gakuen College.

SHORT SERVICE. An Anglican **service** composed in simple **homorhythmic** texture, the most common of the service types, appropriate for ferial days, dating from the mid-16th century. *See also* EVENING PRAYER; FULL SERVICE; GREAT SERVICE; HOLY COMMUNION; MORNING PRAYER; VERSE SERVICE.

SHOUT. *See* SPIRITUAL.

SIDDUR (Heb. "order"). The book of prayer used in synagogue and in Jewish homes for both weekday and Sabbath prayer. Rabbinic authority banned the writing of prayers until the ninth century; the first edited compilation is attributed to Rav Amram c. 875, followed by another of Saddiah Gaon c. 890. The first printed siddur appeared on 7 April 1486 in Rome. The printed siddur is thought to have diminished in Ashkenazic Judaism the role of the *hazan*, who heretofore had sung prayers from memory for the assembly. *See also* MOLIN, JACOB.

SLAVONIC. *See* CHURCH SLAVONIC.

SMART, HENRY THOMAS (26 October 1813, London–6 July 1879, London). Composer of the **hymn** tunes "Regent Square" and "Heathlands," he was the leading concert **organist** of his time and promoted the construction of French-style "symphonic" **pipe organs** in England.

SOLEMN MASS. *See MISSA SOLEMNIS.*

SOLESMES. Name of a small town about 100 km west of Paris, the location of the Benedictine Abbey of St. Pierre, which in the mid-19th century became the most important center for the study and revival of the **Gregorian chant** tradition. *See also* GUÉRANGER, PROSPER.

SONATA DA CHIESA. See CHURCH SONATA.

SONGS OF THE *HAJJ* (*TAHLĪL*). Traditional Islamic songs, approved by juridical Islamic treatises, sung at the departure of pilgrims and at various places in or near Mecca. They may be entirely choral or solo songs with choral refrain. In Egypt, shawms (*mismār*) and **drums** (*tabl baladī*) may accompany them.

SOUTERLIEDEKENS (**Dutch. "little Psalter songs").** An extremely popular collection of **monophonic metrical psalms** for domestic use first published by Symon Cock in Antwerp in 1540. The tunes were largely folk melodies, and the **psalms** were translated into Dutch to fit them. The collection saw nine printings in its first year and 20 subsequent editions. **Clemens non Papa** with Gherardus Mes and Cornelis Buscop arranged the tunes **polyphonically** (publ. 1556–1557).

SOWERBY, LEO (1 May 1895, Grand Rapids, Mich.–7 July 1968, Port Clinton, Oh.). He taught composition at the American Conservatory in Chicago from 1925–1962, was **organist** and choirmaster at the Episcopal Cathedral of St. James from 1927–1962, and was a founding director, from 1962–1968, of the College of Church Musicians in Washington, D. C. He composed more than 120 **anthems** as well as **communion services**, **canticles**, **psalms**, and other choral works.

SPIRITUAL. American religious song first associated with the revival movement sometimes called the Second Awakening at the turn of the 19th century and especially with the large, outdoor, often impromptu camp meetings inspired by itinerant preachers. The songs had to be simple in form and text because of the temporary character of the congregation consisting mostly of illiterate white laborers and African American slaves. Call-and-response forms, simplified well-known texts by **Isaac Watts** and others, and improvised refrains are typical. Because the congregation was biracial, if not integrated, the camp meeting provided a rare but important venue for musical exchange between white and black sacred song.

Another group of spirituals originated among the African American slaves during the 17th, 18th, and 19th centuries, who sang them at formal services, more casually outside of church, and during ecstatic group dances known as "shouts" or "ring-shouts." The shout usually began at the close of a sermon, with movement and singing initiated by a single person and spreading throughout the **congregation**. Because of the significant role of **drumming** in African tribal religions, these spirituals were almost always accompanied by some improvised percussion by striking on pots or other makeshift drum and by using the body: hand-clapping, stomping, body-slapping, and vocal percussion. The most common textual themes were personal salvation expressed in terms of liberation from bondage, as in the Exodus story.

The spiritual quickly moved into established churches. In Philadelphia, in 1803, John Scott published *Hymns and Spiritual Songs for the Use of Christians*, the first printed collection of camp meeting spirituals, and others quickly followed within the decade. It leapt onto the national stage with the 1871–1872 tour of the Fisk Jubilee Singers, a chorus of former slaves studying at Fisk University of Nashville, Tenn., who became something of a sensation after an inspirational rendition of the Northern Civil War song *The Battle Hymn of the Republic* in Boston in 1872. The Fisk chorus embarked on tours of Canada and Europe, introducing the spiritual to the world.

The spirituals of the Fisk singers had been harmonized and arranged by their director George White to be suitable for concert performance. Versions of these appeared in *Jubilee Songs* (New York, 1872) by Theodore F. Seward. Both these and subsequent recording efforts have been criticized as too much influenced by European musical language—and in fact notation captures even less of the spiritual's essence than of most other forms—but on the other hand such efforts brought the spiritual to the wider Western world. Harry Thacker Burleigh (1866–1949) further promoted the spiritual as concert music with his collection arranged for solo voice and piano, *Jubilee Songs of the United States of America* (New York, 1916). In 1929, he published *Old Songs Hymnal* (New York), spirituals arranged very simply for nonprofessionals "to be used in church and home and school, preserving to us this precious heritage." *See also* A COLLECTION OF SPIRITUAL SONGS; GOSPEL SONG; LINING OUT.

SPIRITUAL MADRIGAL. *See MADRIGALE SPIRITUALE.*

SPLIT CHOIR. *See CORI SPEZZATI.*

SPRUCHMOTETTE **(Ger. "saying motet").** Seventeenth-century German motet repertory that set texts from the four Gospels, the **psalms,** or the Song of Songs. Following Johannes Wanning's (1537–1603) cycle of Latin motets published in 1584 and 1590, Andreas Raselius (1563–1602) assembled a cycle of such motets in Ger-

man for the liturgical year in 1594 (five and six voices), as did
Melchior Vulpius (c. 1570–1615) for mostly four voices in 1612–
1621.

STABAT MATER DOLOROSA (**Lat. "His mother stood grieving"**).
Latin poem thought to be of Franciscan origin, traditionally ascribed
to Jacopone da Todi (d. 1306), sung as a **sequence** (since the 15th
century) and an office **hymn** in Roman Catholic liturgy. The **Council
of Trent** excluded it from the liturgy along with most other medieval
sequences, but in 1727 Pope Benedict XIII restored it for use on the
Feast of the Seven Dolours on 15 September.

The 15th-century **Eton Choirbook** contains three **polyphonic** settings and continental composers contributed *stile antico* settings well
into the 18th century, including celebrated compositions of **Giovanni da Palestrina** and **Orlandus Lassus**, both in eight voices.
Today the text is heard most often in concert, set for chorus and **instrumental** or even symphonic accompaniment by composers of
later periods: **Antonio Caldara**, Giovanni Pergolesi (1736), Gioc-
chino Rossini (1841), **Franz Liszt** (part of his **oratorio** *Christus*,
1862–1866), **Antonin Dvořák** (1877), **Giuseppe Verdi** (as the second of his *Quattro Pezzi Sacri*, 1898), **Francis Poulenc** (1950), and
Krzysztof Penderecki (1962).

**STAINER, (SIR) JOHN (6 June 1840, London–31 March 1901, Ve-
rona, Italy). Organist** at St. Paul's Cathedral from 1872 to 1888, he
hastened the reforms of church music championed by the **Oxford
movement** and raised performance standards. He composed three
cantatas, two **oratorios**, and 18 **services** but is remembered today
chiefly for his **hymn tunes** and skilful harmonizations of **hymns**.

**STANFORD, CHARLES VILLIERS (30 September 1852, Dub-
lin–29 March 1924, London).** Active with **Hubert Parry** in the revival of Anglican music, he composed in symphonic style two
oratorios, two **psalms**, two **masses**, one **Requiem**, two **Te Deum**, a
Stabat Mater, and six sets of **service** music, as well as **anthems** and
canticles for chorus with organ, many unpublished.

STEIGER. See MODE.

STICHERON. Byzantine chant originally sung after the verses of a psalm, as are antiphons in the Latin tradition. Later, many became detached and occurred in the morning and evening divine offices. *See also* DIVINE LITURGY; *HESPERINOS*; *ORTHRŌS.*

STILE ANTICO (**It. "ancient style"**). Term used in Italian Baroque theory and criticism to designate the style of high Renaissance **polyphony** or "classical polyphony" as epitomized in the music of **Giovanni da Palestrina**. It was opposed to the *stile moderno*, which referred to the new textures and musical syntax designed for **opera**.

ST. JOHN PASSION, JOHANN SEBASTIAN BACH, BWV 245.
Scored for four-voice choir, vocal soloists, and an orchestra of strings and **continuo** with obbligato **instruments**: two flutes, two oboes, two oboes da caccia, oboe d'amore, lute, two violas d'amore, viola da gamba (the precise scoring of each number is not clear because no score survives from the earliest version). The 67 numbered movements are divided into Parts I and II, and require about one hour and 45 minutes to perform. The work is universally recognized as one of the great exemplars of the **passion** tradition.

    Johann Sebastian Bach first performed this passion at **vespers** on Good Friday, 7 April 1724, in St. Nicholas Church, **Leipzig**. The libretto of this version contains chapters 18 and 19 of St. John's Gospel, two interpolations from St. Matthew that describe Peter's remorse and the miraculous events following Christ's death, and poetic commentary drawn from various sources, including a famous libretto of B. H. Brockes. Bach sets these various texts to four kinds of music: **recitative** for the Gospel, except where speeches by the Apostles or the crowd require a "madrigal" chorus; arioso for the poetry immediately reacting to the Gospel passages, followed immediately by an **aria** for more reflective commentary; and simple, four-voice **chorale** settings for poems that express a more collective response.

    Bach performed the St. John Passion again in 1725, 1732, and 1749, altering the work each time, adding or substituting new movements and changing texts. *See also* ST. MATTHEW PASSION.

ST. MARTIAL. *See* ORGANUM.

ST. MATTHEW PASSION, JOHANN SEBASTIAN BACH, BWV 244. Scored for double four-voice choir, vocal soloists, and a double orchestra of strings, **continuo** and obbligato **instruments**: flutes, oboes, oboes d'amore, oboes da caccia, and viola da gamba. The 78 separate numbers are divided into Parts I and II and require over two and one-half hours to perform. Johann Sebastian Bach's own family members referred to the work as "the great **passion.**" **Felix Mendelssohn** believed it "the greatest of all Christian works," and most critics consider it the greatest exemplar of the passion tradition.

The libretto presents two kinds of text: the Gospel narrative from chapter 26 through chapter 27 and poetic commentary by Picander (pen name of Christian Friedrich Henrici, 1700–1764). Bach sets these to four kinds of music: **recitative** for the Gospel, except where speeches by the Apostles or the crowd require a "madrigal" chorus; arioso for the poetry immediately reacting to the Gospel passages; followed immediately by an **aria** for more reflective commentary; and simple, four-voice **chorale** settings for poems that express a more collective response. Thus the passion story is punctuated by spiritual reflection expressed through poetry and music of great variety at every episode. The entire action is framed by three massive choral numbers at the very beginning, at the end of Part I, and at the end of Part II that bring the level of exegesis to that of Christ's sacrifice considered *in toto.*

Evidence suggests that Bach first performed the St. Matthew Passion as part of a Good Friday **vespers** on 11 April 1727, Parts I and II surrounding a sermon. He revised the entire score in 1736, and this is the version that is almost always performed today. The work was entirely neglected after Bach's death until Mendelssohn's revival in Berlin on 11 March 1829. Most of the arias were left out, but this performance nevertheless ignited the explosive Bach revival of the mid-19th century. *See also* ST. JOHN PASSION.

STOLZER, THOMAS (c. 1480, 'Swidnica, Silesia [modern Poland]–early 1526, Znojmo, Moravia [modern Czech Republic]. A Catholic priest, his compositions, particularly the 14 Latin and four German **psalm** settings were nevertheless a force in the early Reformation, many published by **Georg Rhaw**, and were widely circulated through the early 17th century. *Magister cappellae* at the Hungarian royal court at Ofen from 1522, he composed about 135 sacred works in all the principal genres. *See also* LUTHER, MARTIN; WALTHER, JOHANN.

STRAVINKSY, IGOR (17 June 1882, Oranienbaum near St. Petersburg–6 April 1971, N. Y.). After studying with Nicolai Rimsky-Korsakov from 1903–1908, Stravinsky moved to **Paris** in 1911 after his first major ballet, *Pétrouchka*, opened there. From this point on, he made his living by composing and conducting. He lived in Leysin, Switzerland, from 1914 to June 1920 and then returned to the Paris area. On Easter 1926, he renewed his commitment to the Russian Orthodox Church. He sailed to the United States in September 1938 and settled in West Hollywood, Ca. in spring 1941. From 1969 on, he lived in New York.

Stravinsky's setting of the Roman Catholic **mass ordinary** (1948) for a chorus of boy sopranos, altos, tenors, basses, and double wind quintet is his only major sacred work intended for liturgy. He did compose a **Pater Noster** (1926), **Credo** (1932), and **Ave Maria** (1934), originally in **Church Slavonic** then reworked into Latin in 1949. Other major works include the *Symphony of Psalms* (1930) for four-voiced choir and orchestra; *Canticum Sacrum ad Honorem Sancti Marci Nominis* (**Venice**, 1955) for tenor and baritone soloists, chorus and orchestra; *Lamentations of Jeremiah* (1958) for six soloists, chorus, and orchestra; the **cantata** *A Sermon, a Narrative and a Prayer* for alto and tenor soloists, speaker, chorus and orchestra; *The Flood* (1962), a dramatic work for one tenor and two baritone soloists, three-voiced (SAT) choir, narrator, and orchestra; *Abraham and Isaac* (1963) for baritone solo singing Hebrew text and chamber orchestra; and the **Requiem Canticles** for alto and bass soloists, chorus, and orchestra (1966).

SUBJECT. The melody copied in an **imitative** texture. *See also* FUGUE.

SULZER, SOLOMON (30 March 1804, Hohenems, Austria–17 January 1890, Vienna). Composer and chief **cantor** (*hazan*), first in his hometown at age 13 and then in Vienna from 1826–1891. In the midst of fierce controversy between orthodox and reform Jews about liturgical music, Sulzer brokered a compromise in the "Vienna model," which purged traditional **chanting** of the coloraturas of enthusiastic cantors while introducing the **organ** and contemporary European musical language at the same time. His theories are set out in the preface to a two-volume anthology, *Schir Zion* (1838–1840; 1865–1866).

SWEELINCK, JAN PIETERSZOON (?May 1562, Deventer, the Netherlands–16 October 1621, Amsterdam). He lived almost his entire life in Amsterdam and was **organist** at the Oude Kerk certainly from 1580 (possibly earlier) until his death. Famous as a teacher, his students included **Samuel Scheidt**, Heinrich Scheidemann (c. 1595–1663), and many others who formed the so-called north German **organ** school. He composed 39 **motets** and 153 **psalms**, but Sweelinck is chiefly known for his 32 **fantasias** and **toccatas** and 12 **chorale** settings for keyboard.

SYRIAN CHANT. Chant of the Christian traditions historically descendant of the Patriarchate of Antioch, including Syrian Orthodox, Assyrian (Nestorian), Chaldean, and Maronite Churches, among others. These traditions celebrate a Eucharist or **divine liturgy** analogous to the Latin **mass** and also a cycle of up to eight daily **divine offices** focused on the **psalms**, which are spoken but framed or interpolated with *qale* (**hymns**) and other music. The liturgical chant is like an improvised **recitative**, often on a recitation tone with cadences a tone or semi-tone lower. Hymn forms—*qale, madrasha, sughiatha, ba'utha*—are melodically more elaborate. The offices follow an eight-week **modal** cycle, whereby all the music is sung in Mode 1 for the first week, Mode 2 for the second, etc. *See also* BYZANTINE CHANT; *OKTOĒCHOS*.

– T –

TAHLĪL. See SONGS OF THE *HAJJ.*

TAIZÉ. Interdenominational and international Christian monastic community founded by Roger Louis Schutz-Marsauche (1915–) in 1949,

named for this small village near the site of the great medieval Benedictine monastery at Cluny in Burgundy, France. Because they
wished their many pilgrim guests to participate actively in their liturgies, Brother Roger, Brother Robert Giscard (1922–1993), **Fr. Joseph Gelineau**, and a lay composer, **Jacques Berthier** beginning in
1975 designed a repertory of **chants** and songs that could be easily
learned. Some are **congregational ostinatos**, **canons**, or simple
modal melodies used as **responds** to more professional music. Others give the congregation a simple line to be accompanied by choral
polyphony. Berthier, the principal composer, often borrowed from
Gregorian and **Byzantine chant**. The most common original language is Latin, chosen for its neutrality and *cantabile* qualities, but
Taizé music has since been translated into many languages and is
sung throughout the world. *See also* LITURGICAL MOVEMENT;
SECOND VATICAN COUNCIL.

TAJWĪD. The most learned and precise form of **chanting** of the Qur'ān
in the original Arabic, proceeding in gradually rising and falling
phrases with silences at syntactically appropriate moments. The criteria for proper chanting are textual: prolongation of sound without
falling (*istirsāl*); softening without loss of intonation (*tarkhīm*); am-
plification (*tafkhīm*); breath control (*taqdīr alanfās*); and transition
from stressed to unstressed sound (*tadjrīd*).

Egypt has enjoyed the reputation as the center of *tajwīd* for at least
three centuries. Egyptian *qāri* (**cantors**) are highly respected and
paid and travel widely to teach. *See also QIRĀ'A*; *QIRĀ'A BI'L-
ALHĀ*.

TĀLA. Refers to **metric** organization in Indian classical music and also
the named metric pattern for a particular composition (e.g. *tīntāl*).
The specific *tāla* is defined by the number of duration units and the
manner of their subdivision into smaller groupings. The *tāla* orga-
nizes and constrains the improvisation on the ***rāga*** insofar as structural pitches must coordinate with certain counts of the *tāla*.

TALEA. Pattern of durations in the **tenor** of an **isorhythmic motet**. *See
also COLOR.*

TALLIS, THOMAS (c. 1505, Greenwich–23 November 1585). Composer, **organist** at various churches in Dover and **London**, and Gentleman of the **Chapel Royal**, probably from 1543. He wrote 42 Latin **motets**, including the famous *Spem in alium* for 40 voices, three complete **masses**, and two **Magnificats**, but he was also one of the first important composers to set the new Anglican liturgies of 1547–1553, which realize the ideals of clear syllabic diction. Many of his 24 **anthems** are *contrafacta* of his previously composed motets.

TĀNSEN (fl. c. 1550, probably Gwalior, India). Foundational composer of the Hindustani tradition, he was a member of the court of Mughal Emperor Akbar (ruled 1556–1605) where he introduced the *dhrupad*. His court title, *Miyām* ("master"). has been appended to Hindustani *rāga*s attributed to him (e.g., *Miyām kī Todī*). Modern Hindustani composers frequently claim some relation of discipleship. *See also KIRTANA; KRITI;* TYĀGARĀJA.

TAVENER, (SIR) JOHN (28 January 1944, London). Pianist and **organist**, in January 1962 he began composition studies with Sir Lennox Berkeley (1903–1989) at the Royal Academy of Music, then studied with the Australian David Lumsdaine (1931–   ), and first came to public attention in 1968 with the performance of a **cantata**, *The Whale*. Through the 1970s he composed works deriving from Roman Catholic traditions: *Canciones españolas* (1972), *In Memoriam **Igor Stravinsky** (1971), **Responsorium** in Memory of Annon Lee Silver (1971), **Requiem** for Father Malachy (1973), and the setting of a text from St. John of the Cross in *Ultimos Ritos* (1972). In 1977, he was received into Eastern Orthodoxy, whose liturgy and **Byzantine chants** inspired many of his subsequent works: T*he Great Canon of St. Andrew of Crete* (1981), *Orthodox Vigil Service* (1984), *The Protecting Veil* (1987), **Akathist** *of Thanksgiving* (1988), and *Lamentations and Praises* (2000) are among the best known. His most recent works, influenced by the universalist philosophy of Fritjhof Schuon, may combine references to various world religions. In all, Tavener has composed nearly 100 sacred works for chorus, nearly 60 of them unaccompanied, and another 20 **instrumental** works on religious themes. He was knighted in 2000.

TAVERNER, JOHN (c. 1490, Lincolnshire, England–18 October 1545, Boston, Lincolnshire). Dominant composer in England of his time, he composed 26 **motets**, three **Magnificats**, nine single **mass** movements, and eight **cantus firmus masses** including the "Western Wynde" mass whose tenor is a popular tune of the time. He was a clerk of the choir at the collegiate church at Tattershall (1524–1525), instructor of choristers at Cardinal College (1526–1530), then probably instructor at St. Botolph in Boston (1530–1537).

TA'ZIYE **(Farsi. "mourning").** A Shī'ite religious sung drama, the only indigenous example in the Islamic world, performed during the month of Muharram and commemorating the martyrdom of Hossein, grandson of the Prophet. Dramatic roles are distinguished by **mode** (*dastghāh*). **Drums**, long trumpets, and cymbals may play interludes between dramatic recitations and laments.

The dramas may include processions of flagellants who sing **metrically** strong songs, timed to accord with blows on the back and breast, in **antiphony**. *See also LAUDA; SAMA.*

TCHAIKOVSKY, PIOTR ILYICH (7 May 1840, Votkinsk, Viatka district, Russia–6 November 1893, St. Petersburg). Renowned chiefly for concert music, Tchaikovsky took a serious interest in the condition of Russian Orthodox music, editing the complete sacred choral works of **Dmitri Bortniansky**. He also composed complete settings, unusual for his time, for unaccompanied choir of the two most important Orthodox liturgies, the *Liturgy of St. John Chrysostom* (1878) and the *All-Night Vigil* (1882), the latter using traditional **chants**, a set of nine sacred choruses (1885), and a setting of an Orthodox Easter **hymn** "The Angel Cried Out" (1887). These works, relatively free of Western European traits, initiated a furious period of composition by Russian composers for Orthodox liturgy in the first two decades of the 20th century. *See also VESPERS (ALL-NIGHT VIGIL); ZNAMENNĪY RASPEV.*

TE DEUM. Short title of a Latin **hymn**, *Te Deum Laudamus* (Lat. "We praise you God"), also known as the Ambrosian Hymn, after the tradition that Sts. **Ambrose** and **Augustine** composed it on the occasion of the latter's baptism in 387. Its earliest reference (c. 500) is from the Rule of St. Caesarius.

In the Roman Catholic rite, Te Deum is sung at the end of **matins** on feast days and through the next eight days. It may also be sung on solemn occasions such as the blessing of a pope after **mass** or the **divine office**. The **chant** melody varies in different sources, but the current official version is in the appendix of the Vatican Gradual (1908). **Polyphonic** settings are few; **Giovanni da Palestrina** made one, and **George Frideric Handel** composed two for state victory celebrations, the *Utrecht Te Deum* (1713) and *Dettingen Te Deum* (1743).

Metrical translations into English number about 25, including one by John Dryden, "Thee, Sovereign God, our grateful accents praise," and one by Rev. Clarence A. Walworth, in the *Evangelical Hymnal* of 1853, now commonly used in American Catholic hymnals as "Holy God, We Praise Thy Name." The Anglican rite prescribes Te Deum for **Morning Prayer**.

TELEMANN, GEORG PHILIPP (14 March 1681, Magdeburg, Germany–25 June 1767, Hamburg). A self-taught musician and perhaps the most prolific composer of the 18th century, he entered **Leipzig** University in 1701 and was soon composing for St. Thomas and St. Nicholas, important city churches. In 1704, he was appointed **organist** at the New Church, a third **Leipzig** church, and his productive activities there aroused the ire of **Johann Kuhnau**, the Leipzig **cantor**. By June 1705, he moved to Sorau to be *Kapellmeister* to Count Erdmann II, and by 24 December 1708 he was in Saxe-Eisenach to serve Duke Johann Wilhelm and was appointed concertmaster in August 1709. Desiring the comparative freedom of a church composer, he won the post of *Kapellmeister* at the Barfüsserkirche in Frankfurt and arrived on 18 March 1712. On 17 September 1721, he took up his last post as cantor of the Johanneum Lateinschule and music director of the five main churches of Hamburg.

Because the Hamburg services required **cantatas** before and after the sermon and at the conclusion, it is believed that Telemann composed about 1700, of which 1400 survive, about 12 liturgical cycles. Four cycles were published, highly unusual at the time, and in general his cantatas circulated widely and continued to be heard in Protestant churches throughout Germany until the end of the century. Twenty-three liturgical **passions** exist as well as five other passion **oratorios** and seven sacred oratorios. He also composed about 15 **motets** with **continuo**, a **Magnificat**, and several Latin **masses** and **psalm** settings.

TEMCIT. Turkish songs to the glory of Allah sung at night from minarets during the holy month of Ramadan between the hours of prayer. Some are **proper** to specific nights. *See also 'ADHĀN*; MUEZZIN.

TENEBRAE (Lat. "shadows, darkness"). A special **divine office** combining **matins** and **lauds** sung for Thursday, Friday, and Saturday of Holy Week in the Roman Catholic rite. A total of 15 **psalms** are sung, a candle being extinguished after each until "shadows" remain. The *Cæremoniale episcoporum* of 1752 directed that the offices be anticipated, that is, sung shortly after **Compline** of the previous day, probably in late afternoon, although local practices varied. Texts set **polyphonically** from the 15th century on included the Lamentations of Jeremiah from matins and the **Benedictus** and *Miserere* from Lauds.

TENOR. *See* MOTET.

TĒVĀRAM. Great collection of **hymn** texts dedicated to the Hindu deity Shiva, assembled c. 1000. Their language is Tamil. The hymns may be sung only in temples by a specific class of temple singer, the *odüvar*. The tunes for the texts are called *kattalai*. *See also GĪTA-GOVINDA*; *NĀLĀYIRATIVVIYAPPIRAPANTAM.*

THOMAS, KURT (25 May 1904, Tönning, Germany–31 March 1973, Bad Oeynhausen). Choral conductor and composer who influenced the revival of German Protestant music in the 1920s. He composed a St. Mark **passion**, Christmas and Easter **oratorios**, **cantatas**, **psalms**, and **motets** heavily influenced by Baroque sacred music.

THOMPSON, RANDALL (21 April 1899, New York–9 July 1984, Boston). Composer especially renowned for choral repertory, whose sacred works include settings of the book of Isaiah in *The Peaceable Kingdom* (eight voices, 1936), a famous *Alleluia* (four voices, 1940), *The Last Words of David* (four voices, orchestra, 1949), a *Mass of the Holy Spirit* (eight voices, 1956), a Biblical **Requiem** (12 voices, 1958), *The Passion According to St. Luke* (**oratorio** passion, 1965), as well as other **psalm** and **hymn** settings.

TIBETAN CHANT. There are two religious traditions of **chant** in Tibet. In Bon, a syncretic religion predating the arrival of Buddhism in the eighth century, **metrical** texts may be recited in monotone or in various formulae (*skad*) or in more elaborate chants called *dbyangs*. Notation indicates the kind of formula to be used, but the tradition is essentially oral. Any ceremony must be accompanied by **drums** (*mga*). Cymbals (*rolmo*) and bells (*silsnyan*) may also be heard.

The second tradition of Tibetan **Buddhist chant** is also essentially oral, showing wide variation among localities within at least four distinct subtraditions. Compiled manuals do indicate use of a chorus and **instruments** such as drums, bells, cymbals, clappers, conches, oboes, and trumpets. *Dbyangs* ("vowel") in Buddhist chant are solemn intonations of meaningless vowels inserted among the syllables of the liturgical text. The timbre of the singing is particular to the monastery.

The "Tantric voice" associated particularly with the Gyume and Gyūtō monasteries involves the use of deep fundamental tones whose partials may be heard as biphonic chanting.

TIENTO. See CABEZON, ANTONIO DE.

TINDLEY, CHARLES A. (c. 1859–1933). Methodist preacher, lyricist, and composer of **gospel songs**. His musical direction in Philadelphia and his publication *New Songs of Paradise* (1916) brought gospel music into established evangelical churches.

TIPPETT, (SIR) MICHAEL (2 January 1905, London–8 January 1998, London). Composer for the stage and concert hall who also wrote two **oratorios**: *A Child of Our Time* (1939–1941), a response to world conflict employing black **spirituals**; and *The Vision of St. Augustine* (1963–1965).

TITELOUZE, JEHAN (1562–1563, St. Omer, France–24 October 1633, Rouen). Priest, prize-winning poet, and regarded as the first important composer of **organ** music in France, he was **organist** at the Rouen Cathedral from 1588 until his death. His first collection, *Hymnes de l'Eglise Pour Toucher l'Orgue* ("Church **Hymns** for Organ," 1623), contains **fugal** and **cantus firmus versets** on **plainsong** hymns. His second, *Le Magnificat* (1626), provides eight sets of versets so that the **Magnificat** may be sung in **alternatim** in each of the eight church **modes**. Three **masses** are lost.

TOCCATA (It. "touched"). Keyboard composition that, when played on the **organ**, might have been used as a **prelude** or **verset** in Christian liturgies in Italy and German-speaking countries. "Toccata" connotes rhapsodic passagework and improvisation, although many works so entitled have passages of strict **imitation**. The earliest printed collections appear in 1591 and 1593 in Italy, the latter including works of Claudio Merulo and **Andrea** and **Giovanni Gabrieli**. The dominant figure in the 17th century was **Girolamo Frescobaldi**, particularly in *Recercari et canzoni* (1615) and *Fiori musicali* (1635), whose innovations were brought northward to Austria by Jakob Froberger. The organ toccatas of **Dietrich Buxtehude** and **Johann Sebastian Bach** are linked to a concluding fugal section or separate **fugue**, thus contrasting free and strict compositional methods. In later repertory, the most famous example is probably the "Toccata" concluding the Fifth Organ Symphony (1882) of **Charles Marie Widor**. *See also* CANZONA; RICERCAR.

TOMKINS, THOMAS (1572, St. Davids, Pembrokeshire, England–buried 9 June 1656, Martin Hussingtree, Worcester). Prolific composer of widely circulated Anglican **anthems** (over 120) and **service** music, he studied with **William Byrd** and was a Gentleman of the **Royal Chapel** from at least 1620.

TONE. *See* PSALM TONE.

TONGUE-SINGING. Singing with the gift of tongues, as indicated in 1 Corinthians 14: 15, according to the beliefs of the Pentecostals, a movement that grew out of a revival meeting in Los Angeles in April 1906.

TONUS PEREGRINUS. See PSALM TONE.

TORREJÓN Y VELASCO, TOMÁS DE (baptized 23 December 1644, Villarrobledo near Albacete, Spain–23 April 1728, Lima, Peru). Composer of 20 extant *villancicos* (four **polychoral**) including some for split choir, four **motets** (two polychoral), and one **Magnificat** for 12 voices, he was *maestro di capilla* of Lima Cathedral from 1 January 1676 until his death and exercised a primary influence on sacred music in Latin America.

TRACT. *See* MASS.

TRACTARIANS. *See* OXFORD MOVEMENT.

TRA LE SOLLECITUDINI **(It. "Among the concerns"; also known as *Motu Proprio*).** Papal encyclical promulgated by Pope Pius X on 22 November 1903 that reaffirmed the traditional norms for liturgical music in the Roman Catholic rite. In particular, the encyclical approved **Gregorian chant** as the "supreme model" for sacred music and also "Classical **Polyphony**" as embodied in the works of **Giovanni da Palestrina** (Art. 3, 4). Modern music may provide excellent works for liturgy, but explicit secular influences, such as the theater, are prohibited, including concerted works. **Organ** music is permitted but not as **alternatim**. The length of compositions should not overwhelm liturgical actions. *See also* CECILIAN MOVEMENT; CONSTITUTION ON THE SACRED LITURGY; COUNCIL OF TRENT.

TRENT CODICES. The largest and most significant collection of 15th-century **polyphony**, the codices consist of seven manuscripts of Tyrolean provenance and contain more than 1,500 compositions from the years c. 1400–c. 1480, including works of **Guillaume Du Fay**, **Antoine Busnoys**, and **Johannes Ockeghem**.

TRISAGION **(Gk. "three times holy").** Ordinary Byzantine chant sung at the morning **divine office** (*orthrōs*) and during the **divine**

liturgy before the readings. The text reads: "Holy God, Holy and Mighty, Holy and Immortal, have mercy on us."

TROPARION. Short prayers, usually in strophic form, sung among the verses of a **psalm** in the **Byzantine divine office** since the sixth century. The texts may allude to the feast day and thus make the **psalmody proper**. The melodies are thought to have been simple, and the poetic diction takes after the psalms.

Also a single stanza, three to 13 lines, of a *kontakion* or *kanon*. *See also* ANTIPHON; *STICHERON*.

TROPE. An expansion of a Latin **chant**, accomplished by adding wordless **melismas** to its melody; or, by adding text to original melismas of a chant to produce a syllabic texture; or, by adding both new words and new melody. Medieval sources often term the last two kinds of trope *prosa* or *prosula*. "Trope" can occasionally indicate a chant that replaces another in liturgy, while conveying similar meaning and function.

The sources for the earliest tropes are Frankish, particularly St. Gall and St. Martial, and date from the 10th century and thus are as old as the earliest sources of **Gregorian chant**. Some scholars even doubt the traditional view that tropes expanded older, standard chants, and believe that troped and untroped repertories developed simultaneously.

The liturgical purpose of tropes appears to be multifaceted. They solemnized particular feasts, as did the earliest **polyphony**, which itself could be considered a kind of melodic trope. Tropes of canonical texts often clarified the relation of a chant to its **proper** feast and explained its meaning. Particularly at the **Introit**, tropes act as introductions to the proper chant, an invitation to the choir intoned by the **cantor**. There is an extra-liturgical function too: tropes provided an occasion for liturgical composition after the Gregorian repertory had become more or less fixed.

Chants for the **mass** were most commonly troped in the Middle Ages, with the exception of the Credo, the statement of faith. Of the propers, the **Alleluia** and its concluding wordless *jubilus* provided an exceptional opportunity for troping. Tropes for the **divine office** occur in **responsories** and in the concluding *Benedicamus Domino*.

The liturgical reforms resulting from the **Council of Trent** (1545–1563) eliminated virtually all tropes from the official Roman Catholic rite. However, some very recent popular style settings of the shorter ordinaries show troped texts.

TYĀGARĀJA (4 May 1767, Tiruvarur, Tamil Nadu, India–6 January 1847, Truvaiyaru, Tamil Nadu). Widely regarded as the most important composer of Karnatic music, he studied for 20 years with Sonti Vēnkataramana beginning in 1782, traveled widely, and taught many disciples including Vīnā Kuppayyar who transmitted many of his compositions through notation. Most modern Karnatic composers claim some disciple relation with Tyāgarāja. He is credited with developing a kind of composed variation within the three-part form of the *kriti*. His more than 700 compositions were renowned for their emotional content. *See also BHAJAN; KIRTANA;* TĀNSEN.

– U –

UTASEKKYŌ. Sung Japanese narratives of the Buddha's life and teachings, sung by professionals in a *kabuki* (theater) manner, particularly common in the 17th and 18th centuries.

– V –

VAUGHAN WILLIAMS, RALPH (12 October 1872, Down Ampney, Gloucester, England–26 August 1958, London). Renowned composer and conductor, he composed an *a cappella* **Mass** in G minor (1920–1921), the **oratorio** *Sancta Civitas* ("The Holy City," 1923–1925, based on Revelations), and about 20 other **motets**, **psalms**, and other sacred songs both accompanied and unaccompanied. He is probably best known, however, through his many arrangements of traditional **hymn tunes** and **carols** first published in *The Oxford Book of Carols* (1928), *Songs of Praise* (1931), and *The English Hymnal* (1933), and for several outstanding hymn tunes of his own, including *Down Ampney* ("Come Down, O Love Divine"), *Salva Festa Dies* ("Hail Thee, Festival Day"), *Sine Nomine* ("For All the Saints," all three c.1905), and *King's Weston* ("At the Name of Jesus," 1925).

VENICE. The capital city of the "Most Serene Republic" came to prominence in sacred music in the 16th century, later than most other Italian city-states, but then developed spectacularly into the second most important musical center in Europe after **Rome**. In the 15th century, *laude* might be heard in the confraternities known as *scuole grandi,* and there was occasional ceremonial music at St. Mark's, the doge's private chapel (a basilica from 1520). **Ottaviano Petrucci** (1466–1539) published the first printed collection of **polyphony** in 1501, and in the 16th century Venice became Europe's leading publisher of music. In 1527, the procurators of St. Mark's appointed **Adrian Willaert** as *maestro di cappella* (to 1562), beginning a long series of illustrious *maestri* including Gioseffo Zarlino (1517–1590, *maestro* from 1564–1590), who attracted an outstanding staff including **Andrea** and **Giovanni Gabrieli**. Subsequent *maestri* include **Claudio Monteverdi** (1613–1943), and **Antonio Lotti** (1733–1740). The zenith in sacred music was the Zarlino-Monteverdi period when St. Mark's could have at its disposal a choir of 30 and an **instrumental** ensemble of 20. With such large ensembles and two **organs**, St. Mark's made such a specialty of colorful music for *cori spezzati* that, even without originating in Venice, polychoral music became virtually synonymous with the "Venetian style" of church music and influenced composers as late and as far flung as **Johann Sebastian Bach** and **George Frideric Handel**.

A peculiarly Venetian venue for sacred music were the four *ospedali* of the *Incurabili, Mendicanti, Derelitti,* and *Pietà.* Orphanages that housed mostly illegitimate girls, they trained their inmates in singing, **organ** playing, and, by the late 17th century, string playing; they were renowned all over Europe for the quality of their music. **Sacred concertos**, **oratorios**, and instrumental concertos by Francesco Gasparini (1668–1727) and **Antonio Vivaldi** survive from the *Pietà.*

With the opening of Europe's first commercial **opera** house at San Cassian in 1637, the city's best musical talent increasingly preferred working in the theater to composing for the church.

VERDI, GIUSEPPE (9 or 10 October 1813, Roncole near Busseto, Italy–27 January 1901, Milan). The greatest composer of Italian **opera** in the 19th century contributed *Quattro Pezzi Sacri* ("Four Sacred Pieces," published 1898) and the great **Requiem mass** to the concert choral repertory of sacred music. The *Quattro Pezzi*, evidently composed without commission, include an **Ave Maria** for four-voiced unaccompanied chorus, *Laudi alla Vergine Maria* ("Praises to the Virgin Mary") for women's four-voiced unaccompanied chorus, a *Stabat Mater* for mixed chorus and orchestra, and a **Te Deum** for double chorus and orchestra.

VERSAILLE MOTET. *See GRAND MOTET.*

VERSE ANTHEM. An **anthem** featuring vocal solos, usually in some pattern of alternation with the full choir. The concept coincides with the first major collections of English anthems. The first verse of the anonymous *Now Let the Congregation* in the Wanley Partbooks (c. 1546–1548) is apparently for alto solo, followed by the same verse for full choir. Compositions with more extensive solos date from the 1560s. These most often begin with introductory **organ** solos, followed by a verse for vocal solo(s) with **instrumental** obbligatos, closing the first section with a verse for full chorus, with instruments doubling the vocal parts. Solo/chorus pairs proceed in through-composed manner for as long as the text demands.

The revival of the **Chapel Royal** after the Restoration of Charles II occasioned more elaborate instrumental settings. A string ensemble might further articulate a larger structure by playing ritornellos between the sung verses.

VERSE SERVICE. An Anglican **service** composed with alternation between solo singers and the full choir, after the manner of the **verse anthem**. The earliest examples date from the late 16th century. *See also* FULL SERVICE; GREAT SERVICE.

VERSET. Organ piece that substitutes for a **chant** in liturgy, as in *alternatim*. It may use the original chant melody as a **cantus firmus** or as a subject of **imitation**, or it may be entirely original. *See also* CANZONA; RICERCAR; TOCCATA.

VERSICLE. In Christian liturgies, a short text usually **chanted** by the celebrant or deacon that elicits a response from the choir (e.g., **Benedicamus Domino**). The pairing of versicle and response is called *versus* in Latin liturgical books. *See also* ALLELUIA; *DEUS IN ADJUTORIUM*; DIVINE OFFICE; RESPONSORY.

VERSUS **(Lat. "verse").** *See* VERSICLE.

VESPERS. The major hour of the **divine office** of the Roman Catholic rite sung in the evening. Sundays and important feasts are allotted two vespers services, a first vespers that begins the feast on the preceding evening and second vespers that concludes the feasts on the day itself; ferial days have a single vespers in the evening.

Vespers always begins with the **versicle *Deus in adjutorium***. Then come a number of **proper psalms** with **antiphons**, five in the medieval Benedictine vespers. On Sunday, Psalms 110–114 (Vulgate numeration) are sung, and the weekdays would continue in order through 147, omitting psalms sung at other hours. Solemn feasts might require particular psalms.

The **psalmody** is followed by a brief Bible reading (*Capitulum*, "little chapter") and a proper **hymn**. (In medieval monastic practice an ornate **chant** called a great **responsory** preceded the hymn.) After another versicle comes the **Magnificat** (*see* Appendix A for text) framed by an antiphon for the day, followed by one of the four **Marian antiphons** (*see* Appendix A for texts). The versicle ***Benedicamus Domino*** concludes the service. *See also* EVENING PRAYER; *HESPERINOS;* PSALM TONES.

VESPERS (ALL-NIGHT VIGIL). A setting of the Russian Orthodox night-long service sung in monasteries and, on the eve of holy days, in churches, composed by **Sergei Rachmaninoff** (Op. 37) in two weeks spanning January and February 1915, and premiered on 10 March 1915 in Moscow. Scored for unaccompanied chorus, it requires about 65 minutes. Nine of the 15 prayer settings used melodies drawn from **znamennīy chant**, **Byzantine chant**, and Kievan chant. The music throughout, while clearly of the late 19th century, is syntactically conservative, diatonic, and dominated by step-motion melodies and **homorhythmic** textures that recall the Russian traditions of sacred music.

VESPERS OF 1610 (*VESPRO DELLA BEATA VERGINE*). A setting of a Roman Catholic **vespers** composed by **Claudio Monteverdi** and published in **Venice** in 1610. The scoring of the 13 movements (not including an alternate, simpler six-voiced **Magnificat** and a six-voiced *Missa In Illo Tempore* printed with them) varies from a monody for solo tenor and **continuo** to a **polychoral psalm** for 10 voices in two choirs with accompaniment. A historical performance requires in addition eight vocal soloists and two violins, three violas, one bass violin, one double bass, three cornettos, one large cornetto, three trombones, one contrabass trombone, two tenor recorders, and two transverse flutes or shawms. However, a number of modern editions make possible performances with modern **instruments**. Jeffrey G. Kurtzman has published the most recent and authoritative critical performing edition (Oxford, 1999). Monteverdi's 13 movements require about 90 minutes to perform in concert; a liturgical performance might require an amount of additional **chant**, depending upon how certain controversial matters were resolved.

Monteverdi's Vespers include settings of the response *Domine ad adiuvandum*, five psalms (109, 112, 121, 126, and 147), the **hymn** *Ave Maris Stella*, the Magnificat, and five **sacred concertos** setting Biblical texts (except *Audi coelum*, not Biblical). He included no **antiphons** to frame the psalms and Magnificat, presumably because they would be chosen according to the feast. But some scholars believe that sacred concertos should replace the antiphons; others believe they are independent compositions. Pitch is another controversy. Some movements are notated in *chiavi alte* ("high clefs"); evidence suggests that these should be transposed down a perfect fourth. Questions about when to use the instruments when they are not obbligato, and how many singers on a part in a given movement, as well as the best order of movements all remain unresolved.

Published 13 years after the performance of Jacopo Peri's *Euridice* and three years after Monteverdi's own **opera** *Orfeo*, the Vespers is a unique synthesis of two styles concurrent in early 17th-century Italy: the *stile antico*, the high Renaissance **polyphony** promoted by the **Council of Trent**, and the *stile moderno*, emphasizing the expressivity of the solo voice against a framework of functional harmony. The psalms and Magnificat present this synthesis most clearly. The **cantus firmus** of the ancient **psalm tones** sounds slowly at times against virtuosic solo singing reminiscent of opera, at times against highly **contrapuntal** choral writing reminiscent of the glories of the Venetian school.

VIADANA, LUDOVICO (c. 1560, Viadana near Parma, Italy–2 May 1627, Gualtieri near Parma). *See CENTO CONCERTI ECCLESIASTICI.*

VICTORIA, TOMÁS LUIS DE (1548, Avila–20 August 1611, Madrid). Roman Catholic priest, **organist** and composer noted for his religious devotion, he restricted himself to Latin texts, and thus his *oeuvre* is smaller than that of **Orlandus Lassus** or **Giovanni da Palestrina** with whom his music is often compared: 22 **masses**, 106 **motets** (including polyphonic **antiphons** and **responsories**), 18 **Magnificats** (most are **alternatim**), two **passions**, 38 polyphonic **hymns**, three **sequences** for *cori spezzati* and a famous **Requiem** for his patron the Dowager Empress Maria, sister to the King of Spain, published in 1605. He sang at the Cathedral of Avila and then entered the Jesuit Collegium Germanicum in **Rome** in 1565, where he likely studied with Palestrina; he succeeded him as *maestro* at the Roman seminary in 1571. In the 1560s and 1570s, he held many posts as director and organist in Rome. In 1577, he joined St. Philip Neri's *Congregazione dei Preti dell'Oratorio*, possibly composing music for the *laude* sung there. He returned to Madrid in 1587 and served at the *Monasterio de las Desclazas* until his death.

VIENNA. If its development seems to lag behind that of **Paris** or **London** in the Middle Ages—**polyphony** is mentioned only in 1460—the sacred music of Vienna nevertheless shows some prescient features, such as the reference in 1260 to vernacular **hymn** singing and the foundation by Emperor Rudolf IV (d. 1365) of the Brotherhood of Corpus Christi to chant **liturgical drama**.

The move of Emperor Maximilian's *Hofmusikkappelle* to Vienna in 1498 marks the beginning of a long ascent to world prominence in music. Ferdinand II introduced Italian disciples of **Giovanni Gabrieli** and their Baroque style into the previously conservative court and sacred music after his accession in 1619. Giovanni Valentini's (1582–1649) *sepolcro Santi Risorti* of 1643 began a tradition of **oratorio** particular to Vienna. And alongside the latest in Italian Baroque **operatic** church music was practiced the *stile antico*, especially during Lent.

The two ideals competed for dominance during the 18th century. The archbishop forbad trumpets and **drums** during **mass** in 1753, but Empress Maria Theresa ignored him and favored liturgies whose music was indistinguishable from concerts. **Joseph II**, however, restricted operatic liturgy significantly in the 1780s. A more muted but similar controversy infected Jewish **chant** in the 19th century, resulting in the "Vienna model" of liturgical music engineered by **Cantor Solomon Sulzer**.

By the turn of the 19th century the careers of **Wolfgang Amadeus Mozart** and **Franz Joseph Haydn** and the growing reputation of **Ludwig van Beethoven** established Vienna as the leading musical city of the Western world. But aside from isolated works such as Haydn's *The Creation* and *The Seasons* and Beethoven's *Missa Solemnis* that straddled the sacred and secular, the city's fame rested on **instrumental** concert music and opera. The repertory of sacred music in the great churches of St. Stephen's and St. Augustine's today is little changed, still performed at a **solemn mass** each Sunday by the *Hofmusikkappelle* consisting of the Vienna Boys' Choir, the men of the State Opera Chorus, and players of the Vienna Philharmonic Orchestra.

VILLA-LOBOS, HEITOR (5 March 1887, Rio de Janeiro–17 November 1959, Rio de Janeiro). Founder of Brazilian musical nationalism, he composed the *Missa São Sebastião* (three voices, 1937) and 36 other unaccompanied sacred works.

VILLANCICO. Song of praise using Spanish or other vernacular language. The particular folk element composed into the music specified the type further: *negrilla, calenda, gallego, jácara*. In 17th-century Spain and New Spain, cathedral chapelmasters were expected to compose new *villancicos* each year for certain feasts such as Corpus

Christi and Christmas, and for **matins** of local saint's day as well. The musical form varied, but most examples contain a refrain (*estribillo* or *responsión*) alternating with several stanzas. *See also CHANSON SPIRITUEL; LAUDA.*

VITRY, PHILLIPE DE (31 October 1291, Paris–9 June 1361, Paris). One of the leading intellectuals of his age, he codified the new principles of modern rhythmic (**mensural**) notation in his treatise *Ars Nova* (c. 1322–1323) and composed about a dozen **motets** that may have had some liturgical function.

VIVALDI, ANTONIO (4 March 1678, Venice–28 July 1741, Vienna). Famous composer of **operas** and **instrumental** concertos, his position as *maestro di violino* at the Pio Ospedale della Pietà in Venice allowed the composition of sacred music only when the *maestro di coro* was on leave. He composed 18 **psalms**, a **Magnificat**, 20 **motets**, three **oratorios**, and half a dozen **mass** movements. The most famous of these is his **Gloria in D**.

VOICE. A melody in a **polyphonic** texture.

VOLUNTARY. A free composition or improvisation, usually for **pipe organ**, played before or after an Anglican **service**, at the Offertory of **Holy Communion**, or after the **psalms** or second lesson at **Morning** and **Evening Prayer**. The term dates to c. 1560 and has loose associations with **fugal** writing, but its use varies widely in the sources.

VOTIVE ANTIPHON. Chants unattached to **psalms** whose texts praised the Virgin Mary or other saint, often in rhyme, sung either in the **divine office** or in processions to accompany **litanies** on their feast days. Marian **antiphons** have traditionally concluded **compline** every day since the 13th century. Many were composed in the late Middle Ages, but four of the longer ones—*Alma redemptoris mater, Ave regina coelorum, Regina coelorum laetare,* and *Salve regina* (*see* Appendix A for texts)—have been sung widely down through modern times.

– W –

WALTHER, JOHANN (1496, Kahla, Thuringia, Germany–25 March 1570, Torgau). A critical figure in the development of a **congregational hymnody** for **Lutheranism**, he compiled the *Wittenberger Geystliche Gesangk Buchleyn* (1st edition, 1524) and advised **Martin Luther** on the German **Mass** in 1525. He also composed two Latin **passions**, nine **Magnificats**, eight **psalms**, and 17 Latin **motets**.

WAR REQUIEM. Composed by **Benjamin Britten** for the consecration of the rebuilt Coventry Cathedral, which had been destroyed by German bombing in World War II, the *War Requiem* intersperses poems of Wilfrid Owen (1893–1918, killed in World War I), sung by tenor and baritone soloists accompanied by a chamber orchestra, into the traditional Latin Requiem **mass** text sung by either a boys' choir and **organ** or a four-voiced choir with an occasional soprano solo accompanied by a large orchestra of triple woodwinds, six horns, four trumpets, three trombones, tuba, piano, percussion and strings. The *War Requiem* premiered on 30 May 1962 at the cathedral. It requires about 85 minutes to perform.

WASAN. **Buddhist chant** sung in Japanese. The verses are in traditional five- and seven-syllable lines, set to melodies of eight beats, typical of much Japanese music, articulated by an *ōdaiko* **drum.** Simpler types of *wasan* were used to evangelize the countryside. *See also SHŌMYŌ; UTASEKKYŌ.*

WATTS, ISAAC (17 July 1674, Southampton, England–25 November 1748, Stoke Newington). Influential writer of **hymns** and **psalm** paraphrases. His collection *The Psalms of David Imitated in the Language of the New Testament* (1719) consummated the movement away from literal psalm versifications toward **metrical psalms** more appropriate for **congregational** singing. Altering the text also allowed Watts to reinterpret the psalms in evangelical terms. Watts also published *Horae Lyricae* (1705) and *Hymns and Spiritual Songs* (1707). (at)

WECHSELGESANG (Ger. "exchange song"). Bohemian tradition of singing Christmas songs dating from before the Reformation. Groups of clergy, **instrumentalists**, unison choruses, and **polyphonic** choruses stationed around the church would exchange verses in an elaborated form of **antiphony**. *See also* CAROL; *CORI SPEZZATI*; *NOËL*.

WEELKES, THOMAS (baptized 25 October 1576–buried 1 December 1623, London). Composer, student of **William Byrd**, and **organist** at Chichester Cathedral from between October of 1601 and 1602 until 16 January 1617 when he was dismissed for drunkenness. He composed nine **services**, the most for a single major composer of his time, and completed more than 30 **anthems**.

WESLEY, CHARLES (18 December 1707, Epworth, Lincolnshire, England–29 March 1788, London). An Anglican clergyman and founder, along with his brother **John Wesley**, of Methodism. He wrote the texts for hundreds of **hymns**, among the most celebrated of which are "Hark, the Herald Angels Sing," "Christ the Lord Is Risen Today," and "Love Divine, All Loves Excelling." *See also* WESLEY, JOHN. (at)

WESLEY, JOHN (17 June 1703, Epworth, Lincolnshire, England–2 March 1791, London). Anglican priest who, along with his brother **Charles Wesley**, founded Methodism. He profoundly influenced **hymnody** in England and America through a series of hymnals beginning with *A Collection of Psalms and Hymns* of 1737. He freely adapted popular and even **operatic** tunes for religious texts, which proved very effective in making converts and provided the first large repertory for **congregational** singing in England besides **metrical psalms**. *See also* WESLEY, CHARLES.

WESLEY, SAMUEL (24 February 1766, Bristol, England–11 October 1837, London). Son of **Charles Wesley**, perhaps the finest English **organist** of his time. He greatly admired the Roman Catholic **polyphonic** tradition and composed six **masses** and over 50 **motets** to Latin texts as well as many Anglican **anthems**, **hymns**, and much **service** music as well as **voluntaries** and other works for organ.

WIDOR, CHARLES-MARIE (21 February 1844, Lyons–12 March 1937, Paris). Organist at the prestigious St. Sulpice of Paris from 1870–1934, he studied with Jacques Lemmens (1823–1881) who traced his own pedagogical lineage directly to **Johann Sebastian Bach**. Widor is best known for his 10 **organ** symphonies, published from 1876–1900. He also composed one **mass** and 10 **motets**, often for double choir and large **instrumental** ensembles. *See also CORI SPEZZATI.*

WILLAERT, ADRIAN (ADRIANO) (c. 1490, Bruges or Roulaers, Flanders–7 December 1562, Venice). Through his own compositions and his teaching of following generations, Willaert made the Venetian musical establishment at St. Mark's one of the foremost musical centers of Europe. After trying law at the University of **Paris,** he studied composition with **Jean Mouton**. He served three members of the d'Este family of Ferrara: Cardinal Ippolito I d'Este (1515–1520), Duke Alfonso I (1522), and Cardinal Ippolito II, Archbishop of Milan (1525–1527). On 12 December 1527, the Procurators of St. Mark's appointed him *maestro di cappella*. Among his students were the theorist and teacher Gioseffo Zarlino (1517–1590), the eminent composer Cipriano de Rore (c. 1515–1565), and **Andrea Gabrieli**.

Willaert is best known today for his eight **psalms** composed for *cori spezzati*, the first associated with St. Mark's, published in Venice in 1550, and for a collection of madrigals and **motets**, *Musica nova* (1559, Venice), one of the most famous publications of the century. He also composed nine **masses**, 29 **polyphonic hymn** settings, 18 single choir psalms, and 183 motets. He also published a set of nine **ricercars** for **organ** (1551, Venice). The earlier motets follow the models of Mouton and **Josquin Desprez** with structures clearly articulated by **imitative** pairs. The later ones favor less explicit imitation in order to maintain fuller textures, the trend for the rest of the century.

WILLAN, HEALEY (12 October 1880, Balham, London–16 February 1968, Toronto). A composer who taught at Toronto Conservatory (1913–1937) and at the University of Toronto (1937–1950), he was **organist** and choirmaster at Anglican Church of St. Mary Magdalene (1921–death). His Anglo-Catholicism is reflected in his 14 *Missae Breves* (1928–1963), the *11 Liturgical Motets* (1928–1937), and the Evening **Canticles** (**chant**-with-**fauxbourdons**, from 1928). He also wrote six communion **services**, four full **masses**, other large-scale sacred works (e.g., Te Deum *in B-flat*, 1935–1937), 34 **anthems** and 30 **hymn**-anthems (e.g., *O Lord, Our Governour*, performed at the coronation of Queen Elizabeth II, 1953), about 30 motets, over 30 **canticles**, four sets of organ hymn **preludes**, and other organ music, of which *Introduction, Passacaglia, and Fugue* (1916) is particularly well known. (at)

WILLIAMSON, MALCOLM (21 November 1931, Sydney–2 March 2003, Cambridge). Virtuoso pianist, he settled in **London** (1953) and became Master of the Queen's Music (1975). He taught himself to play the **organ** by studying **Olivier Messiaen**'s music, and he subsequently wrote many organ works (e.g., *Vision of Christ Phoenix*, which includes "Coventry **Carol**" variations (1962) that show Messiaen's influence. After his conversion to Catholicism, he wrote many sacred works: nine **masses** including *Mass of Christ the King* (1977–1978), *Adoremus* (a Christmas **cantata**, 1959), **hymns** and **anthems**, and many others. (at)

WINCHESTER TROPERS. Two manuscripts, provenance of Old Minster, Winchester, England. The earlier, c. 996, contains the oldest version of the **liturgical drama** *Quem quaeritis* **trope** with both text and music. The later, c. 1050, is a revised version of the earlier but also has a supplement of 150 **organa** on mostly **Alleluias** and **responsories** for the **divine office**, composed in parallel note-against-note style with occasional contrary motion. This is the first practical source of **polyphony** in Western music.

WITT, FRANZ XAVER (9 February 1834, Walderbach, Bavaria–2 December 1888, Landshut). Roman Catholic priest and composer, he promoted the revival of ancient traditions of liturgical music through composing in the *stile antico* and by publishing and founding the *Allgemeiner Deutscher Cäcilien-Verein* ("General German **Cecilian** Society") at Bamberg in 1869 and the *Scuola* **Gregoriana** in **Rome** in 1880.

WITTENBERGER GEYSTLICHE GESANGK BUCHLEYN ("Little Spiritual Songbook of Wittenberg," Wittenberg, 1524). The first systematic collection of 38 **chorales** for public worship, arranged by **Johann Walther** for four and five voices in mostly **homorhythmic** but occasionally **contrapuntal** texture, with an introduction by **Martin Luther**. The collection includes 32 texts set to 35 chorale melodies that are given to the tenor voice traditional for German partsongs of the time, and was intended for use in schools and public worship. *See also* RHAW, GEORG.

WOOD, CHARLES (15 June 1866, Armagh, Ireland–12 July 1926, Cambridge). He taught harmony at Royal College of Music (from 1888) and at Cambridge University (1897–1924). Beginning sacred composition in his later years, he wrote four settings of the Communion **service**, 24 **canticles**, and more than 30 **anthems**. His largest church work is *St. Mark's Passion* (1921), which uses **chant** melodies and two **metrical psalm** tunes. (at)

– Y –

YA-YÜEH (Chinese "elegant music"). Refers to the court music of imperial China from 221 B. C. to 1911. This tradition came to incorporate the rituals of Confucianism in the Han dynasties (206 B. C.–220). The nature of the songs—text, number of performers, types of **instruments**, etc.—depended on immediate circumstances. The oldest notation dates from the late 12th century. Confucianists insist on a pentatonic scale (C, D, E, G, A) as the basic compositional material; auxiliary tones could ornament melodic patterns.

YUSHAN. Monastery in the Changshu area of Jiangsu province in China where monks from all over Asia learned the proper methods of **Buddhist chanting**.

– Z –

ZACHOW, FRIEDRICH WILHELM (baptized 14 November 1663, Leipzig, Germany–7 August 1712, Halle). Teacher of

George Frideric Handel, from 11 August 1684 until his death, Zachow was **organist** at the St. Mary's Church in Halle. Surviving from an apparently large *oeuvre* are about 25 **cantatas** in various forms from **sacred concerto** to **operatic**, one **chorale mass**, two Latin **motets**, and about 50 keyboard **chorales**.

ZEMA. Chant of the Ethiopian Church, traditionally ascribed to St. Yared of the sixth century.

ZEMIROT. Songs of Eastern European Jews celebrating the joys of the Sabbath. The melodies, often borrowed from folksong, Jewish and non-Jewish, and cast in simple **meter**, date from roughly 1600–1850, while the poems are much older, from the ninth to 17th centuries of various provenance. *See also PIYYUT.*

ZIMMERMAN, HEINZ WERNER (11 August 1930, Freiburg, Germany). From the late 1950s, he took an interest in the movement to renew Protestant church music in Germany; from 1963–1976, he was director of the *Berliner Kirchenmusikschule* in Spandau. Zimmerman has composed **motets** and **chorale fantasias** for unaccompanied chorus and a larger number of sacred works for chorus with **instruments**. His style combines sacred idioms from **chorales** and **spirituals** with secular elements, e.g., *Missa Profana* (1977), a Latin **mass** for five soloists, chorus, electronic sounds, sirens, Dixieland band, and orchestra.

ZNAMENNĪY RASPEV (Rus. "chanting by signs"). **Chant** of the Russian Orthodox church. The term coincides with chant books of the late 15th century accompanied by *azbuki* ("alphabets") listing neume types with Slavonic names. The earliest Russian sources date from the late 11th century but are written in notation derived from the earliest **Byzantine** type that has not been deciphered, and political turmoil in the 13th century may have prevented the importation of Byzantine innovations. Even the numerous alphabetic tables in the 16th century do not solve the notation problem entirely because they do not agree. A reform associated with Ivan Shaydur about 1600 assigned fixed pitches to the neumes, thus severing all relations with the Byzantine tradition of notating intervals.

When Patriarch Nikon (ruled 1652–1656) promoted the **polyphonic** singing of the chant, groups opposed to it splintered in schism from the Russian Orthodox Church. These "Old Believers" saw polyphony as a threat from Roman Catholicism. The importation of Western staff notation during the reign of Peter the Great (1689–1725) bolstered the new polyphonic chant and marginalized the traditional **monophony**.

ZWINGLI, HULDRYCH (ULRICH) (1 January 1484, Wildhaus, Switzerland–11 October 1531, Cappel). Protestant reformer who, despite extraordinary musical gifts, believed liturgical music to be an obstacle to faith and excluded it entirely from his revised liturgy *Aktion oder Brauch des Nachtmahls* (1525). His ideas resulted in the radical reduction of music in Swiss reform churches, including the wholesale dismantling of **pipe organs**, but a simplified liturgical music based mostly on **metrical psalms** soon returned to reform churches. *See also* CALVIN, JEAN; CONSTANCE SONGBOOK; GENEVAN PSALTER.

Appendix A

Texts of the Roman Catholic Rite

Translations for sections A and B are traditional for the Anglican rite

A. THE ORDINARY PRAYERS OF THE MASS

1. Kyrie eleison

Kyrie eleison	Lord, have mercy upon us.
Christe eleison	Christ, have mercy upon us.
Kyrie eleison	Lord, have mercy upon us.

2. Gloria in excelsis Deo

Gloria in excelsis Deo et in terra pax hominibus bonae voluntatis. Laudamus te. Benedicimus te. Adoramus te. Glorificamus te. Gratias agimus tibi propter magnam gloriam tuam, Domine Deus, rex caelestis, Deus Pater omnipotens. Domine Fili unigenite, Jesu Christe. Domine Deus,

Glory be to God on high and on earth peace, good will towards men. We praise thee, we bless thee, we worship thee, we glorify thee, we give thanks to thee for thy great glory, O Lord God, heavenly King, God the Father Almighty. O Lord, the only begotten son, Jesus

Agnus Dei, Filius Patris. Qui tollis peccata mundi, miserere nobis. Qui tollis peccata mundi, suscipe deprecationem nostram. Qui sedes ad dexteram Patris, miserere nobis.
Quoniam tu solus Sanctus. Tu solus Dominus.
Tu solus Altissimus, Jesu Christe. Cum Sancto Spiritu, in gloria Dei Patris. Amen.

Christ; O Lord God, Lamb of God, Son of the Father, that takest away the sins of the world, have mercy upon us. Thou that takest away the sins of the world, receive our prayer. Thou that sittest at the right hand of God the Father, have mercy upon us. For thou only art holy; thou only art the Lord; thou only, O Christ, with the Holy Ghost, art most high, in the glory of God the Father. Amen.

3. Credo in unum Deum

Credo in unum Deum, Patrem omnipotentem, factorem caeli et terrae, visibilium omnium et invisibilium. Et in unum Dominum, Jesum Christum, Filium Dei unigenitum. Et ex Patre natum ante omnia saecula.
Deum de Deo, lumen de lumine, Deum verum de Deo vero. Genitum, non factum, consubstantialem Patri: per quem omnia facta sunt. Qui propter nos homines et propter nostram salutem descendit de caelis. Et incarnatus est de Spiritu Sancto ex maria Virgine: Et homo factus est. Crucifixus etiam pro nobis: sub Pontio Pilato passus, et sepultus est.
Et resurrexit tertia die, secundum Scripturas. Et ascendit in

I believe in one God, the Father Almighty, maker of heaven and earth, and of all things visible and invisible; And in one Lord Jesus Christ, the only begotten Son of God, born of his Father before all worlds, God of God, Light of Light, very God of very God, begotten, not made, being of one substance with the Father; by whom all things were made; who for us men and for our salvation came down from heaven, and was incarnate by the Holy Ghost of the Virgin Mary, and was made man; and was crucified also for us under Pontius Pilate; he suffered and was buried; and the third day he rose again according to the Scriptures, and ascended into

caelum: sedet ad dexteram patris.
Et iterum venturus est cum gloria, judicare vivos et mortuos: cujus regni non erit finis.
Et in Spiritum Sanctum, Dominum, et vivificantem: qui ex Patre Filioque procedit.
Qui cum Patre et Filio simul adoratur et conglorificatur: qui locutus est per Prophetas. Et unam sanctam catholicam et apostolicam Ecclesiam. Confiteor unum baptisma in remissionem peccatorum. Et expecto resurrectionem mortuorum. Et vitam venturi saeculi. Amen.

heaven, and sitteth on the right hand of the Father; and he shall come again with glory to judge the quick and the dead; whose kingdom shall have no end. And I believe in the Holy Ghost the Lord, and Giver of Life, who proceedeth from the Father and the Son; who with the Father and the Son together is worshipped and glorified; who spake by the prophets. And I believe in one holy Catholic and Apostolic church. I acknowledge one Baptism for the remission of sins; and I look for the resurrection of the dead, and the life of the world to come. Amen.

4. Sanctus

Sanctus, sanctus, sanctus Dominus Deus Sabaoth. Pleni sunt caeli et terra gloria tua. Hosanna in excelsis.
Benedictus qui venit in nomine Domini. Hosanna in excelsis.

Holy, Holy, Holy Lord God of hosts, Heaven and earth are full of thy glory. Glory be to thee, O Lord Most High. Blessed is he that cometh in the name of the Lord. Hosanna in the highest.

5. Agnus Dei

Agnus Dei, qui tollis peccata mundi: miserere nobis.
Agnus Dei, qui tollis peccata mundi: miserere nobis.
Agnus Dei, qui tollis peccata mundi: dona nobis pacem.

O Lamb of God, that takest away the sin of the world, have mercy upon us.
O Lamb of God, that takest away the sin of the world, have mercy upon us.

O Lamb of God, that takest away the sin of the world, grant us thy peace.

6. Ite missa est

Ite, missa est. Deo gratias.

Let us go forth in the name of Christ.
Thanks be to God.

B. THE GOSPEL CANTICLES

1. Benedictus (St. Luke 1: 68–79)

Benedictus Dominus Deus Israel, quia visitavit et fecit redemptionem plebis suae. Et erexit cornu salutis nobis, in domo David pueri sui.
Sicut locutus est per os sanctorum, qui a saeculo sunt, prophetarum ejus.
Salutem ex inimicis nostris, et de manu omnium qui oderunt nos.

Ad faciendam misericordiam cum patribus nostris, et memorari testamenti sui sancti.
Jusjurandum, quod juravit ad Abraham patrem nostrum, daturum se nobis. Ut sine timore, de manu inimcorum nostrorum liberati, serviamus illi. In sanctitate et justitia coram ipso, omnibus deibus nostris.
Et tu puer, propheta Altissimi vocaberis, praeibis enim ante fa-

Blessed be the Lord God of Israel, for he hath visited and redeemed his people. And he hath raised up a mighty salvation for us, in the house of his servant David; And he spake by the mouth of his holy prophets, which have been since the world began; that we should be saved from our enemies and from the hand of all that hate us; to perform the mercy promised to our forefathers and to remember his holy convenant; to perform this oath which He sware to our forefather Abraham, that he would give us; that we being delivered out of the hand of our enemies, might serve him without fear, in holiness and righteousness before him, all the days of our life. And thou, child, shall be called the prophet of the Highest: for

ciem Domini parare vias ejus.
Ad dandam scientiam salutis
plebi ejus, in remissionem peccatorum eorum. Per viscera misericordiae Dei nostri, in quibus
visitavit nos, oriens ex alto. Il-
luminare his qui in tenebris et
in umbra mortis sedent, ad diri-
gendos pedes nostros in viam
pacis.

thou shalt go before the face of
the Lord to prepare His ways,
to give knowledge of salvation
unto his people for the remission of their sins. Through the
tender mercy of our God,
whereby the dayspring from on
high hath visited us, to give
light to them that sit in darkness and in the shadow of
death, and to guide our feet into
the way of peace.

2. Magnificat (St. Luke 1: 46–55)

Magnificat anima mea Dominum. Et exsultavit spiritus meus
in Deo salutari meo. Quia res-
pexit humilitatem ancillae suae;
ecce enim ex hoc beatam me
dicent omnes generationes. Quia
fecit mihi magna qui potens est,
et sanctum nomen eius.
Et misericordia a progenie in
progenies timentibus eum. Fecit
potentiam in brachio suo, dis-
persit superbos mente cordis sui.
Deposuit potentes de sede et ex-
altavit humiles.
Esurientes implevit bonis et div-
ites dimisit inanes.
Suscepit Israel puerum suum re-
cordatus misericordiae suae.
Sicut locutus est ad Patres nostros, Abraham et semini eius in
saecula.

My soul doth magnify the Lord,
and my spirit hath rejoiced in
God my Saviour.
For he hath regarded the lowli-
ness of his handmaiden; for be-
hold, from henceforth all
generations shall call me
blessed. For he that is mighty
hath magnified me; and holy is
his Name. And his mercy is on
those that fear him throughout
all generations. He has showed
strength with his arm; he hath
scattered the proud in the imagination of their hearts. He has
put down the mighty from their
seat, and hath exalted the humble and meek. He hath filled the
hungry with good things; and
the rich he hath sent away
empty. He remembering his
mercy hath holpen his servant
Israel; as he promised to our

forefathers, Abraham and his seed for ever.

3. Nunc Dimittis (St. Luke 2:29–32)

Nunc dimittis servum tuum Domine, secundum verbum tuum in pace. Quia viderunt oculi mei salutare tuum. Quod parasti ante faciem omnium populorum. Lumen ad revelationem gentium, et gloriam plebis tuae Israel.

Lord, now lettest thou thy servant depart in peace, according to they word. For mine eyes have seen thy salvation, which thou hast prepared before the face of all people; to be a light to lighten the Gentiles, and to be the glory of they people Israel.

N.B. To each of the Gospel canticles is appended the lesser doxology:

Gloria Patri et Filio et Spiritui Sancto, sicut erat in principio, et nunc et semper, et in saecula saeculorum. Amen.

Glory be to the Father, to the Son, and to the Holy Spirit, as it was in the beginning, is now and always, forever. Amen.

C. THE MARIAN ANTIPHONS

1. Alma Redemptoris Mater

Alma Redemptoris Mater, quae pervia caeli porta manes, et stella maris succurre cadenti surgere qui curat populo. Tu quae genuisti, nature mirante, tuum sanctum Genitorem. Virgo prius ac posterius, Gabrielis ab ore sumen illud Ave, peccatorum miserere.

Dear Mother of the Redeemer, the gate through which you lead us to heaven, and star of the sea, help the fallen people, those who seek to rise. You who gave birth, with all nature wondering, to your holy Creator, Virgin before and after, who heard from Gabriel's mouth that "Ave," have mercy on us sinners.

2. Ave Regina Caelorum

Ave Regina caelorum, ave Domina Angelorum: salve radix, salve porta, ex qua mundo lux est orta. Gaude Virgo gloriosa, super omnes speciosa. Vale, o valde decora, et pro nobis Christum exora.

Hail Queen of the heavens, hail mistress of the angels, hail root [of Jesse], hail the gate through whom the world's Light is born. Rejoice, glorious Virgin, loveliest of all creatures. Go up on high, and pray for us to Christ.

3. Regina Caeli Laetare

Regina caeli laetare, alleluia. Qua quem meruisti portare, alleluia. Resurrexit, sicut dixit, alleluia. Ora pro nobis Deum, alleluia.

Rejoice, Queen of heaven, alleluia, for Him whom you merited to bear, alleluia. He has risen as he said, alleluia. Pray to God for us, alleluia.

4. Salve Regina

Salve, Regina, mater misericordiae: vita, dulcedo, et spes nostra, salve. Ad te clamamus, exsules, filii Hevae. Ad te suspiramus, gementes et flentes in hac lacrimarum valle. Eia ergo, Advocata nostra, illos tuos misericordes oculos ad nos converte. Et Jesum, benedictum fructum ventris tui, nobis post hoc exsilium ostende. O clemens, O pia, O dulcis Virgo Maria.

Hail, Queen, mother of mercy, our life, sweetness and hope. To you we cry, banished children of Eve. To you we sigh, mourning and weeping in this valley of tears. Therefore, our Advocate, turn your eyes of mercy toward us. And after this our exile show to us the blessed fruit of your womb, Jesus. O clement, o pious, o sweet Virgin Mary.

Appendix B
Shema and *Kaddish*

KADDISH

יתגדל ויתקדש שמה רבא (אמן)
בעלמא די ברא כרעותה
יימליך מלכותה בחייכון
ובומיכון ובחיי דכל בית ישראל
בעגלא ובזמן קריב ואמרו אמן:

יהא שמה רבא מבורך לעולם
ולעלמי עלמיא:

יתברך וישתבך ויתפאר
ויתרומם ויתנשא ויתהדר
ויתעלה ויתהלל שמה דקודשא
בריך הוא
לעלא מן כל ברכתא ושירתא
תושבחתא ונחמתש דאמירן
בעלמא ואמרו אמן:

יהא שלמא רבא מן שמיא וחיים
עלינו ועל כל ישראל
ואמרו אמן:

עושה שלום במרומיו הוא יעשה
שלום עלינו ועל כל ישראל
ואמרו אמן

KADDISH

Yeetgadal v' yeetkadash sh'mey rabbah (Amein).
B'almah dee v'rah kheer'utey v' yamleekh malkhutei,b'chahyeykhohn, uv' yohmeykhohn,
uv'chahyei d'chohl beyt yisrael, ba'agalah u'veez'man kareev, v'eemru: Amein.

May His great Name grow exalted and sanctified (Amen) in the world that He created as He willed.
May He give reign to His kingship in your lifetimes and in your days,
and in the lifetimes of the entire Family of Israel, swiftly and soon. Now respond: Amen.
May His great Name be blessed forever and ever.

(Cong: Amein. Y'hey sh'met rabbah m'varach l'alam u'l'almey almahyah)
Y'hey sh'met rabbah m'varach l'alam u'l'almey almahyah.
Yeet'barakh, v' yeesh'tabach, v' yeetpa'ar, v' yeetrohmam, v' yeet'nasei,
v' yeet'hadar, v' yeet'aleh, v' yeet'halal sh'mey d'kudshah b'reekh hoo
L'eylah meen kohl beerkhatah v'sheeratah,
toosh'b'chatah v'nechematah, da'ameeran b'al'mah, v'eemru: Amein

Blessed, praised, glorified, exalted, extolled,
mighty, upraised, and lauded be the Name of the Holy One, Blessed is He
beyond any blessing and song, praise and consolation that are uttered in the world.

Now respond: Amen.

Y'hei shlamah rabbah meen sh'mahyah,v'chahyeem aleynu v'al kohl yisrael, v'eemru: Amein

May there be abundant peace from Heaven, and life upon us and upon all Israel. Now respond: Amen.

Oseh shalom beem'roh'mahv, hoo ya'aseh shalom, aleynu v'al kohl yisrael v'eemru: Amein

He Who makes peace in His heights, may He make peace, upon us and upon all Israel. Now respond: Amen.

SHEMA

שמע ישראל יי אלוהינו יי אחד:
ברוך שם כבוד מלכותו לעולם ועד:

ואהבת את יי אלוהיך בכל לבבך
ובכל נפשך ובכל מאודך:

והיו הדברים האלה אשר אנוכי
מצווך היום על לבבך:

ושננתם לבניך ודברת בם
בשבתך בביתך ובלכתך בדרך
ובשכבך ובקומך:

וקשרתם לאות על ידך
ו לטוטפות בין עיניך:והי

וכתבתם על מזוזות ביתך
ובשעריך:

SHEMA

Sh'ma yisrael Adonai Eloheinu Adonai echad	Hear, Israel, the Lord is our God, the Lord is One.
Barukh shem k'vod malchuto l'olam va'ed	Blessed be the Name of His glorious kingdom for ever and ever
V'ahavta et Adonai Elohecha b'chol levavcha u'v'chol naf'sh'cha u'v'chol m'odecha	And you shall love the Lord your God with all your heart and with all your soul and with all your might.
V'hayu ha'dvarim ha'ayleh asher anochi m'tzavecha ha'yom al l'vavecha	And these words that I command you today shall be in your heart.
V'shinantam l'vanecha, v'dibarta bam b'shivtecha v'vaytecha, u'v'lechtecha ba'derech, u'v'shachbecha u'v'kumecha	And you shall teach them diligently to your children, and you shall speak of them when you sit at home, and when you walk along the way, and when you lie down and when you rise up.
Uk'shartam l'ot al yadecha, v'hayu l'totafot bayn aynecha	And you shall bind them as a sign on your hand, and they shall be for frontlets between your eyes.
Uchtavtam al mezuzot baytecha u'visharecha	And you shall write them on the doorposts of your house and on your gates.

SHEMA

והיה אם שמוע תשמעו אל
מיצותי אשר אנכי מצווה אתכם
היום לאהבה את יי אלוהיכם
ולעבדו בכל לבבכם ובכל
נפשיכם:

ונתתי מטר ארציכם בעיתו יורה
ומלקוש ואספת דגנך ותירושך
ויצהרך:

ונתתי עשב בשדך לבהמתך
ואכלת ושבעת:

השמרו לכם פן יפתה לבבכם
וסרתם ועבדתם אלוהים אחרים
הישתחויתם להם:ו

וחרה אף יי בכם ועצר את
השמים ולא יהיה מטר והאדמה
לא תיתן את יבולה ואבדתם
מהרה מעל הארץ הטובה אשר
יי נותן לכם:

ושמתם את דברי אלה על
לבבכם ועל נפשכם וקשרתם
אותם לאות על ידכם והיו
לטוטפות בין עיניכם:

ולמדתם אותם את בניכם לדבר
ך ובלכתך בם בשיבתך בבית
בדרך ובשוכבך ובקומך:

וכתבתם על מזוזות ביתך
ובישעריך:

למען ירבו ימיכם וימי בניכם על
האדמה אשר נשבע יי
לאבותיכם לתת לכם כימי
השמים על הארץ:

SHEMA

*V'haya im shamoa tish'meu el mitzvotai asher
anochi m'tzaveh etchem ha'yom, l'ahavah et
Adonai Elohaychem u'l'avdo b'chol l'vavchem
u'v'chol nafshechem*

And it shall come to pass if you surely listen to
the commandments that I command you today,
to love the Lord your God, and to serve him with
all your heart and all your soul,

*V'natati m'tar artzchem b'ito, yoreh u'malkosh
v'asafta d'ganecha v'tirosh'cha v'yitzharecha*

That I will give rain to your land, the early and
the late rains, that you may gather in your grain,
your wine and your oil.

*V'natati aysev b'sad'cha lib'hemtecha v'achalta
v'savata*

And I will give grass in your fields for your
cattle and you will eat and you will be satisfied.

*Hishamru lachem, pen yifteh l'vavchem,
v-sartem va-avadtem elohim achayrim, v-
hishtachavitem lahem.*

Beware, lest your heart be deceived,
and you turn and serve other gods, and worship
them.

*V-charah af Adonai bachem, v-atzar et ha-
shamayim v-lo yihyeh matar,
v-ha-adama lo titayn et y'vulah;
va-avadtem m'hayrah mayal ha-aretz ha-tovah
asher Adonai notayn lachem.*

And anger of the Lord will blaze against you,
and he will close the heavens and there will not
be rain, and the earth will not give you its
fullness, and you will perish quickly from the
good land that the Lord gives you.

*V-sam'tem et d'varai ayleh al l'vavchem v-al
naf'sh'chem;
u-kshartem otam l-ot al yedchem, v-hayu ltotafot
bayn aynaychem.*

So you shall put these, my words, on your heart
and on your soul;
and you shall bind them for signs on your hands,
and they shall be for frontlets between your eyes.

*V-limadtem otam et b'naychem l-daber bam
b-shivt'cha b-vaytecha, u-v-lecht'cha baderech,
u-v-shachb'cha u-v-kumecha.*

And you shall teach them to your children, and
you shall speak of them
when you sit in your house, and when you walk
on the way, and when you lie down, and when
you rise up.

U-ch'tavtam al m'zuzot baytecha u-vi-sharecha.

And you shall write them on the doorposts of
your house and on your gates.

*L'ma'an yirbu y'maychem vi-y'may v'naychem al
ha-adamah asher nishba Adonai
la-avotaychem latayt lahem ki-y'may ha-
shamayim al ha-aretz.*

In order to prolong your days and the days of
your children on the land that the Lord promised
your fathers that he would give them, as long as
the days that the heavens are over the earth.

SHEMA

ויאמר יי אל משה לאמר

דבר אל בני ישראל ואמרת
ועשו להם ציצית על כנפי אלהם
ביגדיהם לדורותם ונתנו על
ציצית הכנף פתיל תכלת

והיה לכם לציצת וראיתם אותו
וזכרתם את כל מצוות יי
ועשיתם אותם ולא תתורו אחרי
לבבכם ואחרי עיניכם אשר
אתם זונים אחריהם

למען תיזכרו ועשיתם את כל
מיצוותי והייתם קדושים
לאלוהיכם

כם אשר הוצאתי אני יי אלוהי
אתכם מארץ מצריים להיות
לכם לאלוהים אני יי אלוהיכם

SHEMA

Vayomer Adonai el Mosheh laymor.

And the Lord spoke to Moses, saying...

Daber el b'nay Yisrael v-amarta alayhem, v-asu lahem tzitzit al can'fay vi-g'dayhem l-dorotam, v-natnu al tzitzit ha-canaf p'til t'chaylet.

Speak to the children of Israel and say to them, they should make themselves tzitzit (fringes) on the corners of their clothing throughout their generations, and give the tzitzit of each corner a thread of blue.

V-hayah lachem l-tzitzit, u-r'iytem oto u-z'chartem et kol mitzvot Adonai, va-asiytem otam v-lo taturu acharay l-vavchem v-acharay aynaychem, asher atem zonim acharaychem.

And they shall be tzitzit for you, and when you look at them you will remember all of the Lord's commandments and do them and not follow after your heart and after your eyes, which lead you astray.

L'ma-an tiz'k'ru v-asitem et kol mitzvotai, vi-h'yiytem k'doshim laylohaychem.

In order to remember and do all My commandments, and be holy for your God.

Ani Adonai Elohaychem, asher hotzaytiy etchem mayeretz Mitzrayim, li-h'yot lahem laylohim. Ani Adonai Elohaychem.

I am the Lord, your God, who lead you from the land of Egypt to be a god to you. I am the Lord, your God.

Bibliography

INTRODUCTION

Because the entries of the dictionary can provide only the most basic information about any item in the vast body of the world's sacred music, the bibliography directs the reader to sources of more detailed and deeper treatments. To this end, the bibliography is organized in top-down fashion, beginning with the most general references about music and religion taken separately, proceeding through general histories of music and histories, dictionaries, and bibliographies of sacred music. Then come biographies and studies of sacred music of specific traditions (e.g., Lutheranism). The last sections, not being strictly bibliographical, are more general: important collections of sacred music, discographies, and electronic sources. Inevitably some items do not fall neatly into any category, or might have fitted sensibly into more than one, e.g., Allan Ho and Dmitry Feofanov's *Biographical Dictionary of Russian/Soviet Composers*, which might have been listed in the **Dictionaries and Bibliographies of Sacred Music** rather than **Studies within Specific Traditions / Byzantine and Orthodox**, where it is found, since nearly all of the composers found there would have written in that specific tradition. To avoid double listings and include as many sources as possible, I hope that the reader may check all plausible subheadings.

The criteria for inclusion begin with the obvious ones of the authors' and publishers' reputations in the various subfields of sacred music. Beyond that I (and the series editor) preferred to include more recent works rather than older ones, works in English, and books rather than articles. Exceptions are made to each of these criteria at times, of course. Some specialized areas have been but little studied as yet, and one must take what one can get. Classic studies and standard references deserve a place almost regardless of their age, and sometimes older editions contain valuable information not retained in later ones, e.g., *The Catholic Encyclopedia*. 1907. [http://www.newadvent.org/cathen/]. Not listed are doctoral dissertations, because they are not nearly as accessible to readers as books, but they nevertheless contain many excellent specialized studies of sacred music (see Adkins, *Doctoral Dissertations in Musicology* in the **General References on Music** and at www.mu sic.indiana.edu/ddm/. Not listed are items written in languages other than those of standard western musicology: English above all, German, French, Italian, Latin, and Spanish. This obviously limits the bibliographies of the non-Western sacred musics; I hope that the interested reader who knows those languages can use the English-language items as stepping stones to publications written in them.

For English speakers, the most useful of the **General References** to be found in most libraries are *The New Grove*, a music encyclopedia of 29 volumes, recently revised and updated, the *RILM* index of periodical literature, the *RISM* catalog of musical sources, and *Baker's* biographical dictionaries.

Both practitioners and scholars of sacred music must understand at least in its fundamentals the religious tradition to which that music belongs. The **General References on Religion** provides the standard references for each of the world's major religions, as well as some general references useful for comparing across religions.

Histories of Music Comprising Sacred Music combines two kinds of books: those concentrating on sacred music not limited to a specific religious tradition, e.g., Stephen A. Marini's *Sacred Song in America: Religion, Music, and Public Culture*, and more general histories of music whose purview would automatically include significant emphasis on sacred music. Of these, Alan Atlas's *Renaissance Music*, Richard Crawford's *America's Musical Life*, Richard Hoppin's *Medieval Music*, Eileen Southern's *The Music of Black Americans*, Reinhard Strom's *The Rise of European Music, 1380–1500*, and Peter Williams' *The Organ in Western Culture* would provide good starting points for most topics in sacred music of the west.

Items concentrating on sacred music whose titles contain the words "bibliography," "dictionary," or "encyclopedia" should be found in **Dictionaries and Bibliographies of Sacred Music**, although there are other items, such as catalogs, if they do not focus on one religious tradition. Sectarian items, such as handbooks for hymnals, are found further on in **Studies within Specific Traditions**.

The biographical section includes principally composers but also anyone who has influenced the course of sacred music history, e.g., Prosper Guéranger. It has a subheading for each person with three or more entries. Items about less significant personages are grouped together under "Others," listed alphabetically by author as usual. In recent years have appeared a great number of books devoted to single works, such as the *Mass in B Minor* of J. S. Bach, and these are duly listed, especially if there is a corresponding entry in the historical dictionary. Of particular interest to scholars are the "Guides to Research" for individual composers, usually published by Garland Press but occasionally by Routledge and others. The Cambridge Handbooks are also excellent bibliographical references.

It only made sense to subdivide by religious tradition the **Studies within Specific Traditions**. Because of all the sacred musics it prizes written notation, Christian music naturally has been studied the most. This vast literature is further subdivided by sect (e.g., Roman Catholic, Byzantine, etc.) or other convenient grouping (e.g., American Protestant) when the sects become too small. This is the best section to locate studies of non-Western sacred musics, e.g., Islamic.

The bibliography concludes with resources that are not books, strictly speaking: important collections of music, including complete works collections of major composers; discographies, including some general guides and discographies of specific composers of important sacred works; and internet sites, some of which correspond to the most important general references (e.g., *RISM*).

GENERAL REFERENCES ON MUSIC

Adkins, Cecil, and Alis Dickinson. *Doctoral Dissertations in Musicology.* 2nd series. 1st cumulative ed. Philadelphia, Pa.: American Musicological Society; Basel: International Musicological Society, 1990. Supplements, 1991.

Arom, Simha. *African Polyphony and Polyrhythm: Musical Structure and Methodology.* Cambridge: Cambridge University Press, 1991.

Benjamin, Thomas. *The Craft of Tonal Counterpoint.* New York: Routledge, 2003.

Cohen, Aaron I. *International Encyclopedia of Women Composers.* 2nd ed., vol. 1. New York: Books and Music, 1987.

De Lerma, Dominique-René. *A Bibliography of Black Music.* 4 vols. Westport, Conn.: Greenwood, 1981–1984.

Duckles, Vincent H., and Ida Reed. *Music Reference and Research Materials: An Annotated Bibliography.* 5th ed. New York: Schirmer, 1997.

Finscher, Ludwig. *Musik in Geschichte und Gegenwart: allgemeine Enzyklopädie der Musik.* 2nd ed., rev. 20 vols. Kassel, Germany: Bärenreiter, 1994–2004.

The Garland Encyclopedia of World Music. James Porter and Timothy Rice, eds. 10 vols. New York: Routledge, 1997–2002.

Griffiths, Paul. *Thames and Hudson Encyclopedia of Twentieth Century Music.* New York: Thames and Hudson, 1986.

Kennedy, Michael, and Joyce Bourne. *The Oxford Dictionary of Music.* 2nd ed. Oxford: Oxford University Press, 1994.

Randel, Don Michael. *The New Harvard Dictionary of Music.* Cambridge, Mass.: Belknap Press of Harvard University Press, 1986.

Répertoire International de Littérature Musicale. RILM Abstracts of Music Literature. New York: International *RILM* Center, 1967– . Vol. 1.

Répertoire International des Sources Musicales [RISM]. Munich: G. Henle, 1960–.

Sadie, Julie Anne, and Rhian Samuel. *The New Grove Dictionary of Women Composers.* London: Macmillan, 1994.

Sadie, Stanley. *The New Grove Dictionary of Music and Musicians.* 29 vols. New York: Macmillan, 2001.

Slonimsky, Nicolas. *Baker's Biographical Dictionary of Musicians.* New York: Schirmer, 1991.

Slonimsky, Nicolas, Laura Diane Kuhn, and Nicholas Slonimsky. *Baker's Biographical Dictionary of Musicians.* 6 vols. New York: Schirmer, 2001.

GENERAL REFERENCES ON RELIGION

Bowker, John, ed. *The Oxford Dictionary of World Religions.* Oxford: Oxford University Press, 1997.

Eliade, Mircea, et al., eds. *The Encyclopedia of Religion.* New York: Macmillan, 1987.

Festivals and Holidays. New York: Macmillan Library Reference USA, 1999.

Johnston, William M., ed. *Recent Reference Books in Religion: A Guide for Students, Scholars, Researchers, Buyers & Readers.* Chicago: Fitzroy Dearborn, 1998.

Smith, Jonathan Z., et al., eds. *The HarperCollins Dictionary of Religion.* San Francisco: Harper San Francisco, 1995.

I. Buddhism

Bunce, Fredrick W. *A Dictionary of Buddhist and Hindu Iconography, Illustrated: Objects, Devices, Concepts, Rites, and Related Terms.* New Delhi: D. K. Printworld, 1997.

Keown, Damien. *A Dictionary of Buddhism.* Oxford: Oxford University Press, 2003.

Murthy, K. Krishna. *A Dictionary of Buddhist Terms and Terminologies.* New Delhi: Sundeep Praskashn, 1999.

Prebish, Charles. S. *A Historical Dictionary of Buddhism.* Metuchen, N. J.: Scarecrow, 1993.

Singh, Nagendra Kumar, ed. *International Encyclopedia of Buddhism.* New Delhi: Anmol Publications, 1996.

II. Christianity

Andrews, Dean Timothy. *The Eastern Orthodox Church: A Bibliography.* 2nd ed. Brookline, Mass.: Holy Cross Orthodox Theological School, 1957.

Balmer, Randall, and John R. Fitzmier. *The Presbyterians.* Westport, Conn.: Greenwood, 1993.

Bard Thompson. *Liturgies of the Western Church.* Philadelphia: Fortress Press, 1961. Rpt. 1980.

Blumhofer, Edith, and Randall H. Balmer. *Modern Christian Revivals.* Urbana, Ill.: University of Illinois Press, 1993.

Blumhofer, Edith L., et al., eds. *Pentecostal Currents in American Protestantism.* Urbana, Ill.: University of Illinois Press, 1999.

Bodensieck, Julius, ed. *The Encyclopedia of the Lutheran Church.* Minneapolis: Augsburg, 1965.

Brockway, Robert W. *A Wonderful Work of God: Puritanism and the Great Awak-*

ening. Bethlehem, Pa.: Lehigh University Press; London: Associated University Presses, 2003.

Carlen, Claudia, ed. *The Papal Encyclicals*. Ann Arbor: Pierian Press, 1990.

Clark, Stephen R. L. *God's World and the Great Awakening*. Oxford: Clarendon Press and Oxford University Press, 1991.

Constantelos, Demetrio J. *Understanding the Greek Orthodox Church: Its Faith, History, and Practice*. New York: Seabury Press, 1982.

Cross. F. L., and E. A. Livingstone, eds. *The Oxford Dictionary of the Christian Church*. 2nd edition. Oxford: Oxford University Press, 1958, 1983.

Crumb, Lawrence N. *The Oxford Movement and its Leaders: A Bibliography of Secondary and Lesser Primary Sources*. Metuchen, N. J.: Scarecrow, 1988.

Di Berardino, Angelo, ed. *Encyclopedia of the Early Church*. Trans. Adrian Walford. New York: Oxford University Press, 1992.

Elliot, Peter J. *Ceremonies of the Modern Roman Rite: The Eucharist and the Liturgy of the Hours*. San Francisco: Ignatius Press, 1995.

Ellis, Jane. *The Russian Orthodox Church: A Contemporary History*. Bloomington, Ind.: Indiana University Press, 1986.

Farmer, David H. *The Oxford Dictionary of Saints*. 4th ed. New York: Oxford University Press, 1997.

Farmer, David H. and Paul Burns. *Butler's Lives of the Saints*. 12 vols. Collegeville, Minn.: Liturgical Press, 1995–2000.

Fennell, John L. I. *A History of the Russian Church to 1448*. London: Longman, 1995.

Frey, Sylvia R., and Betty Wood. *Come Shouting to Zion: African American Protestantism in the American South and British Caribbean to 1830*. Chapel Hill, N.C.: University of North Carolina Press, 1998.

Gallagher, Edward J., and Thomas Werge. *Early Puritan Writers: A Reference Guide*. Boston: G. K. Hall, 1976.

Gamber, Klaus. *The Reform of the Roman Liturgy: Its Problems and Background*. San Juan Capistrano: Una Voce Press, 1993.

General Instruction of the Roman Missal. Washington, D.C.: United States Conference of Catholic Bishops, 2003.

Glazier, Michael, and Thomas J. Shelley, eds. *The Encyclopedia of American Catholic History*. Collegeville, Minn.: Liturgical Press, 1997.

Herbermann, Charles G., et al., eds. *The Catholic Encyclopedia; An International Work of Reference on the Constitution, Doctrine, Discipline, and History of the Catholic Church*. New York: Appleton, 1907–1914.

Jedin, Hubert. *Ecumenical Councils of the Catholic Church*. New York: Herder and Herder, 1960.

Johnson, Paul E., ed. *African-American Christianity: Essays in History*. Berkeley: University of California Press, 1994.

Jungmann, Josef. A. *Missarum Sollemnia: Eine genetische Erklärung der römi-*

schen Messe. Vienna: Herder, 1949. Trans. *The Mass of the Roman Rite*. Westminster, Md.: Christian Classics, 1951. Rpt. 1986.

Kazhdan, Alexander. *The Oxford Dictionary of Byzantium*. New York: Oxford University Press, 1991. (vol. 1, 507; vol. 2, 1354–1355).

Lang, Jovian P. *Dictionary of the Liturgy*. New York: Catholic Book Publishing Co., 1989.

New Catholic Encyclopedia. 2nd ed. Detroit: Thompson/Gale; Washington, D. C.: Catholic University, 2003–.

Nockles, Peter B. *The Oxford Movement in Context: Anglican High Churchmanship, 1760–1857*. Cambridge: Cambridge University Press, 1994.

Pettegree, Andrew, Alastair Duke, and Gillian Lewis, eds. *Calvinism in Europe, 1540–1620*. Cambridge: Cambridge University Press, 1994.

Pfaff, Richard W. *Medieval Latin Liturgy: A Select Bibliography*. Toronto: University of Toronto Press, 1982.

Prokurat, Michael, Alexander Golitzin, and Michael D. Peterson, eds. *A Historical Dictionary of the Orthodox Church*. Lanham, Md.: Scarecrow, 1996.

Robinson, Thomas A., et al. *The Early Church: An Annotated Bibliography of Literature in English*. Metuchen, N. J.: Scarecrow, 1993.

Scribner, William, et al. *Anthology of Presbyterian & Reformed Literature*. 5 vols. Dallas, Tex.: Naphtali Press, 1988–1992.

Spurr, John. *English Puritianism, 1603–1689*. New York: St. Martin's Press, 1998.

Stelton, Leo F. *Dictionary of Ecclesiastical Latin: With an Appendix of Latin Expressions Defined and Clarified*. Peabody, Mass.: Hendrickson, 1995.

Taft, Robert, S. J. *The Liturgy of the Hours in East and West*. Collegeville: Liturgical Press, 1986.

White, James F. *Roman Catholic Worship: Trent to Today*. Collegeville, Minn.: Liturgical Press, 2003.

Wilson, John Frederick. *Religion and the American Nation: Historiography and History*. Athens, Ga.: University of Georgia Press, 2003.

III. Hinduism

Bunce, Fredrick W. *A Dictionary of Buddhist and Hindu Iconography, Illustrated: Objects, Devices, Concepts, Rites, and Related Terms*. New Delhi: D. K. Printworld, 1997.

Garg, Ram Ganga, gen. ed. *Encyclopaedia of the Hindu World*. New Delhi: Concept 1992.

Lochtefeld, James G. *The Illustrated Encyclopedia of Hinduism*. New York: Rosen, 2002.

Pruthi, Raj Kumar, and Rameshwari Devi, eds. *Encyclopaedia of Indian Society and Culture*. Jaipur, India: Mangal Deep Publications, 2002.

Soundara, Rajan. *Concise Classified Dictionary of Hinduism*. New Dehli: Concept, 2001.

Sullivan, Bruce M. *Historical Dictionary of Hinduism*. Lanham, Md.: Scarecrow, 1997.

William, George M. *Handbook of Hindu Mythology*. Santa Barbara, Calif.: ABC-CLIO, 2003.

IV. Islam

Adamec, Ludwig W. *A Historical Dictionary of Islam*. Lanham, Md.: Scarecrow Press 2001.

Bearman, Peri J., ed. *The Encyclopaedia of Islam*. 5th ed. Leiden: Brill, 2003.

Douglass, Susan L., ed. *The Rise and Spread of Islam, 622–1500*. Detroit: Gale Group, 2001.

Esposito, John L., ed. *The Oxford Dictionary of Islam*. New York: Oxford University Press, 2003.

Esposito, John L., ed. in chief. *The Oxford Encyclopedia of the Modern Islamic World*. New York: Oxford University Press, 1995.

Geddes, Charles L. *An Analytical Guide to the Bibliographies on Islam, Muhammed, and the Qu'rān*. Denver, Colo.: American Institute of Islamic Studies, 1973.

Haddad, Yvonne Yazbeck, et al., eds. *The Islamic Revival Since 1988: A Critical Survey and Bibliography*. Westport, Conn.: Greenwood, 1997.

Index Islamicus. East Grinstead, West Sussex, UK: Bowker-Saur, 1994– .

Martin, Richard C., ed. *The Encyclopedia of Islam and the Muslim World*. New York: Macmillan Reference USA, 2003.

Nanji, Azim. *The Muslim Almanac: A Reference Work on the History, Faith, Culture, and Peoples of Islam*. Detroit: Gale Research, 1996.

Taher, Mohamed. *Encyclopaedic Survey of Islamic Culture*. New Delhi: Anmol Publications, 1997–.

Winchester, Faith. *Muslim Holidays*. Mankato, Minn: Bridgestone Books, 1999.

V. Judaism

De Lange, Nicholas R. M. *Atlas of the Jewish World*. New York: Facts on File, 1984.

Griffiths, David B. *A Critical Bibliography of Writings on Judaism*. Lewiston, N. Y.: E. Mellen Press, 1988.

Jacobs, Louis. *The Jewish Religion: A Companion*. Oxford: Oxford University Press, 1995.

Karkhanis, Sharad. *Jewish Heritage in America: An Annotated Bibliography*. New York: Garland, 1988.

Lemche, Niels Peter. *Historical Dictionary of Ancient Israel*. Lanham, Md.: Scarecrow, 2004.

Nadell, Pamela Susan. *Conservative Judaism in America: A Biographical Dictionary and Sourcebook.* New York: Greenwood, 1988.

Nulman, Macy. *The Encyclopedia of Jewish Prayer: Ashkenazic and Sephardic Rites.* Northvale, N. J.: Jason Aronson, 1993.

Olitzky, Kerry M., et al., eds. *Reform Judaism in America: A Biographical Dictionary and Sourcebook.* Westport, Conn.: Greenwood, 1993.

Roth, Norman, ed. *Medieval Jewish Civilization: An Encyclopedia.* New York: Routledge, 2003.

Sherman, Moshe D. *Orthodox Judaism in America: A Biographical Dictionary and Sourcebook.* Westport, Conn.: Greenwood, 1996.

Werblowsky, R. J. Zwi, and Geoffrey Wigoder, eds. *The Oxford Dictionary of the Jewish Religion.* New York: Oxford University Press, 1997.

Wigoder, Geoffrey, ed. in chief. *The New Encyclopedia of Judaism.* New York: New York University Press, 2002.

VI. Other

Bretzke, James T. *Bibliography on East Asian Religion and Philosophy.* Lewiston, N. Y.: E. Mellen Press, 2001.

Glazier, Stephen D., ed. *The Encyclopedia of African and African-American Religions.* New York: Routledge, 2000.

Hirschfelder, Arlene. *Encyclopedia of Native American Religions.* New York: Facts on File, 2000.

Lopez, Donald S. *Religions of China in Practice.* Princeton, N. J.: Princeton University Press, 1996.

McGreal, Ian P., ed. *Great Thinkers of the Eastern World: The Major Thinkers and the Philosophical and Religious Classics of China, India, Japan, Korea, and the World of Islam.* New York: HarperCollins, 1995.

Melton, J. Gordon. *The Encyclopedia of American Religions.* 7th ed. Detroit: Gale, 2003.

Murphy, Larry G., J. Gordon Melton, and Gary L. Ward, eds. *Encyclopedia of African American Religions.* New York: Garland, 1993.

Queen, Edward L. II, Stephen R. Prothero, and Gardiner H. Shattuck, Jr. *Encyclopedia of American Religious History.* New York: Facts on File, 2001.

Schwade, Arcadio. *Shintō Bibliography in Western Languages: Bibliography on Shintö and Religious Sects, Intellectual Schools and Movements Influenced by Shintöism.* Leiden: E. J. Brill, 1986.

Yao, Xinzhong, ed. *RoutledgeCurzon Encyclopedia of Confucianism.* London: Routledge, 2003.

Histories of Music Comprising Sacred Music

Apel, Willi. *The History of Keyboard Music to 1700.* Trans. and rev. Hans Tischler. Bloomington: Indiana University Press, 1972.

Atlas, Alan. *Renaissance Music: Music in Western Europe 1400–1600*. New York: W. W. Norton, 1998.

Badin, Paul. *Ricercar*. Coaraze: Amourier, 2000.

Béhague, Gerard. *Music in Latin America: An Introduction*. Englewood Cliffs, N. J.: Prentice-Hall, 1979.

Bernstein, Jane A. *Print Culture and Music in Sixteenth-Century Venice*. New York: Oxford University Press, 2001.

Brooks, Tilford. *America's Black Musical Heritage*. Englewood Cliffs, N. J.: Prentice-Hall, 1984.

Buelow, George J. *A History of Baroque Music*. Bloomington: Indiana University Press, 2004.

Butt, John and Tim Carter, eds. *The Cambridge History of Seventeenth-Century Music*. Cambridge: Cambridge University Press, 2005.

Chase, Gilbert. *America's Music: From the Pilgrims to the Present*. Urbana: University of Illinois Press, 1987.

———. *A Guide to the Music of Latin America*. 2nd ed. Washington, D. C.: Library of Congress and the Pan American Union, 1962.

Christensen, Thomas S. *The Cambridge History of Western Music Theory*. Cambridge: Cambridge University Press, 2001.

Cook, Nicholas, and Anthony Pople, eds. *The Cambridge History of Twentieth-Century Music*. Cambridge: Cambridge University Press, 2004.

Crawford, Richard. *America's Musical Life: A History*. New York: Norton, 2001.

Crocker, Richard, and David Hiley. *The Early Middle Ages to 1300*. New York: Oxford University Press, 1990.

Cusic, Don. *The Sound of Light: A History of Gospel and Christian Music*. Milwaukee, Wis.: Hal Leonard, 2002,

Ellinwood, Leonard. *The History of American Church Music*. New York: Da Capo Press, 1970.

Everist, Mark. *Music Before 1600*. Oxford: Blackwell Reference, 1992.

Foley, Edward. *Foundations of Christian Music*. Chicago: Liturgical Press, 1996.

Gangwere, Blanche M. *Music History from the Late Roman through the Gothic Periods, 313–1425: A Documented Chronology*. Westport, Conn.: Greenwood, 1986.

Gangwere, Blanche M. *Music History during the Renaissance Period, 1425–1520: A Documented Chronology*. Westport, Conn.: Greenwood, 1991.

Godwin, Joscelyn. *The Harmony of the Spheres: A Sourcebook of the Pythagorean Tradition in Music*. Rochester, Vt.: Inner Traditions International, 1993.

Grout, Donald J., and Claude V. Palisca. *A History of Western Music*. 6th ed. (1st ed., 1960). New York: W. W. Norton, 2001.

Harper, John. *The Forms and Orders of Western Liturgy from the Tenth to the Eighteenth Century: A Historical Introduction and Guide for Students and Musicians*. Oxford: Clarendon Press, 1991.

Hitchcock, H. Wiley. *Music in the United States: A Historical Introduction*. Englewood Cliffs, N. J.: Prentice Hall, 1988.

Hoppin, Richard. *Medieval Music*. New York: W. W. Norton, 1978.

Hughes, Andrew. *Style and Symbol in Medieval Music, 800–1453*. Ottawa: Institute of Medieval Music, 1989.

Hyatt King, Alec. *Four Hundred Years of Music Printing*. London: British Museum, 1964.

Kavanaugh, Patrick. *The Music of the Angels: A Listener's Guide to Sacred Music from Chant to Christian Rock*. Chicago: Loyola Press, 1999.

Kmetz, John. *Music in the German Renaissance*. Cambridge: Cambridge University Press, 1994.

Landels, John G. *Music in Ancient Greece and Rome*. London: Routledge, 1999.

Landon, H. C. Robbins, and John Julius Norwich. *Five Centuries of Music in Venice*. New York: Schirmer, 1991.

Lang, Paul Henry. *Music in Western Civilization*. New York: W. W. Norton, 1941.

Launay, Denise. *La Musique Religieuse en France du Concile de Trente à 1804*. Paris: Société Française de Musicologie, 1993.

Marini, Stephen A. *Sacred Song in America: Religion, Music, and Public Culture*. Urbana: University of Illinois Press, 2003.

Mayer-Serra, Otto. *Música y músicos de Latinoamérica*. 2 vols. Mexico City: Editorial Atlante, 1947.

Morgan, Robert P. *Twentieth Century Music*. New York: Norton, 1991.

The New Oxford History of Music. 10 vols. London: Oxford University Press, 1954–90.

Owen, Barbara. *The Registration of Baroque Organ Music*. Bloomington: Indiana University Press, 1997.

Pahlen, Kurt, et al. *The World of the Oratorio: Oratorio, Mass, Requiem, Te Deum, Stabat Mater, and Large Cantatas*. Portland, Ore.: Amadeus, 1990.

Price, Curtis A. *The Early Baroque Era: From the Late 16th Century to the 1660s*. Englewood Cliffs, N. J.: Prentice Hall, 1993.

Quasten, Johannes. *Music and Worship in Pagan and Christian Antiquity*. Washington, D. C.: Catholic University Press, 1983.

Rice, John A. *Empress Marie Therese and Music at the Viennese Court, 1792–1807*. Cambridge: Cambridge University Press, 2003.

Routley, Erik. *Twentieth Century Church Music*. New York: Oxford University Press, 1964.

Samson, Jim, ed. *The Cambridge History of Nineteenth-Century Music*. Cambridge: Cambridge University Press, 2001.

Sitsky, Larry. *Music of the Twentieth-Century Avant-garde: A Biocritical Sourcebook*. Westport, Conn.: Greenwood, 2002.

Smither, Howard E. *A History of the Oratorio*. Chapel Hill: University of Northern Carolina Press, 1977.

Southern, Eileen. *The Music of Black Americans: A History.* 3rd ed. New York: Norton, 1977.

Stevenson, Robert. *A Guide to Caribbean Music History.* Lima: Ediciones "CULTURA," 1975.

———. *Latin American Colonial Anthology.* Washington, D. C.: Organization of American States, 1975.

———. *The Music of Peru.* Washington, D. C.: Pan American Union, 1960.

Strimple, Nick. *Choral Music in the Twentieth Century.* Portland, Ore.: Amadeus Press, 2002.

Strohm, Reinhard. *The Rise of European Music, 1380–1500.* Cambridge: Cambridge University Press, 1993.

Strohm, Reinhard, and Bonnie Blackburn. *Music as Concept and Practice in the Late Middle Ages.* Oxford: Oxford University Press, 2001.

Strunk, Oliver, and Leo Treitler. *Source Readings in Music History.* 1st ed.: 1950. Rev. ed. New York: W. W. Norton, 1998.

Taruskin, Richard. *Oxford History of Western Music.* 6 vols. New York: Oxford University Press, 2005.

Thistlethwaite, Nicholas. *The Making of the Victorian Organ.* Cambridge: Cambridge University Press, 1990.

Tokita, Alison McQueen, and David W. Hughes, eds. *Japanese Music.* Cambridge: Cambridge University Press, 2005.

Ulrich, Homer. *A Survey of Choral Music.* New York: Harcourt Brace Jovanovich, 1973.

White, John D. *Theories of Musical Texture in Western History.* New York: Garland, 1995.

Williams, Peter. *The Organ in Western Culture.* New York: Cambridge University Press, 1993.

Wilson-Dickson, Andrew. *The Story of Christian Music: From Gregorian Chant to Black Gospel.* Oxford: Lion, 1992.

Yudkin, Jeremy. *Music in Medieval Europe.* Englewood Cliffs, N. J.: Prentice-Hall, 1989.

DICTIONARIES AND BIBLIOGRAPHIES OF SACRED MUSIC

(Handbooks for specific religions are found in **Studies within Specific Traditions**)

Adler, Samuel. *American Sacred Choral Music: Overview and Handbook.* Brewster, Mass.: Paraclete Press, 2001.

Arnold, Corliss R. *Organ Literature: A Comprehensive Survey.* Metuchen, N. J.: Scarecrow, 1995.

Bieri, Martin. *Ricercare: Verzeichnis cantus-firmus-gebundener Orgelmusik.* Wiesbaden: Breitkopf & Härtel, 2001.

Bowers, Roger. *English Church Polyphony: Singers and Sources from the 14th to the 17th Century*. Aldershot, Hampshire, England: Ashgate/Variorum, 1999.

Brown, Howard Mayer. *Instrumental Music Printed Before 1600: A Bibliography*. Cambridge, Mass.: Harvard University Press, 1965.

Carroll, J. Robert. *Compendium of Liturgical Music Terms*. Toledo, Oh.: Gregorian Institute of America, 1964.

Chase, Robert. *Dies Irae: A Guide to Requiem Music*. Lanham, Md.: Scarecrow, 2003.

Claghorn, Gene. *Women Composers and Hymnists: A Concise Biographical Dictionary*. Metuchen, N. J.: Scarecrow, 1984.

The Concordia Hymn Prelude Series Index. St. Louis, Mo.: Concordia, 1986.

Davidson, James Robert. *A Dictionary of Protestant Church Music*. Metuchen, N. J.: Scarecrow, 1975.

Ellinwood, Leonard W., and Elizabeth Lockwood. *Bibliography of American Hymnals Compiled from the Files of the Dictionary of American Hymnology, a Project of the Hymn Society of America*. 27 microfisches. New York: University Music Editions, 1983.

Floyd, James Michael, and Avery T. Sharp. *Church Music: A Research and Information Guide*. New York: Routledge, 2005.

Gellerman, Robert F. *The American Reed Organ and the Harmonium: A Treatise on its History, Restoration and Tuning, with Descriptions of Some Outstanding Collections, Including a Stop Dictionary and a Directory of Reed Organs*. Vestal, N. Y.: Vestal Press, 1996.

Hardwick, Peter. *British Organ Music of the Twentieth Century*. Lanham, Md.: Scarecrow, 2003.

Hays, Alfreda. *Passion Settings of the German Baroque: A Guide to Printed Editions*. New York: American Choral Foundation, 1975.

Hettinger, Sharon L. *American Organ Music of the Twentieth Century: An Annotated Bibliography of Composers*. Warren, Mich.: Harmonie Park Press, 1997.

Hsieh, Fang-Lan. *An Annotated Bibliography of Church Music*. Lewiston, N. Y.: Edwin Mellen, 2003.

Hughes, Anselm. *Liturgical Terms for Music Students: A Dictionary*. 1st ed. 1940. Rpt. St. Clair Shores, Mich.: Scholarly Press, 1972.

Jackson, Irene V. *Afro-American Religious Music: A Bibliography and Catalogue of Gospel Music*. Westport, Conn.: Greenwood, 1979.

Julian, John. *A Dictionary of Hymnology, Setting forth the Origin and History of Christian Hymns of All Ages and Nations*. 1st ed. 1892. Rev. ed. 1907. Rpt. Grand Rapids, Mich.: Kregel, 1985.

Laster, James. *Catalogue of Choral Music Arranged in Biblical Order*. 2nd ed. Lanham, Md.: Scarecrow, 1996.

———. *Catalogue of Vocal Solos and Duets Arranged in Biblical Order*. Metuchen, N. J.: Scarecrow, 1984.

Leaver, Robin A. "Hymnals, Hymnal Collections and Collection Development." *Notes* 47 (1990): 331–54.

McCutchan, Robert G. *Hymn Tune Names, Their Sources and Significance.* 1st ed. 1957. Rpt. St. Clair Shores, Mich.: Scholarly Press, 1976.

Porte, Jacques. *Encyclopédie des Musique Sacrées.* 3 vols. Paris: Édition Labergerie, 1968–1970.

Poultney, David. *Dictionary of Western Church Music.* Chicago: American Library Association, 1991.

Powell, Mark A. *Encyclopedia of Contemporary Christian Music.* Peabody, Mass.: Hendrickson, 2002.

Ray, James D. *The Chorus Reference Manual: A Comprehensive Guide to Choruses and Praise Songs for Music Leaders and Worship Planners.* North Charleston, S. C.: SoftRay Resources, 1991.

————. *The Hymnal Reference Manual: An Index of Hymns, Hymn Tunes, Classifications, Key Words, Meter, Scripture References, and Key.* North Charleston, S. C.: SoftRay Resources, 1991.

Segre, Marcella. *Bibliography of Jewish Music Bibliographies.* Haifa: Haifa Music Museum & AMLI Library, 1970.

Sendrey, Alfred. *Bibliography of Jewish Music.* New York: Columbia University Press, 1951. Rpt. New York: Kraus, 1968.

Szövérffy, Joseph, and Eva C. Topping. *A Guide to Byzantine Hymnography: A Classified Bibliography of Texts and Studies.* 2 vols. Brookline, Mass.: Classical Folia Editions.

Von Ende, Richard C. *Church Music: An International Bibliography.* Metuchen, N. J.: Scarecrow, 1980.

Weisser, Albert. *Bibliography of Publications and Other Resources on Jewish Music.* New York: National Jewish Music Council, 1969.

Yahalom, Joseph. *Palestinian Vocalised Piyyut Manuscripts in the Cambridge Genizah Collections.* Cambridge: Cambridge University Press. 1997.

Yeats-Edwards, Paul. *English Church Music: A Bibliography.* London: White Lion, 1975.

BIOGRAPHIES OF MUSICIANS, INCLUDING STUDIES OF SPECIFIC WORKS

Bach, Johann Sebastian, and family

Boyd, Malcolm, ed. *J. S. Bach.* Oxford Composer Companions. Oxford: Oxford University Press, 1999.

Butt, John. *Bach: Mass in B Minor.* Cambridge: Cambridge University Press, 1991.

Crist, Stephen A. *Bach in America.* Urbana: University of Illinois Press, 2002.

Du Bouchet, Paule. *Magnificat: Jean-Sébastien Bach, le Cantor*. Paris: Gallimard, 1991.

Dürr, Alfred. *Johann Sebastian Bach's St. John Passion: Genesis, Transmission and Meaning*. Trans. Alfred Clayton. Oxford: Oxford University Press, 2000.

Forkel, Johann Nikolaus. *Johann Sebastian Bach: His Life, Art, and Work*. 1st. ed. 1802. [trans] New York: Da Capo Press, 1970.

Humphreys, David. *The Esoteric Structure of Bach's Clavierübung III*. Cardiff: University College of Cardiff Press, 1983.

Leaver, Robin. *J. S. Bach as Preacher*. St. Louis, Mo.: Concordia, 1982.

Melamed, Daniel R., and Michael Marissen. *An Introduction to Bach Studies*. New York: Oxford University Press, 1998.

Meyer, Ulrich. *Biblical Quotation and Allusion in the Cantata Libretti of Johann Sebastian Bach*. Lanham, Md.: Scarecrow, 1997.

The New Bach Reader: A Life of Johann Sebastian Bach in Letters and Documents. Hans T. David and Arthur Mendel, eds. Rev. and enlarged, Christoph Wolff. New York: W. W. Norton, 1998.

Schmieder, Wolfgang. *Thematisch-systematisches Verzeichnis der musikalischen Werke von Johann Sebastian Bach: Bach-Werke-Verzeichnis (BWV)*. Wiesbaden: 1950. 2nd ed. 1990.

Schulze, Hans-Joachim, and Chrisoph Wolff. *Bach Compendium: Analytisch-bibliographisches Repertorium der Werke Johann Sebastian Bachs (BC)*. Leipzig: 1985.

Spitta, Phillipp. *Johann Sebastian Bach: His Work and Influence on the Music of Germany*. 3 vols. Trans. Clara Bell and J. A. Fuller-Maitland. Englewood Cliffs, N. J.: Dover, 1992.

Stauffer, George B. *Bach: The Mass in B Minor (The Great Catholic Mass)*. Monuments of Western Music. G. B. Stauffer, ed. New York: Schirmer Books, 1997.

———. *J. S. Bach as Organist: His Instruments, Music, and Performance Practices*. Bloomington: Indiana University Press, 1986.

Stinson, Russell. *Bach, the Orgelbüchlein*. New York: Schirmer Books, 1996.

———. *J. S. Bach's Great Eighteen Organ Chorales*. New York: Oxford University Press, 2001.

Williams, Peter F. *The Organ Music of J. S. Bach*. 2nd ed. New York: Cambridge University Press, 2004.

Wolff, Christoph. *Johann Sebastian Bach: The Learned Musician*. New York: W. W. Norton, 2002.

Wolff, Christoph, et al. *The New Grove Bach Family*. New York: W. W. Norton, 1983.

Beethoven, Ludwig van

Cooper, Barry. *Beethoven*. Oxford: Oxford University Press, 2000.

Drabkin, William. *Beethoven, Missa Solemnis*. Cambridge: Cambridge University Press, 1991.

Lockwood, Lewis. *Beethoven: The Music and the Life*. New York: Norton, 2003.
Mellers, Wilfrid Howard. *Beethoven and the Voice of God*. New York: Oxford University Press, 1983.
Thayer, Alexander Wheelock. *The Life of Beethoven*. Ed. Elliott Forbes. 2 vols. Princeton, N. J.: Princeton Unversity Press, 1964.

Berlioz, Hector

Bloom, Peter. *The Life of Berlioz*. Cambridge: Cambridge University Press, 1998.
Findlay, Meredith Claire. *The Requiem Masses of Luigi Cherubini and Hector Berlioz: Their Place in History*. Northampton, Mass.: Smith College, 1974.
Rushton, Julian. *The Music of Berlioz*. Oxford: Oxford University Press, 2001.

Billings, William

McKay, David Phares, and Richard Crawford. *William Billings of Boston: Eighteenth-Century Composer*. Princeton, N. J.: Princeton University Press 1975.
Barbour, James Murray. *The Church Music of William Billings*. 1st ed. 1960. New York: Da Capo Press, 1972.
Kroeger, Karl. *Catalog of the Musical Works of William Billings*. New York: Greenwood, 1991.

Brahms, Johannes

Beller-McKenna, Daniel. *Brahms and the German Spirit*. Cambridge, Mass.: Harvard University Press, 2004.
Musgrave, Michael. *Brahms, A German Requiem*. New York: Cambridge University Press, 1996.
Swafford, Jan. *Johannes Brahms: A Biography*. New York: Alfred A. Knopf, 1997.

Britten, Benjamin

Cooke, Mervyn. *Britten, War Requiem*. New York: Cambridge University Press, 1996.
Elliott, Graham. *Benjamin Britten: The Spiritual Dimension*. London: Oxford University Press, 2006.
Kendall, Alan. *Benjamin Britten*. London: Macmillan, 1973.
Rupprecht, Philip. *Britten's Musical Language*. Cambridge: Cambridge University Press, 2002.

Byrd, William

Andrews, H. K. *Technique of Byrd's Vocal Polyphony*. London: Oxford University Press, 1964.

Fellowes, Edmund H. *William Byrd*. London: Oxford University Press, 1948.

Holst, Imogen. *Byrd*. London: Faber, 1972.

Kerman, Joseph. *The Masses and Motets of William Byrd*. Berkeley: University of California Press, 1978.

Turbet, Richard. *William Byrd: A Guide to Research*. Garland Composer Resource Manuals 7. New York: Garland, 1987.

Dufay, Guillaume

Cumming, Julie E. *The Motet in the Age of Du Fay*. New York: Cambridge University Press, 1999.

Fallows, David. *Dufay*. London: Dent, 1982.

Gülke, Peter. *Guillaume Du Fay: Musik des 15. Jahrhunderts*. Stuttgart: Bären-reiter, 2003.

Planchart, Alejandro Enrique. "The Early Career of Guillaume Du Fay." *Journal of the American Musicological Society* 46 (1993): 341–68.

Wright, Craig. "Dufay's *Nuper rosarum flores*, King Solomon's Temple, and the Veneration of the Virgin." *Journal of the American Musicological Society* 47 (1994): 395–441.

Elgar, Edward

Foster, Michael. *Elgar's Gigantic Work: The Story of the Apostles Trilogy*. London: Thames, 1995.

Grimley, Daniel M., and Julian Rushton, eds. *The Cambridge Companion to Elgar*. Cambridge: Cambridge University Press, 2005.

Kennedy, Michael. *The Life of Elgar*. Cambridge: Cambridge University Press, 2004.

McGuire, Charles E. *Elgar's Oratorios: The Creation of an Epic Narrative*. Aldershot, Hampshire, England: Ashgate, 2002.

Moore, Jerrold N. *Edward Elgar: A Creative Life*. Oxford: Oxford University Press, 1984.

Young, Percy M. *Elgar, Newman, and the Dream of Gerontius: In the Tradition of English Catholicism*. Aldershot, Hampshire, England: Scolar Press, Ashgate, 1995.

Handel, George Frederic

Burrows, Donald. *Handel*. The Master Musicians Series. Stanley Sadie, ed. New York: Schirmer, 1994.

———. "Handel and the 1727 Coronation." *The Musical Times* 118 (1977): 269.

———. *Handel and the English Chapel Royal.* London: Church Music Society, 1985. Rpt. London: Oxford University Press, 2005.

———. *Handel: Messiah.* Cambridge Music Handbooks. Julian Rushton, gen. ed. Cambridge: Cambridge University Press, 1991.

Dean, Winton. *Handel's Dramatic Oratorios and Masques.* London: Oxford University Press, 1959.

Deutsch, Otto Erich. *Handel: A Documentary Biography.* London: Adam and Charles Black, 1955.

Eisen, Walter and Margret Eisen. *Händel-Handbuch, herausgegeben vom Kuratorium der Georg-Friedrich-Händel-Stiftung.* 4 vols. Kassel: Bärenreiter, 1978–1985.

Hurley, David R. *Handel's Muse: Patterns of Creation in his Oratorios and Musical Dramas, 1743–1751.* Oxford: Oxford University Press, 2001.

Parker, Mary Ann. *G. F. Handel: A Guide to Research.* New York: Routledge, 2005.

Shaw, Watkins. *A Textual and Historical Companion to Handel's "Messiah."* London: Novello, 1965.

Shaw, Watkins, and Graham Dixon. "Handel's Vesper Music. *The Musical Times* 126 (1985): 132.

Tovey, Donald Francis. "Handel: 'Israel in Egypt.'" *Essays in Music Analysis* Vol. 5. London: Oxford University Press, 1937.

Young, Percy M. *The Oratorios of Handel.* London: Dobson, 1949.

Haydn, Franz Joseph

Drury, Jonathan D. *Haydn's Seven Last Words: An Historical and Critical Study.* Urbana, Ill.: Drury, 1975.

Grave, Floyd K. and Margaret G. Grave. *Franz Joseph Haydn: A Guide to Research.* New York: Garland, 1990.

Haydn, Joseph, et al. *The Creation and the Seasons: The Complete Authentic Sources for the Wordbooks.* Cardiff: University College of Cardiff Press, 1985.

MacIntyre, Bruce C. *Haydn, The Creation.* New York: Schirmer and Prentice Hall International, 1998.

Temperley, Nicholas. *Haydn, The Creation.* Cambridge: Cambridge University Press, 1991.

Josquin des Prez

Elders, Willem, and Frits De Haen, eds. *Proceedings of the International Josquin Symposium, Utrecht 1986.* Amsterdam: Vereniging voor Nederlandse Muziekgeschiedenis, 1991.

Godt, Irving. "Motivic Integration in Josquin's Motets," *Journal of Music Theory* 21 (1977): 264–92.

Lowinsky, Edward E., and Bonnie Blackburn, eds. *Josquin Des Prez: Proceedings of the International Festival-Conference Held at The Julliard School at Lincoln Center in New York City, 22–25 June 1971.* London: Oxford University Press, 1976.

Noble, Jeremy. "The Function of Josquin's Motets." *Tijdschrift van de Vereniging voor Nederlandse Muziekgeschiedenis* 35 (1985): 9–31.

Osthoff, Helmuth. *Josquin Desprez.* 2 vols. Tutzing: Schneider, 1962–1965.

Robinson, Sydney Charles. *Josquin des Prez: A Guide to Research.* New York: Garland, 1983.

Sherr, Richard, ed. *Josquin Companion.* New York: Oxford University Press, 2000.

Lassus, Orlandus (Orlando di Lasso, Roland Lassus)

Bergquist, Peter, ed. *Orlando di Lasso Studies.* Cambridge: Cambridge University Press, 1999.

Bötticher, Wolfgang. *Orlando di Lasso und seine Zeit, 1532–1594.* Kassel: Bärenreiter, 1958.

Bossuyt, Ignace, Eugeen Schreurs, and Annelies Wouters. eds. *Orlandus Lassus and His Time: Colloquium Proceedings, Antwerpen 24–26.08.1994.* Peer: Alamire Foundation, 1995.

Crook, David. *Orlando DiLasso's Imitation Magnificats for Counter-Reformation Munich.* Princeton, N. J.: Princeton University Press, 1994.

Erb, James. *Orlando di Lasso: A Guide to Research.* New York: Garland, 1990.

Leuchtmann, Horst. *Orlando di Lasso.* 2 vols. Wiesbaden: Breitkopf & Härtel, 1976–1977.

Roche, Jerome. *Lassus.* Oxford Studies of Composers 19. London: Oxford University Press, 1982.

Machaut, Guillaume de

Earp, Lawrence M. *Guillaume de Machaut: A Guide to Research.* New York: Garland, 1995.

Leech-Wilkinson, Daniel. *Machaut's Mass: An Introduction.* Oxford: Clarendon Press, 1990.

Robertson, Anne Walters. *Guillaume de Machaut and Reims: Context and Meaning in His Musical Works.* Cambridge: Cambridge University Press, 2002.

Mendelssohn, Felix

Edwards, Frederick George. *The History of Mendelssohn's Oratorio "Elijah."* London: Novello, Ewer, 1896.

Mercer-Taylor, Peter. *The Cambridge Companion to Mendelssohn*. Cambridge: Cambridge University Press, 2004.

Todd, R. Larry. *Mendelssohn and His World*. Princeton, N. J.: Princeton University Press, 1991.

Werner, Jack. *Mendelssohn's "Elijah"; A Historical and Analytical Guide*. London: Chappell, 1965.

Messiaen, Olivier

Bruhn, Siglind. *Messiaen's Language of Mystical Love*. New York: Garland, 1998.

Hill, Peter. *The Messiaen Companion*. Portland, Ore.: Amadeus Press, 1994.

Griffiths, Paul. *Olivier Messiaen and the Music of Time*. Ithaca, N. Y.: Cornell University Press, 1985.

Morris, David. *Oliver Messiaen: A Comparative Bibliography of Material in the English Language*. Coleraine, Northern Ireland: University of Ulster, 1991.

Nichols, Roger. *Messiaen*. Oxford: Oxford University Press, 1986.

Monteverdi, Claudio

Adams, K. Gary, and Dyke Kiel. *Claudio Monteverdi: A Guide to Research*. New York: Garland, 1989.

Arnold, Denis. *Monteverdi*. 3rd ed. Rev. Tim Carter. 1st ed. 1963. London: J. M. Dent, 1990.

Chafe, Eric, *Monteverdi's Tonal Language*. New York: Schirmer, 1992.

Fabri, Paolo. *Monteverdi*. 1st ed. 1985. Trans. Tim Carter. Cambridge: Cambridge University Press, 1994.

Kurtzman, Jeffrey. *The Monteverdi Vespers of 1610: Music, Context, Performance*. New York: Oxford University Press, 1999.

Whenham, John. *Monteverdi Vespers (1610)*. Cambridge: Cambridge University Press, 1997.

Mozart, Wolfgang Amadeus

Rosselli, John. *The Life of Mozart*. Cambridge: Cambridge University Press, 1998.

Gutman, Robert W. *Mozart: A Cultural Biography*. New York: Harcourt Brace, 1999.

Solomon, Maynard. *Mozart: A Life*. New York: HarperCollins, 1995.

Wolff, Christoph. *Mozart's Requiem: Historical and Analytical Studies, Documents, Score*. Berkeley: University of California Press, 1994.

Palestrina, Giovanni da

Bianchi, Lino. *Iconografia Palestriniana: Giovanni Pierluigi da Palestrina: Immagini e Documenti del suo Tempo.* Lucca, Italy: Libreria Musicala Italiana, 1994.

Boyd, Malcolm. *Palestrina's Style: A Practical Introduction.* Oxford: Oxford University Press, 1973.

Garratt, James. *Palestrina and the German Romantic Imagination: Interpreting Historicism in Nineteenth-Century Music.* Cambridge: Cambridge University Press, 2002.

Hall, Alison. *Palestrina: an Index to the Casimiri, Kalmus, and Haberl Editions.* Philadelphia, Pa.: Music Library Association, 1980.

Jeppesen, Knud. *Counterpoint: The Polyphonic Vocal Style of the Sixteenth Century.* Trans. Glen Haydon. New York: Prentice-Hall, 1939. Rpt. Dover, 1992.

Lockwood, Lewis, ed. *Palestrina Pope Marcellus Mass.* Norton Critical Scores. New York: W. W. Norton, 1975.

Marvin, Clara. *Giovanni Pierluigi da Palestrina: A Guide to Research.* New York: Routledge, 2002.

Roche, Jerome. *Palestrina.* London: Oxford University Press, 1971.

Poulenc, Francis

Keck, George. *Francis Poulenc: A Bio-bibliography.* New York: Greenwood, 1990.

Mellers, Wilfrid H. *Francis Poulenc.* Oxford: Oxford University Press, 1993.

Schmidt, Carl B. *Entrancing Muse: A Documented Biography of Francis Poulenc.* Hillsdale, N. Y.: Pendragon Press, 2001.

Purcell, Henry

Adams, Martin. *Henry Purcell: The Origins and Development of his Musical Style.* Cambridge: Cambridge University Press, 1995.

Homan, Peter. *Henry Purcell.* Oxford: Oxford University Press, 1994.

Zimmerman, Franklin B. *Henry Purcell: A Guide to Research.* New York: Garland, 1989.

Schütz, Heinrich

Buelow, George J. *A Schütz Reader: Documents on Performance Practice.* New York: American Choral Foundation, 1985.

Moser, Hans Joachim. *Heinrich Schütz: His Life and Work.* Trans. and ed. Derek McCulloch. New York: St. Martin's Press, 1967. 1st ed. 1959.

Skei, Allen B. *Heinrich Schütz: A Guide to Research*. New York: Garland Press, 1981.
Smallman, Basil. *Schütz*. New York: Oxford University Press, 2000.

Stravinsky, Igor

Cross, Jonathan. *The Cambridge Companion to Stravinsky*. Cambridge: Cambridge University Press, 2003.
Joseph, Charles M. *Stravinsky Inside Out*. New Haven, Conn.: Yale University Press, 2001.
Walsh, Stephen. *Stravinsky: A Creative Spring: Russia and France, 1882–1934*. New York: Alfred A. Knopf, 1999.
Zama, Alberta. *Strawinksy e il Sacro*. Florence: Athaneum, 1997.

Vaughn Williams, Ralph

Day, James. *Vaughan Williams*. London: J. M. Dent, 1972.
Hurd, Michael. *Vaughan Williams*. London: Faber and Faber, 1970.
Kennedy Michael. *The Works of Ralph Vaughan Williams*. London: Oxford University Press, 1964.

Verdi, Giuseppe

Phillips-Matz, Mary Jane. *Verdi, A Biography*. Oxford: Oxford University Press, 1993.
Rosen, David. *Verdi, Requiem*. Cambridge: Cambridge University Press, 1995.
Rosselli, John. *The Life of Verdi*. New York: Cambridge University Press, 2000.

Wesley, Charles, John and Samuel

Dallimore, Arnold A. *A Heart Set Free: The Life of Charles Wesley*. Wheaton, Ill: Crossway Books, 1988.
Horton, Peter. *Samuel Sebastian Wesley: A Life*. London: Oxford University Press, 2004.
Kassler, Michael, and Philip Olleson, eds. *Samuel Wesley (1766–1837): A Source Book*. Burlington, Vt.: Ashgate, 2001.
Olleson, Philip. *Samuel Wesley: The Man and His Music*. Woodbridge, Suffolk, England: Boyden Press, 2003.
Routley, Erik. *The Musical Wesleys*. New York: Oxford University Press, 1968.
Young, Carlton R. *Music of the Heart: John & Charles Wesley on Music and Musicians: An Anthology*. Carol Stream, Ill.: Hope, 1995.

Others

Adrian, Thomas. *Górecki*. Oxford: Oxford University Press, 1997.

Allis, Michael. *Parry's Creative Process*. Aldershot, Hampshire, England: Ashgate, 2003.

Arnold, Ben. *The Liszt Companion*. Westport, Conn.: Greenwood, 2002.

Arnold, Denis. *Giovanni Gabrieli and the Music of the Venetian High Renaissance*. Oxford: Oxford University Press, 1979.

Beckerman, Michael B. *Dvořák and his World*. Princeton, N. J.: Princeton University Press, 1993.

Benham, Hugh. *John Taverner: His Life and Music*. Aldershot, Hampshire, England: Ashgate, 2003.

Benser, Caroline C. and David F. Urrows. *Randall Thompson: A Bio-Bibliography*. Westport, Conn.: Greenwood, 1991.

Bent, Margaret. *Dunstaple*. London: Oxford University Press, 1981.

Bianchi, Lino. *Carissimi, Stradella, Scarlatti e l'Oratorio Musicale*. Rome: De Santis, 1969.

Brown, David. *Thomas Weelkes: A Biographical and Critical Study*. New York: Praeger, 1969.

Bumgardner, Thomas A. *Norman Dello Joio*. Boston: Twayne, 1986.

Burkholder, J. Peter. *Charles Ives, the Ideas Behind the Music*. New Haven, Conn.: Yale University Press, 1985.

Cessac, Catherine. *Marc-Antoine Charpentier*. Trans. E. Thomas Glasow. Portland, Ore.: Amadeus, 1995.

Chadwick, Henry. *Boethius, the Consolations of Music, Logic, Theology, and Philosophy*. Oxford: Clarendon Press and Oxford University Press, 1981.

Charteris, Richard. *Giovanni Gabrieli: A Thematic Catalogue of His Music*. Thematic Catalogue Series 20. Stuyvesant, N. Y.: Pendragon Press, 1996.

Clarke, F. R. C. *Healey Willan: Life and Music*. Toronto: University of Toronto Press, 1983.

Cooper-White, Pamela. *Schoenberg and the God-idea: The Opera Moses und Aron*. Ann Arbor, Mich: UMI Research Press, 1985.

Copley, I. A. *The Music of Charles Wood: A Critical Study*. London: Thames, 1978.

Cramer, Eugene C. *Studies in the Music of Tomás Luis de Victoria*. Aldershot, Hampshire, England: Ashgate, 2001.

———. *Tomás Luis de Victoria: A Guide to Research*. New York: Garland, 1998.

Crews, C. Daniel. *Johann Friedrich Peter and His Times*. Winston-Salem, N. C.: Moravian Music Foundation, 1990.

Cross, Charlotte M., and Russell A. Berman. *Political and Religious Ideas in the Works of Arnold Schoenberg*. New York: Garland, 2000.

Davis, Paul. *Isaac Watts: His Life and Works*. New York: Dryden, 1943.

De Boer, Kee, and John B. Ahouse. *Daniel Pinkham: A Bio-Bibliography*. New York: Greenwood, 1988.

Dibble, Jeremy. *C. Hubert H. Parry: His Life and Music*. New York: Clarendon Press and Oxford University Press, 1992.

Dirksen, Pieter. *The Keyboard Music of Jan Pieterszoon Sweelinck: Its Style, Significance and Influence*. Utrecht: Koninklijke Vereniging voor Nederlandse Muziekgeschiedenis, 1997.

Dirksen, Pieter. *Sweelinck Studies: Proceedings of the International Sweelinck Symposium, Utrecht 1999*. Utrecht: STIMU, Foundation for Historical Performance Practice, 2002.

Dixon, Graham. *Carissimi*. Oxford: Oxford University Press, 1986.

Doe, Paul. *Tallis*. Oxford Studies of Composers 4. London: Oxford University Press, 1968.

Ebrecht, Ronald. *Maurice Duruflé, 1902–1986: The Last Impressionist*. Lanham, Md.: Scarecrow, 2002.

Findlay, James F. *Dwight L. Moody: American Evangelist, 1837–1899*. Chicago: University of Chicago Press, 1969.

Fitch, Fabrice. *Johannes Ockeghem, Masses and Models*. Paris: H. Champion, 1997.

Garside, Charles. *Zwingli and the Arts*. New Haven, Conn.: Yale University Press, 1966.

Gibbs, Christopher H. *The Life of Schubert*. Cambridge: Cambridge University Press, 2000.

Guttman, Hadassah. *The Music of Paul Ben-Haim: A Performance Guide*. Metuchen, N. J.: Scarecrow, 1992.

Halbreich, Harry and Reinhard G. Pauly. *Arthur Honegger*. Portland, Ore.: Amadeus Press, 1999.

Hamilton, Kenneth, ed. *The Cambridge Companion to Liszt*. Cambridge: Cambridge University Press, 2005.

Hammond, Frederick. *Girolamo Frescobaldi*. Cambridge, Mass.: Harvard University Press, 1983.

———. *Girolamo Frescobaldi: a Guide to Research*. New York: Garland, 1988.

Hand, Colin. *John Taverner: His Life and Music*. London: Eulenburg Books, 1978.

Harley, John. *Orlando Gibbons and the Gibbons Family of Musicians*. Aldershot, Hampshire, England: Ashgate, 1999.

Harrán, Don. *Salamone Rossi: Jewish Musician in Late Renaissance Mantua*. Oxford: Oxford University Press, 1999.

Heller, Karl, and David Marinelli. *Antonio Vivaldi: The Red Priest of Venice*. New York: Amadeus Press, 1997.

Hillier, Paul. *Arvo Pärt*. Oxford: Oxford University Press, 1997.

Hitchcock, H. Wiley. *Marc-Antoine Charpentier*. Oxford: Oxford University Press, 1990.

Hofmann, John. *Flor Peeters, His Life and His Organ Works*. Fredonia, N. Y.: Birchwood, 1978.

Howes, Frank Stewart. *The Music of William Walton*. London: Oxford University Press, 1973.

Johnson, Cuthbert. *Prosper Gueranger (1805–1875): A Liturgical Theologian: An Introduction to his Liturgical Writings and Work*. Rome: Pontificio Ateneo S. Anselmo, 1984.

Jones, Andrew V. *The Motets of Carissimi*. Ann Arbor, Mich.: UMI Research Press, 1982.

Jones, Ralph H. *Charles Albert Tindley, Prince of Preachers*. Nashville, Tenn.: Abingdon Press, 1982.

Josephson, David S. *John Taverner: Tudor Composer*. Ann Arbor, Mich.: UMI Research Press, 1979.

Keeble, Brian, ed. *The Music of Silence: A Composer's Testament/John Tavener*. London: Faber and Faber, 1999.

Kemp, Ian. *Tippett, the Composer and His Music*. London: Eulenburg Books and Da Capo Press, 1984.

King, Charles. W. *Frank Martin: A Bio-Bibliography*. New York: Greenwood, 1990.

Kirkman, Andrew and Dennis Slavin. *Binchois Studies*. Oxford: Oxford University Press, 2000.

Klessmann, Eckart. *Telemann in Hamburg: 1721–1767*. Hamburg: Hoffman und Campe, 1980.

Labounsky, Ann. *Jean Langlais: The Man and his Music*. Portland, Ore.: Amadeus Press, 2000.

La Croix, Richard R. *Augustine on Music: An Interdisciplinary Collection of Essays*. Lewiston, N. Y.: Mellen Press, 1988.

Morosan, Vladimir. "A Stranger in a Strange Land: Tchaikovsky as a Composer of Church Music." *Tchaikovsky and His Contemporaries: A Centennial Symposium*. Ed. Alexander Mihailovic. Westport, Conn.: Greenwood, 1999, pp. 197–227.

Maier, Elisabeth. *Anton Bruckner zum Gedenken*. Vienna: Wiener Katholische Akademie, 1997.

Matthews, Theodore K. *The Masses of Anton Bruckner: A Comparative Analysis*. Ann Arbor, Mich.: University Microfilms, 1975.

Mattos, Cleofe Person de. *José Maurício Nunes Garcia: Biografia*. Rio de Janeiro: Ministéro da Cultura, 1997.

McGrath, Alister E. *A Life of John Calvin*. New York: Blackwell, 1990.

Meconi, Honey. *Pierre de la Rue and Musical Life at the Hapsburg-Burgundian Court*. Oxford: Oxford University Press, 2003.

Minear, Paul Sevier. *Death Set to Music: Masterworks by Bach, Brahms, Penderecki, Bernstein*. Atlanta, Ga.: John Knox Press, 1987.

Murray, Michael. *Marcel Dupré, the Work of a Master Organist*. Boston: Northeastern University Press, 1985.

Nectoux, Jean Michel. *Gabriel Fauré: A Musical Life*. Cambridge: Cambridge University Press, 1991.

Newbould, Brian. *Schubert, The Music and the Man*. Berkeley: University of California Press, 1997.

Noske, Frits. *Sweelinck*. Oxford: Oxford University Press, 1988.

Osmond-Smith, David. *Berio*. Oxford: Oxford University Press, 1991.

Palmer, Christopher. *Herbert Howells: A Centenary Celebration*. London: Thames, 1992.

Patterson, Donald L., and Janet L. Patterson. *Vincent Persichetti: A Bio-Bibliography*. New York: Greenwood, 1988.

Pemberton, Carol A. *Lowell Mason: A Bio-Bibliography*. New York: Greenwood, 1988.

Peterson, John W., and Richard Engquist. *The Miracle Goes On*. Grand Rapids, Mich.: Zondervan, 1976.

Peyser, Joan. *Bernstein: A Biography*. Rev. ed. New York: Billboard Books, 1998.

Phillips, Edward R. *Gabriel Fauré: A Guide to Research*. New York: Garland, 1999.

Picker, Martin. *Johannes Ockeghem and Jacob Obrecht: A Guide to Research*. New York: Garland, 1988.

Poznansky, Alexander and Brett Langston. *The Tchaikovsky Handbook: A Guide to the Man and His Music*. Bloomington: Indiana University Press, 2002.

Pritchard, Brian W. *Antonio Caldara: Essays on His Life and Times*. Aldershot, Hampshire, England: Scolar Press, 1987.

———. *Henricus Isaac: A Guide to Research*. New York: Garland, 1991.

Rifkin, Joshua. *North German Baroque Masters: Schütz, Froberger, Buxtehude, Purcell, Telemann*. London: Macmillan, 1985.

Robinson, Ray, and Regina Chlopicka, eds. *Studies in Penderecki*. Princeton, N. J.: Prestige, 1998.

Rubio, Samuel. *Crisóbal de Morales: Estudio Crítico de su Polifonia*. Madrid: Biblioteca "La Ciudad de Dios," 1969.

Saffle, Michael. *Franz Liszt: A Guide to Research*. New York: Routledge, 2004.

Sankey, Ira D. *My Life and the Story of the Gospel Hymns and of Sacred Songs and Solos*. New York: Harper, 1906. Rpt. AMS Press, 1974.

Sarwas, Joachim. *Helmut Bornefeld Studien zu seinem "Choralwerk" mit einem Verzeichnis seiner Werke*. Frankfurt am Main: Lang, 1991.

Sawkins, Lionel. "Chronology and Evolution of the *Grand Motet* at the Court of Louis XIV: Evidence from the *Livres du Roi* and the Works of Perrin, the *sous-maîtres* and Lully." *Jean-Baptiste Lully and the Music of the French Baroque*. Ed. J. H. Heyer. Cambridge: Cambridge University Press, 1989: 41–79

Schwerm, Jules. *Got to Tell It: Mahalia Jackson, Queen of Gospel*. Oxford: Oxford University Press, 1992.

Scott, R. H. F. *Jean-Baptiste Lully*. London: Owen, 1973.

Selfridge-Field, Eleanor. *The Music of Benedetto and Alessandro Marcello: A The-*

matic Catalogue with Commentary on the Composers, Works and Sources. New York: Oxford University Press, 1990.

Short, Michael. *Gustav Holst: The Man and His Music.* Oxford: Oxford University Press, 1990.

Smith, Rollin. *Saint-Saëns and the Organ.* Stuyvesant, N. Y.: Pendragon Press, 1992.

———. *Toward an Authentic Interpretation of the Organ Works of César Franck.* Hillsdale, N. Y.: Pendragon Press, 2002.

Snyder, Kerala J. *Dietrich Buxtehude, Organist in Lübeck.* New York: Schirmer, 1987.

Steed, Graham. *The Organ Works of Marcel Dupré.* Stuyvesant, N. Y.: Pendragon Press, 1999.

Steiman, Sidney. *Custom and Survival: A Study of the Life and Work of Rabbi Jacob Molin (Moelln) Known as the Maharil (c. 1360–1427), and His Influence in Establishing the Ashkenazic Minhag (Customs of German Jewry).* New York: Bloch, 1963.

Swafford, Jan. *Charles Ives: A Life With Music.* New York: Norton, 1996.

Thomerson, Kathleen. *Jean Langlais: A Bio-Bibliography.* New York: Greenwood, 1988.

Tomaszewksi, Mieczyslaw, ed. *The Music of Krzysztof Penderecki: Poetics and Reception.* Cracow: Akademia Muzyczna w Krakowie, 1995.

Tunley, David. *François Couperin and "the Perfection of Music."* Aldershot, Hampshire, England: Ashgate, 2004.

Vidali, Carole Franklin. *Alessandro and Domenico Scarlatti: A Guide to Research.* New York: Garland, 1993.

Vogelsänger, Siegfried. *Michael Praetorius beim Wort genommen: zur Entstehungsgeschichte seiner Werke.* Aachen: Herodot Rader Verlag, 1987.

Voss, Hans Dieter. *Arthur Honegger, "Le Roi David": Ein Beitrag zur Geschichte des Oratoriums im 20. Jahrhundert.* Munich: Musikverlag Katzbichler, 1983.

Warren, Edwin B. *Life and Works of Robert Fayrfax, 1464–1521.* Musicological Studies and Documents 22. Dallas, Tex.: American Institute of Musicology, 1969.

Webber, Geoffrey. *North German Church Music in the Age of Buxtehude.* Oxford: Oxford University Press and Clarendon Press, 1996.

Wegman, Robert C. "Another 'Imitation' of Busnoys's *Missa L'Homme armé*: and Some Observations on *Imitatio* in Renaissance Music. *Journal of the Royal Musicological Association* 114 (1989): 189–202.

———. *Born for the Muses: The Life and Masses of Jacob Obrecht.* Oxford: Clarendon Press, 1996.

Weyer, Martin. *Die Orgelwerke Joseph Rheinbergers: Ein Handbuch für Organisten.* Wilhelmshaven: F. Noetzel Verlag, 1994.

———. *Die Orgelwerke Max Regers: Ein Handbuch für Organisten.* Wilhelmshaven: F. Noetzel Verlag, 1989.

Zimmermann, Petra. *Musik und Text in Max Regers Chorwerken 'grossen Styls.'* Wiesbaden: Breitkopf & Härtel, 1997.

STUDIES WITHIN SPECIFIC TRADITIONS

I. Christian

Adey, Lionel. *Hymns and the Christian Myth.* Vancouver: University of British Columbia Press, 1986.

Arnold, Corliss Richard. *Organ Literature: A Comprehensive Survey.* Metuchen, N. J., Scarecrow, 1973.

Bradshaw, Murray C. *The Origin of the Toccata.* Dallas, Tex.: American Institute of Musicology, 1972.

Douglass, Fenner. *The Language of the Classical French Organ: A Musical Tradition Before 1800.* New Haven, Conn.: Yale University Press, 1978.

Guentert, Kenneth. *The Christian Music Directories.* San Jose, Calif.: Resource Publications, 1993.

Hughes, Charles H. *American Hymns Old and New.* Vol. 2. New York: Columbia University Press, 1980.

Johanson, John H. *Moravian Hymnody.* Winston-Salem, N. C.: Moravian Music Foundation, 1980.

Lovelace, Austin. *Anatomy of Hymnody.* Abingdon Press, 1965.

McKinnon, James W. *Music in Early Christian Literature.* Cambridge: Cambridge University Press, 1987.

Ochse, Orpha Caroline. *The History of the Organ in the United States.* Bloomington: Indiana University Press, 1975.

Redman, Robb. *The Great Worship Awakening: Singing a New Song in the Postmodern Church.* San Francisco: Jossey-Bass, 2002.

Reynolds, William. *Survey of Christian Hymnody.* 3rd ed. Carol Stream, Ill.: Hope Publishing, 1987.

Routley, Erik. *The Music of Christian Hymns.* Chicago: G.I.A. Publications, 1981.

———. *Panorama of Christian Hymnody.* Minneapolis, Minn.: Liturgical Press, 1979.

Schlick, Arnolt. *Spiegel der Orgelmacher und Organisten.* Trans. Elizabeth Berry Barber. Buren, Netherlands, 1980.

Sumner, William Leslie. *The Organ: Its Evolution, Principles of Construction and Use.* 4th ed. New York: St. Martin's Press, 1981.

Thistlethwaite, Nicholas, and Geoffrey Webber, eds. *The Cambridge Companion to the Organ.* Cambridge: Cambridge University Press, 1998.

Wackernagel, Philipp. *Das deutsche Kirchenlied von der ältesten Zeit bis zu Anfang es 17. Jahrhunderts.* 5 vols. Leipzig: Teubner, 1864–1877. Rpt.: Hildesheim: Olms, 1964.

Wenk, Arthur. *Musical Resources for the Revised Common Lectionary.* Metuchen, N. J.: Scarecrow, 1994.

Whitney, Craig R. *All the Stops: The Glorious Pipe Organ and Its American Masters.* New York: Public Affairs, 2003.

Williams, Peter F. *The European Organ, 1450–1850.* London: Batsford, 1966

———. *A New History of the Organ from the Greeks to the Present Day.* Bloomington: Indiana University Press, 1980.

———. *The Organ in Western Culture, 750–1250.* Cambridge: Cambridge University Press, 1993.

ROMAN CATHOLIC

1. General

Day, Thomas. *Why Catholics Can't Sing: The Culture of Catholicism and the Triumph of Bad Taste.* New York: Crossroad, 1992.

Fellerer, Karl Gustav. *The History of Catholic Church Music.* Trans. Francis A. Brunner. 1st printing 1961. Westport, Conn.: Greenwood, 1979.

Hayburn, Robert F. *Papal Legislation on Sacred Music 95 A. D. to 1977 A. D.* Collegeville, Minn.: Liturgical Press, 1979.

Higginson, J. Vincent. *A Handbook for American Catholic Hymnals.* Springfield, Tex.: Hymn Society of America, 1976.

Nohl, Paul-Gerhard. *Lateinische Kirchenmusiktexte: Geschichte, Übersetzung, Kommentar.* Kassel: Bärenreiter, 1996.

Roche, Jerome L. *North Italian Church Music in the Age of Monteverdi.* Oxford: Oxford University Press, 1984.

Scott, Darwin Floyd. *The Roman Catholic Liturgy: Liturgical Books: A Musical Guide.* Los Angeles: University of California, 1980.

Terrien, Samuel L., and Bruce Gebert. *The Magnificat: Musicians as Biblical Interpreters.* New York: Paulist Press, 1995.

2. Chant

Bailey, Terence. *The Ambrosian Alleluias.* Egham, Surrey: Plainsong & Mediaeval Music Society, 1983.

———. *Antiphon and Psalm in the Ambrosian Office.* London: Institute of Medieval Music, 1994.

———. *The Transitoria of the Ambrosian Mass: Compositional Process in Ecclesiastical Chant.* Ottawa: Institute of Mediaeval Music, 2003.

Bailey, Terence, and Paul Merkley. *The Antiphons of the Ambrosian Office.* Ottawa: Institute of Mediaeval Music, 1989.

Barr, Cyrilla. *The Monophonic Lauda and the Lay Religious Confraternities of Tus-*

cany and Umbria in the Late Middle Ages. Kalamazoo, Mich.: Medieval Institute Publications, Western Michigan University, 1988.

Berschin, Walter, and David Hiley. *Die Offizien des Mittelalters: Dichtung und Musik.* Tutzing: Schneider, 1999.

Bryden, John R., and David G. Hughes. *An Index of Gregorian Chant.* Cambridge, Mass.: Harvard University Press, 1969.

Carroll, Joseph R. *The Technique of Gregorian Chironomy.* Toledo: Gregorian Institute of America, 1955.

Chevalier, Ulysse. *Repertorium Hymnologicum: Catalogue de chants, hymnes, proses, séquences, tropes en usage dans l'église latine depuis les origines jusqu'à nos jours.* 6 vols. Louvain, Belgium: Société des Bollandistes, 1892–1920. Rpt. 1959.

Crocker, Richard L. *The Early Medieval Sequence.* Berkeley: University of California Press, 1977.

———. *An Introduction to Gregorian Chant.* New Haven, Conn.: Yale University Press, 2000.

Evans, Paul. *The Early Trope Repertory of Saint Martial de Limoges.* Princeton, N. J.: Princeton University Press, 1970.

Fassler, Margot E. and Rebecca Baltzer, eds. *The Divine Office in the Latin Middle Ages: Methodology and Source Studies, Regional Developments, Hagiography: Written in Honor of Professor Ruth Steiner.* New York: Oxford University Press, 2000.

Gallagher, Sean. *Western Plainchant in the First Millenium: Studies in the Medieval Liturgy and Its Music.* Aldershot, Hampshire, England: Ashgate, 2003.

Gajard, Dom Joseph. *The Solesmes Method: Its Fundamental Principles and Practical Rules of Interpretation.* Trans. R. Ecile Gabain. Collegeville, Minn.: Liturgical Press, 1960.

Greene, Richard L. ed. *The Early English Carols.* Oxford: Clarendon Press, 1935; rev. 1977.

Haberl, Ferdinand. *Das gregorianische Alleluia der heiligen Messe.* Regensburg: n.p., 1983.

Hiley, David. *Western Plainchant: A Handbook.* Oxford: Clarendon Press; New York: Oxford University Press, 1993.

Jeffrey, Peter. *Ethnomusicology in the Study of Gregorian Chant.* Chicago: University of Chicago Press, 1995.

———. "Liturgical Chant Bibliography." *Plainsong and Medieval Music* 1 (1992): 175–196.

———. *Prophecy Mixed with Melody: From Early Christian Psalmody to Gregorian Chant.* (forthcoming)

Jeffrey, Peter, ed. *The Study of Medieval Chant: Paths and Bridges, East and West: in Honor of Kenneth Levy.* Woodbridge, Suffolk, England: Boydell Press, 2001.

Karp, Theodore. *An Introduction to the Post-Tridentine Mass Proper.* Middleton, Wis.: American Institute of Musicology, 2005.

————. *Aspects of Orality and Formularity in Gregorian Chant*. Evanston, Ill: Northwestern University Press, 1998.

Kelly, Thomas F. *The Beneventan Chant*. New York: Cambridge University Press, 1989.

————. *Plainsong in the Age of Polyphony*. Cambridge: Cambridge University Press, 1992.

Levy, Kenneth. *Gregorian Chant and the Carolingians*. Princeton, N. J.: Princeton University Press, 1998.

Markus, R. A. *Gregory the Great and His World*. New York: Cambridge University Press, 1997.

McKinnon, James. *The Advent Project: The Later Seventh-Century Creation of the Roman Mass Proper*. Berkeley:: University of California Press, 2000.

Nowacki, Edward. "Antiphonal Psalmody in Christian Antiquity and Early Middle Ages." *Essays on Medieval Music*. Graeme M. Boone, ed. Cambridge: Harvard University Press, 1995. (293–294).

Odelman, Eva. *Les Prosules Limousines de Wolfenbüttel: Edition Critique des Prosules de l'Alleluia du Manuscrit Wolfenbüttel*. Stockholm: Almqvist & Wiksell International, 1986.

Planchart, Alejandro. *Repertoire of Tropes at Winchester*. Princeton, N. J.: Princeton University Press, 1976.

Plumley, Yolanda. *The Music of the Medieval Liturgical Drama in France and England*. New York: Garland, 1989.

Randel, Don Michael. *An Index to the Chant of the Mozarabic Rite*. Princeton, N. J.: Princeton University Press, 1973.

Rankin, Susan, ed. *Music in Medieval English Liturgy*. Oxford: Oxford University Press, 1993.

Soltner, Louis. *Solesmes and Dom Guéranger, 1805–1875*. Orleans, Mass.: Paraclete Press, 1995.

Steiner, Ruth. *Studies in Gregorian Chant*. Aldershot, Hampshire, England: Ashgate, 1999.

Szövérffy, Joseph. *Repertorium hymnologicum novum*. Berlin: Classical Folia Editions, 1983–.

Van der Werf, Henrik. *The Emergence of Gregorian Chant: A Comparative Study of Ambrosian, Roman, and Gregorian Chant*. Rochester, N. Y.: H. van der Werf, 1983.

3. Polyphony

Apel, Willi. *The Notation of Polyphonic Music, 900–1600*. 5th ed. Cambridge, Mass.: Mediaeval Academy of America, 1961.

Bent, Margaret. *Counterpoint, Composition, and Music Ficta*. New York: Routledge, 2002.

Berger, Karol. *Musica Ficta: Theories of Accidental Inflections in Vocal Polyphony from Marchetto da Padova to Gioseffo Zarlino*. Cambridge: Cambridge University Press, 1987.

———. *Theories of Chromatic and Enharmonic Music in Late Sixteenth-Century Italy*. Studies in Musicology 10. Ann Arbor, Mich.: UMI Research Press, 1980.

Bossuyt, Ignace. *Flemish Polyphony*. Leuven, Belgium: Davidsfonds, 1994.

Bradshaw, Murray C. *The Origin of the Toccata*. Rome: American Institute of Musicology, 1972.

Carver, Anthony F. *"Cori Spezzati": The Development of Sacred Polychoral Music to the Time of Schütz*. 2 vols. Cambridge: Cambridge University Press, 1988.

Cummings, Anthony M. "Toward an Interpretation of the Sixteenth-Century Motet." *Journal of the American Musicological Society* 34 (1981): 43–59.

Everist, Mark. *French Motets in the Thirteenth Century*. Cambridge: Cambridge University Press, 1994.

Falck, Robert. *The Notre Dame Conductus: A Study of the Repertory*. Henryville, Pa. Institute of Mediaeval Music, 1981.

Fuller, Sarah. "Defending the *Dodecachordon*: Ideological Currents in Glarean's Modal Theory." *Journal of the American Musicological Society* 49 (1996): 191–224.

Gombosi, Otto. "About Organ Playing the Divine Service, circa 1500." *Essays on Music in Honor of Archibald Thompson Davison*. Cambridge, Mass.: Harvard University Press, 1957.

Huot, Sylvia. *Allegorical Play in the Old French Motet: The Sacred and the Profane in Thirteenth-Century Polyphony*. Stanford, Calif.: Stanford University Press, 1997.

Karp, Theodore. *The Polyphony of Saint Martial and Santiago de Compostela*. Berkeley: University of California Press, 1992.

Köhler, Rafael. *Die Cappella Sistina under den Medici-Päpsten, 1513–1534*. Kiel: Ludwig, 2001.

Kurtzmann, Jeffrey G. "Tones, Modes, Clefs, and Pitch in Roman Cyclic Magnificats of the 16th Century." *Early Music* 22 (1994): 641–64.

Leichtentritt, Hugo. *Geschichte der Motette*. 1st ed. 1908. Hildesheim: Georg Olms, 1967.

Lockwood, Lewis. *The Counter-Reformation and the Masses of Vincenzo Ruffo*. Venice: Fondazione Giorgio Cini, 1970.

Lowinsky, Edward E. *Medici Codex of 1518: A Choirbook of Motets Dedicated to Lorenzo de' Medici, Duke of Urbino*. Chicago: University of Chicago Press, 1968.

Luce, Harold T. *The Requiem Mass from its Plainsong Beginnings to 1600*. Tallahassee: Florida State University Press, 1958.

Macey, Patrick. "Savonarola and the Sixteenth-Century Motet." *Journal of the American Musicological Society* 36 (1983): 442–52.

———. "The Lauda and the Cult of Savonarola." *Renaissance Quarterly* 45 (1992): 439–83.

McGee, Timothy J. *Medieval and Renaissance Music: A Performer's Guide*. Toronto: Toronto University Press, 1985.

Meconi, Honey, ed. *Early Music Borrowing*. New York: Routledge, 2003.

Meier, Bernhard. *The Modes of Classical Vocal Polyphony*. Trans. Ellen S. Beebe. New York: Broude Bros., 1988. Original 1974.

Mielke, Andreas. *Untersuchungen zur Alternatim-Orgelmesse*. Kassel: Bärenreiter, 1996.

Moll, Kevin N. *Counterpoint and Compositional Process at the Time of Dufay: Perspectives from German Musicology*. New York: Garland, 1997.

Owens, Jessie Ann. *Composers at Work: The Craft of Musical Composition, 1450–1600*. Oxford: Clarendon Press, 1996.

Pesce, Dolores. *Hearing the Motet: Essays on the Motet of the Middle Ages and Renaissance*. Oxford: Oxford University Press, 1996.

Pozzi, Giovanni. *Alternatim*. Milan: Adelphi, 1996.

Reynolds, Christopher. *Papal Patronage and the Music of St. Peters, 1380–1513*. Irvine: University of California Press, 1995.

Robertson, Alec. *Requiem: Music of Mourning and Consolation*. New York: Praeger, 1968.

Roche, Jerome. *North Italian Church Music in the Age of Monteverdi*. Oxford: Clarendon Press, 1984.

Sanders, Ernest H. *French and English Polyphony of the 13th and 14th Centuries: Style and Notation*. Aldershot, Hampshire, England: Ashgate, 1998.

Saunders, Suparmi Elizabeth. *The Dating of the Trent Codices from their Watermarks: With a Study of the Local Liturgy of Trent in the Fifteenth Century*. New York: Garland, 1989.

Selfridge-Field, Eleanor. *Venetian Instrumental Music from Gabrieli to Vivaldi*. Oxford: Blackwell, 1975. Rpt. Dover: 1994.

Sherr, Richard. *Papal Music and Musicians in Late Medieval and Renaissance Rome*. Oxford: Clarendon Press, 1998.

Southern, Eileen. *The Buxheim Organ Book*. Brooklyn, N. Y.: Institute of Mediaeval Music, 1963.

Sparks, Edgar H. *Cantus Firmus in Mass and Motet, 1420–1520*. Berkeley: University of California Press, 1963.

Stephan, Wolfgang. *Die burgundisch-niederländische Motette zur Zeit Ockeghems*. Kassel: Bärenreiter, 1937. Rpt. 1973.

Stevenson, Robert M. *Spanish Cathedral Music in the Golden Age*. Berkeley: University of California Press, 1961.

Tischler, Hans. *Conductus and Contrafacta*. Ottawa: Institute of Mediaeval Music, 2001.

Tinctoris, Johannes. *Terminorum Musical Diffinitorium / Dictionary of Musical Terms*. Trans. Carl Parrish. New York: Norton, 1963.

Van der Werf, Hendrik. *Integrated Directory of Organa, Clausulae, and Motets of the Thirteenth Century*. Rochester, N. Y.: H. van der Werf, 1989.

Van Wye, Benjamin D. "Ritual Use of the Organ in France." *Journal of the American Musicological Society* 33 (1980): 287–325.

Ward, Lynn Halpern. "The *Motetti Missales* Repertory Reconsidered." *Journal of the American Musicological Society* 39 (1986): 491–523.

Weber, Edith. *Le Concile de Trente et la Musique: De la Réforme à la Contre-Réform.* Paris: H. Champion, 1982.

Wiering, Frans. *The Language of the Modes. Studies in the History of Polyphonic Modality.* New York: Routledge, 2001.

Wright, Craig. *Music and Ceremony at Notre Dame of Paris, 500–1550.* New York: Cambridge University Press, 1991.

4. Since 1700

Archbold, Lawrence, and William J. Peterson. *French Organ Music: from the Revolution to Franck and Widor.* Rochester, N. Y.: University of Rochester Press, 1995.

Arnold, Denis and Elsie Arnold. *The Oratorio in Venice.* London: Royal Musical Association, 1986.

Balado, J. L. Gonzalez. *The Story of Taizé.* 3rd rev. ed. Collegeville, Minn.: Liturgical Press, 1988.

Daly, Kieran Anthony. *Catholic Church Music in Ireland, 1878–1903: the Cecilian Reform Movement.* Dublin: Blackrock, 1995.

Joncas, J. Michael. "Musical Semiotics and Liturgical Musicology: Theoretical Foundations and Analytic Techniques." *Ecclesia Orans* 8 (1991): 181–206.

Koch, Jakob Johannes. *Traditionelle mehrstimmige Messen in erneuerter Liturgie— ein Widerspruch?* Regensburg: Pustet, 2002.

Kubicki, Judith M. and Jacques Berthier. *Liturgical Music as Ritual Symbol: A Case Study of Jacques Berthier's Taizé Music.* Leuven, Belgium: Peeters, 1999.

Laird, Paul R. *Towards a History of the Spanish Villancico.* Warren, Mich.: Harmonie Park Press, 1997.

Love, Andrew Cyprian. *Musical Improvisation, Heidegger and the Liturgy—A Journey to the Heart of Hope.* Lewiston, N. Y.: Edwin Mellen, 2003.

MacIntyre, Bruce C. *The Viennese Concerted Mass of the Early Classic Period.* Ann Arbor, Mich.: UMI Research Press, 1986.

Madden, Lawrence J. *The Awakening Church: 25 Years of Liturgical Renewal.* Collegeville, Minn.: Liturgical Press, 1992.

Murray, Michael. *French Masters of the Organ: Saint-Saëns, Franck, Widor, Vierne, Dupré, Langlais, Messiaen.* New Haven, Conn.: Yale University Press, 1998.

Pierre, Constant. *Histoire du Concert Spirituel: 1725–1790.* Paris: Société Française de Musicologie, 1975.

Unverricht, Hubert. *Der Caecilianismus: Anfänge, Grundlagen, Wirkungen: Inter-*

nationales Symposium zur Kirchenmusik des 19. Jahrhunderts. Tutzing, Germany: H. Schneider, 1988.

5. Transcultural

Duncan, Stephen F. *A Genre in Hindusthani Music (Bhajans) as Used in the Roman Catholic Church*. Lewiston, N. Y.: Edwin Mellen Press, 1999.

Klein, Christopher. *Messkompositionen in Afrika: ein Beitrag zur Geschichte und Typologie der katholischen Kirchenmusik Afrikas*. Göttingen: Edition Re, 1990.

Worst, John. *A Nigerian Journal*. Grand Rapids, Mich.: Calvin College, 1984.

BYZANTINE AND ORTHODOX

Arhipov, Sergei. *The Apostol: Epistle Readings, Prokimena, Alleluia Verses and Antiphons for the Entire Liturgical Year*. South Canaan, Pa.: St. Tikhon's Seminary Press, 1996.

Biezen, J. van. *The Middle Byzantine Kanon-notation of Manuscript H.: A Paleographic Study With a Transcription of the Melodies of 13 Kanons and a Triodon*. Bilthoven: A. B. Creyghton, 1969.

Brill, Nicholas P. *History of Russian Church Music, 988–1917*. Bloomington, Ill.: Brill, 1980.

Conomos, Dimitri E. *Byzantine Trisagia and Cheroubika of the Fourteenth and Fifteenth Centuries: A Study of Late Byzantine Liturgical Chant*. Thessaloniki: Patriarchal Institute for Patristic Studies, 1974.

———. *Byzantine Hymnography and Byzantine Chant*. Brookline, Mass.: Hellenic College Press, 1984.

———. *The Late Byzantine and Slavonic Communion Cycle: Liturgy and Music*. Washington, D. C.: Dumbarton Oaks Research Library and Collection, 1985.

Cooper, Henry R. *Slavic Scriptures: The Formation of the Church Slavonic Version of the Holy Bible*. Madison, N. J.: Fairleigh Dickinson University Press, 2003.

Duichev, Ivan. *Kiril and Methodius: Founders of Slavonic Writing: A Collection of Sources and Critical Studies*. Boulder, Colo.: East European Monographs, distrib. Columbia University Press, 1985.

Duncan, Stephen F. *The History of the Sacred Musical Life of an Orthodox Church in America*. Lewiston, N. Y.: Edwin Mellen, 2004.

Farrow, Michael G. *Psalm Verse of the Orthodox Liturgy: Antiphonal, Entrance, Prokeimena, Alleluia, and Comminion [sic] Hymn Verses and their Biblical Citations According to Both the Greek and Slav Usages*. Torrance, Calif.: Oakwood Publications, 1997.

Gardiner, S. C. *Old Church Slavonic: An Elementary Grammar*. Cambridge: Cambridge University Press, 1984.

Gardner, Johannes von. *Russian Church Singing*. 2 vols. Guilford, Conn.: Orthodox Music Press, 1980.

Habbi, Antun. *Short Course in Byzantine Ecclesiastical Music*. Newton, Mass.: Greek Melkite Catholic Diocese of Newton, 1988.

Hannick, Christian. "Reference Materials on Byzantine and Old Slavic Music and Hymnography." *Journal of the Plainsong and Medieval Music Society* 13 (1990): 83–89.

Ho, Allan and Dmitry Feofanov. *Biographical Dictionary of Russian/Soviet Composers*. Westport, Conn.: Greenwood, 1989.

Louth, Andrew. *St. John Damascene: Tradition and Originality in Byzantine Theology*. Oxford: Oxford University Press, 2002.

Morosan, Vladimir. *Choral Performance in Pre-Revolutionary Russia*. Ann Arbor, Mich.: UMI Research Press, 1986.

Raasted, Jürgen. "Compositional Devices in Byzantine Chant." *Cahiers de L'Institut du Moyen-Age Grec et Latin* 59 (1989): 247–270.

———. "Koukouzeles Revision of the Sticherarion and Sinai gr. 1230." *Laborare fratres in unum: Festschrift László Dobszay zum 60. Geburtstag*. Ed. Janka. Szendrei and David Hiley. Hildesheim: Weidmann, 1995), pp. 261–77.

Roccasalvo, Joan. I. *The Plain Chant Tradition of Southwestern Rus'*. Boulder, Co.: East European Monographs, 1986.

Romanou, Kaite. "A New Approach to the Work of Chrysanthos of Madytos: The New Method of Musical Notation in the Greek Church and the *Mega theoretikon tes mousikes*." *Studies in Eastern Chant* 5. Ed. Dimitri E. Conomos. Crestwood, N. Y.: St. Vladimir's Seminary Press, 1991, pp. 89–100.

Smrzík, Stephen. *The Glagolitic or Roman-Slavonic Liturgy*. Cleveland, Oh.: Slovak Institute, 1959.

Svövérffy, Joseph, and Eva C. Topping. *A Guide to Byzantine Hymnography: A Classified Bibliography of Texts and Studies*. Brookline, Mass.: Classical Folia Editions; Leyden: E. J. Brill, 1979–.

Swan, A. J. *Russian Music and its Sources in Chant and Folksong*. London: 1973.

The Oxford Dictionary of Byzantium. 3 vols. Ed. Alexander P. Kazhdan, et al. New York: Oxford, 1991.

Taft, Robert F. *The Liturgy of the Hours in East and West: The Origins of the Divine Office and Its Meaning for Today*. Collegeville, Minn.: Liturgical Press, 1986.

Touliatos-Banker, Diane. "The Byzantine Orthros." *Byzantina* 9 (1977): 324–83.

Vaporis, N. M. *Three Byzantine Sacred Poets: Studies of Saint Romanos Melodos, Saint of Damascus, Saint Symeon the New Theologian*. Brookline, Mass.: Hellenic College Press, 1979.

Wolfram, Gerda, et al. *Die Erotapokriseis des Pseudo-Johannes Damaskenos zum Kirchengesang*. Vienna: Verlag der Österreichischen Akademie der Wissenschaften, 1997.

Wellesz, Egon. *A History of Byzantine Music and Hymnography*. Rev. ed. London: Oxford University Press, 1961.

ANGLICAN

Baldwin, David. *The Chapel Royal: Ancient and Modern*. London: Duckworth, 1990.

Benham, Hugh. *Latin Church Music in England, c. 1460–1575*. London: Barrie & Barrie, 1975.

Caldwell, John. *Oxford History of English Music: Vol. 1: From the Beginnings to c. 1715*. Oxford: Clarendon Press, 1991.

Daniel, Ralph T. *The Sources of English Church Music, 1549–1660*. London: Stainer and Bell for the British Academy, 1972.

Dearnley, Christopher. *English Church Music, 1650–1750*. New York: Oxford University Press, 1970.

Dexter, Keri. *'A good Quire of voices': The Provision of Choral Music at St George's Chapel, Windsor Castle, and Eton College, c. 1640–1733*. Aldershot, Hampshire, England: Ashgate, 2002.

Frost, Maurice. *Historical Companion to Hymns Ancient and Modern*. London: Printed for the Proprietors by William Cleves and Sons, 1962.

Gatens, William J. *Victorian Cathedral Music in Theory and Practice*. Cambridge: Cambridge University Press, 1986.

Glover, Raymond F., gen. ed. *The Hymnal 1982 Companion*. 4 vols. New York: Church Hymnal Corporation, 1990–.

Harrison, Frank Ll. *Music in Medieval Britain*. 4th ed.. Buren, The Netherlands: Knuf, 1980.

Hatchett, Marion J. *A Liturgical Index to The Hymnal 1982*. New York: Church Hymnal, 1986.

Hutchings, Arthur. *Church Music in the Nineteenth Century*. London: Herbert Jenkins, 1967.

Illing, Robert, and Thomas Sternhold. *The English Metrical Psalter 1562: A Catalogue of the Early Editions, an Index to their Contents, and a Comparative Study of their Melodies*. Adelaide: South Australian Government Printer, 1983.

Le Huray, Peter. *Music and the Reformation in England: 1549–1660*. New York: Oxford University Press, 1967.

Lindley, Simon. *Muse and the Mass: The Choral Repertory and the Service of Holy Communion in the Anglican Church: Yesterday, Today and Tomorrow*. Croydon, England: Royal School of Church Music for the Church Music Society, 1991.

Long, Kenneth. *The Music of the English Church*. London: Hodder and Stoughton, 1991.

Parks, Edna D. *Early English Hymns: An Index*. Metuchen, N. J.: Scarecrow, 1972.

Perry, David W. *Hymns and Tunes Indexed by First Lines, Tune Names, and Metres Complied from Current English Hymnbooks*. Croydon, England: Hymn Society of Great Britain and Ireland and Royal School of Church Music, 1980.

Phillips, Peter. *English Sacred Music 1549–1649*. Oxford: Gimell, 1991.

Rainbow, Bernard. *The Choral Revival in the Anglican Church, 1839–1872*. New York: Oxford University Press, 1970.

Routley, Erik. *A Short History of English Church Music*. London: Mowbrays, 1977.

Scott, David. *The Music of St. Paul's Cathedral*. London: Stainer and Bell and Galaxy Music Corp., 1972.

Sharp, Ian. *The Liturgical Use of the Organ Voluntary*. Croydon, England: Royal School of Church Music, 1984.

Shaw, H. Watkins *Eighteenth Century Cathedral Music*. London: Hodder and Stoughton, 1970.

Spink, Ian. *Restoration Cathedral Music 1660–1714*. Oxford: Clarendon Press; New York: Oxford University Press, 1995.

Stevens, Denis. *Tudor Church Music*. New York: Merlin, 1955. Rpt. 1966.

Tamke, Susan S. *Make a Joyful Noise unto the Lord: Hymns as a Reflection of Victorian Social Attitudes*. Athens: Ohio University Press, 1978.

Temperley, Nicholas. *The Music of the English Parish Church*. New York: Cambridge University Press, 1983.

Turbet, Richard. *Tudor Music: A Research and Information Guide*. New York: Garland, 1994.

Wienandt, Elwyn A., and Robert H. Young. *The Anthem in England and America*. New York: Free Press, 1970.

Wilson, Ruth Mack. *Anglican Chant and Chanting in England, Scotland, and America, 1660 to 1820*. Oxford: Clarendon Press and Oxford University Press, 1996.

Yeats-Edwards, Paul. *English Church Music: A Bibliography*. London: White Lion, 1975.

Zim, Rivkah. *English Metrical Psalms: Poetry as Praise and Prayer, 1535–1601*. Cambridge: Cambridge University Press, 1987.

LUTHERAN

Blume, Friederich. *Protestant Church Music: A History*. German ed. 1965. New York: Norton, 1974.

Daniel, Thomas. *Der Choralsatz bei Bach und seiner Zeitgenossen: eine historische Satzlehre*. Cologne: Dohr, 2000.

Dürr, Alfred, and Walther Killy. *Das Protestantische Kirchenlied im 16. und 17. Jahrhundert: Text-, musik- und theologiegeschichtliche Probleme*. Wiesbaden: In Kommission bei O. Harrasowitz, 1986.

Gissel, Siegfried. *Untersuchungen zur mehrstimmigen protestantischen Hymnenkomposition in Deutschland um 1600*. Kassel: Bärenreiter, 1983.

Hendrickson, Marion Lars. *Musica Christi: A Lutheran Aesthetic*. Peter Lang, 2005.

Herl, Joseph. *Worship Wars in Early Lutheranism: Choir, Congregation, and Three Centuries of Conflict*. Oxford: Oxford University Press, 2004.

Krummacher, Friedhelm. *Die Choralbearbeitung in der protestantischen Figural-musik zwischen Praetorius und Bach.* Kassel: Bärenreiter, 1978.

Leaver, Robin A. "The Lutheran Reformation." *The Renaissance.* Iain Fenlon, ed. London: Macmillan, 1989.

Liemohn, Edwin. *The Chorale through Four Hundred Years.* Philadelphia, Pa.: Muhlenberg Press, 1953.

Mahrenholz, Christhard, and Oskar Söhngen. *Handbuch zum evangelischen Kir-chengesangbuch.* 3 vols. Göttingen: Vandenoeck & Ruprecht, 1953–1970.

Marshall, Robert L. *Luther, Bach, and the Early Reformation Chorale.* Atlanta, Ga.: Pitts Theological Library, 1995.

Nettl, Paul. *Luther and Music.* Trans. Frida Best and Ralph Wood. Philadelphia, Pa.: Muhlenberg Press, 1948.

Riedel, Johannes. *The Lutheran Chorale: Its Basic Traditions.* Minneapolis, Minn.: Augsburg Publishing House, 1967.

Schacht-Pape, Ute. *Das Messenschaffen von Alessandro Scarlatti.* Frankfurt am Main: P. Lang, 1993.

Schalk, Carl. *Luther and Music: Paradigms of Praise.* St. Louis, Mo.: Concordia, 1988.

Stevenson, Robert M. *Patterns of Protestant Church Music.* Durham, N. C.: Duke University Press, 1953.

Stulken, Marilyn Kay. *Hymnal Companion to the Lutheran Book of Worship.* Phila-delphia, Pa.: Fortress Press, 1981.

Walker, Paul. *Church, Stage, and Studio: Music and its Contexts in Seventeenth-Century Germany.* Ann Arbor, Mich.: UMI Research Press, 1990.

Werning, Daniel J. *A Selected Source Index for Hymn and Chorale Tunes in Lu-theran Worship Books.* St. Louis, Mo.: Concordia, 1985.

CALVINIST (REFORMED)

Bouwsma, William J. *John Calvin: A Sixteenth-Century Portrait.* Oxford: Oxford University Press, 1988.

Haeussler, Armin. *The Story of Our Hymns: The Handbook to the Hymnal of the Evangelical and Reformed Church.* St. Louis, Mo.: Eden Publishing House, 1952.

Leaver, Robin A. *Goostly Psalmes and Spirituall Songes: English and Dutch Metri-cal Psalms from Coverdale to Utenhove: 1535–1566.* Oxford: Oxford University Press, 1991.

Potter, George R. *Zwingli.* Cambridge: Cambridge University Press, 1976.

Pratt, Waldo Selden. *The Music of the French Psalter of 1562.* New York: Columbia University Press, 1939.

Vischer, Lukas. *Christian Worship in Reformed Churches Past and Present.* Grand Rapids, Mich.: W. B. Eerdmans, 2003.

AMERICAN PROTESTANT

Adams, Charles B. *Our Moravian Hymn Heritage: Chronological Listing of Hymns and Tunes of Moravian Origin in the American Moravian Hymnal of 1969*. Bethlehem, Pa.: Moravian Church of America, 1984.

Anderson, E. Byron. *Worship Matters: A United Methodist Guide to Ways to Worship*. Nashville, Tenn.: Discipleship Resources, 1999.

Bruce, Dickson, Jr. *And They All Sang Hallelujah: Plain-Folk Camp Meeting Religion, 1800–1845*. Knoxville: University of Tennessee Press, 1974.

Buechner, Alan. *Yankee Singing Schools and the Golden Age of Choral Music in New England, 1760–1800*. Boston: Boston University for The Dublin Seminar for New England Folklife, 2003.

Christ-Janer, Albert, Charles W. Hughes, and Carleton Sprague Smith. *American Hymns, Old and New*. New York: Columbia University Press, 1980.

Cobb, Buell E., Jr. *The Sacred Harp: A Tradition and its Music*. Athens: University of Georgia Press, 1989.

Cornwall, J. Spencer. *Stories of Our Mormon Hymns*. Salt Lake City, Utah: Deseret Book Company, 1975.

Daniel, Ralph T. *The Anthem in New England before 1800*. Evanston, Ill.: Northwestern University Press, 1966.

Diehl, Katharine Smith. *Hymns and Tunes: An Index*. New York: Scarecrow, 1966.

Ellinwood, Leonard W. *Dictionary of American Hymnology: First Line Index: A Project of the Hymn Society of America*. 179 microfilm reels with printed guide. New York: University Music Editions, 1984.

Forbes, Bruce D., and Jeffrey H. Mahan. *Religion and Popular Culture in America*. Berkeley: University of California Press, 2000.

Howard, Jay R. *Apostles of Rock: The Splintered World of Contemporary Christian Music*. Lexington, Ky.: University Press of Kentucky, 1999.

Hoge, Dean R., Benton Johnson, and Donald A. Luidens. *Vanishing Boundaries: The Religion of Mainline Protestant Baby Boomers*. Westminster, Oh.: John Knox, 1994.

Hostetler, Lester. *Handbook to the Mennonite Hymnary*. Newton, Kans.: General Conference of the Mennonite Church of North America, 1949.

Jackson, George Pullen. *White Spirituals in the Southern Uplands*. Chapel Hill: University of North Carolina Press, 1933.

Klepper, Robert E. *A Concordance of the Pilgrim Hymnal*. Metuchen, N. J.: Scarecrow, 1989.

———. *Methodist Hymnal Concordance*. Metuchen, N. J.: Scarecrow, 1987.

Marini, Stephen A. *Sacred Song in America: Religion, Music, and Public Culture*. Urbana: University of Illinois Press, 2003.

McKim, LindaJo H. *The Presbyterian Hymnal Companion*. Louisville, Ky.: Westminster/John Knox Press, 1993.

Miller, Kiri, et al. *The Chattahoochee Musical Convention, 1852–2002: A Sacred Harp Historical Sourcebook*. Carrollton, Ga.: Sacred Harp Museum, 2002.

Mouw, Richard J. *Wonderful Words of Life: Hymns in American Protestant History and Theology*. Grand Rapids, Mich.: Eerdmans, 2004.

Neufeld, Bernie. *Music in Worship: A Mennonite Perspective*. Scottdale, Pa.: Herald Press and Faith and Life Press, 1998.

Stevenson, Robert. *Protestant Church Music in America*. New York: Norton, 1970.

Turner, Ronald A. *A Study Guide to Anthem Literature: History and Performance Practice*. Louisville, Ky.: Southern Baptist Theological Seminary, 1981.

Temperley, Nicholas. *The Hymn Tune Index: A Census of English-Language Hymn Tunes in Printed Sources from 1535 to 1820*. Oxford: Clarendon Press; New York, Oxford University Press, 1998.

Young, Carlton R. *Companion to the United Methodist Hymnal*. Nashville, Tenn.: Abingdon Press, 1993.

AFRICAN AMERICAN

Abbington, James. *Readings in African American Church Music and Worship*. Chicago, Ill.: GIA Publications, 2001.

Anderson, Robert and Gail North. *Gospel Music Encyclopedia*. New York: Sterling, 1979.

Boyer, Horace Clarence. *How Sweet the Sound: The Golden Age of Gospel*. Washington, D.C.: Elliott & Clark, 1995.

Cone, James H. *The Spirituals and the Blues*. 2nd ed. Maryknoll, N. Y.: Orbis Books, 1991.

Cusic, Don. *The Sound of Light: A History of Gospel Music*. Bowling Green, Oh.: Bowling Green State University Popular Press, 1990.

Epstein, Dena. *Sinful Tunes and Spirituals*. Urbana: University of Illinois Press, 1977.

Goff, James R. *Close Harmony: A History of Southern Gospel*. Chapel Hill: University of North Carolina Press, 2002.

Harris, Michael W. *The Rise of Gospel Blues: The Music of Thomas Andrew Dorsey in the Urban Church*. New York : Oxford University Press, 1992

Harvey, Louis-Charles. "Black Gospel Music and Black Theology." *The Journal of Religious Thought* 43:2 (Fall–Winter, 1986–1987), 19–37.

Jackson, Irene V. *Afro-American Religious Music*. Greenwood, 1979.

Johnson, Jason M. et al. *Soul Sanctuary: Images of the African American Worship Experience*. Bulfinch, 2006.

Jones, Arthur C. *Wade in the Water: The Wisdom of the Spirituals*. Maryknoll, N. Y.: Orbis Books, 1993.

Jones, Ferdinand, and Arthur C. Jones, eds. *The Triumph of the Soul: Cultural and Psychological Aspects of African American Music*. Westport, Conn.: Praeger, 2001.

Leonard, Neil. *Jazz: Myth and Religion*. New York: Oxford University Press, 1987.

Lovell, John, Jr. *Black Song, The Forge and the Flame: The Story of How the Afro-American Spiritual Was Hammered Out.* 2nd ed. New York: Paragon House, 1986.

Marsh, J. B. T. *The Story of the Fisk Jubilee Singers.* Boston: Houghton, 1880.

Moore, Allan, ed. *The Cambridge Companion to Blues and Gospel Music.* Cambridge: Cambridge University Press, 2003.

Nielsen, Aldon L. *Black Chant: Languages of African-American Postmodernism.* Cambridge: Cambridge University Press, 1997.

Reagon, Bernice Johnson. *If You Don't Go, Don't Hinder Me: The African American Sacred Song Tradition.* Lincoln: University of Nebraska Press, 2001.

Reagon, Bernice Johnson, ed., *"We'll Understand It Better By and By": Pioneering African American Gospel Composers.* Washington, D. C.: Smithsonian Institution Press, 1992.

Roberts, John Storm. *Black Music of Two Worlds.* New York: Praeger, 1972.

Sankey, Ira D. *My Life and the Story of the Gospel Hymns.* New York: Harper and Brothers, 1907.

Sizer, Sandra. *Gospel Hymns and Social Religion: The Rhetoric of Nineteenth-Century Revivalism.* Philadelphia, Pa.: Temple University Press, 1978.

Spencer, Jon Michael. *Protest & Praise: Sacred Music of Black Religion.* Minneapolis, Minn.: Fortress Press, 1990.

Turner, Steve. *Amazing Grace: The Story of America's Most Beloved Song.* New York: Ecco, 2002.

Young, Alan. *Woke Me Up This Morning: Black Gospel Singers and the Gospel Life.* Jackson: University Press of Mississippi, 1997

Jewish

Egger, Ellen M. *A Singing Haggadah: An Illustrated Passover Haggadah with Traditional Chants and Melodies.* Princeton, N. J.: L'Rakia Press, 1986.

Flender, Reinhard. *Hebrew Psalmody: A Structural Investigation.* Jerusalem: Magnes Press, Hebrew University, 1992.

Gradenwitz, Peter. *The Music of Israel: From the Biblical Era to Modern Times.* Rev. ed. Portland, Ore.: Amadeus Press, 1996.

Hoffman, Lawrence A. and Janet R. Walton. *Sacred Sound and Social Change: Liturgical Music in Jewish and Christian Experience.* South Bend, Ind.: University of Notre Dame Press, 1992.

Idelsohn, A. Z. *Jewish Music in its Historical Development.* New York: Schocken Books, 1967.

Jacobson, Joshua R. *Chanting the Hebrew Bible: The Art of Cantillation.* Philadelphia: Jewish Publication Society, 2002.

Lehnardt, Andreas. *Qaddish: Untersuchungen zur Entstehung und Rezeption eines rabbinischen Gebetes.* Tübingen: Mohr Siebeck, 2002.

Levine, Lee I. *The Synagogue in Late Antiquity.* Philadelphia: American Schools of Oriental Research, 1987.

Neusner, Jacob. *Judaism's Theological Voice: The Melody of the Talmud.* Chicago: University of Chicago Press, 1995.

Nulman, Macy. *Concise Encyclopedia of Jewish Music.* New York: McGraw-Hill, 1975.

Petuchowski, Jakob J. *Theology and Poetry: Studies in the Medieval Piyyut.* London: Routledge and K. Paul, 1977.

Portnoy, Marshall. *The Art of Torah Cantillation: A Step-by-Step Guide to Chanting Torah.* New York: UAHC, 2000.

Schach, Stephen R. *The Structure of the Siddur.* Northvale, N. J.: Jason Aronson, 1996.

Schiller, David M. *Bloch, Schoenberg, and Bernstein: Assimilating Jewish Music.* Oxford: Oxford University Press, 2003.

Shelemay, Kay Kaufman. *Pizmon: Syrian–Jewish Religious and Social Song.* Hohokus, N. J.: Shanachie, 1985.

———. *Studies in Jewish Musical Traditions: Insights from the Harvard Collection of Judaica Sound Recordings.* Cambridge, Mass.: Harvard College Library, 2001.

Shiloah, Amnon. *Jewish Musical Traditions.* Detroit: Wayne State University Press, 1992.

———. *The Performance of Jewish and Arab Music in Israel Today.* Amsterdam: Harwood Academic Press, 1997.

Staiman, Mordechai. *Niggun: Stories Behind the Chasidic Songs that Inspire Jews.* Northvale, N. J.: Jason Aronson, 1994.

Swados, Elizabeth and Eli Wiesel. *The Haggadah.* New York: S. French, 1982.

Telzner, David, and Gabriel Sivan. *The Kaddish: Its History and Significance.* Jerusalem: Tal Orot Institute, 1995.

Tietze, Andreas, and Joseph Yahalom. *Ottoman Melodies, Hebrew Hymns: A 16th Century Cross-Cultural Adventure.* Budapest: Akadémiai Kiadó, 1995.

Werner, Eric. *A Voice Still Heard . . . : The Sacred Songs of the Askenazic Jews.* University Park, Pa.: Pennsylvania State University Press, 1976.

———. *From Generation to Generation: Studies of Jewish Musical Tradition.* New York: American Conference of Cantors, 1967.

Wickes, William. *Two Treatises on the Accentuation of the Old Testament.* New York: Ktav, 1881, 1970.

Zeitlin, S. Z., and Haim Bar-Dayan. *The Hebrew Calendar and the Cantillations for the Festivals of the Year.* Tel-Aviv: S. Z. Zeitlin, 1984.

Islamic

Arcangeli, Piero G. *Musica e Liturgia nella Cultura Mediterranea: Atti del Convegno Internazionale di Studi (Venezia 2–5 Ottobre 1985).* Florence: L. S. Olschki, 1988.

Avery, Kenneth S. *Psychology of Early Sufi Sama': Listening and Altered States.* London: RoutledgeCurzon, 2004.

Çagatāy, N. "The Tradition of Mavlid Recitations in Islam Particularly in Turkey," *Studia Islamica* 28 (1868): 127–.

During, Jean. "Revelation and Spiritual Audition in Islam," *World of Music* 3 (1982): 68–84.

———. "What is Sufi Music?" *The Legacy of Mediaeval Persian Sufism.* Ed. Leonard Lewisohn. London: Khaniqahi-Nimatullahi, 1992, pp. 277–87.

Ernst, Carl W. *The Shambhala Guide to Sufism.* Boston, Mass.: Shambhala, 1997.

Farmer, H. G. "The Religious Music of Islam," *Journal of the Royal Asiatic Society* (1952): 60–65.

Faruqi, L. I. "The Cantillation of the Qur'ān," *Asian Music* 19:1 (1987): 2–25.

Kaptein, N. J. G. *Muhammad's Birthday Festival: Early History in the Central Muslim Lands and Development in the Muslim West until the 10th–16th Century.* Leiden: E. J. Brill, 1993.

Kilpatrick, Hilary. *Making the Great Book of Songs: Compilation and the Author's Craft in Abu l-Faraj al-Isbahani's Kital al-Aghani.* London: RoutledgeCurzon, 2003.

Muhaiyaddeen, M. R. Bawa. *Dhikr: The Remembrance of God.* Narbeth, Pa.: Fellowship Press, 1999.

Nasr, S. H. "Islam and Music," *Studies in Comparative Religion* 10 (1976): 37–45.

Nayyar, Adam. *Qawwali.* Islamabad: Lok Virsa Research Centre, 1988.

Nelson, Kristina. *The Art of Reciting the Qur'an.* Austin: University of Texas Press, 1985.

Pacholczyk, Jósef M. *Regulative Principles in the Koran Chant of Shaikn 'Abdu'l-Basit 'Abdu's-Samad.* Los Angeles: University of California, 1970.

Qureshi, Regula Burckhardt. "Sounding the Word: Music in the Life of Islam." *Enchanting Powers: Music in the World's Religions.* Ed. Lawrence Sullivan. Cambridge, Mass.: Harvard University Press, 1997, pp. 263–98.

———. *Sufi Music of India and Pakistan: Sound, Context and Meaning in Qawwali.* Cambridge Studies in Ethnomusicology. John Blacking, ed. Cambridge: Cambridge University Press, 1986.

Sadler, A. W. *Mysticism and Devotion in the Music of the Qawwali.* New York: Performing Arts Program of the Asia Society, 1974.

Shiloah, Amnon. *Music in the World of Islam: A Socio-cultural Study.* Detroit: Wayne State University Press, 1995

Simms, Rob. *The Repertoire of Iraqi Maqam.* Lanham, Md.: Scarecrow, 2004.

Sunbul, Sharif. *Mulid!: Carnivals of Faith.* Cairo: American University in Cairo Press, 1999.

Surty, Muhammad Ibrahim Hafiz Ismail. *A Course in 'ilm al-Tajwid, the Science of Reciting the Qu'ran.* Leicester, England: Islamic Foundation, 1992.

Touma, Habib, et al. *The Music of the Arabs.* Portland, Ore.: Amadeus Press, 1996.

Waugh, Earle H. *Memory, Music, and Religion Morocco's Mystical Chanters.* Charleston, S. C.: University of South Carolina Press, 2005.

Buddhist and Shinto

Abe, Ryuichi. *The Weaving of Mantra: Kukai and the Construction of Esoteric Buddhist Discourse.* New York: Columbia University Press, 1999.

Averbuch, Irit. *The Gods Come Dancing: A Study of the Japanese Ritual Dance of Yamabushi Kagura.* Ithaca, N. Y.: East Asia Program, Cornell University, 1985.

Giesen, Walter. *Zur Geschichte des buddhistischen Ritualgesangs in Japan.* Kassel : Bärenreiter, 1977.

Gold, Lisa. *Music in Bali.* New York: Oxford University Press, 2005.

E. Harich-Schneider. "Dances and Songs of the Japanese Shinto Cult." *World of Music* 25: 1 (1983), 16–29.

Kaufmann, Walter. *Tibetan Buddhist Chant: Musical Notations and Interpretations of a Song Book by the Bkah Brgyud Pa and Sa Skya Pa Sects.* Bloomington: Indiana University Press, 1975.

Kiehnle, Catharina. *The Conservative Vaisnava: Anonymous Songs of the Jñandev Gātha.* Stuttgart: F. Steiner Verlag, 1997.

Lee, Byong Won. *An Analytical Study of Sacred Buddhist Chant of Korea.* Ann Arbor, Mich.: Xerox University Microfilms, 1974.

Malm, William P. *Traditional Japanese Music and Musical Instruments.* New Edition. Tokyo: Kodansha International, 2000.

Ortolani, Benito. *The Japanese Theatre: From Shamanistic Ritual to Contemporary Pluralism.* Leiden, Netherlands: E. J. Brill, 1990.

Tamba, Akira. *Musique Traditionnelles du Japon: Des Origines au XVIe Siècle.* Arles: Cité de la Musique, 1995.

Hindu

Bhagyalekshmy, S. *Carnatic Music Compositions: An Index.* Trivandrum, India: CBH Publications, 1994.

Chandra, Moti. *Gīta Govinda.* New Delhi: Lalit Kala Akademie, 1980.

Clayton, Martin. *Time in Indian Music: Rhythm, Metre, and Form in North Indian Rag Performance.* Oxford: Oxford University Press, 2000.

Gaston, Anne-Marie. *Krishna's Musicians: Musicians and Music Making in the Temples of Nathdvara, Rajasthan.* New Dehli: Manoshar, 1997.

Gautam, M. R. *Evolution of Raga and Tala in Indian Music.* New Delhi: Munshiram Manoharial, 1989.

Howard, Wayne. *Sāmavedic Chant.* New Haven, Conn.: Yale University Press, 1977.

Jackson, William J. *Tyagaraja, Life and Lyrics*. Delhi and New York: Oxford University Press, 1991.

Lohan, Marie. *Kirtana*. Montreux: Minerva Press, 1996.

Nijenhuis, Emmie te, et al. *Sacred Songs of India: Diksitar's Cycle of Hymns to the Goddess Kamala*. Wintherthur, Switz: Amadeus, 1987.

Ranade, Ashok D. *Keywords and Concepts: Hindustani Classical Music*. New Dehli: Promilla: 1990.

Sundaram, B. M. *Tala Sangraha: Compendium of Talas in Karnatak Music*. Bangalore: Percusive Arts Centre, 1987.

Tirtha, B. B. and B. V. Tripurari. *Bhajan: Mantras of Mercy*. Novato, Calif.: Mandala, 2002.

Viswanathan, T., and Matthew Harp Allen. *Music in South India*. New York: Oxford University Press, 2004.

Wade, Bonnie C. *Music in India: The Classical Traditions*. Rev. ed. New Dehli: Manohar, 1999.

Tribal

Carrington, John F. *Talking Drums of Africa*. New York: Negro Universities Press, 1949. Rpt. 1969.

Harvey, Graham and Karen Ralls. *Indigenous Religious Musics*. Aldershot, Hampshire, England: Ashgate, 2000.

Friedson, Steven M. *Dancing Prophets: Musical Experience in Tumbuka Healing*. Chicago: University of Chicago Press, 1996.

Nketia, J. H. Kwabena. *Drumming in Akan Communities in Ghana*. Edinburgh: T. Nelson, 1963.

Stillman, Amy K. *Sacred Hula: The Historical Hula Ala Apapa*. Honolulu: Bishop Museum Press, 1998.

Summers, Bill. *Studies in Bata: Sacred Drum of the Yoruba: Havana to Matanzas*. N.P., n.p. 2002.

Turner, Victor. *The Drums of Affliction: a Study of Religious Processes among the Ndumbu of Zambia*. New York: Oxford University Press, 1968.

Comparative

Irwin, Joyce, ed. *Sacred Sound: Music in Religious Thought and Practice*. Chico, Calif.: Scholars Press, 1983.

IMPORTANT COLLECTIONS OF MUSIC

Analecta Hymnica Medii Aevi. 55 vols. 1st ed. G. M. Dreves, Clemens Blume, and H. M. Bannister. Leipzig: 1886–1922.

Analecta Hymnica Medii Aevi: Register. Dorothea Baumann and Max Lütolf, eds. 2 vols. Bern: Francke, 1978.

Antiphonale Monasticum pro Diurnis Horis. Tournai, Belgium: Desclée, 1934.

Antiphonale Sacrosanctae Romanae Ecclesiae pro Diurnis Horis. Tournai, Belgium.: Desclée, 1949.

Bach, Johann Sebastian. *Neue Ausgabe sämtlicher Werke.* Ed. Johann-Sebastian-Bach-Institut Göttingen and the Barch-Archiv Leipzig. Kassel: 1954.

Byrd, William. *The Byrd Edition.* 17 vols. Eds. Philip Brett et al. London: Stainer & Bell, 1970–.

Corpus Mensurabilis Musicae. Rome: American Institute of Musicology, 1948.

Du Fay, Guillaume. *Opera Omnia.* Ed. Heinrich Bessler. *Corpus Mensurabilis Musicae.* Rome: American Institute of Musicology, 1964.

Idelsohn, Abraham Z. *Thesaurus of Hebrew Oriental Melodies.* 10 vols. New York: Ktav, 1973.

Graduale Sacrosanctae Romanae Ecclesiae. Tournai, Belgium: Desclée, 1908.

Johann Sebastian Bachs Werke. Ed. Bach-Gesellschaft. 46 vols. Leipzig: 1851–1899.

Josquin Desprez. *Werken.* Ed. Albert Smijers. Amsterdam: Kistner & Siegel, 1921–1956.

———. *Opera Omnia: Editio Altera.* Eds. Myroslaw Antonowycz and Willem Elders. Amsterdam: Verenigung vor Nederlandse Muziekgeschiedenis, 1957–1959.

Kurtzmann, Jeffrey G. *Vespers and Compline Music for Six Principal Voices.* New York: Garland, 2000.

Lasso, Orlando di. *Sämtliche Werke.* 21 vols. Kassel: Bärenreiter, 1956.

The Liber Usualis with Introduction and Rubrics in English. New York, 1952.

Monteverdi, Claudio. *Tutte le Opere.* Ed. G Francesco Malipiero. 17 vols. Asola, Italy: G. F. Mailipiero, 192–42; Vienna: Universal Edition, 1966.

Monumenta Monodica Medii Aevi. Ed. Bruno Stäblein. Kassel: Bärenreiter, 1956.

Monumentae Polyphoniae Liturgicae Sanctae Ecclesiae Romanae. Rome: Societas Universalis Sanctae Cecilae, 1948– .

Monuments of Renaissance Music. Chicago: University of Chicago Press, 1964–

Morosan, Vladimir. *One Thousand Years of Russian Church Music, 988–1988.* Washington, D. C.: Musica Russica, 1991.

Palestrina, Giovanni Pierluigi da. *Le Opere Complete.* Eds. Raffaele Casimiri, Knud Jeppesen, and Lino Bianchi. 35 vols. Rome: Istituto Italiano per la Storia della Musica, 1939–.

———. *Werke.* Ed. F X. Haberl. 32 vols. Leipzig: Breitkopf & Härtel, 1862–1907.

Van den Borren, Charles. *Polyphonia Sacra: A Continental Miscellany of the Fourteenth Century.* London: Plainsong & Medieval Society, 1962.

Victoria, Tomas Luis di. *Opera Omnia.* Ed. Felipe Pedrell. 7 vols. Leipzig: Breitkopf & Härtel, 1902–1913.

DISCOGRAPHIES

Bibilographic and General

A Bibliography of Discographies. 3 vols. New York: R. R. Bowker, 1977–1983.
Schwann Opus. Santa Fe, N. M.: Stereophile, 1991–2001.

Specific Discographies Including Sacred Music

Barnett, Elise B. *A Discography of the Art Music of India*. Ann Arbor, Mich.: Society for Ethnomusicology, 1975.

Blyth, Alan, ed. *Choral Music on Record*. Cambridge: Cambridge University Press, 1991.

Bodman, Ellen-Fairbanks, and Lorrain Sakata. *The World of Islam, Images and Echoes: A Critical Guide to Films and Recordings*. New York: American Council of Learned Societies, 1980.

Croucher, Trevor. *Early Music Discography: From Plainsong to the Sons of Bach*. Phoenix, Az.: Oryx Press, 1981.

Day, Timothy. *A Discography of Tudor Church Music*. London: British Library Association, 1989.

Dols, Nancy, et al. *Musics of the World: A Selective Discography*. 4 vols. Los Angeles: Ethnomusicology Archive, UCLA Music Library, 1977.

Faw, Marc Taylor. *A Verdi Discography*. Norman, Okla.: Pilgrim Books, 1982.

Gombert, Greg. *A Guide to Native American Music Recording*. Fort Collins, Colo: Multi Cultural Publishing, 1994.

Graham, Ronnie. *The Da Capo Guide to Contemporary African Music*. New York: Da Capo Press, 1988.

Kinnear, Michael S. *A Discography of Hindustani and Karnatic Music*. Westport, Conn.: Greenwood, 1985.

Kratzenstein, Marilou and Jerald Hamilton. *Four Centuries of Organ Music: From the Robertsbridge Codex Through the Baroque Era: An Annotated Discography*. Detroit: Information Coordinators, 1984.

Lovallo, Lee T. *Anton Bruckner: A Discography*. Berkeley, Calif.: Fallen Leaf Press, 1991.

Maguire, Marsha. *A List of Long-Playing Recordings of Sacred Harp and other Shape Note Singing*. Washington, D. C.: Library of Congress, Archive of Folk Song, 1979.

Minegishi, Yuki. *A Discography of Japanese Music*. Tokyo: Japan Foundation, 1980.

Parsons, Charles H. *A Benjamin Britten Discography*. Lewsiton, Me.: E. Mellen Press, 1990.

Tinnell, Roger D. *An Annotated Discography of Music in Spain Before 1650.* Madison, Wis.: Hispanic Seminary of Medieval Studies, 1980.

Turner, Patricia. *Afro-American Singers: An Index and Preliminary Discography of Long-Playing Recordings of Opera, Choral Music, and Song.* Minneapolis, Minn.: Challenge, 1977.

Weber, Jerome F. *Benjamin Britten.* Utica, N. Y.: J. F. Weber, 1975.

———. *A Gregorian Chant Discography.* 2 Vols. Utica, N. Y.: J. F. Weber, 1990.

Westerlund, Gunnar, and Eric Hughes. *Music of Claudio Monteverdi: A Discography.* London: British Institute of Recorded Sound, 1972.

Internet Sites

Archives of African American Music and Culture. (Indiana University) [http://www.indiana.edu/~aaamc/index.html]

Buddhist Sound Files. [http://www.sinc.sunysb.edu/Clubs/buddhism/music/music.html]

CANTUS: Database of Latin Ecclesiastical Chants. Terence Bailey, director. [http://publish.uwo.ca/~cantus/]

The Catholic Encyclopedia. 1907. [http://www.newadvent.org/cathen/]

Doctoral Dissertations in Musicology. (Indiana University, Thomas J. Mathiesen, director) [http://www.music.indiana.edu/ddm/]

The Gregorian Chant Home Web Page. (Princeton University) [http://silvertone.princeton.edu/chant_html/]

Jewish Encyclopedia.com. [http://www.jewishencyclopedia.com/index.jsp]

Medieval Music Database: An Integration of Electronic Sources. [http://www.lib.latrobe.edu.au/MMDB/]

Monumenta Musicae Byzantinae. [http://www.igl.ku.dk/MMB/Welcome.html]

Renaissance Liturgical Imprints. (University of Michigan, David Crawford, director) [http://www-personal.umich.edu/~davidcr.]

Répertoire International des Sources Musicales. http://www.nisc.com/factsheets/qrism.asp

RILM Abstracts of Music Literature. http://www.csa.com/factsheets/rilm-set-c.php?SID=c4fg6rpjg3v5nmn09k2kml

Thesaurus of Musicarum Latinarum. (Indiana University) Thomas J. Mathiesen, director. [http://www.music.indiana.edu/tml/start.html]

About the Author

Joseph P. Swain has taught music history and theory for more than 25 years at Phillips Academy and Colgate University. He is organist and director of music at St. Malachy's Church in Sherburne, New York, and Music Director of Tapestry, the All-Centuries Singers, based in Clinton, New York. He has also written *Harmonic Rhythm* (Oxford, 2002), *The Broadway Musical* (Oxford, 1990; rev. ed. Scarecrow, 2002), which won ASCAP's Deems Taylor Award in 1991, *Musical Languages* (Norton, 1997), and *Sound Judgment* (San Francisco, 1987).